Professional
Excel® Services

Professional
Excel® Services

Shahar Prish

Wiley Publishing, Inc.

Professional Excel® Services

Published by
Wiley Publishing, Inc.
10475 Crosspoint Boulevard
Indianapolis, IN 46256
www.wiley.com

Copyright © 2007 by Wiley Publishing, Inc., Indianapolis, Indiana

Published simultaneously in Canada

ISBN: 978-0-470-10486-6

Manufactured in the United States of America

10 9 8 7 6 5 4 3 2 1

Library of Congress Cataloging-in-Publication Data

Prish, Shahar, 1975-
  Professional Excel Services / Shahar Prish.
     p. cm.
  Includes bibliographical references.
  ISBN 978-0-470-10486-6 (paper/website)
  1. Microsoft Excel (Computer file)--Handbooks, manuals, etc. 2. Business--Computer programs. I. Title.
  HF5548.4.M523P76 2007
  005.54--dc22

                    2007006215

For general information on our other products and services please contact our Customer Care Department within the United States at (800) 762-2974, outside the United States at (317) 572-3993 or fax (317) 572-4002.

Trademarks: Wiley, the Wiley logo, Wrox, the Wrox logo, Programmer to Programmer, and related trade dress are trademarks or registered trademarks of John Wiley & Sons, Inc. and/or its affiliates, in the United States and other countries, and may not be used without written permission. Microsoft and Excel are registered trademarks of Microsoft Corporation in the United States and/or other countries. All other trademarks are the property of their respective owners. Wiley Publishing, Inc., is not associated with any product or vendor mentioned in this book.

Wiley also publishes its books in a variety of electronic formats. Some content that appears in print may not be avail-able in electronic books.

To my parents, Tzila and Danny — thank you

About the Author

Shahar Prish was born and raised in Israel. He was playing around with computers for 10 years or so when suddenly and unexpectedly it became a useful skill to have. At the age of 16, Shahar started working in a company that did various backup and encryption applications for the PC. When he turned 18 he was drafted to the army where he defended his country from behind a keyboard, a monitor, and way too much non-dairy chocolate bread-spread. When he got out of the army, he tried to get a degree in CS, but failed miserably due to work getting in the way. He worked for a big telecommunication company (where he developed software for international calls fraud detection) and in a small startup (which did something with browsers — it was never really clear). In 1998 he was the first employee in a small company called "Maximal Innovative Intelligence" that developed Business Intelligence software. In 2001 Maximal was purchased by Microsoft and the product it was selling was rebranded and sold as "Microsoft Data Analyzer". From Maximal, eleven employees moved over to the US where they started working in the Office group. A year after moving, Shahar started working with the rest of the team on Excel Services (then called Excel Server). After spending most of his life writing code, Shahar intends to keep doing so until the medics pry the keyboard from his dead cold hands.

Credits

Acquisitions Editor
Katie Mohr

Senior Development Editor
Tom Dinse

Technical Editor
Justin Rockwood

Production Editor
Debra Banninger

Copy Editor
Foxxe Editorial Services

Editorial Manager
Mary Beth Wakefield

Production Manager
Tim Tate

Vice President and Executive Group Publisher
Richard Swadley

Vice President and Executive Publisher
Joseph B. Wikert

Compositor
Laurie Stewart, Happenstance Type-O-Rama

Proofreader
Sossity Smith

Indexer
Melanie Belkin

Anniversary Logo Design
Richard Pacifico

Acknowledgments

Thanks to:

- ❑ The team at Wrox and especially Katie and Tom for making this book possible
- ❑ Justin for giving me great feedback when editing the book and for making sure all my t's were crossed
- ❑ Eran for helping when it was difficult to transform what I was thinking into words and for helping with ideas for some of the solutions in the book
- ❑ The Excel Services team for helping with some of the issues that came up during the writing of the book.

Content

Contents

Contents

Contents

Contents

Contents

Introduction

Excel spreadsheets are used practically everywhere — they are the cornerstone of many applications and businesses. Excel Services revolutionizes the spreadsheet world by introducing server-side spreadsheet calculation and rendering with unparallel Excel fidelity. This book will guide developers through understanding what Excel Services is, how to work with it, and how to develop applications on top of it.

It is rather embarrassing to say, but it took me a whole three years to understand just how useful Excel Services is. It was after I gave (what I thought was) a well-received demo at Office DevCon in Redmond with Danny Khen, a program manager on the Excel Services team. I remember going through the parts of the demo: One of the first things I showed was how to extract a column of data from an Excel worksheet and utilize it in an ASP.NET application. The crowd applauded, which threw me off-guard because I thought I hadn't really gotten to the cool part yet. A few days later I was at a birthday party for the daughter of Boaz Chen, a friend and coworker who moved here from Israel with me (and who also happens to work on Excel Services). I remember standing in the doorway on our way out when it suddenly hit me. Even that simple operation of getting a column of data from Excel is incredibly useful. It basically means you can use Excel Services just like the client version is used — as a miniature database application. This opens up a world of new scenarios! See, until that moment, from a programmatic point of view, I was looking at Excel Services only from the "Excel model" angle — as a really neat way of calculating a complex model without having to resort to rewriting it or to creating whole Excel farms.

Shortly after the presentation I started getting emails from people who found out about me through my blog. And there again it was revealed to me just how blind I was. People were using Excel Services for various things I never thought about, everything from building an auditing mechanism for charging for usage of Excel models to running iterative simulations in financial markets.

One of the things that these exchanges confirmed was the fact that I really like working with other developers and trying to help them find solutions to their problems. And here I was in a perfect position to do this, and since this is Excel we are talking about, I figured I was in a perfect position to help a potentially large number of developers. That is around the time when the idea of writing this book came along — a way of giving many developers a starting point when trying to attack a problem with Excel Services.

Who This Book Is For

If you are an independent developer and have built applications on Excel or have used a spreadsheet as a starting point for code, this book is for you. If you are a developer working in an organization which relies on Excel spreadsheets for modeling, handling, and storing data and you want to see how these processes can be streamlined and be leveraged more than ever before, this book is for you. If you are a developer who likes new technologies and are looking for new ways to solve both old problems and new ones, this book is for you.

This book is targeted at developers who are comfortable in the .NET environment. The coding examples in the later chapters use mostly C# — however, they can all be implemented in pretty much any other .NET-supporting language. While this book assumes some knowledge of .NET, the first examples in the book also go through the basics of creating projects. One project (in Chapter 10) is written using C++/CLI (managed extensions for C++) for technical reasons. That chapter can be skipped by readers with no C++ knowledge — the solution can be used as is. The details are given for people who are more interested in the intricacies of how the solution actually works.

What This Book Covers

The first half of this book provides detailed explanations about the various programmability options Excel Services offers. It delves into specifics as well as warning against problematic areas developers have to look out for. This includes Excel Web Services, the Excel Services UDF (User Defined Functions) extension mechanism and a bit of information about the EWA (Excel Web Access). When they're done reading this part, developers will have a good grasp of how to extend and work against Excel Services.

The second half of the book gives some ideas for solutions that can be written by using Excel Services. Some of the solutions are more generic than others and may be usable as is by developers. Other solutions are good "stepping stones" towards other, more elaborate solutions. Furthermore, some solutions complement each other and have more value when used together.

How This Book Is Structured

The parts that explain Excel Web Services and UDFs both have three chapters each. The first chapter of each part presents a small "hello world" example that makes use of the technology. The second chapters provide deep, detailed explanation about the technology. The third chapters in each of these parts shows how to code a useful solution that can be reused by developers (in the case of the Excel Web Services part) or by users (in the case of the UDF part).

The second half of the book contains examples of reusable projects — each chapter here is divided into three main sections. The first section shows how the example can be used. The second section goes into detail about how the example is coded. The last section, where it exists, talks about some of the possible improvements that can be made in the example.

Generally speaking the examples in the second half of the book require you to understand the explanations shown in the first half.

What You Need to Use This Book

To make full use of this book, the following products and resources are needed:

- ❑ Access to a Microsoft Office SharePoint Server (Enterprise edition) installation.
- ❑ Visual Studio 2005 (or newer). Developers can make do with any other development environment that can create .NET 2.0 assemblies for UDFs. Older versions of Visual Studio 2003 can be used to access Excel Web Services; however, the experience may be different from that described in the book.
- ❑ Excel 2007

Conventions

To help you get the most from the text and keep track of what's happening, we've used a number of conventions throughout the book.

> **Boxes like this one hold important, not-to-be forgotten information that is directly relevant to the surrounding text.**

Tips, hints, tricks, and asides to the current discussion are offset and placed in italics like this.

As for styles in the text:

❑ We *highlight in italic type* new terms and important words when we introduce them.

❑ We show keyboard strokes like this: Ctrl+A.

❑ We show file names, URLs, and code within the text like so: `persistence.properties`.

❑ We present code in two different ways:

```
In code examples we highlight new and important code with a gray background.
The gray highlighting is not used for code that's less important in the present
context, or has been shown before.
```

Source Code

As you work through the examples in this book, you may choose either to type in all the code manually or to use the source code files that accompany the book. All of the source code used in this book is available for download at `www.wrox.com`. Once at the site, simply locate the book's title (either by using the Search box or by using one of the title lists) and click the Download Code link on the book's detail page to obtain all the source code for the book.

Because many books have similar titles, you may find it easiest to search by ISBN; this book's ISBN is 978-0-470-10486-6.

Once you download the code, just decompress it with your favorite compression tool. Alternately, you can go to the main Wrox code download page at `www.wrox.com/dynamic/books/download.aspx` to see the code available for this book and all other Wrox books.

Errata

We make every effort to ensure that there are no errors in the text or in the code. However, no one is perfect, and mistakes do occur. If you find an error in one of our books, such as a spelling mistake or faulty piece of code, we would be very grateful for your feedback. By sending in errata you may save another reader hours of frustration and at the same time you will be helping us provide even higher-quality information.

To find the errata page for this book, go to www.wrox.com and locate the title using the Search box or one of the title lists. Then, on the book details page, click the Book Errata link. On this page you can view all errata that has been submitted for this book and posted by Wrox editors. A complete book list including links to each book's errata is also available at www.wrox.com/misc-pages/booklist.shtml.

If you don't spot "your" error on the Book Errata page, go to www.wrox.com/contact/techsupport.shtml and complete the form there to send us the error you have found. We'll check the information and, if appropriate, post a message to the book's errata page and fix the problem in subsequent editions of the book.

p2p.wrox.com

For author and peer discussion, join the P2P forums at p2p.wrox.com. The forums are a web-based system for you to post messages relating to Wrox books and related technologies and interact with other readers and technology users. The forums offer a subscription feature to e-mail you topics of interest of your choosing when new posts are made to the forums. Wrox authors, editors, other industry experts, and your fellow readers are present on these forums.

At http://p2p.wrox.com you will find a number of different forums that will help you not only as you read this book but also as you develop your own applications. To join the forums, just follow these steps:

1. Go to p2p.wrox.com and click the Register link.

2. Read the terms of use and click Agree.

3. Complete the required information to join as well as any optional information you wish to provide, and click Submit.

4. You will receive an e-mail with information describing how to verify your account and complete the joining process.

You can read messages in the forums without joining P2P but in order to post your own messages, you must join.

Once you join, you can post new messages and respond to messages other users post. You can read messages at any time on the web. If you would like to have new messages from a particular forum e-mailed to you, click the Subscribe to this Forum icon by the forum name in the forum listing.

For more information about how to use the Wrox P2P, be sure to read the P2P FAQs for answers to questions about how the forum software works as well as many common questions specific to P2P and Wrox books. To read the FAQs, click the FAQ link on any P2P page.

Professional
Excel® Services

Part I: Introducing Excel Services

Introduction to Excel Services

So why do you care about Excel Services? Well, since you bought this book, there is a chance your organization uses Excel in its day-to-day operation. Who can blame them? Excel is the most popular modeling tool and the most popular database tool. It is so versatile that the same person can use it for both a complex financial model and a simple task list. In the Excel organization, for example, it is not uncommon to use Excel for managing tasks, project milestones, and bug reports. Over the years, Excel has gathered a very large set of features ranging from advanced formatting to advanced data acquisition mechanisms. With Excel 2007, this set of features has been bolstered even more to allow Excel to be a first-class BI (business intelligence) tool.

Why Use Excel Services

While Excel is a great tool, it really lacks in one specific area: it is a client application. It was designed to be a client application from the get-go, and in all probability it will stay that way. That means it is focused on one user getting whatever Excel functionality that user needs on a PC. There are many indicators showing that organizations will want to run Excel on the server:

❑ For one, a lot of people go to great lengths to try to get Excel client to work in a server environment — at great cost and with great frustration.

❑ People want one version of the truth — but when workbook files are used with Excel client, there is no real protection against people modifying them. With only the client at the users' disposal, it is much harder to keep a single version that will be the "single point of entry" to the data.

❑ Intellectual property is expensive, and companies want to guard it. Excel models can become extremely complex and give a real edge to their owners. Those owners do not want others to be able to access the models — only the results of the models. Excel does not really supply such protection.

❑   Running a lot of models, whether as part of a mechanized process or because a lot of users need to get at the data, is virtually impossible to do in a scalable manner with Excel.

❑   To see any part of an Excel file, the entire file must be opened. This can put a strain on even the fastest networks and can be completely impractical when people are connecting over a WAN.

More accurately, in some cases Excel is smart enough to delay-load some types of data caches such as pivot tables.

❑   People want to see and navigate Excel worksheets inside a browser. But they also want those worksheets to be up to date, and they want the ability to navigate them and do simple operations such as drilling down through information or filtering lists.

❑   Administrators want more manageability of what Excel does. Some workbooks have complex data queries that, when executed by too many users at the same time, can bring databases to their knees. Conversely, some data sources are accessible only to specific users. For these reasons, workbooks that are distributed may sometimes only have copies of data rather than actual live data. This raises the "one version of the truth" problem — how can organizations know what data is current?

For these reasons and others, organizations end up producing various creative solutions to the problem. These solutions usually come in two flavors: large, custom-built farms of Excel client applications and rewriting the underlying models.

The Excel Client Farms

Excel farms are relatively large farms (or computing clusters) that run multiple instances of Excel on request. People usually build some kind of protocol that allows them to extract information from the Excel processes and transfer it back to the user in whatever form is desired.

These solutions, while creative and impressive, do not scale well and are not fun to maintain. They require a lot of hardware due to various Excel limitations (again that pesky "was not designed for the server" thing), and managing the whole thing is really hard to do.

Rewriting the Models

The other solution organizations come up with, which is no less painful (and in some ways, more painful), is to take tried-and-true models written in Excel and rewrite them in some other language so that they can be used without Excel. This is of course a huge time investment — not only can the models be excessively complex, but when a model changes, the code needs to be updated appropriately, which takes a lot of time (testing alone is a major time sink, since one needs to make sure that the model behaves the same way that it does in Excel).

Note that, in some cases at least, the reason for transferring models into code does not have to do with the inability to get server capabilities but rather is done to squeeze every ounce of performance out of a model. Excel Services may or may not help in these cases. Some organizations will retain their need to rewrite Excel models.

How Excel Services Comes to the Rescue

Excel Services has been created to solve all these problems and more. While still using portions of Excel code that have been rewritten to be serverworthy, large amounts of work has been done around that code to make it into an actual server product.

Excel Services solves some of the problems simply by virtue of being a server product — intellectual property is protected because users do not have access to the actual workbook (unless the admin allows them to see it). Since all the calculations are done on the server, it is not even an issue — there is no need to transfer the model itself to the user. This also takes care of the "one version of the truth" issue — there is a central repository for information, and only people who are allowed to update that repository will. Furthermore, because Excel Services is leveraging the SharePoint infrastructure, it can make use of such features as "view-only rights" where some users can access the complete file (by loading it in Excel or by saving it to their hard drive), while others can only view it through the server.

Because it is a server, it can also do various things that the client was never designed to do, such as sharing information across users. The file itself need not be loaded more than once. This not only reduces network traffic, but it also means that the actual process of loading the file, which can be very long and CPU-intensive for large models, is only done once. This is doubly true for models that rely on getting data from databases — Excel Services can figure out what data is sharable among which users and make sure that it does not query the database too many times. On top of that, the administrators can also instruct Excel Services to only hit the database server periodically — say, not more than once every 5 minutes — giving them much more control over how many times the database will be hit by requests.

Since Excel Services was built from the ground up to have multiple instances of the same workbook open at any given time, it is possible for multiple users to open any number of workbooks and work with them. The same goes for processes that need concurrent access to workbooks. The number of workbooks that can be interacted with at a given moment is only limited by memory and CPU.

Finally, because the server supplies the means to access parts of loaded workbooks, people who are across the WAN will not need to take the hit of loading the entire file — they can just request a small part of the workbook. This also ties into EWA (Excel Web Access), which is a Web Part that allows people to navigate Excel workbooks inside a browser (*no* ActiveXs, I repeat, no ActiveXs at all, just plain old HTML and JavaScript, honest).

Excel Services Goals

It is important to understand what our goals were when we started thinking and designing Excel Services. Understanding the goals explains a lot of the technical decisions we made throughout the project. I am only listing the goals that have specific bearings on our server product — obviously goals such as customer satisfaction are there by default.

First Goal — 100% Fidelity with Excel

Our first and foremost goal was to have 100% fidelity with Excel in every Excel feature we support. That is to say, if we support a given Excel feature, our goal is to support it in exactly the same manner that Excel 2007 supports it. It does not mean, though, that we support all of Excel's features.

That said, sometimes when things are transferred to a server environment, "100% fidelity" stops being a clear-cut thing. As an example, take the Data Refresh feature. In Excel, when the user refreshes the data, Excel will go and grab new data from the database back end. On the server, as described before, the administrator can place a limit on how often refreshes may occur.

Second Goal — Security

It is incredibly important that Excel Services does not expose information to unauthorized users. If a user does not have access to a workbook, that person should never be able to use Excel Services to circumvent that principle (unless the administrator specifically set up the server for that). Similarly, if a workbook is set up such that users should not be able to see the actual models and formulas of the workbook, Excel Services should never supply that information to users.

Additionally, users should never be able to see information that belong to other users. So, if a user accesses data and gets a set of results and a second user gets a different set of results, neither of them should be able to see the results of the other.

Third Goal — Robustness and Reliability

Since this is a server product, robustness and reliability are paramount — we want to be able to keep the server up and running for as long as possible. If there is a feature in Excel that is impossible to translate well to the server because it will reduce robustness or reliability, there is a good chance we will preemptively decide not to do it at all.

2

User and Administrator Cheat Sheet

This chapter gives an overview of the differences between Excel 2007 and Excel Services, what Excel Server can do right out of the box, the various topologies available when deploying Excel Services, and a cheat sheet for how to do basic administration of Excel Services.

Excel 2007 and Excel Services

Excel and Excel Services can process the same files and come up with the exact same results. This sometimes leads people to think that Excel Services is simply "Excel running on the server." This misconception can give rise to expectations that Excel Services cannot satisfy.

> *Throughout the book I will use "Excel" as shorthand for "Microsoft Excel 2007" — the client software — and "Excel Services" as shorthand for "Microsoft Office SharePoint Server — Excel Services."*

It is important to understand that the fact that Excel runs on a client machine, with one user, makes it wildly different from Excel Services, which has many users all at the same time. This brings us to the first major difference between Excel Services and Excel: there is no object model in Excel Services.

Object Model Support

Yes, you read correctly: Excel Services does not expose an automation object model (OM) in the traditional manner. There is no endless list of objects with properties and collections. There is not even a short list of them. The only way to automate Excel Services is through the supplied set of methods exposed by Excel Web Services. Those methods contain a set of primitives that allow developers not so much to automate Excel features but to work with the Excel model embedded in a workbook. In the first version of Excel Services, it was a not a goal to allow people to author workbooks on the server but rather to allow them to make use of workbooks. Therefore, it became far less important to supply an OM. Furthermore, given the way that Excel Services is programmed (and because it does not support VBA) adding an OM would have meant creating an object model in .NET. Implementing an object model that diverges from that of Excel would have created an instant backward-compatibility issue. When we do create an OM, it should be something that works both on the client and on the server so that solutions written for one can be leveraged by the other.

Addin Model Support

With the exception of support for UDFs (user defined functions), there is no real support for addins on the server. This means that there is no way to extend Excel Services the way that some solutions extend Excel — from within.

This does not prevent people from using Excel Services inside their solutions, however. On the contrary; it is much easier, and by far more scalable, to do that with Excel Services than it is with Excel. However, the standard addins that people write for Excel cannot be used with this version of Excel Services.

Excel Services Out of the Box

There are three primary ways to interact with Excel Services. The only one that works "out of the box," though, is Excel Web Access (EWA), which allows you to see workbooks rendered inside a browser in a truly thin manner. The other two are the Excel Web Services and UDFs. I will touch on those later.

Excel Web Access

Much the same way that Outlook Web Access (OWA) allows users to see their Exchange inbox in a browser, EWA allows users to see, navigate, and interact with workbooks on the server. EWA is implemented as a Web Part in SharePoint, where it can be used to build dashboard and SharePoint applications.

The EWA team did a truly amazing job at keeping Excel Services faithful to Excel 2007, where humanly (and sometimes even inhumanly) possible, which is no small feat when you consider all the new visual features of Excel Services. Almost all visual features that are supported by Excel Services have near-complete fidelity to the way things look in Excel 2007, when using Internet Explorer 6 (IE 6) or above.

Although Firefox 1.5 is a supported browser, some visual features are only available in IE 6 or above.

See if you can detect which one of the images in Figure 2.1 is from EWA and which one is from Excel Services.

For integration inside SharePoint smart-pages, EWA also supports the part-to-part SharePoint feature, allowing you to connect it to other Web Parts to create an integrated application.

Being a Web Part, the EWA can also be used in applications. It has properties that can be modified to change its behavior and so on. I will give a few examples of the ways you can utilize it inside and outside SharePoint.

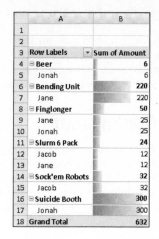

Figure 2.1

Topologies

Excel Services can be deployed in various ways, each targeting a different scenario. The diagram in Figure 2.2 shows the general-case deployment.

The back-end server(s) are running Excel Services. The front-end server(s) are running the SharePoint portal product and the EWA Web Part, which together allow you to build dashboards that contain Excel Services features.

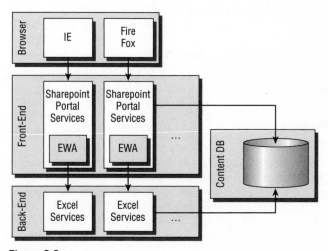

Figure 2.2

Departmental Deployment

In some cases the back end, front end, and content DB will all be installed on the same machine. This is especially useful in cases where there is a small group of trusted people using the server (that is where "departmental" comes from). This is also the way I would recommend you test your Excel Services solution because there will be less noise when debugging.

Large Scale Deployment

Excel Services scales well both up and out. Scaling up means that administrators can throw better hardware at an Excel Services machine and expect to get better performance. Scaling out means that they can add more machines to a server farm that will be able to handle extra load. Excel Services has a few schemes for load balancing that allow the administrator to determine how Excel Services will handle traffic coming in to multiple machines. (You can see them in the "Excel Services Settings" section later in this chapter.)

Unsupported Features

When we started out with Excel Services, we knew that our goal was to support almost all of the features of Excel. However, we also knew that this is something we would not be able to get into the product with the first version. So, we have tried to have a clear story about what we support and what we do not support. While what's unsupported is well documented, I thought I would touch on some items and explain the logic behind them. I believe that most of the features that are currently unsupported will be added in a future version or service pack. The only one that I am pretty sure will never make its way onto the server is VBA support.

Excel Services has two types of features it does not support:

❑ **Roundtrip-only features.** Excel Services will load workbooks containing these features and will even know how to create workbooks containing these features when the user opens the workbook through the Open in Excel toolbar button. However, these features will not be displayed in EWA or be accessible through the API.

❑ **Unsupported features.** These features are completely unsupported, meaning that workbooks containing them will fail to load in the EWA or through the application programming interface (API).

Old File Format

Early in the process we decided to support only the new .xlsx and .xlsb Excel file formats. This was mainly due to the fact that we did not want to rewrite all the old Excel code to make it serverworthy. We had a chance to start from scratch and get code with high reliability and robustness that could be used on the server, so we went with that route. Since Excel 2007 comes with converters that allow you to mass convert files, this should not be painful for most users.

VBA

Visual Basic for Applications (VBA) was the one feature we knew for a fact would not make it into the product. There was never even a question about it. Bringing VBA into the server would have been colossal work, if it even would have even been possible. Remember, in addition to fidelity to Excel 2007, other very important features are reliability and robustness. VBA is a pretty antiquated technology that was never intended to run on a server. As such, it would have been impossible to get it up and running with server quality without a total rewrite.

We knew from the beginning that this was going to be a painful point for our users. However, in the long run it was the right thing to do. Had we tried to patch VBA to work properly on the server, we probably would have missed many of our deadlines and would have ended up with a subpar server to boot. Which brings us to the next painfully missing feature: query tables.

Query Tables

Query tables are the Excel feature that allows users to bring in tabular data from relational databases. PivotTables are a more elaborate feature that allows users to slice and dice the data in a table, where the rows and columns originate from the data itself (or from an Analysis Services cube).

Excel Services does not currently support query tables When we started out, it was obvious to us that we had to choose between that and PivotTables. In the end, PivotTables won (mainly because at least some of the functionality that query tables has can be exposed by PivotTables).

External Workbooks

Excel allows people to reference cells and ranges from other workbooks. With Excel Services, this poses quite a few problems. You reference workbooks by their path. With Excel Services and SharePoint document libraries as our preferred storage, this does not make much sense. On top of that, in Excel, when multiple workbooks are open, they share the calculation chain. This mechanism would have been difficult to translate to the server in version 1.

One of the sample solutions presented in this book will allow you to get data from external workbooks that are accessible to Excel Services.

Real-Time Data

Excel supports a feature called Real Time Data (RTD). This is basically a push-model cell data feature where a custom component notifies Excel when it has new data. Excel will then go and get that data and update the sheet, causing a recalculation. This has the net effect of making Excel update its calculation, potentially very often, due to new incoming data.

Since both "clients" of Excel Services (that is, EWA and the Web Service API) are pull models (i.e., calls are made from client to server and the server cannot notify client on changes), there was very little sense in adding support for the RTD feature.

That said, this book will provide an example showing how you can still leverage existing RTD servers with Excel Services, with some limitations.

Images and Shapes

Excel Services will not load workbooks that contain images or shapes — another of the things that would have been nice to have but just did not make the final cut.

Protection/Encryption

Excel Services comes with built-in protection — if administrators do not wish for a workbook to be accessed, they are provided with various tools to ensure this.

Other Unsupported Features

This is a partial list of the other features that are unsupported in Excel Services:

❑ ActiveX controls

❑ Comments

❑ Controls/forms

❑ Embedded OLE objects

❑ Ink annotations

❑ Pictures/clipArt/shapes

❑ SmartTags

❑ Text queries

❑ Web queries

❑ XLM sheets (macros)

❑ XML mapping

Roundtrip-Only Features

The following features will not prevent a workbook from loading, but they will not be accessible either:

❑ Freeze panes

❑ Split windows

❑ Custom views

❑ XML expansion packs

How to Administer Excel Services

As this is a "how to program Excel Services" type of book and is not meant as a detailed administration guide, this section will only go into those details that are appropriate for the content of the book. It will discuss a standalone deployment and assumes that Excel Services is already installed. When there is a major difference between a standalone deployment and a more complex one, I will call that out specifically. That said, I will be providing an overview of what Excel Services deployments one can expect and what to look out for with them.

Various parts of this book may require you to make changes to the configuration of Excel Services. The main entry point for that can be found in the following location on your server:

```
http://<servername>:<port>/ssp/admin/default.aspx
```

To find your port (and get to the main administration site of your SharePoint server), you can go to Start/Control Panel/Administrative Tools/Microsoft Windows SharePoint Services 3.0. That will bring you to the Central Administration page of your SharePoint server. When that page comes up, you will find your port number in the address bar. Another way of getting to the Excel Services administration site is to click the link under Shared Services Administration on the left side of the Central Administration page.

Regardless to how you get there, you should see the configuration options for all your installed servers. In this example, the server has only Excel Services installed, so that is the only option shown in Figure 2.3.

From this page, you can reach all the possible configuration options of Excel Services.

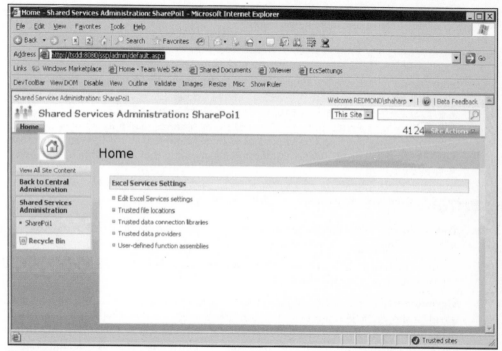

Figure 2.3

Excel Services Settings

This section contains the basic Excel Server settings. The only option that may affect the various examples in this section is the Maximum Sessions Per User option.

Sessions will be discussed more thoroughly later when session and state are discussed (see the next chapter for more information), but for now it is enough to understand that each time a user or process interacts with Excel Services, it does so from within a session. A session can be discarded in one of two ways — either the caller explicitly closes it or it will time out. This setting limits the amount of *concurrently* opened sessions a user can have. For most purposes, the defaults should be enough. However, in some cases, the same user identity may need to open many concurrent sessions that stay open for a long time on the server. In such cases, this value may need to be increased.

Trusted File Locations

Excel Services will not open files from just any location. The administrator needs to specify what locations are available for users. Any attempt to open a file that resides in storage other than a trusted location (TL for short), will fail. For that reason, when developing and testing your solutions, it is important to make sure that the place from which you are loading files is trusted. Each trusted location has its own settings. This is especially useful in installations where some locations are safer and more secure than others. For example, say that you have two trusted locations — one that contains "Administrator-sanctioned" workbooks and one to which employees can upload any old file. You can see that the "Administrator-sanctioned" location is a "safer" location that is more frequently tested and checked for problems, so it will not have any adverse effects on the server. Settings such as Maximum Workbook Size and Maximum Request Timeout can be increased considerably to allow more functionality.

The important configuration options are:

❏ Address and Location Type. This is the actual URL that points to your trusted location. This can either be a network share (`\\server\share\directory`), an HTTP location (`http://www.fileserver.com/ExcelFiles`), or a SharePoint document library (`http://companyweb/sites/accounting/Shared Documents`). Some features may only work when a file is published to a SharePoint site. It is important to understand that this is the server name should never be localhost or 127.0.0.1 — it has to be something that's reachable by the user.

   The most notable such feature is workbook parameters support in EWA. This feature will only work when an Excel Workbook was published to a SharePoint document library.

❏ **Trust Children.** When this is checked, all folders under the one specified in the Address setting will also be treated as trusted locations.

❏ **Session Timeout and Short Session Timeout.** This is explained in detail in the next chapter, where sessions are discussed in depth.

❏ **Maximum Request Duration.** When a request reaches the server, there is a limit on how long it will be allowed to execute. Once that time has passed, the server will do its best to cancel the request and return it to the caller. If your solution requires you to often make calls to the server that take a long time to execute, you may want to change this value. The default is 300 seconds (which is 5 minutes).

   Some operations on the server cannot be canceled immediately. This is why you may at times see requests timing out after the allotted time.

❏ **Volatile Functions Cache Lifetime.** This is explained in detail in the next chapter.

❏ **Allow User Defined Functions.** The administrator can decide for each trusted location whether or not it allows UDFs to run inside its workbooks. If this option is not checked, any advanced UDFs you added to Excel Services will not work. This is the number one gotcha when writing UDFs — if you forget to check this, your UDFs will not execute in your workbook.

User Defined Function Assemblies

User defined functions are managed .NET assemblies that contain functions that are callable from within cells. This allows the developer to augment the existing Excel Services function library and is one of the ways we can add features back into Excel Services. Each such assembly needs to be registered in this part of the configuration.

Make sure to choose the correct option here — either File or GAC (Global Assembly Cache) — choosing an incorrect one will cause your assembly to fail when loading and leave you scratching your head as to why this is happening.

Summary

When developing software that works with Excel Services, it is useful for developers to understand how to administer the server, both when they want to test edge cases and when they need the server to be configured a certain way for their solution to work optimally. This chapter discussed the most common administration tasks developers will undertake — more advanced configurations may sometimes be needed but are out of the scope of this book.

3

Inside Excel Services

There are various technical details one needs to understand about Excel Services for the rest of the book to make sense. Even though some of this information may not have an immediate impact on how you use, or even program against, Excel Services, it will help you understand what happens under the hood.

Session, State, and Workbooks

When programming Excel Services, it is incredibly important to understand exactly how sessions fit in.

All interaction with Excel Services revolves around workbooks that are loaded, queried, and manipulated. When a workbook is needed, it is loaded into a session. What happens internally is this:

1. The server brings up the file and copies it locally (more on that when I discuss workbook caches) if it has not already done so.

2. It loads the workbook into memory if it has not already done so. This loaded workbook will be used as a "template" or as an "initial state."

3. Finally, a session is opened, and the workbook "template" is assigned to the session where it will be used. The session will have its own private copy as needed, and it will not affect the globally loaded workbook. In that way, the changes users make to the workbooks they load are isolated. A user making a change to a workbook will not see changes made to that same workbook by a different user.

No interaction with workbooks can be achieved without a session, and no session can exist that does not refer to a specific workbook. When a session expires (for any reason), all the information it holds expires with it. That means that if you make changes to a workbook and the session you work against is closed, all your changes will be lost. Open sessions on the server have a unique ID (Session ID) associated with them. That ID is used to interact with the session throughout its lifetime.

To further explain this, consider the simple workbook shown in Figure 3.1. It has two cells, A1 and A2.

Figure 3.1

A2 contains a very simple formula. In this case, it would be equal to 2. For this example, say that you have two users loading the workbook, one after another and manipulating it:

❑   **Jay opens a session asking for Workbook1.xlsx.** If the workbook is not available, the server will load it and go through the stages of making it available for users.

❑   **Jay gets the cell in A2.** The value Jay will see is "2" since that value was originally loaded with the workbook.

❑   **Jay sets the cell in A1 to "40.9" and gets the cell in A2.** The value Jay will get from A2 will now be "41.9", just as if Jay were to open the file in Excel and place "40.9" in A1.

❑   **From a different computer, Zoe also opens a session asking for Workbook1.xlsx.**

❑   **Zoe gets the value from A2.** Zoe will see the value "2" — she will not see any of the changes Jay made to the workbook since the two versions are isolated; they start out the same but they do not affect each other in any way.

It is important to understand that, from the users' point of view, they are the only one interacting with the workbook — nobody else can affect what they see in the workbook. The server makes sure to keep the workbooks isolated.

Generally speaking, Excel Services will not allow more than one request to a session at the same time. That is why the EWA may sometimes display a message saying that "there is currently a request running on this session, please try again later." That said, there are a few types of requests that can be made concurrently on a session. For more information about that, see the API references in Chapter 5.

Caches

Excel Services employs multiple levels of caching to ensure that requests can be executed as fast and with as little impact on the system as possible.

Workbook Caches

As stated before, Excel Services caches what data it can to provide faster response to users. Workbooks are cached on various levels.

Workbook Disk Cache

When a user asks for a workbook for the first time, that workbook is fetched from its remote location to the local disk. Once in the disk cache, the workbook will be deleted only when it is stale (i.e., when a newer workbook is available) or if space is needed in the cache (and since the cache defaults to 40GB, it is rare that additional space will be needed). Because memory is scarcer than disk space, there are cases in which workbooks that were in memory will be discarded (since they are not being used anymore) only to be reloaded from the local disk when requested again. This saves us from having to bring the file over the network every time the file is needed. The server also makes sure that it has current files. Whenever a workbook is opened, the server checks the "Last modified" property of the workbook. If there is a new workbook available, the server will fetch the new one.

Loaded Workbook Cache

Once a workbook has been brought to the local server, it will be loaded into memory. This loaded representation of the file will continue to exist in memory for as long as somebody is still using the workbook. Like most Excel Services caches, it may continue to exist in memory as long as there is no memory pressure on the server. Only the first request for the workbook will take the hit of going through the loading process — subsequent requests will use the loaded workbook.

Workbooks that are loaded under two different locales or in different time zones may need to be loaded more than once into memory. For example, a workbook loaded by a user using the Japanese locale and one loaded by a user using the Hebrew locale will cause two copies of the workbook to be loaded into memory. This is due to the fact that some very basic things behave differently with some locales and so have potentially completely different memory representations.

Shared Workbook Cache

It often happens that multiple users can share the same workbook. The obvious example is a workbook that is completely devoid of data queries or other volatile data. All users who open such a workbook will get the same result, no matter what. In those cases, Excel Services will only ever have one copy of that workbook in memory, which will be shared among users. This holds true in more complex cases, too. If Excel Services detects that two different users can share the same piece of data (and from that deduce that the whole workbook is identical for both users), it will make sure that only one copy of that workbook exists in memory.

Data Caches

When workbooks contain external data, that data may or may not be sharable by two different users. Moreover, say that a workbook contains two data queries — one sharable and one not. Excel Services will manage separate caches for each data source, allowing users to share results where possible.

Caching Calculations

Calculations are cached as part of the *Shared Workbook Cache* described previously. The important thing to note is that Excel Services is configured by default to minimize calculations of volatile functions.

Volatile functions are defined as functions that may return different results for the same parameters. A good example is the Excel built-in NOW() function. It has no parameters and yet it returns different results each time it gets called. The Volatile Function Cache Lifetime setting determines how often Excel Services make calls to volatile functions. The default setting is 300 seconds, which means that, in the example of NOW(), a workbook will only be recalculated for users asking for the workbook (or for users manually recalculating it) once every 5 minutes.

Some solutions in this book will require that you reduce this number to "0," which means that, whenever a user requests a workbook, that workbook will be recalculated to get the new value for the volatile functions.

Changing this setting to "0," however, also means that Excel Services is not reusing the workbooks it caches as often as it could be. This, in turn, can reduce the throughput of the server. Note that because this setting (Volatile Function Cache Lifetime) is bound to a trusted location, it is easy to partition files in such a way that only the ones that need to be recalculated often will be allowed to be.

Summary

Excel Services does its best to share resources among users as much as it can. This is one reason a single Excel Services server can service many more users on the same hardware than Excel Client ever could. While not strictly needed for writing code against the server, this chapter may help developers understand why Excel Services behaves in a certain way in various scenarios.

Programmability Options

There are three programmability interfaces you can use when you want to extend or work against Excel Services. Each one stands alone, although some can be used together to develop more complex solutions. Because each programmability option is aimed at solving a completely different problem, they require different skill sets. This chapter enumerates these different interfaces and gives a short explanation about what they can be used for. The next chapters in the book will go into more detail about these subjects.

Excel Web Services

The Excel Web Services are exposed as a set of methods that allow the developer to interact with workbook primitives and work against models that are embedded in Excel workbooks. The primitives allow you to open a workbook on the server, interact with it and close it. At times I will also refer to the Excel Web Services as EWS or the API.

Opening and Closing the Workbook

Before any other interaction can take place, the caller needs to open the workbook on the server. This will produce a "Session ID" that can be used throughout the lifetime of the opened workbook to interact with it. If no interaction is made with a specific session ID for a predefined length of time, Excel Services will timeout the session and get rid of it.

When opening a workbook, other than passing the location of the workbook, the caller can also supply what locale is needed for the operation. Opening a workbook under the French Canadian locale will potentially produce different results from opening it under a Farsi locale.

When a workbook is opened, there are various operations the server takes to prepare it. One example is data refreshes. If a workbook has a PivotTable on it, that PivotTable may be set up to refresh whenever the workbook is opened. If that is the case, the call will return only once the workbook has been refreshed. Note that, as in Excel, failure to refresh does not mean that the workbook cannot be opened. In those cases, the caller will get a warning as a result from the server explaining what failures occurred. If a workbook cannot be opened at all (say, because it does not exist, or if the user does not have access to it), the call to opening the workbook will fail, which translates to an exception being thrown in most cases.

The server allows the same workbook to be opened multiple times, even by the same user. In all such cases, the user starts from the "template" of the workbook, meaning the workbook will contain the information it was initially loaded with from disk. The only limit is the number of sessions per user that the administrator allows on the server.

The API contains a method to allow the caller to close an open workbook. In most cases, it is important to call this function explicitly so that the server can reclaim the session memory as soon as possible.

Getting Values from the Workbook

Once a session is opened, the developer is free to read values from it. There are several methods that allow the caller to get values from a workbook, each one tailored for a specific scenario. Developers can request either ranges or single cells and can do that in a variety of ways. As an example, when using the GetRangeA1() method call, the caller can pass in either an Excel reference string (such as A1) or a named range (such as NamedRange1). Excel will use the same logic it uses to resolve calls to figure out what the user wants.

While it's possible to get values from the Excel workbook, there is currently no way to get any formatting data.

> *Because it is possible to get the actual workbook from Excel Services (the binary representation), it is possible to use the* System.Packaging *assembly shipped with .NET 3.0 to crack open the workbook and read any information from it, including formatting. The book has an example of how to use* System.Packaging *but does not have a specific sample illustrating formatting.*

Writing Values to the Workbook

There are several methods that allow the developer to write values into the workbook. These values are placed in the cells specified and may or may not cause a recalculation to be fired (depending on how the workbook is authored). The same rules that apply to named ranges and Excel references when getting ranges apply in these methods as well.

Note that in this version of Excel Services you may only write into cells that do not contain formulas.

Workbook-level Interaction

The API contains methods to refresh data connections embedded in the workbook, as well as methods for recalculating the workbook.

Getting a Whole Workbook

You can use the API to get the workbook as it is currently in the session. Furthermore, the API can either retrieve a snapshot of the workbook (containing only the calculated values) or the full workbook (formulas and all).

This feature is incredibly useful for solutions that require continued interaction with a modified workbook in Excel. The result gets sent back in the format the workbook was originally saved in.

Miscellaneous Methods

There are a few other methods available for the caller. They allow you to get information about a session or about the server (such as server version or the locale the session is using).

The developer can also cancel a request that is currently running on the server by using the `CancelRequest()` call.

User Defined Function Assemblies

Excel Services allows solution providers to write a UDF assembly that can be used to augment the functions that can be used in formulas in Excel, much like XLLs and Automation Addins.

Since this is a new model and since Excel Services does not sport an OM (object model), there are several restrictions that are put on the UDFs. I will go into those in details in the section about UDFs.

EWA Web Part

The Excel Web Access Web Part allows people to embed live workbooks as part of their web application. While the control a developer has is somewhat limited, it does do a good job with showing workbooks and allowing the user to navigate them.

Summary

While the programmability story of Excel Services is not as rich as that of Excel, it still gives the developer ample opportunity to extend and drive the server. The next few chapters will take each of these programmability areas and expand on them, further explaining what they are most useful for and giving examples on how to use them.

Part II: Excel Web Services

5

Hello World Sample

In this chapter, you write your first "Hello World" program using Excel Web Services. You learn how to achieve the following:

- ❑ Add a reference to Excel Web Services by using Visual Studio 2005 to gain access to the Excel Services APIs.
- ❑ Use the APIs to open a workbook on the server and get back a Session ID.
- ❑ Extract values from cells in the workbook and set values into them.
- ❑ Use a model inside the workbook by setting values into some cells and getting results from another.

Hello World Overview

To keep it simple, a console application will make use of Excel Web Services. The workbook for this example contains a very simple Excel model, which is shown in Figure 5.1.

This workbook contains three cells that will be used in the example:

- ❑ A1 contains a string.
- ❑ A2 contains the string from A1 prefixed with the word "Hello".
- ❑ A3 contains a Boolean that will be "true" if A2 equals "Hello World" and "false" otherwise.

(The B2 and B3 cells are there to show you what the formulas in A2 and A3 are.)

When it's done, the Hello World application will be able to set a value it gets from the command line into A1, read the string from A2, display it in the console window, and then also display whether the message that was printed was actually "Hello World." As a final step, this chapter will show how changing the model does not require the developer to change any code in the application.

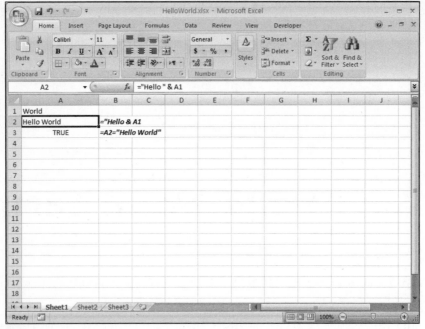

Figure 5.1

Preparing the Project and Opening a Workbook

The first step is to place the workbook in a trusted location (for more information about trusted locations, see Chapter 2). For this example, the trusted location will be `http://OSS/Shared Documents/HelloWorld.xlsx`. Depending on the setup, the location can, of course, be different. To save a workbook into SharePoint, users can either use the Excel 2007 Save As feature to save the file to the server, the Publish to Excel Services feature, or the SharePoint Web user interface to upload the file there.

Making Sure the File Can Be Accessed by Excel Services

Once the file has been saved to the server, the server should be able to access it. It is always a good idea to make sure that the trusted locations are working. Excel Services will not distinguish in its error messages between the case where a location is not trusted (i.e., not on the Trusted Location list) and when the file does not exist. Both these errors will produce the same error text and error code. This ambiguity exists for security reasons. If a different error message were given, malicious users could use it to snoop around and use Excel Services to check which files exist in document libraries they do not have access to. There are a few ways to check if a file can be loaded by Excel Services — the easiest is to use a browser to navigate to EWA (Excel Web Access) and ask it to load the file. To do that, you can simply navigate to the SharePoint document library where you stored the file, use the dropdown on the file name and choose the View in Web Browser option (see Figure 5.2). Once that is done, the workbook should be rendered in the browser as shown in Figure 5.3.

Figure 5.2

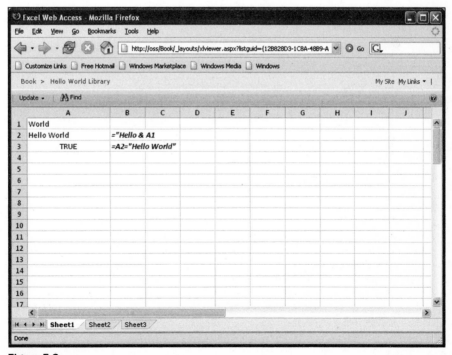

Figure 5.3

Now that you know the workbook can be opened by Excel Services, you can go to the next stage — using the API to access it.

Preparing the Project for Use with Excel Services

As described previously in the "Hello World Overview" section, this chapter shows you the steps for creating a console application that can access information on the server. The first step is accomplished with the Visual Studio New Project Wizard. For this example, the Console Application option (shown in Figure 5.4) should be used to create the project.

Once that is done, use the Visual Studio Add Web Reference option, as shown in Figure 5.5, so the project will contain a proxy that will be used to access the Web Service.

In Visual Studio, proxies ease the use of Web Services for developers. While they are relatively easy to use even without a proxy, it makes everything cleaner and smoother (and type safe!)

Right-clicking on the project and choosing the Add Web Reference option presents the user with a dialog box (see Figure 5.6) for the address of the Web Service. The address to the appropriate Excel Services Web Service will be `http://<server name>/vti_bin/ExcelService.asmx`. When adding web references in Visual Studio though, developers will need the WSDL (Web Services Description Language) that corresponds to the Web Service. To gain access to that, you need to append `?wsdl` to the URL. In this case, the address will be:

```
http://OSS/_vti_bin/ExcelService.asmx?wsdl
```

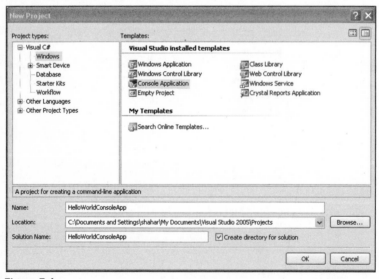

Figure 5.4

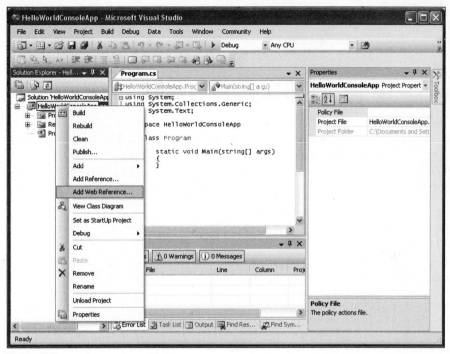

Figure 5.5

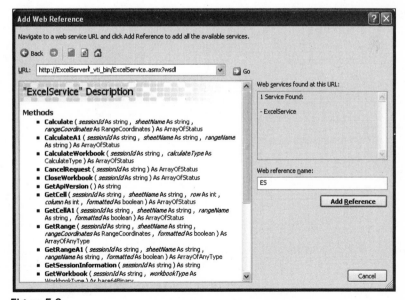

Figure 5.6

The last important part here is the Web reference name text box on this dialog. When Visual Studio prepares the proxy that allows the developer to access Excel Services, it will place it in a namespace by that name. In this case, you will use ES for that namespace.

Opening a Workbook on the Server

Now that everything set up, the developer can finally start working against Excel Services. The first step is to open a workbook on the server and get back a Session ID. This Session ID will be usable with the Excel Web Services methods. The method that will be used to open the workbook is appropriately named `OpenWorkbook` and will be called from the `ExcelService` class that was created previously:

```
private const string Workbook =
        "http://OSS/Shared Documents/HelloWorld.xlsx";
static void Main(string[] args)
{
    // Create the proxy instance.
    ES.ExcelService s = new ES.ExcelService();
    s.SoapVersion = SoapProtocolVersion.Soap12;
string sessionId;
    try
    {
        // Make sure your user credentials are used.
        s.Credentials = System.Net.CredentialCache.DefaultCredentials;
        ES.Status[] status;
        Console.WriteLine("Opening workbook {0}", Workbook);

        // Open the workbook.
        sessionId = s.OpenWorkbook(Workbook,
            String.Empty, String.Empty,
            out status);

        Console.WriteLine("Session ID is: {0}", sessionId);
    }
    catch (SoapException e)
    {
        Console.WriteLine("Got server error: {0}", e.SubCode.Code.Name);
    }
    catch (Exception e)
    {
        Console.WriteLine("Got unknown error: {0}", e);
    }
}
```

Running the program should show the output depicted in Figure 5.7.

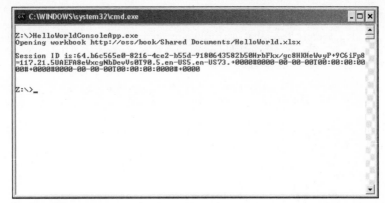

Figure 5.7

This is what the code is doing:

1. First the proxy is prepared for usage.

- ❑ The proxy that was created by importing the WSDL is instantiated (`new ES .ExcelService()`). This will allow the developer to make calls into Excel Web Services.

- ❑ The proxy is then set up to use the SOAP (Simple Object Access Protocol) version 1.2 protocol (that is what the enum value of `Soap12` stands for). This is done so that the developer can get more granular errors from calls to the Web Service. If this value were not set, the protocol would have been SOAP version 1.1, which would not have allowed for error sub codes.

See www.w3.org/TR/soap *for more information about the additions to the protocol.*

- ❑ Finally, the developer needs to make sure that the proxy uses the appropriate user credentials to access the server. This step is not always necessary (for example, if the Web Service is completely public), but in most Excel Services deployments, the code would fail to run without this line.

2. Next, the workbook is opened for use.

- ❑ Two variables need to be defined for usage with the `OpenWorkbook` call — one for holding the status array and one for holding the Session ID that will be created.

- ❑ The call is then made to `OpenWorkbook` method with the name of the workbook passed in. There are two empty strings that get passed in — these determine what locale will be used for the session and will be discussed in detail in Chapter 6.

3. Finally, the program takes care of errors that may occur:

  ❑ SoapExceptions that are thrown mean that an actual server error has occurred. For example, if an incorrect file name was to be passed, or if the caller does not have access rights to that workbook, SoapExceptions exceptions would be thrown.

  ❑ Other exceptions may signify that other errors are occurring, such as being unable to reach the server or not having rights to access the Web Service.

At the end of the try block, the caller is left with a Session ID that can be used to make other calls into Excel Services to communicate with the server.

Getting a Cell from the Workbook

Now that the program has the Session ID, it is very easy to ask Excel Services to get a value from the workbook. In this example, a call is made to GetCellA1(), which fetches the A2 cell (the one containing the concatenated greeting string).

```
// Grab the cell from A2.
Console.WriteLine("Reading cell from Sheet1!A2");
object greeting = s.GetCellA1(sessionId,
      "Sheet1", "A2", true, out status);
Console.WriteLine("Greeting is: {0}", greeting);
```

The first parameter that is passed in is the Session ID that was retrieved from opening the workbook — almost all the methods in the Web Service take this as their first parameter. Next, the cell reference that is wanted is passed in as a parameter — in this case, cell A2 on Sheet1. The rest of the parameters will be discussed in detail in Chapter 6.

Running the application now will display the output shown in Figure 5.8.

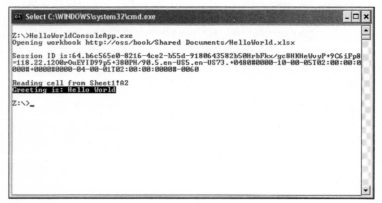

Figure 5.8

Writing Values into Cells in the Workbook

Excel Services also allows developers to write values into cells in the workbook. This is the key to leveraging models written in Excel workbooks on the server. In this case, the program will take the first argument passed to it and write it into the A1 cell. That, in turn, should cause the value in A2 to change and display the new greeting message.

To do this, the program will call the SetCellA1() method exposed by the proxy. The code will be placed before the code added in the "Getting a Cell from the Workbook" section.

```
// Set the first argument to the program into A1
if (args.Length >= 1)
{
    string greetingSubject = args[0];
    Console.WriteLine("Setting {0} into Sheet1!A1", greetingSubject);
    s.SetCellA1(sessionId, "Sheet1", "A1", greetingSubject);
}
```

First, the program checks to see that there are arguments passed to it — if there are, it will use the first one (args[0]) in a call to SetCellA1(). The Session ID is again passed as the first parameter. Much as with GetCellA1, the target of the operation is also passed in as a reference to a cell (Sheet1, A1). Finally, the greetingSubject variable, which contains the value that needs to be set, is passed as an argument as well.

If the program was to be called with the string "Nasty" as the first argument, it would produce a result similar to that shown in Figure 5.9.

Notice how the resulting string is now "Hello Nasty" instead of the somewhat more mundane "Hello World."

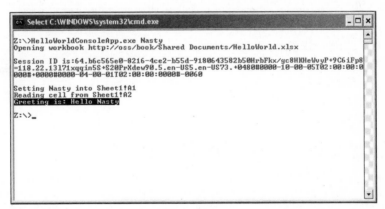

Figure 5.9

Using the Model Part of the Workbook

This brings this section to the last functional part of the "Hello World" example — making sure the value is "correct." This is what cell A3 will be used for. A3 contains a formula that returns a value indicating whether or not the value equals "Hello World." Of course, that model could be written into the code, but that would defeat the purpose of this demo. Furthermore, at the end of the chapter, it will be shown how the fact that this simplistic model is embedded in Excel can come in handy.

Toward the end of the `try` block, the following code needs to be added:

```
Console.WriteLine("Reading cell from Sheet1!A3");
bool valid = (bool)s.GetCellA1(sessionId,
     "Sheet1", "A3", false, out status);
if (valid)
     Console.WriteLine("Value is valid!");
else
     Console.WriteLine("Value is invalid!");
```

Running the program once with "Nasty" and once with "World" outputs "Value is invalid!" and "Value is valid!" respectively, as shown in Figure 5.10.

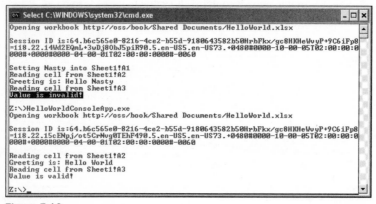

Figure 5.10

Finishing the Sample Project

The final part that will be added to the project is to close the Session ID that was opened. This is very important, since sessions take memory on the server, and while the server will close them in due time, it is much healthier for the overall system if they are close when no longer needed.

The method used to close the workbook, will be the `CloseWorkbook()` method. To make sure that the code always runs, it will be placed inside a `finally` block (that way, even if one of the other calls fails, the session will still be closed):

```
finally
{
    if (!String.IsNullOrEmpty(sessionId))
    {
        Console.WriteLine("Closing the workbook...");
        s.CloseWorkbook(sessionId);
    }
}
```

Updating the Model

Now that the "Hello World" sample is working, it is easy to see how powerful Excel Services is. The simplistic model outputs `true` if the string is what the model writer expected and `false` if it is not. Because that logic is embedded inside a workbook, it is incredibly easy to change the behavior of the sample program without changing any of the actual code. If the model in the workbook was to be changed to expect the string "Hello Mondo" instead of "Hello World," and then the same binary was to be executed again, the string will now only be valid if A2 has "Hello Mondo" in it.

The modified workbook would look like Figure 5.11.

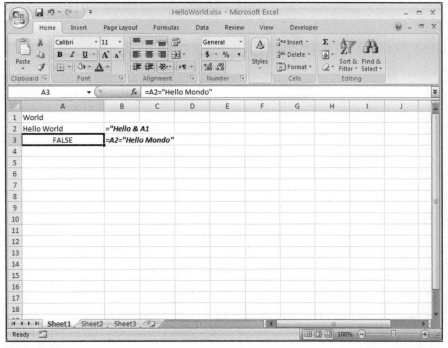

Figure 5.11

If the program was executed after the workbook modification, with World as a parameter, the result would be the string "Value is invalid."

Extras

There are a few "best practices" that were omitted from the code to make it shorter.

For one, the CloseWorkbook() call should be made inside its own try/catch block. Consider what happens if the session times out or if the session was forcibly closed on to the server due to an unrecoverable error. In those cases, calling CloseWorkbook() on a now invalid Session ID will throw an exception. This try/catch block was added to the complete listing at the end of this chapter.

It would have also been useful for the program to use named ranges instead of actual cell references. This adds a level of abstraction that gives the workbook author much more flexibility as to how the workbook looks. In this case, if the workbook author were to move the cells around (because they wanted to pretty it up and add labels to each cell by adding a column at the right), the program would stop working. If you used named ranges, however, the author could move the names around with the cell and the program would continue to work.

Final Program

This section shows you the final "Hello World" program, in both C# and VB.NET.

C# Hello World Program

```
class Program
{
    private const string Workbook = "http://OSS/Shared Documents/HelloWorld.xlsx";
    static void Main(string[] args)
    {
        // Create the proxy instance.
        ES.ExcelService s = new ES.ExcelService();
        s.SoapVersion = SoapProtocolVersion.Soap12;
        string sessionId = null;

        try
        {
            // Make sure your user credentials are used.
            s.Credentials = System.Net.CredentialCache.DefaultCredentials;
            ES.Status[] status;
            Console.WriteLine("Opening workbook {0}", Workbook);

            // Open the workbook.
            sessionId = s.OpenWorkbook(Workbook,
                String.Empty, String.Empty,
                out status);
```

```
                    Console.WriteLine("Session ID is:{0}", sessionId);

                    // Set the first argument to the program into A1.
                    if (args.Length >= 1)
                    {
                        string greetingSubject = args[0];
                        Console.WriteLine("Setting {0} into Sheet1!A1",
greetingSubject);
                        s.SetCellA1(sessionId, "Sheet1", "A1", greetingSubject);
                    }

                    // Grab the cell from A2.
                    Console.WriteLine("Reading cell from Sheet1!A2");
                    object greeting = s.GetCellA1(sessionId,
                        "Sheet1", "A2", true, out status);
                    Console.WriteLine("Greeting is: {0}", greeting);

                    // Get the value that says if the model is valid.
                    Console.WriteLine("Reading cell from Sheet1!A3");
                    bool valid = (bool)s.GetCellA1(sessionId,
                        "Sheet1", "A3", false, out status);
                    if (valid)
                        Console.WriteLine("Value is valid!");
                    else
                        Console.WriteLine("Value is invalid!");
                }
                catch (SoapException e)
                {
                    Console.WriteLine("Got server error:{0}", e.SubCode.Code.Name);
                }
                catch (Exception e)
                {
                    Console.WriteLine("Got unknown error:{0}", e);
                }
                finally
                {
                    if (!String.IsNullOrEmpty(sessionId))
                    {
                        Console.WriteLine("Closing the workbook...");
                        try
                        {
                            s.CloseWorkbook(sessionId);
                        }
                        catch
                        {
                        }
                    }
                }
            }
        }
```

VB.NET Sample Code

```vb.net
Const Workbook As String = "http://OSS/Shared Documents/HelloWorld.xlsx"

Sub Main(ByVal Args() As String)
    ' Create the proxy instance.
    Dim service As ES.ExcelService = New ES.ExcelService()
    service.SoapVersion = Web.Services.Protocols.SoapProtocolVersion.Soap12
    Dim sessionId As String
        Try
            ' Make sure your user credentials are used.
            service.Credentials = System.Net.CredentialCache.DefaultCredentials
            Dim status() As ES.Status
            Console.WriteLine("Opening workbook {0}", Workbook)

            ' Open the workbook.
            sessionId = service.OpenWorkbook(Workbook, "", "", status)

            Console.WriteLine("Session ID is: {0}", sessionId)

            ' Set the first argument to the program into A1.
            If (Args.Length >= 1) Then
                Dim greetingSubject = Args(0)
                Console.WriteLine("Setting {0} into Sheet1!A1",
greetingSubject)
                service.SetCellA1(sessionId, "Sheet1", "A1", greetingSubject)
            End If

            ' Grab the cell from A2.
            Console.WriteLine("Reading cell from Sheet1!A2")
            Dim greeting As Object = service.GetCellA1(sessionId, _
              "Sheet1", "A3", False, status)
            Console.WriteLine("Greeting is: {0}", greeting)

            ' Get the value that says if the model is valid.
            Console.WriteLine("Reading cell from Sheet1!A3")
            Dim valid As Boolean = CBool(service.GetCellA1(sessionId, _
              "Sheet1", "A3", False, status))

            If (valid) Then
                Console.WriteLine("Value is valid!")
            Else
                Console.WriteLine("Value is invalid!")
            End If
        End With
    Catch ex As SoapException
        Console.WriteLine("Got server error:{0}", ex.SubCode.Code.Name)
    Catch ex As Exception
        Console.WriteLine("Got unknown error:{0}", ex)
```

```
        Finally
            If (Not (String.IsNullOrEmpty(sessionId))) Then
                Console.WriteLine("Closing the workbook.")
                Try
                        service.CloseWorkbook(sessionId)
                Catch
                End Try
            End If
        End Try

    End Sub
```

Summary

Excel Services lets the developer write code that can open, manipulate, and get values back from a work-book. While the range of functionality is not near as wide as it is with Excel, Excel Services still provides very compelling capabilities when it comes to calculating models on the server. The next chapters will expand further on these abilities.

6

Excel Web Services Reference

As described in the introduction to this book, programming against Excel Services is generally done through the Excel Services Web Service. This chapter will dive into more details about how to use Excel Services via the API. This will also set the stage for the next project, Excel Web Services Wrapper, creating a library that will help you make better use of Excel Web Services.

Direct Linking

While, the main way to program against the Excel Web Services is via Web services, there are some cases where that is impossible. Consider for example a Web Part solution that is deployed on your SharePoint web front-end web server. To use the API, this solution needs, essentially, to loop back to the front-end machine and invoke the Excel Web Services (since the Excel Services Web Service API is located there). In some cases, this would be impossible. Due to security issues, administrators sometimes block the ability of a machine to loop back to the farm it belongs to through HTTP. To solve this problem, the Excel Web Services can be directly linked (.NET reference) by an assembly, which can then make direct calls (as opposed to Web service calls that go over HTTP). This technique will be shown when the book shows how to create the Excel Web Services Wrapper project. This has the added bonus of being somewhat faster, since there is one less out-of-process call to be made.

Notations Used in the API Reference

The calls that Visual Studio 2005 will generate for you may look different from the way they look in other tools. For some reason, the Web service importer of VS promotes out-parameters into return values. This can cause some inconsistencies in the generated VS proxy. For example, almost all web methods take a `Status` array as their last parameter to report any warnings with the calls. When imported into VS, some of the methods will have a `Status` array as a return value — these are the methods that do not have a return value, such as the `SetCellA1` used in the Hello World example in this section. The original method signature contained an extra parameter, much like the `OpenWorkbook` call and the `GetCellA1` call. When they are different, I will include both signatures for each function, since they may be used from tools that do not make this modification.

Session Management Methods

There are three methods that are used to manage sessions and gain information about them. The two important ones are of course the `OpenWorkbook` and `CloseWorkbook` methods. The third one, `GetSessionInfo`, is used to get some basic information about the session.

OpenWorkbook

To be able to do anything programmatically with Excel Services, you first need to call `OpenWorkbook`. The result of a successful `OpenWorkbook` call is a Session ID that will be used throughout the interaction of the caller with the workbook.

```
string OpenWorkbook(string workbookPath,
string uiCultureName,
string dataCultureName,
out Status[] status)
```

The arguments are:

❑ `workbookPath` — This is the URL or URN to the workbook that needs to be opened. See the "Remarks" section following this list for what types of URLs/URNs are supported. In any case, for this method to be successful, the workbook specified needs to be located in a TL (trusted location) (see Chapter 2 for more information about trusted locations).

❑ `uiCultureName` — A language code (i.e., "en-US") that will govern the UI aspect of strings that come back from the server. For example, if this string was "he-IL," the error strings that would come back when an error occurs will be in the Hebrew language.

See `http://msdn.microsoft.com/library/default.asp?url=/workshop/author/dhtml/reference/language_codes.asp` *for a complete list.*

❑ `dataCultureName` — Also a language code, this one governs the way data will be formatted in workbooks that are loaded. For example, passing in "de-DE" (German locale) will cause the decimal point to become a comma so that a cell containing 3.1415 would come back as 3,1415 when formatted as a string.

❑ `status` — Workbooks may contain elements such as data connections. In some cases, workbooks are designed to refresh their data when they load. Due to the fickle nature of some networks, there may be errors when trying to do the refresh operation. In those cases, the *OpenWorkbook* operation will succeed (the caller will get a valid Session ID), however, the warnings about the parts that failed will be contained in the `Status` array — an entry for each problem discovered while loading the workbook. Note that if there are errors that prevent the workbook from opening, the method will throw an exception instead of using the status array.

❏   `Return Value` — The string that returns from Excel Services is the Session ID that will be used to communicate with Excel Services.

Remarks

Workbook URLs and URNs can be of one of the following forms:

```
http://servername/folder/workbook.xlsx
https://servername/folder/workbook.xlsx
\\fileserver\share\workbook.xlsx
file://fileserver/share/workbook.xlsx
```

Excel Services supports all these and will successfully load the file (if it is in a TL).

You can pass in empty strings for both `dataCultureName` and `uiCultureName`. When you do that, Excel Services will use the SharePoint locales for the root web site.

Example — Opening a Workbook and Checking for Warnings

This example shows how to open a workbook. If any warnings are detected, they will be output to the console window for display to the user.

```
s = new ExcelService();
Status[] status;
string sessionId = s.OpenWorkbook(
    "http://Company/Shared Documents/Model.xlsb",
    "", "", out status);
if (status.Length > 0)
{
    Console.WriteLine("There were {0} warnings when opening the workbook.",
        status.Length);
}
```

Example — Opening a Workbook with Different Locales

In this case, the workbook will be opened using the German Germany locale for UI and the U.S. English locale for data. If an exception is raised, its message will be in German.

```
s = new ExcelService();
Status[] status;
try
{
    string sessionId = s.OpenWorkbook(
        "http://Company/Shared Documents/NonExistantFile.xlsb",
        "de-DE", "en-US", out status);
}
catch (SoapException ex)
{
    MessageBox.Show(ex.Message);
}
```

In this case, the message box that appears will contain an error in the German language.

Of course, this requires that the German language locale be installed on the server. If it is not, Excel Web Services will fall back to another suitable culture or to the language pack included with the installation.

CloseWorkbook

When you are done with a session, it is good practice to close it so that the server can reclaim the memory that it uses:

```
// VS2005 imported signature
Status[] CloseWorkbook(string sessionId)
// Real signature
void CloseWorkbook(string sessionId, out Status[] sessionId)
```

The arguments are:

❑   `sessionId` — A session that was previously opened using the `OpenWorkbook` call.

❑   `Return Value` — An array of `Status` objects. In this version, this will always be an empty array.

Note about request concurrency: `CloseWorkbook` *can be called while Excel Services is still busy processing other requests on the session. If there is a request running in the session, the server will issue an implicit cancel call and return immediately. From that moment, the session will be inaccessible to callers even though it may still exist on the server for the duration of the canceled operation.*

> **Always put your `CloseWorkbook` call in the final part of your code so that it will be called even when there is an error in the flow of your calls to Excel Services. That will make sure you always close the session. Furthermore, always wrap it in a `try/catch` block. Sometimes sessions will close (due to unrecoverable errors or server failures) — failing to do so will cause the call to fail and can potentially cause your program to terminate.**

CancelRequest

Operations on Excel Services such as data refreshes can take a long time to complete. In such cases, the caller may at times wish to cancel the request:

```
// VS2005 imported signature
public Status[] CancelRequest(string sessionId)
// Real signature
public void CancelRequest(string sessionId, out Status[] status)
```

The arguments are:

❑   `sessionId` — A session that was previously opened using the `OpenWorkbook` call.

❑   `Return value` — An array of `Status` objects. With this version of Excel Services, this array will always be empty.

Note about request concurrency: `CancelRequest` *can be called on any valid session, even if it is already processing a request.*

This method is usually called from a different thread than the one you wish to cancel or, alternatively, it can be called from the same thread if you called the original request in an asynchronous manner. There are a few important things to note about canceling requests on Excel Services:

❑ Since there is no request ID, you can only cancel the currently running request — there is no way to cancel a specific request.

❑ Some requests cannot be canceled immediately and will require some more processing before canceling — that is why you may not get an immediate cancellation.

❑ Depending on timing, a request may not be canceled even though Excel Services got a cancellation request. This usually happens when the ongoing operation is almost finished when the cancellation call comes in — Excel Services will usually opt to finish the request if all that is left to be done is cleaning up and sending the response back to the caller.

❑ When canceling a request, the call to `CancelRequest` will return immediately in a successful manner. The other call (the one that is being canceled) will return with an error saying that it was canceled.

The request may take time to return if the Web front end (WFE) machine you are using for your API calls is stressed.

Example

This example uses the generated asynchronous functionality of the proxy to issue a refresh request to the server. If the request takes too long to finish, the code will call `CancelRequest` on it.

```
void IssueTimeLimitedRequest()
{
    // Assign a callback to when the callback is complete.
    s.RefreshCompleted +=
        new RefreshCompletedEventHandler(RefreshCompleted);

    // Create an event - we will use that to signal the completeness of
    // the request.
    using (ManualResetEvent e = new ManualResetEvent(false))
    {
        Console.WriteLine("Issuing refresh request.");
        s.RefreshAsync(m_sessionId, "", e);

        Console.WriteLine(
            "Waiting for request to finish or 5 seconds to pass");
        bool signalled = e.WaitOne(5000, true);

        // If we timed out, it means the request did not finish
        // after the allotted 5 seconds. Attempt to cancel it.
        if (!signalled)
        {
            Console.WriteLine(
                "5 seconds passed - cancelling request");
            s.CancelRequest(m_sessionId);
```

```
                        // Wait again for the request to return so that we know
                        // we can continue working with the server.
                        // Note: In some cases, you may wish to completely abandon
                        // the session - in those cases, you can just call
                        // CloseWorkbook() on the sessionId and not have to wait for
                        // the request to finish.
                        e.WaitOne();
            }
            else
            {
                        // Depending on what the error is in the refresh result
                        // we can figure if there was an exception or not.
                        if (m_refreshResult.Error == null)
                        {

                                Console.WriteLine(
                                        "Refresh request finished succesfuly");
                        }
                        else
                        {
                                Console.WriteLine(
                                        "Refreh request failed.");
                        }
                }
        }
}

void RefreshCompleted(object sender, RefreshCompletedEventArgs e)
{
        // Assign the event arguments to a member variable so we can
        // access them.
        m_refreshResult = e;
        ManualResetEvent completionEvent = (ManualResetEvent)(e.UserState);
        completionEvent.Set();
}
```

GetSessionInfo

This method can be used to get information about a Session ID. When successful it will return some basic information such as the locales the session was opened with.

```
// VS2005 imported signature
public string GetSessionInformation(string sessionId,
        out string uiCultureNameUsed,
        out string dataCultureNameUsed,
        out Status[] status)
// Real Signature
public void GetSessionInformation(string sessionId,
        out string uiCultureNameUsed,
        out string dataCultureNameUsed,
        out Status[] status,
 out string sessionInfo)
```

The arguments are:

❑   `sessionId` — A session that was previously opened using the `OpenWorkbook` call.

❑   `uiCultureUsed` — Will contain the UI culture that was used to open the session.

❑   `dataCultureUsed` — Will contain the data culture that was used to open the session.

❑   `status` — Will always be empty.

❑   `Return Value` — The version of the Excel Services being used.

Note that this is different than the version of the API. The API version is retrieved by calling the `GetAPIVersion` *method and is the version of the product running on the web front end, serving requests. This method returns the version of the server that is running inside the Shared Service Provider (SSP) — the actual Excel Services server.*

This method call is mostly useful to check if a Session ID is still valid (and as a way to keep it alive). It is also useful if code gets handed a Session ID that another piece of code created and needs to find the locales that were used to open it, or if the server had to fall back to other locales.

Cell Retrieval Methods

Excel Services supplies four methods for retrieving data from Excel Services, each being slightly different from the other but all sharing the same functionality. The following table maps out the four methods and their usage. The next few pages will elaborate on each method.

Function Name	Usage
`GetCell`	Used for getting a cell from the workbook using an x,y coordinate for the cell. Calling this function with the 2,2 coordinates will retrieve the cell located in C3.
`GetCellA1`	Retrieves a single value based on an Excel references or named range. Calling this function with the string "B3" as the range parameter will retrieve the cell located in B3. Calling it with the string "Price" as the range parameter will retrieve value that the named range "Price" represents.
`GetRange`	Used to retrieve a whole range of cells by numeric coordinates.
`GetRangeA1`	Used to retrieve a range based on an Excel reference or named range.

Common Characteristics for GetXXX Methods

There are a few common characteristics when it comes to all four data retrieval methods, which are described in the following sections.

Cell/Range Differences

The methods that have `Cell` in their names can only retrieve a single value. If you try to retrieve an Excel Reference or a named range that contains more than one cell, they will fail.

Methods with `Range` in their names can retrieve any number of cells. There is an upper limit of 1,000,000 (1 million) cells on the range that can be retrieved.

Accessing Multi-cell Ranges

The value returned from the `GetRange` and `GetRangeA1` methods is always a jagged array. The return value type will be `object[]` (object array). We call this array the "outer array." Each element in the outer array will always be an object array as well (the "inner arrays"). The easiest way to look at this is to consider the outer array as the rows collection and the inner array as the cells or columns in each row. Figure 6.1 illustrates the structure that will be returned when a request for the range G4:J7 is made, and how it looks in memory.

In this case, to access the cell in G6, you could use the following code:

```
object[] rows;
// ... Get the range G4:J7 into the rows variable.
// Index 2 corresponds to row 6.
object[] row = (object[])rows[2];
// Index 0 in the row corresponds to the G column.
object cell = row[0];
```

It is important to note that callers can rely on the jagged array that is returned to always have the same number of cells in every row. Excel Services will always return rows multiplied by columns as the number of cells, regardless of their contents.

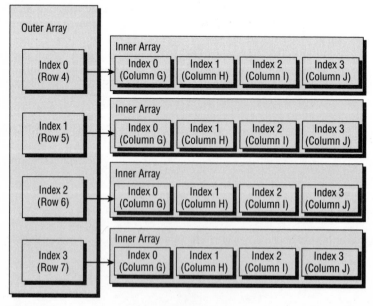

Figure 6.1

Supported Range Names

The `GetCellA1` and `GetRangeA1` methods support any range that the `INDIRECT` Excel function knows how to handle, namely:

❏ Any global or sheet-bound named range.

❏ Any A1-style range — for example, Sheet1!A1:Z30.

❏ Any structured reference construct. For example, calling `GetRangeA1` with the range name `ProductTable[ProductName]` will return all the cells in the table ProductTable that are located under the column called ProductName.

Cell Formatting

All value retrieval methods have a Boolean parameter called `formatted`. The value passed in that parameter will determine how the data comes back. When `formatted` is set to `true`, all cell contents come back formatted as strings. The resulting string depends both on the formatting style applied to the cell in the workbook and on the locale that was used to open the workbook. If the parameter is set to `false`, however, the data will come back bearing the actual type — be it `System.Double` (for numbers), `System.String`, `System.DateTime`, or `System.Boolean`. There is also a fifth type, which is used when a cell contains an error — that is an enumeration type that is defined in the Web Service and is called `CellError`. The following table shows how various cells will look when retrieved in their formatted or unformatted form.

Cell Contents	Formatted	Notes	Result
The number 9.0210	True	"Number" cell formatting with 2 decimal places. The workbook was opened using the en-US locale.	Type:System.String Value: "9.02"
The number 9.0210	True	"Number" cell formatting with three decimal places. The workbook was opened using the de-DE locale (German, Germany)	Type: System.String Value: "9,021"
The number 9.0210	False	Any number cell formatting, any locale	Type:System.Double Value: 9.0210
The string "Hello World"	True/false		Type: System.String Value: "Hello World"
The date 04/18/2006	True	"Date" cell formatting with only month and day. Workbook was opened using the "en-US" locale (English, U.S.).	Type:System.String Value: "4/18"
The date 04/18/2006	True	"Date" cell formatting with only month and day. Workbook was opened using the "he-IL" locale (Hebrew, Israel)	Type:System.String Value: "18/04"

Continued

Cell Contents	Formatted	Notes	Result
The date 04/18/2006	True	"Date" cell formatting with only month and day. Workbook was opened using the "he-IL" locale (Hebrew, Israel)	Type:System.String Value: "18/04"
The date 04/18/2006	False	Any date format, any locale	Type: System.DateTime Value: 18th April 2006
The error #DIV/0	False		Type: CellErrorValue: CellError.Div0
The error #DIV/0	True		Type: System.String Value: "#DIV/0"

GetCell

The GetCell method is used to retrieve a single cell using a numerical coordinate:

```
public object GetCell(string sessionId,
    string sheetName,
    int row,
    int column,
    bool formatted,
    out Status[] status)
```

❑   sessionId — A session that was previously opened using the OpenWorkbook call.

❑   sheetName — The name of the sheet that contains the information. Omitting this parameter will return values from the default sheet. You should always pass this parameter in — otherwise, you may not be able to rely on the results coming back. The "default" sheet in this case is the sheet that was active when the workbook was opened. Since this is liable to change as people save the workbook, it is not recommended that code rely on it.

❑   row — Zero-based row index of the cell that is wanted. Index 0 corresponds to row 1 in an Excel worksheet. Index 1 corresponds to row 2, and so on.

❑   column — Zero-based column index of the cell that is wanted. Index 0 corresponds to column A, index 1 corresponds to column B, and so on.

❑   formatted — Specifies whether or not the value returned should be formatted.

❑   status — An array of Status objects retrieved from the server. This array will always be empty.

About request concurrency: This method can be called with the other Get functions at the same time. That means that you can get data from multiple ranges at the same time.

Example

The following example takes a value from the cell B8 (row 7, column 1) in the "Matrix" sheet and returns it if it is a double. If it is not, it throws an exception.

Note how the row parameter is 7 even though we write into a cell that is on the eighth row. This is due to the fact that the Excel Web Services API is zero-based when it comes to indices, while the Excel sheet is one-based.

While it may seem like a weird technical decision to make the API zero-based, it actually makes sense when you think about it. For users who want to use Excel notations, we supply the methods postfixed with the A1 notation. If users want to access the workbook using a coordinate method, we supply them with one that is consistent with most .NET languages, that is, zero-based.

```
object o = s.GetCell(m_sessionId, "Matrix", 7, 1, false, out status);
if (o.is double)
{
    return (double)o;
}
throw new InvalidOperationException(
    "Value retrieved from Workbook was not a number!");
```

GetCellA1

When a value is needed from Excel Services and the caller has an Excel-style reference to it (A1) or a name of a range, the GetCellA1 method can be used to gain access to that cell:

```
public object GetCellA1(string sessionId,
    string sheetName,
    string rangeName,
    bool formatted,
    out Status[] status)
```

❑   sessionId — A session that was previously opened using the OpenWorkbook call.

❑   sheetName — The name of the sheet in which rangeName resides. Can be ommitted if the range is global or if it contains the name of the sheet.

❑   rangeName — Named range requested.

❑   formatted — Specifies whether the result should be formatted or not.

❑   Status — An array of Status objects returned from Excel Services. This array will always be empty.

Calling this method with a range that contains more than one cell will fail. Calling it with a range that would not work with the Excel INDIRECT function will also fail.

If formatted is true, the returned object will always be a string. Otherwise, the type may vary, depending on the type of the value inside the cell.

About request concurrency: This method can be called with the other Get functions at the same time. That means you can get data from multiple ranges at the same time.

Example

The following example takes a double that represents dollars and then uses a workbook to grab how many yens to a dollar the current exchange rate is. It then uses that number to calculate how many yens the dollar amount is equal to.

Notice how the sheet name is left empty:

```
double ConvertDollarToYen(double dollars)
{
    // Get the value from the DollarToYenRate named range.
    object o = s.GetCellA1(m_sessionId,
        "",
        "DollarToYenRate",
        false,
        out status);

    // Calculate how many yens.
    return dollars * (double)o;
}
```

GetRange

The GetRange method is similar to the GetCell call, but returns a full range:

```
public object[] GetRange(string sessionId,
    string sheetName,
    RangeCoordinates rangeCoordinates,
    bool formatted,
    out Status[] status)
```

The arguments are:

❑ sessionId — A session that was previously opened using the OpenWorkbook call.

❑ sheetName — The name of the sheet that contains the information. Omitting this parameter will return values from the default sheet.

❑ rangeCoordinates — Instance of a RangeCoordinates class — contains the top, left, width, and height coordinates of the requested range.

❑ formatted — Specifies whether or not the value returned should be formatted.

❑ status — An array of status objects retrieved from the server. This array will always be empty.

❑ Return Value — A jagged array containing the requested range.

About request concurrency: This method can be called with the other Get functions at the same time. That means you can get data from multiple ranges at the same time.

Example

The following example gets a range that corresponds to the C4:D6 range on the workbook. It will then iterate all cells in the range and process them.

```
// Create a RangeCoordinates object corresponding to
// C4:D6
RangeCoordinates rangeCoordinates = new RangeCoordinates();
c.Column = 2;
c.Row = 3;
c.Height = 3;
c.Width = 2;
// Get the range from the server.
object[] rows = s.GetRange(m_sessionId, "Matrix", rangeCoordinates,
    true, out status)
// Iterate over all the rows and process each cell in each row.
foreach (object[] row in rows)
{
    foreach (object cell in row)
    {
        ProcessCell(cell);
    }
}
```

GetRangeA1

The GetRangeA1 method is used to get a range of values based on an Excel-style reference (A1:B2) or on named ranges. The value returned is a jagged array.

```
object[] GetRangeA1(string sessionId,
    string sheetName,
    string rangeName,
    bool formatted,
    out Status[] status)
```

The arguments are:

❑   sessionId — A session that was previously opened using the OpenWorkbook call.

❑   sheetName — The name of the sheet that contains the range. If omitted, Excel Services will try extrapolating the name from the range. Failing that, the default sheet will be used to get the range.

❑   rangeName — An Excel-type reference (A1:B2) or other named range reference ("MyNamedRange").

❑   formatted — Specifies whether or not the value returned should be formatted.

❑   status — An array of Status objects. In this version of Excel Services, this array will always be empty.

❑   Return value — A jagged array containing the range.

About request concurrency: This method can be called with the other Get functions at the same time. That means you can get data from multiple ranges at the same time.

Example

The following example uses the new structured reference feature in Excel 2007 to get a list of products from a workbook. In this case, there is a data table in a workbook called ProductTable that contains a column called ProductName. To reference the whole column of cells, the developer can use the notation Table[Column] — in this case ProductTable[ProductName] — to get the entire column of cells. The result can then be iterated over and the data outputted to the console.

```
// Get a list of products from a workbook
// and output them to the console.
object[] rows;
rows = s.GetRangeA1(m_sessionId, "",
    "ProductTable[ProductName]", true,
    out status);

foreach (object[] row in rows)
{
    Console.WriteLine(row[0].ToString());
}
```

Workbook Retrieval

Excel Services allows callers to retrieve the workbook that is currently opened inside a session. Using this functionality sends back a byte array that, when saved to disk, can be opened by Excel (or Excel Services) to see the workbook as it was in the session at the time this method was called.

This feature is incredibly useful when there's a need for a file that can be further analyzed in Excel or when reports are being published to SharePoint. In those cases, the caller opens a workbook that serves as a template, then modifies cells or initiates updates by using the Refresh or Calculate methods, and gets back the workbook that was generated with those changes.

On top of that, the retrieved workbook can take one of three forms:

1. **Full Workbook:** This option is only available if the user has full access to the workbook. It will return the workbook, complete with formulas and data connections.

2. **Full Snapshot:** This option will return a workbook that will look like the full workbook but will not have any formulas or embedded data connections. In a sense, it will be equivalent to taking every sheet on the workbook and copying only the values that are visible.

3. **Published Items Snapshot:** Some workbooks have published items in them (usually named ranges, PivotTables, or charts). When this option is used, a workbook is created with a sheet for each such published item. When the snapshot is opened in Excel, each such sheet will contain only the information that was available in each published item.

GetWorkbook

```
public byte[] GetWorkbook(
    string sessionId,
    WorkbookType workbookType,
    out Status[] status)
```

The arguments are:

❑   `sessionId` — A session that was previously opened using the `OpenWorkbook` call.

❑   `WorkbookType` — An enumeration that can be one of the following values: `FullWorkbook`, `FullSnapshot`, or `PublishedItemsSnapshot`.

❑   `status` — An array of `Status` objects. In this version of Excel Services, this array will always be empty.

❑   `Return Value` — An array of bytes that when saved to disk can be opened by Excel 2007.

Writing Values into Cells

Excel Services supports some data writeback from the Excel Web Services API. Callers are limited with what cells they may write into, however. Calls can only be made to set values into cells that do not contain formulas or other Excel objects inside them — that includes cells that "belong" to a PivotTable. For example, it is impossible to change the filter of a PivotTable to something other than what the pivot was authored with. On the other hand, it is possible to use Excel 2007's cube functions to achieve similar results.

Cube functions allow workbook authors to include free-form and unstructured data from Online Analytical Processing (OLAP) models inside their workbooks. Similarly, it is impossible to use Excel Web Services to do any kind of other interaction with the workbook such as drilling down or filtering.

The methods described in this section illustrate the possibilities Excel Services presents for writing data back into an Excel Workbook. There are four methods (each equivalent to one of the cell retrieval methods described in the "Cell Retrieval Methods" section earlier in this chapter).

The same rules that apply to the behavior of the `Get` family of methods apply to the `Set` family of methods — this includes how references work, how ranges are handled (as jagged arrays), and so on.

Type and Content Restrictions with Set Methods

Values going into single cells can only be one of the following: `String`, all numeric types other than 64-bit integers and .NET decimals, `Boolean`, and `DateTime`. The caller can also pass in a null reference — this will empty the cell of contents and is the equivalent of passing in an empty string.

When calling `SetRange` or `SetRangeA1`, the range passed in must be a jagged array where each inner array contains the correct number of instances and the size of the range must conform to the size of the range it was called on. For example, calling `SetRange()` when the size of the target range on the workbook is eight columns by two rows and passing in a jagged array that has three items in its outer array will fail to work. The passed in jagged array must consist of an outer array containing two items and each inner array containing eight items.

SetCell

The equivalent of `GetCell`, `SetCell` allows the caller to set values into a cell that is identified by x,y-type coordinates:

```
// VS2005 Imported signature
public Status[] SetCell(string sessionId,
    string sheetName,
    int row,
    int column,
    object cellValue)
// Real  signature
public void SetCell(string sessionId,
    string sheetName,
    int row,
    int column,
    object cellValue,
out Status[] status)
```

The arguments are:

❑   `sessionId` — A session that was previously opened using the `OpenWorkbook` call.

❑   `sheetName` — The name of the sheet that contains the range. If omitted, the default sheet will be used to get the range.

❑   `row` — Zero-based index of the row into which the cell value will be placed (index 0 corresponds to the first row in Excel. Index 1 corresponds to the second row, and so on).

❑   `column` — Zero-based index of the column into which the cell value will be placed.

❑   `cellValue` — The value that will be placed inside the cell. The type of the passed object can be `double`, `Boolean`, `string`, or `DateTime`, or the parameter can contain a null reference.

❑   `Return value` — An array of `Status` objects containing warnings about the operation.

Example

This example takes the value "true" and places it in B3 by using the `SetCell` method.

```
// Set the value in cell B3 to contain the
// boolean value of true (which in turn will place
// the number 1 in the cell)
s.SetCell(m_sessionId, "Sheet1", 2, 1, true);
```

SetCellA1

SetCellA1 is similar to the SetCell method, but SetCellA1 uses Excel References.

```
// VS2005 Imported signature
public Status[] SetCellA1(string sessionId,
     string sheetName,
     string rangeName,
     object cellValue)
// Real signature
public void SetCellA1(string sessionId,
     string sheetName,
     string rangeName,
     object cellValue,
out Status[] status)
```

The arguments are:

❑   sessionId — A session that was previously opened using the OpenWorkbook call.

❑   sheetName — The name of the sheet in which rangeName resides. Can be ommitted if the range is global or if it contains the name of the sheet.

❑   rangeName — Named range or Excel reference to set the value into.

❑   cellValue — The value to set into the cell.

❑   Return value — Array of Status returned from Excel Services.

If rangeName corresponds to a range that is larger than a single cell, this call fails to execute.

Example

Note that the sheet name is not passed in this example — Excel Services does not require a sheet name when the rangeName is a global named range in Excel.

The preceding statement results from a somewhat unfortunate incident of overloaded terms. A "named range" in Excel is any Excel range that was named in the workbook. The RangeName parameter refers to any valid string that corresponds to a range in Excel such as "A1" or "Interest" (if the workbook contains a named range called interest) or "Table1[Column1]" if the workbook contains a table named Table1 and a column named Column1).

```
// Set the value in the range corresponding to
// the name "Interest" to 0.05
s.SetCellA1(m_sessionId, "", "Interest", 0.05);
```

SetRange

The SetRange call allows the user to set a range of cells in the workbook based on a coordinate system:

```
// VS2005 Imported signature
public Status[] SetRange(string sessionId,
     string sheetName,
```

```
        RangeCoordinates rangeCoordinates,
        object[] rangeValues)
// Real signature
public void SetRange(string sessionId,
    string sheetName,
    RangeCoordinates rangeCoordinates,
    object[] rangeValues,
out Status[] status)
```

The arguments are:

❑   sessionId — A session that was previously opened using the OpenWorkbook call.

❑   sheetName — The name of the sheet in which rangeName resides. If the sheet name is omitted, the server will use the default sheet.

❑   rangeCoordinates — Contains an instance of the RangeCoordinates class that describes a range using the top-left coordinate and width and height of the range.

❑   rangeValues — The range to set into the cell — this must be a jagged array, according to the rules described in the "Accessing Multi-cell Ranges" section earlier in the chapter.

❑   Return value — An array of Status objects returned from Excel Services. This array will always be empty.

SetRangeA1

SetRangeA1 sets a range in an Excel workbook with values from the caller:

```
// VS2005 imported signature
public Status[] SetRangeA1(
    string sessionId,
    string sheetName,
    string rangeName,
    object[] rangeValues)
// Real Signature
public void SetRangeA1(
    string sessionId,
    string sheetName,
    string rangeName,
    object[] rangeValues,
out Status[] status)
```

The arguments are:

❑   sessionId — A session that was previously opened using the OpenWorkbook call.

❑   sheetName — The name of the sheet in which rangeName resides. Can be ommitted if the range is global or if it contains the name of the sheet.

❑   rangeName — A named range or Excel reference to set the value into.

❑   rangeValues — A jagged array of values to insert into the workbook.

❑   Return value — Array of Status objects returned from Excel Services.

Example

The following example sets values into a range that is 2 columns by 12 rows:

```
// Create the outer array.
object[] rows = new object[12];
// Now, read data from our source
// And create an inner array for each month
for (int month = 0; month < 12; month++)
{
    DateTime depositDate;
    double depositAmount;
    GetDepositInfo(out depositDate, out depositAmount);
    rows[month] = new object[] { depositDate, depositAmount };
}
// Finally, set the value into Excel Services.
s.SetRangeA1(m_sessionId, "", "PaymentData", rows);
```

Workbook Updating Methods

Excel Services allows the caller to refresh data on the workbook and recalculate a potentially dirty workbook. The Calculate, CalculateA1, and CalculateWorkbook methods will cause Excel Services to recalculate a workbook (the Calculate and CalculateA1 methods allow for finer control over what portions of the workbook are to be recalculated). This feature is most useful if the workbook is set up for manual recalculation or when it contains volatile functions that need to be recalculated so that they can get their new values.

With workbooks that have automatic recalc turned on, this call can still be useful if the workbook has any kind of volatile data in it. Take, for example, Excel's NOW() function, which gives the current date and time. Calling any of the Calculate() functionality on such a workbook will potentially cause the function to be reevaluated and provide new results.

When a workbook is set to auto-recalc, each call to one of the methods in the SetXXX family will cause a recalculation of everything that is based on that cell. Since that can be inefficient with large models when multiple cells need to be set into the workbook, developers should work with their workbook authors to make sure that in those cases the workbook is not set to automatically recalculate.

> *When multiple cells need to be changed in a workbook before data is extracted out of it, it is a good idea to set it to manual recalculation. However, it is worth noting that for small models the overhead of setting cells and getting ranges will overshadow the recalculation by several orders of magnitude. In those cases, it may make sense to keep the automatic recalculation setting on so that the workbook is more usable when loaded in Excel.*

Employ caution when using the Calculate and CalculateA1 methods — they will only calculate the range passed into them. Consider the workbook shown in Figure 6.2, which has auto-recalc turned off.

If the value "6" was to be set into B3 (inside "Section 1"), the cell in D3 ("Section 2") and cell F3 ("Section 3") would not be updated because the workbooks auto recalc is disabled. If the caller were to call the CalculateA1 on cell F3, nothing would change — the value there would still be 4 (since D3 is 2).

To get the correct value — which is 24 — the `Calculate` method will need to be called on the range of D3:F3 so that both numbers would be recalculated.

The `CalculateA1` and `Calculate` methods are usually used when there is a specific order in which the caller wants to calculate areas in the workbook.

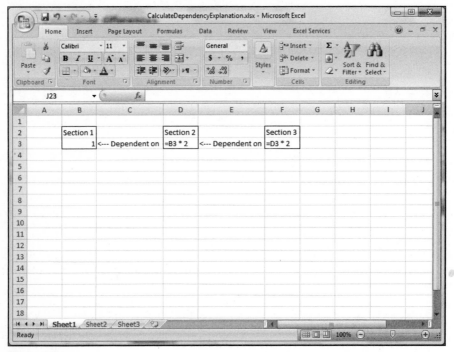

Figure 6.2

Calculate

The `Calculate` method allows the caller to recalculate a specific range in the workbook that is coordinate-based.

```
// VS2005 Imported signature
public Status[] Calculate(string sessionId,
    string sheetName,
    RangeCoordinates rangeCoordinates)
// Real signature
public void Calculate(string sessionId,
    string sheetName,
    RangeCoordinates rangeCoordinates,
out Status[] status)
```

The arguments are:

- ❑   `sessionId` — A session that was previously opened using the `OpenWorkbook` call.

- ❑   `sheetName` — The name of the sheet in which `rangeName` resides. If the sheet name is omitted, the server will use the default sheet.

- ❑   `rangeCoordinates` — Contains an instance of the `RangeCoordinates` class, which describes a range using the top-left coordinate and width and height of the range.

- ❑   `Return value` — An array of `Status` objects with warnings that occurred when trying to recalculate.

CalculateA1

`CalculateA1` is similar to the `Calculate()` method, but `CalculateA1` uses Excel References.

```
// VS2005 Imported signature
public Status[] CalculateA1(string sessionId,
    string sheetName,
    string rangeName)
// Real signature
public void CalculateA1(string sessionId,
    string sheetName,
    string rangeName,
out Status[] status)
```

The arguments are:

- ❑   `sessionId` — A session that was previously opened using the `OpenWorkbook` call.

- ❑   `sheetName` — The name of the sheet in which `rangeName` resides. Can be ommitted if the range is global or if it contains the name of the sheet.

- ❑   `rangeName` — Named range requested.

- ❑   `Return value` — An array of `Status` objects with warnings that occurred when trying to recalculate.

Example

The following example sets various values into the workbook and then reads a single value and returns it:

```
// Set values into the model
s.SetCellA1(m_sessionId, "", "InterestRate", GetInterestRate());
s.SetCellA1(m_sessionId, "", "Principal", GetPrincipal());

// Recalculate the model so we will have accurate results.
s.CalculateA1(m_sessionId, "", "MonthlyPayment");

// Now we can get the calculated value of MonthlyPayment.
return (double)s.GetCellA1(m_sessionId, "", "MonthlyPayment", false, out status);
```

CalculateWorkbook

Callers who want to recalculate the whole workbook can use the `CalculateWorkbook` method:

```
// VS2005 Imported signature
public Status[] CalculateWorkbook(string sessionId, CalculateType calculateType)
// Real signature
public void CalculateWorkbook(string sessionId,
    CalculateType calculateType,
Out Status[] status)
```

The arguments are:

❑ `sessionId` — A session that was previously opened using the `OpenWorkbook` call.

❑ `calculateType` — Enumeration value. Can either be `CalculateType.CalculateFull` or `CalculateType.Recalculate`.

❑ `Return value` — An array of `Status` objects with warnings that occurred when trying to recalculate.

For the most part, callers can just use the `CalculateType.Recalculate` enumeration value when calling this method — it will make sure that the whole workbook is recalculated.

`CalculateType.CalculateFull` is a more thorough version of `CalcualteType.Recalculate` — it does extra operations behind the scenes, namely, it rebuilds dependency chains and clears any prior knowledge about the workbook calculation. For the most part, callers should not use this value, but it can be useful in rare cases when developers want to make sure that their workbook behaves properly. For example, calls with `CalculateType.CalculateFull` can be compared to calls with `CalculateType.Recalculate` to make sure that models are being calculated correctly.

Example

The following code will calculate the whole workbook:

```
s.CalculateWorkbook(m_sessionId, CalculateType.Recalculate);
```

Refresh

Workbooks may contain parts that are driven by data from back-end database servers. On the server, this can either be PivotTables or cube functions. Callers may need to refresh data sources that are embedded in the workbook. With Excel 2007, it is very easy to manage connections. To see the names of all the connections a workbook contains, the Connection Manager option can be used. It brings up a dialog box that shows all of the connections embedded in the workbook, as shown in Figure 6.3.

This functionality is accessible by flipping to the Data tab on the ribbon and then clicking the Connections button in the Manage Connections group.

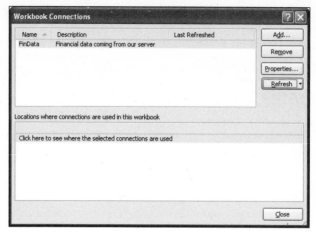

Figure 6.3

```
// VS2005 Imported signature
public Status[] Refresh(string sessionId,
     string connectionName)
// Real signature
public void Refresh(string sessionId,
     string connectionName,
Status[] status)
```

The arguments are:

- ❑ sessionId — A session that was previously opened using the OpenWorkbook call.

- ❑ connectionName — The name of the connection to refresh. If empty, all connections on the workbook will be refreshed.

- ❑ Return value — An array of Status objects with warnings that occurred when trying to refresh.

It is important to understand that the allowed data refresh frequency is controlled by the administrator — if the settings of the trusted data source do not allow frequent refreshes, calls to this method will succeed with no warning being issued, but no refresh will occur. Only when enough time passes that the connection can be refreshed again, will it cause a refresh to occur.

Example

This example refreshes the "FinData" connection inside a workbook:

```
s.Refresh(m_sessionId, "FinData");
```

Support Classes and Enumerations

There are a few support classes imported with the Excel Web Services. The discussion of the methods earlier in this chapter touched on them briefly — this section will supply more information about them.

RangeCoordinates

RangeCoordinates is used by methods that take numeric coordinates for defining ranges, such as Calculate, GetRange, and SetRange. The class simply contains members for the top-left origin point (represented as Row and Column in the class) and the width/height of the range.

See the example in the GetRange section earlier in the chapter for more information on how to use this class.

Status

The Status class contains various warnings and supportive information about the calls into Excel Services. The primary functionality of this class is to report when calculations fail or when data sources fail to query. The class has three properties:

❑   Name — This is a string that represents the code for the warning or alert. It is not localized (it will always be in English regardless of what locale was used to open the workbook). For a list of potential values, see the list of error codes in the section about exceptions in this chapter.

❑   Severity — This value is used for reporting what the severity of the status message is. The potential string values for this property can be one of the following: Error, Warning, or Information. At the time of writing, Excel Services will never return the string "Information" in this class.

Since the book was written before the product was released, this might change by the time you read this. Service packs may also change this behavior.

❑   Message — The Message property contains a localized message string with verbose information about the warning/error that occurred. Developers can use this value to display more information to the user.

Exceptions and Errors

Excel Web Services (when accessed through SOAP or direct linking) exposes a relatively rich set of error codes when things go wrong. Different mechanisms may consume these errors in different ways. However, if you are using Visual Studio to access the API, the errors will be presented in the form of a SoapException thrown from the call.

Note that even when using direct linking, callers will still see SoapExceptions being thrown — the same as when using a generated proxy.

Callers of Excel Web Services must also expect different types of exceptions other than SoapExceptions. These can occur for various reasons — such as network problems, unresponsive servers, errors in authentication, and so on. None of these extra exceptions are unique to Excel Web

Services, since developers may encounter them when using any other Web Service. However, as explained earlier, applicative exceptions (those that occur due to an error in the processing of requests in Excel Services) will be exposed as SoapExceptions.

SoapException

When raised from Excel Services, SoapException instances have two interesting members — the Message property and the SubCode property. The Message property contains a verbose error message localized according to the UI locale used when opening the workbook.

The SubCode property contains a short string that corresponds to the error that occurred. This property is especially useful because it can be used programmatically to figure out what went wrong with the call. Because it is not verbose (there is no need to do any parsing) and not localized, it is very simple to use.

To be able to access the SubCode property on the SoapException instance, the developer needs to instruct the proxy instance that it needs to use the SOAP 1.2 standard. If that step is not taken, the SubCode property will always be null. To instruct the proxy, the SoapVersion property on the proxy needs to be set to be the enum value of Soap12:

```
ES.ExcelService s = new ES.ExcelService();
s.Url = "http://server/_Vti_bin/ExcelService.asmx";
s.SoapVersion = System.Web.Services.Protocols.SoapProtocolVersion.Soap12;
s.Credentials = System.Net.CredentialCache.DefaultCredentials;
```

Visual Studio 2003 does not supply access to the SubCode element of a Soap fault, as it only supports SOAP version 1.1.

Example

The following example shows how to access the error code that Excel Services returns. In this case, when the call recognizes that the session has timed out, it will try to reopen the workbook and reread the data from it:

```
double ReadValueFromSession()
{
    bool tryAgain;
    bool failedOnce = false;
    double result = 0;
    Status[] status;
    do
    {
        tryAgain = false;
        try
        {
            // Make the call, try getting the value.
            result = (double)s.GetCellA1(m_sessionId,
                "", "FinalResult", false, out status);
        }
        catch (SoapException ex)
        {
            // If this is the first time we failed, reopen the workbook.
```

```
                    if (!failedOnce)
                    {
                        if (ex.SubCode.Code.Name == "InvalidOrTimedOutSession")
                        {
                            failedOnce = true;
                            m_sessionId = s.OpenWorkbook(
                                "http://server/docs/workbook.xlsx",
                                "", "", out status);
                            tryAgain = true;
                        }
                    }
                }
            } while (tryAgain);
            return result;
    }
```

SubCode List

There are over 100 errors that can potentially return from Excel Services. Luckily, most of them are not used when the APIs are accessed but are used internally in various parts of the system. The following table is a partial list of the error codes that are most common. It is worth remembering that these codes are used both in `SoapExceptions` raised from Excel Web Services and inside the `Status` class instances that Excel Web Services uses to report information about successful method calls.

Error Code	Notes
NotMemberOfRole	The caller does not have the rights to access the server.
ExternalDataRefreshFailed	Refreshing a data source inside a workbook failed.
FileOpenSecuritySettings	OpenWorkbook failed because the administrator security settings prevented it from opening (for example, the file was too big).
FileOpenNotFound	OpenWorkbook failed because the file does not exist.
FileOpenAccessDenied	OpenWorkbook failed because the user does not have access to the file.
FileCorrupt	OpenWorkbook failed because the file is corrupt.
WorkbookNotSupported	The workbook is not supported.
GenericFileOpenError	Excel Services failed to open the file for an unknown reason.
IRMedWorkbook	OpenWorkbook failed because the workbook has Information Rights Management on it.
FormulaEditingNotEnabled	Caller tried writing a formula into the workbook.

Error Code	Notes
DimensionAndArrayMismatch	Caller tried setting a range into a workbook, but the parameter that contains the array values does not match the target range.
SetRangeFailure	Caller tried to write values into a range that has protected cells (for example, a formula).
ObjectTypeNotSupported	Caller tried to write values into a range, but the values were not of a supported type.
RangeParseError	The range that was passed into a method with the A1 postfix could not be parsed.
SpecifiedRangeNotFound	The range that was passed into a method with the A1 postfix could not be found.
InvalidSheetName	The sheet name was not found or was invalid.
DiscontiguousRangeNot-Supported	When trying to set or get a range of cells, a range that is not contiguous was supplied. Excel Services only supports contiguous ranges.
RangeRequestAreaExceeded	The range requested contained more than the 1 million cell limit.
SheetRangeMismatch	The sheet name that was passed in a sheetName parameter does not match a sheet specified in the rangeName parameter.
ApiInvalidArgument	An argument passed into the API call was invalid.
ApiInvalidCoordinate	The contents of the RangeCoordinates class or the row and column parameters on a Get or Set call to Excel Services were not legal.
MultipleRequestsOnSession	Sessions can only support a single request at any given time (with a few exceptions). Multiple requests have been issued on the same session.
InvalidOrTimedOutSession	The Session ID the call was made on is either invalid or has since timed out.
MaxSessionsPerUserExceeded	The limit set by the administrator on how many sessions a user can have open at any given time has been exceeded.
OperationCanceled	When a user calls the CancelRequest method on a session, the operation that is currently taking place will error out with this code.

Continued

Error Code	Notes
OperationCanceled	When a user calls the CancelRequest method on a session, the operation that is currently taking place will error out with this code.
MaxRequestDurationExceeded	The request took longer to process than the administrator allowed.
RetryError	Excel Services may at times reach a state where it is strapped for resources. In those cases, it may start denying requests. Such denied requests will return an error with this code.
SaveFailed	A generic error code used when the GetWorkbook call fails.

Summary

The Excel Web Services API is not an all-encompassing mechanism for manipulating workbooks on the server. It lacks numerous functions that the Excel client OM has. However, it is an excellent lightweight tool for running and utilizing Excel models on the server. My personal bet is that in future versions more and more features will find themselves into the server and into the API.

In the next chapter, I show you a comprehensive library that will have a few advantages over the usage of the Excel Web Services API in the manner that was described in the "Hello World" and API reference examples.

7

Building the Excel
Services Library (ESL)

In the "Hello World" example from Chapter 5, the Excel Web Services API was imported directly into the project. While there is nothing wrong with that, it is not the most maintainable way of using it. Here are some of the reasons why using a wrapper around the APIs is a good idea:

❑ **Direct linking** — When using direct linking to communicate with Excel Services, the methods that are used will look somewhat different from the generated Web Service proxy. For the same piece of code to work against a directly linked Excel Services library, recompilation will always be needed. More than that, in some cases, even recompilation will not help as the signatures of the methods will be different. It is better to have a mechanism that will allow developers to write the same code whether they are working against the actual SOAP server or if they are using the server via direct linking.

❑ **Tool import differences** — VS 2005 imports Web services one way. WSDL.EXE can import it in different ways. Other environments may have still other ways. Keeping the calls consistent is important so that future projects can be written the same way, reducing the time needed to get used to a new way of doing them.

❑ **Multiple projects** — As developers start writing more projects for Excel Services, they may need multiple projects to interact with Excel Services. Because Excel Web Services uses a string for the Session ID, this is probably not going to be a problem from the technical sense, but it does mean developers will end up having multiple namespaces each containing the same functionality.

❑ **Snags and "gotchas"** — While the Excel Web Services is a relatively simple API, there are a few snags to watch for. For example, one of the most common problems is remembering to call the CloseWorkbook method when you are done with a workbook. Writing a wrapper that will remember to do that for you goes a long way toward writing better and more scalable code.

❑ **Excel Web Services is not object oriented** — Due to the nature of SOAP services, they are exposed as a set of functions rather than an object hierarchy. In the case of Excel Web Services, this is not too bad, but abstracting the calls into an object hierarchy can simplify some cases and make the code more maintainable and easier to read.

❑ **Some parameters are rarely used** — In the Excel Web Services interface, a few of the parameters that are used to call methods are often ignored. This falls into two categories — parameters that are returned (out parameters) but are usually not inspected and parameters where the caller passes in a value that tells Excel Services to behave in some default manner. An example for the first category is the `Status[]` parameter that almost all methods contain. It is not really needed in most cases and will actually be empty in quite a few of the methods. The second example is the `sheetName` parameter in the methods that have the A1 postfix (`GetCellA1`, `SetRangeA1`, etc.). In those methods, the `sheetName` is usually not really useful and in most cases will be passed in as an empty string. Because Web Services do not support overriding function names, easier versions of the calls could not be offered to the developers. Having the library allows us to have overloads that are easier to use.

The Excel Services Library (ESL) was designed to handle these issues and more.

This chapter will walk through the process of creating the ESL, giving you a greater understanding (for those who need it) about how Web services work and how to debug applications using the ESL. While it's possible to skip this chapter and use the library as it is on the companion CD, it is worthwhile to take a look through the design so that you at the very least know how it works.

Project Design

The ESL will be built as a C# library (choosing the .NET library option from the New Project dialog should create one from a default template). The main entry point will be the `ExcelServices` object, which will contain the functionality needed to open a workbook in a session on the server. Sessions are represented by the `Session` class, which exposes all of the methods of Excel Web Services. When instantiating the `ExcelServices` class, it will be possible to choose between the two activation models (direct linking and SOAP Web Services). Once instantiated, the object will present a unified interface for working with Excel Services, regardless of what connection model is used. The diagram shown in Figure 7.1 shows the basic class structure that will be used for the `ExcelServices` object (the arrows in the diagram denote a reference held).

The `ExcelServices` object will use either the direct linking wrapper or the Web Service wrapper via a standard interface called `IExcelServicesWrapper` (where all the functionality is exposed). The `ExcelService` object will then add some functionality over that interface.

Abstraction Classes

As discussed, there will be a few abstraction classes that will give the API the object-oriented feel that it lacks. These classes include the `Session` class, which encapsulates the Session ID that was returned from the server. Using the `Session` class frees the developer from having to pass in the Session ID on

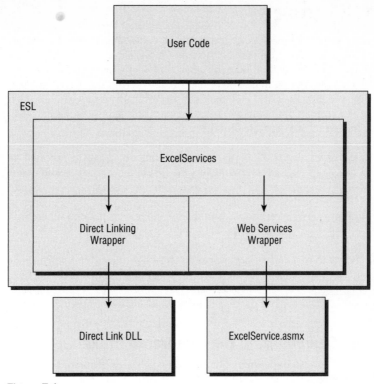

Figure 7.1

each method call. It also makes cleanup better by closing the server session when the instance of the class is disposed or garbage collected.

The second abstraction revolves around ranges. As discussed in a previous chapter, ranges extracted from the server (or those that are written back to the server) use a jagged array for transferring the data. Using the RangeResult class to abstract that jagged array allows the caller to use the range in a more Excel-like fashion by supplying a great many methods that allow the user to enumerate rows or cells, to access cells by index, and so on. It also provides easy access to information about the structure of the result (how many columns and rows it has, for example).

Furthermore, RangeResults are potentially live objects — meaning that they can be requeried after they have been created to refresh them and get new results.

Namespace

ExcelServicesLibrary will be used as the main namespace in this solution. There will be some nested namespaces for things such as resources and helper classes, but for the most part, the user of the library will only use the ExcelServicesLibrary namespace.

Support Classes

Some of the code that will be produced may look a bit confusing. This is due to the fact that when using the Direct Link feature of the Excel Web Services assembly, names similar to the ones already existing are imported into the ESL assembly. Take the `Status` class, for example: when the project is done, the assembly will have two of those in it. One of them will be written in the assembly and the other will be imported by direct linking the Excel Web Services assembly. Even though these two types are called by the same name and contain the same members, they are different — they exist on two different namespaces and are indeed in two separate binaries.

The `Status` class that will be defined and used by developers using the ESL will have the full name of `ExcelServicesLibrary.Status`, while the one inside the directly linked assembly will be called: `Microsoft.Office.Excel.Server.CalculationServer.Status`.

To create the support classes, you should cannibalize the ones generated when the WSDL was imported into VS 2005.

> *We could have had three classes for each support class — one in the Web Services proxy, one in the directly linked assembly, and one that we would write ourselves. That would have been the purest approach. While pureness is commendable, there is very little we lose by using the generated classes for both the public-facing support classes and the ones used to interact with the Web Services.*

Generating and Cannibalizing the Generated Proxy

In the "Hello World" example shown in Chapter 5, a proxy was generated for Excel Web Services by using the Add Web References option of VS 2005. The same thing should be done here, importing a definition of the Web Service, but instead of using the automatically generated code, it will be readded to the server as a regular file:

1. Create a folder in the project called "Soap" — it will contain all the files that are specific for the wrapper that calls into Excel Web Services.

2. Import Excel Web Services into the project using the Add Web Reference option. Name the Web service "ES". (The name is not really important — it will be deleted shortly.)

3. Next, add the generated C# file to the project by right-clicking the `Soap` folder and choosing the Add Existing Item option. When the dialog box opens, go into the directory containing the generated proxy under the project's directory (it will be in a directory called `ES` under a directory called `Web References` in this case) and select the file called `Reference.cs`. This will copy the file to the project's directory.

4. Delete the reference to the Web Service from the project tree — it is not needed anymore.

5. Rename the file added to the `Soap` folder to `ExcelServiceSoap.cs`.

6. Rename the main class inside that file to `ExcelServiceSoap` instead of `ExcelService`:

```
[System.Xml.Serialization.XmlIncludeAttribute(typeof(object[]))]
public class ExcelServiceSoap :
System.Web.Services.Protocols.SoapHttpClientProtocol
```

7. Open `ExcelServiceSoap.cs` and remove the comment that says the file was auto-generated. Delete from the file the following properties/methods:

   ❑ `useDefaultCredentialsSetExplicitly` field

   ❑ The constructor

   ❑ `Url` property

   ❑ `UseDefaultCredentials` property

8. Change the namespace to `ExcelServicesLibrary.Soap` instead of `ExcelServicesLibrary.ES`.

The project now has support for connecting to Excel Services via SOAP. The next step is to extract the support classes and enumerations from the file and add them to the project under the main namespace.

Extracting Enumerations

To do this, add a new file to the project's root and call it `Enums.cs`. The namespace for that file should be `ExcelServicesLibrary`.

There are three enumerations that need to be moved over to this file — `CellError`, `CalculateType`, and `WorkbookType`. These enumerations are in the `ExcelServiceSoap.cs` file and will need to be copied over (making sure they are deleted from the original file). These enumerations should retain their serialization attributes when copied. After moving the `CalculateType` enumeration, the file should look like Listing 7-1.

Listing 7-1: Enums.cs

```
namespace ExcelServicesLibrary
{
    [System.SerializableAttribute()]
    [System.Xml.Serialization.XmlTypeAttribute(Namespace =
"http://schemas.microsoft.com/office/excel/server/webservices")]
    public enum CalculateType
    {

        /// <remarks/>
        Recalculate,

        /// <remarks/>
        CalculateFull,
    }
}
```

The other two enumerations should be moved into this file as well.

Extracting the Support Classes

Two support classes will need to be moved into the main namespace from the `ExcelService-Soap.cs` file — the `Status` class and the `RangeCoordinates` class. Files named `Status.cs` and `RangeCoordinates.cs` should be created in the project root for each of these support classes. The namespace will be `ExcelServicesLibrary` as it was for the enumerations that were moved.

After moving the `Status` class, the file will look like Listing 7-2.

Listing 7-2: Status.cs

```
namespace ExcelServicesLibrary
{
    [System.SerializableAttribute()]
    [System.Diagnostics.DebuggerStepThroughAttribute()]
    [System.ComponentModel.DesignerCategoryAttribute("code")]
    [System.Xml.Serialization.XmlTypeAttribute(Namespace =
"http://schemas.microsoft.com/office/excel/server/webservices")]
    public class Status
    {
        private string nameField;
        private string severityField;
        private string messageField;

        public string Name
        {
            get { return this.nameField; }
            set { this.nameField = value; }
        }

        public string Severity
        {
            get { return this.severityField; }
            set { this.severityField = value; }
        }

        public string Message
        {
            get { return this.messageField; }
            set     { this.messageField = value; }
        }
    }
}
```

The same operation should be done for the `RangeCoordinates` class, while making sure that the original is deleted from the `ExcelServiceSoap.cs` file.

Once moving the support constructs is complete and a functioning Web Service proxy is available, the developer will need an interface that will be used to abstract both the direct linked assembly and the SOAP proxy for callers of the ESL.

Method Call Abstraction

An interface will be used to achieve the abstraction of calls. The same call, from the point of view of the developer, will either go to the SOAP interface Excel Services exposes or to the directly linked assembly.

IExcelServiceWrapper

The IExcelServiceWrapper interface will be implemented by the two components that know how to supply Excel Services functionality. The signatures of the methods will be true to the original signatures as they are defined in the WSDL of Excel Web Services. The snippet shown in Listing 7-2 is the definition of the interface.

The interface contains only the full method signature — it does not contain the easy-to-use overloads. The main reason for this is that the overrides can easily be done in the outer class (the one exposed to the caller) and so less code needs to be written in each class that implements the IExcelServiceWrapper interface.

Listing 7-2: IExcelServiceWrapper interface

```
internal interface IExcelServiceWrapper
{
     string GetApiVersion(out Status[] status);
     string OpenWorkbook(string workbookPath,
          string uiCultureName, string dataCultureName,
          out Status[] status);
void CloseWorkbook(string sessionId,
          out Status[] status);
     void Refresh(string sessionId,
          string connectionName, out Status[] status);
     void Calculate(string sessionId,
          string sheetName, RangeCoordinates rangeCoordinates,
          out Status[] status);
     void CalculateA1(string sessionId,
          string sheetName, string rangeName,
          out Status[] status);
     object[] GetRange(string sessionId,
          string sheetName, RangeCoordinates rangeCoordinates, bool formatted,
          out Status[] status);
     object[] GetRangeA1(string sessionId,
          string sheetName, string rangeName, bool formatted,
          out Status[] status);
     object GetCell(string sessionId,
          string sheetName, int row, int column, bool formatted,
          out Status[] status);
     object GetCellA1(string sessionId,
          string sheetName, string rangeName, bool formatted,
          out Status[] status);
     void SetRange(string sessionId,
          string sheetName, RangeCoordinates rangeCoordinates, object[]
rangeValues,
          out Status[] status);
     void SetRangeA1(string sessionId,
          string sheetName, string rangeName, object[] rangeValues,
          out Status[] status);
     void SetCell(string sessionId,
          string sheetName, int row, int column, object cellValue,
```

Continued

```
            out Status[] status);
    void SetCellA1(string sessionId,
            string sheetName, string rangeName, object cellValue,
            out Status[] status);
    void CalculateWorkbook(string sessionId,
            CalculateType calculateType, out Status[] status);
    string GetSessionInformation(string sessionId,
            out string uiCultureNameUsed, out string dataCultureNameUsed,
            out Status[] status);
    void CancelRequest(string sessionId,
            out Status[] status);
    byte[] GetWorkbook(string sessionId,
            WorkbookType workbookType, out Status[] status);
}
```

As you can see, the interface defines all the functionality that Excel Services exposes.

IWrapperCredentials

The IWrapperCredentials interface, shown in Listing 7-3, allows the concrete implementations to support modifying the credentials used to make the call. When using direct linking, this functionality is not needed. The SOAP version, though, could potentially need it. The SOAP wrapper will implement this and allow the callers to set what credentials to use. The direct link wrapper will not.

Listing 7-3: IWrapperCredentials interface

```
Internal interface IWrapperCredentials
{
    ICredentials ServiceCredentials
    {
        get;
        set;
    }
}
```

The next step is to create the class that will expose through this interface access to the SOAP interface of Excel Web Services.

Modifying ExcelServiceSoap

In a previous section, a class called ExcelServiceSoap was created in the ExcelServicesLibrary .Soap namespace and placed in a folder named Soap. This file should be modified to serve as one of the concrete implementations of the IExcelServiceWrapper interface.

To do that, the interface will be added to the inheritance list of the class:

```
[System.Xml.Serialization.XmlIncludeAttribute(typeof(object[]))]
public class ExcelServiceSoap :
    System.Web.Services.Protocols.SoapHttpClientProtocol,
```

```
IExcelServiceWrapper,
IWrapperCredentials
```

If the project is compiled now, the compiler will complain, with errors proclaiming that some of the methods in the IExcelServiceWrapper interface are not implemented in this class.

Not all functions will need to be reimplemented — those that happen to have the same signature in both generated proxy and in the interface will assume the identity of the method in the interface, eliminating the need to add them. Those that are not will have to be added. Take the CloseWorkbook method as an example. In the generated proxy it is defined as:

```
public Status[] CloseWorkbook(string sessionId)
```

Note how the Status[] parameter has been promoted to a return value. An overload that conforms to the signature in the IExcelServiceWrapper interface will have to be added:

```
public void CloseWorkbook(string sessionId, out Status[] status)
{
    status = CloseWorkbook(sessionId);
}
```

The same will need to be done for the following methods (all of which have void as a return value in the interface): Refresh, Calculate, CalculateA1, SetRange, SetRangeA1, SetCell, SetCellA1, CalculateWorkbook, CancelRequest.

The IWrapperCredentials interface also needs to be implemented:

```
#region IWrapperCredentials Members

public ICredentials ServiceCredentials
{
    get { return Credentials; }
    set { Credentials = value; }
}

#endregion
```

Once this modification is done, the project should compile properly.

Another static method needs to be added to the class, one that will create it. The method instantiates the class, sets it up, and returns to the caller:

```
internal static IExcelServiceWrapper Create(string server)
{
    ExcelServiceSoap service = new ExcelServiceSoap();
    service.Url = server;
    service.Credentials = System.Net.CredentialCache.DefaultCredentials;
    service.SoapVersion = SoapProtocolVersion.Soap12;
    service.Timeout = System.Threading.Timeout.Infinite;
    return service;
}
```

Exception Classes

There are three exception classes defined in the project. The `ExcelServicesException` class acts as the base for the other two. The `UnsupportedException` is thrown when the wrong value is passed to the creation method of the `ExcelServices` class. The `CannotRefreshException` is thrown when a `Range` object is not connected to a session and thus cannot be refreshed.

All three exception classes are pretty straightforward and contain constructors that follow the suggested .NET exception construction pattern.

ExcelServices Class

The `ExcelServices` class is the main entry point to users of the ESL. The next step is to add it to the project. For that, the Add/Class option should be selected on the project. The new file should be named `ExcelServices.cs`.

ExcelServicesType

The project will also require an enumeration that will allow the caller to specify what type of Excel Services they want to use (direct linking or SOAP). Add a file called `ExcelServicesType.cs` that contains an enumeration defined in the following manner:

```
public enum ExcelServicesType
{
    Automatic = 0,
    DirectLinking = 1,
    Soap = 2
}
```

The `DirectLinking` and `Soap` values were already discussed. Later, more code will be added. It will recognize the `Automatic` value and try to deduce whether the caller will benefit most from a direct linking or SOAP and choose appropriately.

Implementing ExcelServices

The new class will receive information in its constructor parameters that will govern how the class will behave. Note that the constructor does not really do much other than storing the information:

```
public class ExcelServices
{
    private ExcelServicesType m_type;
    private string m_server;

    protected ExcelServices(ExcelServicesType type, string server)
    {
        m_type = type;
        m_server = server;
    }
    // ...
```

Once a properly constructed ExcelServices object exists, it can be used for one of two things — either to get the version of the APIs or to open a session. The class also contains two read-only properties that return the m_type and m_server fields (called Type and Server, respectively). At the heart of both of these calls is the CreateWrapper method call, which knows how to create the correct class that implements the IExcelServicesWrapper interface. Since so far the only implemented mechanism is the SOAP one, this method is relatively simple:

```
private IExcelServiceWrapper CreateWrapper()
{
    IExcelServiceWrapper wrapper = null;
    switch (Type)
    {
        case ExcelServicesType.Soap:
            wrapper = Soap.ExcelServiceSoap.Create(Server);
            break;
        case ExcelServicesType.Automatic:
        case ExcelServicesType.DirectLinking:
        default:
            break;
    }

    if (wrapper == null)
    {
        throw new UnsupportedException();
    }

    return wrapper;
}
```

The CreateWrapper method checks the type of the requested connection and uses it to figure out what class to instantiate. In this case, it only supports the ExcelServiceSoap class that was just created. Once created, the new instance is returned.

For a simple example of how this is used, see this GetApiVersion method:

```
public string GetApiVersion(out Status[] status)
{
    IExcelServiceWrapper wrapper = CreateWrapper();
    return wrapper.GetApiVersion(out status);
}
```

In this case, the wrapper is created and used to make the GetApiVersion call.

Incidentally, there is an overload of this method that does not utilize the Status array as a parameter:

```
public string GetApiVersion()
{
    Status[] status;
    return GetApiVersion(out status);
}
```

The more interesting example, however, is how the Open method works.

ExcelServices.Open()

The ExcelServices.Open method has a few overloads, all using the one Open method that has the most parameters. The following is the signature of the Open method:

```
public Session Open(string workbookPath,
string uiCultureName, string dataCultureName, out Status[] status)
```

Each of the overloads available will pass default values to a combination of these parameters.

The method returns a Session object to the caller. This object is an instance of the Session ID wrapper we discussed before.

The implementation of this method does the following:

```
public Session Open(string workbookPath,
string uiCultureName, string dataCultureName, out Status[] status)
{
    IExcelServiceWrapper wrapper = CreateWrapper();
    string sessionId = wrapper.OpenWorkbook(workbookPath,
uiCultureName, dataCultureName, out status);
    Session session = null;
    try
    {
        // Create a workbook object and initialize it with the session ID.
        session = new Session(wrapper, sessionId);
    }
    catch
    {

        // If an exception occurs, we want to close the session.
        try
        {
            Status[] closeWorkbookStatus;
            wrapper.CloseWorkbook(sessionId, out closeWorkbookStatus);
        }
        catch
        {
        }
        throw;
    }
    return session;
}
```

This Open method makes a call to the wrapper object and asks it to open a workbook. If successful, it returns a Session object that wraps the Session ID and gives access to most of the methods.

Notice also how the code closes the workbook if the creation of the Session object fails. This guarantees that in the case of errors, no opened sessions will be leaked.

Overload Example

The following example shows the simplest overload in the class:

```
public Session Open(string workbookPath)
{
    Status[] status;
    return Open(workbookPath,
        Thread.CurrentThread.CurrentUICulture.Name,
        Thread.CurrentThread.CurrentCulture.Name,
        out status);
}
```

The overload requires only a path to a workbook file. The method will "fill in the blanks" by making assumptions about the call.

ExcelServices.FromSessionId()

The `ExcelServices` class exposes another method that allows the developer to create a `Session` object out of a Session ID. This is useful where your code interacts with other code that uses Excel Web Services that supplies you with the Session ID string.

```
public Session FromSessionId(string sessionId)
{
    return new Session(CreateWrapper(), sessionId);
}
```

The Session Class

Most of the methods are located in the `Session` class. The methods look similar to those available through the Excel Web Services, but they do not take the Session ID parameter because the class already has it as a member. That makes the usage easier and more streamlined. In addition, the class supports the `IDisposable` interface, which will allow callers to use the class inside a `using` statement. Here is an example of how to use this class:

```
static void Main(string[] args)
{
    ExcelServices s =
new ExcelServices(ExcelServicesType.Soap, "http://oss");
    s.Credentials = GetCredentials();
    using (Session session = s.Open("http://oss/Documents/Book1.xlsx"))
    {
        Console.WriteLine("A1 is " + session.GetCellA1("Sheet1!A1").ToString());
    }
}
```

A few things are apparent:

❑ There was no need to pass in any extra parameters to the OpenWorkbook method — the call to Open, which is the equivalent, simply takes the name of the workbook as a parameter.

❑ There is no need to call CloseWorkbook. The using statement automatically calls Dispose() on the object and closes the session.

❑ The call to GetCellA1 looks simpler than the original four parameter call.

The next few sections will go over how the implementation of Session looks. Note that since there is a lot of repetition in the overloads of the methods, only a few methods will be shown to help illustrate the concept.

The Session class will contain the Session ID and an instance of the wrapper that will be used to issue the actual requests:

```csharp
public sealed class Session : IDisposable
{
    private string m_sessionId;
    private IExcelServiceWrapper m_wrapper;
    private bool m_closeSessionOnDispose = true;
    private bool m_disposed;

    internal Session(IExcelServiceWrapper wrapper, string sessionId)
    {
        m_sessionId = sessionId;
        m_wrapper = wrapper;
    }
    public bool Disposed
    {
        get { return m_disposed; }
    }

    public bool CloseSessionOnDispose
    {
        get { return m_closeSessionOnDispose; }
        set { m_closeSessionOnDispose = value; }
    }

    internal IExcelServiceWrapper InternalWrapper
    {
        get { return m_wrapper; }
        set { m_wrapper = value; }
    }

    public string SessionId
    {
        get { return m_sessionId; }
        set { m_sessionId = value; }
    }
    // ...
}
```

The `m_closeSessionOnDispose` member will be used to determine if the session needs to be closed when the object is disposed. This is useful when developers want to use the `Session` class to make calls on a Session ID they do not own.

Dispose Code

The code that executes when the object is disposed (or finalized) is tied to the `Close()` method the class exposes. The following code sample shows the `Dispose()` method and the finalizer — both of them calling a method that takes care of closing the workbook if necessary and resetting its state:

```
~Session()
{
    IntenralDispose();
}

public void Dispose()
{
    InternalDispose();
    GC.SuppressFinalize(this);
}
```

Depending on how the instance is set up, `Dispose(bool)` calls the `Close()` method, which ultimately calls into the `CloseWorkbook()` method. If the `Close()` method is not called, `Dispose(bool)` makes sure that it resets the members of the class so that it knows it is disposed of:

```
protected virtual void InternalDispose()
{
    if (CloseSessionOnDispose)
    {
        Close();
    }
    else
    {
        ResetMembers();
    }
}
private void ResetMembers()
{
    m_disposed = true;
    m_sessionId = null;
    m_wrapper = null;
}
```

The `Close()` method makes sure that the object has not yet been disposed of. Once it asserts that this is the case, it makes a call into the `CloseWorkbook()` method on the `IExcelServicesWrapper` interface. Notice that it catches all exceptions and only rethrows if the caller required it. Since, for the most part, there is no course of action that needs to (or even can) be taken when a session fails to close, it makes sense in most cases to simply ignore the error:

```
public void Close()
{
    Status[] status;
```

```
        Close(out status, false);
    }

public void Close(out Status[] status, bool throwOnError)
{
    status = null;
    if (Disposed || InternalWrapper == null)
    {
        status = new Status[0];
        return;
    }
    try
    {
        InternalWrapper.CloseWorkbook(SessionId, out status);
        Utils.FixStatusArray(ref status);

    }
    catch
    {
        if (throwOnError)
        {
            throw;
        }
    }
    finally
    {
        ResetMembers();
    }
}
```

Note how `Close` also takes care to reset the member variables you no longer require. This will make sure that subsequent calls will fail immediately.

The rest of the work on this class has to do with writing all the correct overloads that will make life easier for callers. The following two sections are examples for such overloads — one for the `Refresh` method and one for the `GetRangeA1` method.

Every time you call a function in `IExcelServiceWrapper` *that returns a* `Status` *array, you will also immediately call the* `Utils.FixStatusArray()` *method on it. This method checks to see if the* `Status` *array is null, and if it is, it replaces it with an empty array. That makes code more uniform when using the returned arrays (there is no need to check for null — one can immediately access the* `Length` *property to see if there are any items.*

The following method is defined in the `Session` class and is used to make sure that the state of the session is valid:

```
private void ThrowIfNeeded()
{
    if (m_disposed)
    {
        throw new ObjectDisposedException("Session");
    }
```

```
    if (InternalWrapper == null)
    {
        throw new InvalidOperationException();
    }
}
```

Refresh Functionality

Workbooks that have data sources in them may need to be refreshed by code. To do that, Excel Web Services supplies the callers with the Refresh method. The first overload that will be added to the Session class will be a method that duplicates the entire functionality of the Refresh() method:

```
public bool Refresh(string connectionName, out Status[] status)
{
    ThrowIfNeeded();
    InternalWrapper.Refresh(m_sessionId, connectionName, out status);
    Utils.FixStatusArray(ref status);
    return status.Length == 0;
}
```

The method is relatively simple. It makes sure that the object state is valid (by calling ThrowIfNeeded()). It then makes a call into the wrapper, passing in the Session ID that the Session object wraps as the first parameter and passing through the parameters passed to it. Finally, it returns a Boolean that represents whether or not any Status object returned from the call — this will enable callers to write more simplified code when refreshing data. Here's an example of using Refresh() and checking the Status array:

```
ExcelServices s = new ExcelServices(ExcelServicesType.Soap, "http://oss");
s.Credentials = GetCredentials();
using (Session session = s.Open("http://oss/Documents/Book1.xlsx"))
{
    Status[] status;
    if (!session.Refresh("MyConnection", out status))
    {
        foreach (Status warning in status)
        {
            Console.WriteLine(warning.Message);
        }
    }
}
```

The Refresh() method has four overloads — the one described above and three more. The first overload simply allows the caller to omit the Status array:

```
        public bool Refresh(string connectionName)
        {
            Status[] status;
            return Refresh(connectionName, out status);
        }
```

The second one will refresh the whole workbook by passing in an empty string to the `Refresh()` call and return a `Status` array:

```
public bool Refresh(out Status[] status)
{
    return Refresh("", out status);
}
```

The last one will refresh the whole workbook and allow the caller to ignore the `Status` array:

```
public bool Refresh()
{
    Status[] status;
    return Refresh("", out status);
}
```

Overall, this makes the code much more readable and removes some of the tedium of repeating ignorable code.

GetRangeA1 Functionality

The `GetRangeA1` set of overloads return an instance of the `RangeResult` class. The following is the basic method `GetRangeA1()`:

```
public RangeResult GetRangeA1(string sheetName, string rangeName, bool formatted,
out Status[] status)
{
    ThrowIfNeeded();
    RangeA1Updater updater = new RangeA1Updater();
    updater.Session = this;
    updater.SheetName = sheetName;
    updater.RangeName = rangeName;
    updater.Formatted = formatted;
    RangeResult result = new RangeResult(this, updater.UpdateFunction);
    status = result.Refresh();
    return result;
}
```

The method prepares a `RangeA1Updater` instance (explained later in this chapter) and fills it with the appropriate information. It then creates a new instance of the `RangeResult` class and returns that instance. The infrastructure around the `RangeResult` class will be discussed in the next section, for now, this section discusses the other three overloads available for the callers. None of them (except for the first one, which was just discussed) will return a `Status` array because the `GetXXX` family of methods will never return anything there. The first overload is similar to the basic call:

```
public RangeResult GetRangeA1(string sheetName, string rangeName, bool formatted)
{
    Status[] status;
    return GetRangeA1(sheetName, rangeName, formatted, out status);
}
```

The second overload ignores the sheet name in the call. Because the rangeName can be any Excel type reference, there is usually no real reason to use it — to get cell A1 from Sheet1, the caller may pass in Sheet1!A1. In addition, named ranges are usually global in scope, and so it is unnecessary to pass in a sheet name either:

```
public RangeResult GetRangeA1(string rangeName, bool formatted)
{
    Status[] status;
    return GetRangeA1("", rangeName, formatted, out status);
}
```

Finally, the last overload will default to returning unformatted data (see the section discussing the GetXXX Excel Web Services methods in Chapter 6).

```
public RangeResult GetRangeA1(string rangeName)
{
    Status[] status;
    return GetRangeA1("", rangeName, false, out status);
}
```

Session Class Summary

The rest of the methods available in this class will supply the rest of the functionality of Excel Web Services. The overloads will always consist of a fully featured call that contains all of the parameters the method it is based on contains (except for the Session ID, which will always be implicitly passed in). Each set of overloads will also have a version of the method where the Status array is not passed in. Then the rest of the overloads in each set (if more exist) will consist of passing reasonable defaults to the fully featured call. The full source code is available online and on the companion CD.

The RangeResult Class

Chapter 5 describes how multi-cell ranges returned from Excel Web Services are used. While using jagged arrays is pretty simple, it could be made to be more readable by fashioning some structure around it. As shown in Figure 7.2, ESL uses the RangeResult class to do that — the class wraps the raw data coming back from Excel Web Services and builds an object model on top of it.

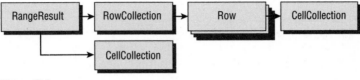

Figure 7.2

Example

The workbook shown in Figure 7.3 has a list of products a gaming store sells and has in stock. The next few sections will show code that will extract the list of products from the workbook and fill a .NET WinForms application with it.

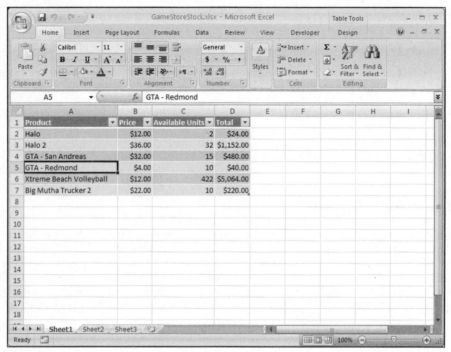

Figure 7.3

As you can see, the table content is selected and in the Named Range box (top-left part of the screen) you can see the name ProductTable. That is the name of the contents of the table on this Excel workbook. This name will be used in the code so that if the table gets bigger or smaller, the form will always get the correct amount of data (as opposed to what would have happened if the code were using an Excel reference such as Sheet1!A2:D7).

The following code will be attached to the Refresh button on the form — when it is clicked, the code will use ESL to ask the server for the "ProductTable" range.

```
private void refreshButton_Click(object sender, EventArgs e)
{
    ExcelServices s =
        new ExcelServices(ExcelServicesType.Soap, "oss");

    using (Session session =
        s.Open("http://oss/Documents/GameStoreStock.xlsx"))
    {
```

```
        RangeResult range = session.GetRangeA1("ProductTable", true);
        productListView.Items.Clear();
        foreach (Row row in range.RowCollection)
        {
            ListViewItem item = new ListViewItem(row.ToStringArray());
            productListView.Items.Add(item);
        }
    }
}
```

The code no longer handles a jagged array — instead, it uses the `Row` and `RowCollection` object to access the data. The infrastructure is relatively simple, but it provides some structure and some utility functionality. When the code runs, the ListView control gets filled with the relevant data from the Excel workbook, as shown in Figure 7.4.

Figure 7.4

How RangeResult Works

Since `RangeResult` is just a wrapper to the jagged array, its functionality is fairly simple. To allow callers to refresh the result, however, it needs to store enough information in itself to be able to reissue the request. To do that, there is a delegate that knows how to requery data from Excel Web Services:

```
public delegate object[] RangeResultUpdateHandler(out Status[] status);
```

This delegate will be implemented by two updater classes — one for `GetRange()` and one for `GetRangeA1()`, called `RangeUpdater` and `RangeA1Updater`, respectively. Both classes will inherit from a base class called `BaseUpdater` that has some of the common information both classes will need:

```
public abstract class BaseUpdater
{
    private Session m_session;
    private string m_sheetName;
    private bool m_formatted;

    public Session Session
    {
        get { return m_session; }
```

```
                set { m_session = value; }
        }

        public bool Formatted
        {
                get { return m_formatted; }
                set { m_formatted = value; }
        }

        public string SheetName
        {
                get { return m_sheetName; }
                set { m_sheetName = value; }
        }

}
```

The `RangeUpdater` class will add to these the `RangeCoordinates` property, while the `RangeA1Updater` will add a string property that will be used to store the named range passed in. Each will also have to implement the delegate that will do the requerying. This section discusses the `RangeA1Updater` class only — the `RangeUpdater` is almost identical.

```
public class RangeA1Updater : BaseUpdater
{
        private string m_rangeName;

        public object[] UpdateFunction(out Status[] status)
        {
                object[] result = Session.InternalWrapper.GetRangeA1(
                        Session.SessionId,
                        SheetName,
                        RangeName,
                        Formatted,
                        out status);
                Utils.FixStatusArray(ref status);
                return result;
        }

        public string RangeName
        {
                get { return m_rangeName; }
                set { m_rangeName = value; }
        }
}
```

The delegate implementation is simple — it makes a call to the `IExcelServiceWrapper` with the members it has and returns the results.

Previously, when this chapter discussed how the various overloads for `GetRangeA1()` in the `Session` class, the code created an instance of the `RangeA1Updater` class:

```
RangeA1Updater updater = new RangeA1Updater();
updater.Session = this;
updater.SheetName = sheetName;
```

```
updater.Formatted = formatted;
updater.RangeName = rangeName;
RangeResult result = new RangeResult(this, updater.UpdateFunction);
status = result.Refresh();
return result;
```

The first thing the code does is to create the updater. It then initializes it with the information it will need to rerun the query. Finally, it creates a `RangeResult` instance, which takes the delegate as a parameter and asks it to refresh itself.

"Versioning" of the RangeResult Class

The `RangeResult` class keeps track of what version it is. In this context, a version is defined as a single requery of the range; therefore, when the `RangeResult` is first created, its version number will be 1. The second time it is requeried, the version will be 2, and so on.

This versioning mechanism is in place so that objects that are created off a `RangeResult` object and could potentially cause problems if used after a requery. By using this versioning mechanism, they will know that they are no longer connected to the correct object.

```
public class RangeResult
{
private object[] m_rawData;
private RowCollection m_rowCollection;
private Session m_session;
private RangeResultUpdateFunction m_updateFunction;
private RangeCellCollection m_cellCollection;
private int m_version;
    internal int Version
    {
        get { return m_version; }
    }
    public bool CanRefresh
    {
        get
        {
            bool result = UpdateFunction != null && !Session.Disposed;
            return result;
        }
    }

//...
    public Status[] Refresh()
    {
        if (!CanRefresh)
        {
            throw new CannotRefreshException();
        }
        Status[] status;
        m_rawData = UpdateFunction(out status);
        m_version++;
        return status;
    }
}
```

Currently, the only class in the system that tracks versions is the Row class. When callers ask for a specific row in the range, the row will be tagged with the current version. If a call is made into Row when the versions do not match, an exception will be thrown to warn the user that the row was created in a previous version of the RangeResult instance.

RowCollection Class

The RowCollection class holds a reference to the RangeResult class and allows the caller to use indexing to either access a given row in the returned range or, alternately, enumerate the rows.

```
public class RowCollection : IEnumerable<Row>
{
// ...
    public Row this[int index]
    {
        get
        {
            if (index < 0 || index >= RangeResult.RowCount)
            {
                throw new IndexOutOfRangeException();
            }

            Row row = new Row(RangeResult, index);
            return row;
        }
    }

    private IEnumerable<Row> EnumerateRows()
    {
        for (int i = 0; i < RangeResult.RowCount; i++)
        {
            yield return this[i];
        }
    }
// ...
    public IEnumerator<Row> GetEnumerator()
    {
        return EnumerateRows().GetEnumerator();
    }
// ...
}
```

The indexer of the RowCollection class returns a Row instance for the appropriate inner array from the jagged array result. The private EnumerateRows() method uses C#'s iterator functionality to create an enumerator that gives all the items in the list. Since the class implements the IEnumerable<> interface, it also implements the GetEnumerator() method, which calls into the EnumerateRows() method.

Row Class

Each Row instance represents a single row in the returned range. The Row class provides access to the content of the returned range — the cells.

The two interesting members of this class are the Cells property and the ToStringArray() method.

The `Cells` property will return a `CellCollection` object that can be iterated and returns all the cells in the row.

```
public CellCollection CellCollection
{
    get
    {
        ThrowOnVersion();
        if (m_cellCollection == null)
        {
            m_cellCollection = new RowCellCollection(this);
        }
        return m_cellCollection;
    }
}
```

The `ToStringArray()` provides an easy way of getting all the cells in the row as an array of strings. The array will always have the same number of cells as in the original row (empty cells are turned into empty strings).

```
public string[] ToStringArray()
{
    string[] strings = new string[Count];
    for (int i = 0; i < Count; i++)
    {
        if (this[i] == null)
            strings[i] = "";
        else
            strings[i] = this[i].ToString();
    }
    return strings;
}
```

CellCollection

`CellCollection` is an abstract class that supplies a generic implementation for iterating over cells. It is implemented by two concrete classes — the `RowCellCollection` and the `RangeCellCollection`. The first one is used from within a `Row` class to access the cells inside a row. The latter can be accessed off a `Range` object and can be used to access all the cells in a range as if they were a contiguous block of data items.

The class has two abstract members — an indexer that needs to be implemented to give access to the cells by index and a `GetEnumerator()` method that returns an enumeration of all the items:

```
public abstract object this[int index]
{
    get;
}

public abstract IEnumerator<object> GetEnumerator();
```

A method called `NonEmptyCells()` is also supplied by the base class. It returns only the cells that contain information. This method uses the enumerator returned by `GetEnumerator()` to go over all the cells and only return those that have values in them (and thus it can be shared between both concrete implementations).

RangeResult exposes a property called CellCollection that returns the RangeCellCollection concrete class. The indexer of that class uses a flattened index to figure out which cell is needed:

```
public override object this[int index]
{
    get
    {
        if (index < 0)
        {
            throw new IndexOutOfRangeException();
        }

        int row = index / RangeResult.ColumnCount;
        int col = index % RangeResult.ColumnCount;
        if (row >= RangeResult.RowCount)
        {
            throw new IndexOutOfRangeException();
        }

        return RangeResult.RowCollection[row].CellCollection[col];
    }
}
```

The GetEnumerator override iterates over all the rows and returns each of the objects returned:

```
public override IEnumerator<object> GetEnumerator()
{
    foreach (object[] row in RangeResult.RawData)
    {
        foreach (object cell in row)
        {
            yield return cell;
        }
    }
}
```

The implementation of RowCellCollection is even simpler — the indexer returns the *n*th item in the inner object array in the jagged array. The GetEnumerator() calls into the Array.GetEnumerator() method and passes it through.

WorkbookData Class

The current binary representation of a workbook that was changed inside a session can be retrieved from the server. This is especially useful when callers want to save a workbook that is usable by Excel. The method used for that is called GetWorkbook(), returning an array of bytes. WorkbookData wraps that array of bytes and adds the ability to save the array into a file.

The following is an example of how usage of this class may look:

```
ExcelServices s = new ExcelServices(ExcelServicesType.Soap, "http://oss");
s.Credentials = GetCredentials();
using (Session session = s.Open("http://oss/Documents/Book1.xlsx"))
{
    session.SetCellA1("Sheet1!A1", 4.45);
    WorkbookData wbd = session.GetWorkbook(WorkbookType.FullSnapshot);
    string fileName =
Environment.GetFolderPath(Environment.SpecialFolder.Personal);
    fileName = System.IO.Path.Combine(fileName, "MyFile.xlsx");
    wbd.Save(fileName);
}
```

The code sets a value into the workbook and then calls the GetWorkbook() method on the session. The resulting WorkbookData object is then used to save the file to disk into the My Documents folder.

Summary

The ESL greatly simplifies working with the two versions of the API. It hides quite a bit of the nitty-gritty details from developers and makes the code that uses Excel Web Services more readable and maintainable.

Throughout the rest of the book, when usage examples of the API are given, the ESL will be used in most implementations.

Part III: User Defined Functions

UDF Sample

Excel Services allows developers to extend the library of cell functions with their own code. This is very similar to XLLs, automation addins, and VBA work. When a workbook has a formula in it that contains unrecognized names that look like function calls, Excel Services will search for that name in the UDF assemblies that the administrator registered and if the same name is found, Excel Services will try to call into it. As mentioned before, Excel Services does not have an object model — this means that when UDF code is executing, there is very little information it can know about the environment in which it executes. The next chapter will delve more into the limitations of UDFs.

What This Sample Contains

Because this is a "teach by example" chapter, the UDFs presented will not have a cohesive thread that links them. They are, for the most part, relatively simple pieces of code that will augment Excel Services with functions it does not contain by default.

The first step though, is to create the actual UDF library that will be used.

Creating a UDF Assembly

UDF assemblies are .NET 2.0 libraries. When using Visual Studio 2005, use the New Project option to create a new library, as shown in Figure 8.1.

Of course, the language selected can be any of the languages supported by your environment. In this case, it is a C# library called UDFExample.

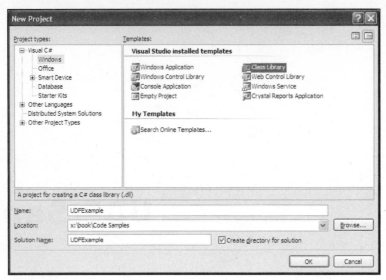

Figure 8.1

Required References

The next step is to add a reference to `Microsoft.Office.Excel.Server.Udf.dll`. There are two ways to do that, depending on where the development occurs: on the server in which Excel Services is installed, or on another machine.

Server Box Development

If the development occurs on a box where Excel Services is installed, the .NET tab on the Add References dialog can be used to choose the appropriate assembly. That entry in the list will be called "Excel Services UDF Framework." Clicking OK will add that assembly to the list.

Nonserver Box Development

When developing on a machine that does not contain a server or when developing in an environment where a direct path to a referenced assembly is required, developers will need to copy over the appropriate assembly to their build-trees for consumption. The assembly can either be found in the GAC on the server or, more conveniently, in the following directory:

```
%Program Files%\Common Files\Microsoft Shared\web server extensions\12\ISAPI
```

Most developers will probably go with the "Non-server box development" option. This is the more common case in most organizations and is probably more reliable from a build-environment point of view.

Once the assembly is copied to the build directory, the developer can use the "Browse" tab in the Add Reference dialog box to select the assembly, as shown in Figure 8.2.

Once this stage is done, the project is ready to be a UDF assembly.

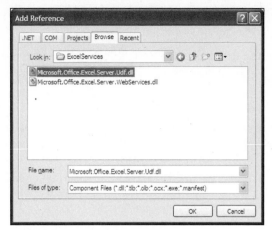

Figure 8.2

Adding the UDF Class

The Visual Studio wizards usually create a default class when creating a library (Class1 in a C# project). That default can be used and renamed, or a wholly new class that will contain the UDF can be created. It is important to make sure that the class is defined as *public* and that it is decorated by the UdfClass attribute that resides in the Microsoft.Office.Excel.Server.Udf namespace:

```
using Microsoft.Office.Excel.Server.Udf;

namespace UDFExample
{
    [UdfClass]
    public class MyUdfClass
    {
    }
}
```

This is the absolute minimum needed to create a UDF class. However, it does not yet have any methods that can run. That will be the next step.

The name of the class is not really important, it can be pretty much anything that will actually compile. It is, however, recommended that you properly name classes and namespaces so in future versions, when fully qualified names would potentially be supported, the UDF assembly will still be usable.

Adding the First UDF

One of the things UDFs are useful for is replacing overly elaborate Excel formulas with a more simplistic one. Take, for example, a formula that finds the last string in a word. You could use the following Excel Formula to write it:

```
=RIGHT(A1,LEN(A1)-FIND(CHAR(255),SUBSTITUTE(A1,"
",CHAR(255),LEN(A1)-LEN(SUBSTITUTE(A1," ","")))))
```

In the following steps, the original string in A1 would be "This book is awesome." The formula goes through the following steps:

1. It finds the number of spaces in the string (call that `AmountOfSpaces`):

```
AmountOfSpaces := LEN(A1)-LEN(SUBSTITUTE(A1," ",""))
```

(In the example: 3)

2. It then substitutes the last space (which would correspond to the number in `AmountOfSpaces`) for a character that is usually unused in strings — the 255th character in the ASCII table. In the example, the "^" will be used to represent it (call the resulting string `LastSpaceChanged`):

```
LastSpaceChanged : = SUBSTITUTE(A1," ",CHAR(255), AmountOfSpaces)
```

(In the example: "This book is^awesome")

3. Next, the formula finds the location of the character in the string:

```
LocationOfLastSpace := FIND(CHAR(255), LastSpaceChanged)
```

(In the example, that will equal 13.)

4. The last calculation returns the number of characters to that character from the end of the string:

```
PositionFromRight := LEN(A1)-LocationOfLastSpace
```

(In the example, equals 7)

5. Finally, the `RIGHT` formula is used to get the end of the string:

```
LastWord := RIGHT(A1, PositionFromRight)
```

(In the example, the word "awesome")

Now, this is not too bad: it's a relatively simple Excel formula — but if a lot of copy and paste is involved and if the formula is being used very often, it can become quite cumbersome. Furthermore, once workbook authors start using this in other workbooks, even more cutting and pasting happens. It would have been much easier to just have a function called `GetLastWord`.

Adding the Method to the Class

In the class that was created, the developer will add a public method that receives a string as a parameter and returns a string that represents the last word.

To make the method consumable as a UDF, it needs to be decorated by the `UdfMethod` attribute class. This is how the empty method will look:

```
[UdfMethod]
public string GetLastWord(string phrase)
{
}
```

The last part is to actually fill in the implementation of the method:

```
[UdfMethod]
public string GetLastWord(string phrase)
{
    int lastSpace = phrase.Trim().LastIndexOf(" ");
    if (lastSpace == -1)
        return phrase;

    string result = phrase.Substring(lastSpace + 1);
    return result;
}
```

This method is even better than the Excel one we came up with because it makes sure there is no white-space around the string (that's what the call to `Trim()` does).

Now that the method is up and running, it needs to be tested.

Adding the UDF to Excel Services

Before Excel Service can use a UDF, two things need to happen. The first is that the UDF needs to be added to the list of assemblies Excel Services is aware of, and the second is that the trusted location that will be used for storing the workbook containing the call to the function needs to have UDFs turned on. While Chapter 2 contains some information on how to get to the relevant configuration areas, this section will show exactly what needs to be done.

The GAC will not be used for this example. Instead, the UDF assembly will be placed in a local path (there will be more information about these options in Chapter 9). A good location would be:

```
C:\UDFs
```

The DLL will need to be copied into this directory.

It is also possible to instruct Visual Studio to compile the assembly directly to this folder.

Once the assembly is compiled and properly placed, a UDF entry needs to be added to the list of available assemblies by clicking the User-defined function assemblies link in the Excel Services Configuration screen. Initially, a blank list will appear. Clicking on Add User-Defined Function Assembly will take you to a form that can be used to add a UDF, as shown in Figure 8.3.

The three important settings here are the name of the assembly, the fact that it's a file path (as opposed to one residing in the GAC), and the fact that it's enabled. Once OK is clicked at the bottom of the page, the assembly will be added to the list of assemblies available to Excel Services.

Access to the trusted locations is also explained in Chapter 9. The workbook that will use the UDF in this example resides in a trusted location (like all files Excel Services can access). Navigating to the setting of that trusted location will provide access to the User-defined functions allowed option shown in Figure 8.4, which needs to be enabled in order for the UDF to be executed by the server.

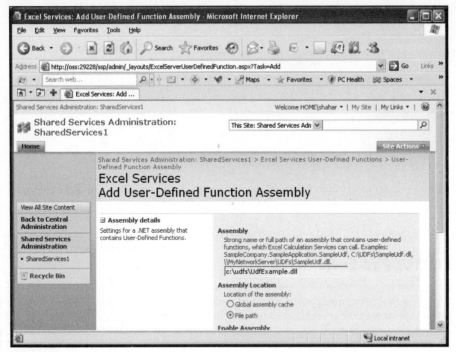

Figure 8.3

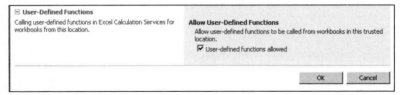

Figure 8.4

Creating the Workbook

The workbook (shown in Figure 8.5) will be relatively simple — cell A1 contains a sentence, and cell A2 contains a formula that calls into the newly created UDF.

The workbook now contains a call to the UDF. However, since the client does not know such a function exists, it will display the error #NAME.

> *Excel 2007 does not support Excel Services UDFs right out of the box. Chapter 10 shows how to develop an addin for Excel 2007 that will provide this functionality and allow users to see real results of UDFs when authoring workbooks.*

Uploading the workbook to the trusted location with the enabled UDF execution on it and viewing that file in the browser, however, shows that the UDF was actually called successfully on the server, as shown in Figure 8.6.

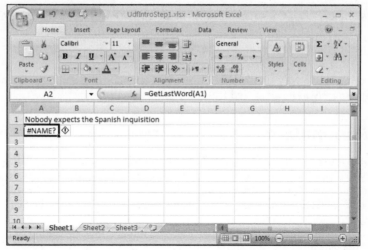

Figure 8.5

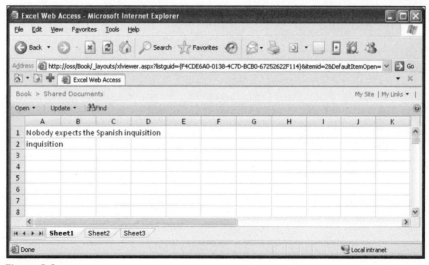

Figure 8.6

VB.NET Version of the UDF

The following code is the equivalent UDF, but in VB.NET:

```
<UdfClass> _
Public Class MyUdfClass
    <UdfMethod> _
    Function GetLastWord(ByVal phrase As String) As String
        Dim lastSpace As Integer = phrase.Trim().LastIndexOf(" ")
        If lastSpace = -1 Then Return phrase
```

```
                Dim result As String = phrase.Substring(lastSpace + 1)
                Return result
        End Function
End Class
```

That was an example of a very simple UDF — one that takes a string and returns a string. The next UDF will show some slightly more advanced features.

Optional Parameters

While optional parameters are not supported with Excel Services UDFs, the .NET ParamArray is. This means that calls can be made to have seemingly varying amounts of parameters. In reality, the last argument to the method is actually an array — the compiler takes care to take all the parameters that come after the one-before-last and pack them into an array that is then passed as the last parameter.

The example will use this feature to add a parameter that will allow the setting of the delimiter that is used between the words. The new method will be called GetLastWord2:

```
[UdfMethod]
public string GetLastWord2(string phrase, params string[] args)
{
    string delimiter = " ";
    if (args.Length > 0)
    {
        delimiter = args[0];
        if (delimiter.Length > 1)
        {
            throw new InvalidOperationException();
        }
    }
    int lastDelimiter = phrase.Trim().LastIndexOf(delimiter);
    if (lastDelimiter == -1)
        return phrase;

    string result = phrase.Substring(lastDelimiter + 1);
    return result;
}
```

Very similar to the previous version, this UDF checks to see if there is an extra parameter inside the args parameter and if there is, it will use it as the delimiter (as long as it's one-character long).

After compiling the assembly and placing it in the aforementioned location, the server should be able to use the newly created method.

> If your server has just been running the previous example, you may get an error that the file is currently in use. You will need to restart Excel Services to be able to upload the new version. In the UDF references chapter, I will go into detail about the various ways this can be achieved, but for now, running IISRESET.EXE from a command prompt on the server should suffice.

If the workbook was to be modified now to contain a comma-delimited list such as "Rum, Wine, Bourbon, Whiskey" this UDF can be used with a comma as the second parameter to return the last item in the list, as shown in Figure 8.7.

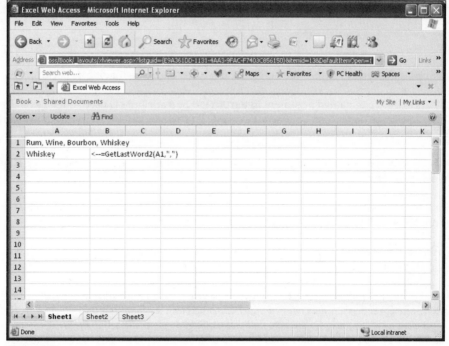

Figure 8.7

Getting External Data

One of the best uses for UDFs is to bring external information to the workbook — the following example will grab stock information from a Web Service and return it to the sheet.

Of course, this can be done by using any Web Service that supplies such functionality; a publicly available one is located at:

```
http://ws.cdyne.com/delayedstockquote/delayedstockquote.asmx?wsdl
```

Before using the Web Service, though, it needs to be imported into the project. (In this example, the namespace used will be StockQuote. Chapter 5 provides an example of how to do this. Instead of importing Excel Web Services though, the supplied address should be used.)

Once imported, the following UDF method should compile successfully:

```
[UdfMethod(IsVolatile = true)]
public double GetStockQuote(string symbol)
{
    StockQuote.DelayedStockQuote s =
        new StockQuote.DelayedStockQuote();
```

```
    decimal result = s.GetQuickQuote(symbol, "");

    return (double)result;
}
```

The call passes the symbol to the Web Service and returns the value that it gets back.

The IsVolatile=true named argument in the UdfMethod attribute is used to tell Excel Services that this UDF can change depending on when it's called. This will be discussed in length in Chapter 9 when UDF references are discussed.

A new workbook will contain a list of symbols and calls to this new UDF for each of the symbols, as shown in Figure 8.8.

As with the workbook that was previously shown, Excel shows the error #NAME in each of the cells, since it does not know of the function written for the server.

Navigating to this workbook on the server should show the values for each of the stock symbols, as shown in Figure 8.9.

If you find that the code does not execute properly for you, it may mean that your computer is behind a proxy. Since Excel Services does not run under a user account, it cannot take advantage of the IE settings to figure out what the proxy is. You may find that you need to manually set up the proxy before making calls into the Web Service. See the Proxy property on the StockQuote.DelayedStockQuote Web Service class for more information.

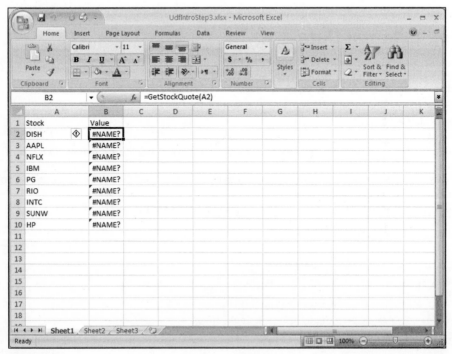

Figure 8.8

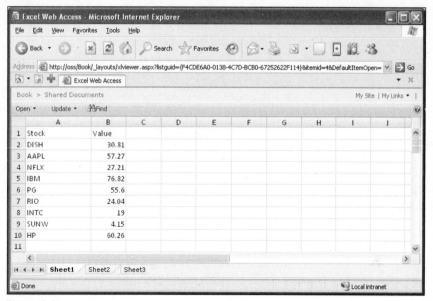

Figure 8.9

With only a few lines of code, it was possible to add completely new capabilities to Excel Services. The next section discusses how cell ranges can come into play with UDFs.

Using Ranges with UDFs

Excel Services UDFs allow methods to receive and return arrays of data. This is especially useful when callers want to exchange a large amount of information between a UDF and Excel. The same rules that apply to ranges in an Excel native function apply to UDFs — you can use any notation Excel supports, including other array formulas to get information into UDFs.

Taking the example shown with the stock quotes, it is important to understand what actually happens under the hood. For each cell that contains a formula (the calls to GetStockQuote), Excel Services makes a call to the assembly shown. That means that if there are 100 symbols that need to be looked up, 100 calls will occur to the UDF. That in itself is not so bad. However, in the particular case of calling into Web Services each of those calls will go off-box to try to get back data.

To make this UDF more efficient, it needs to be changed so that it works with ranges — instead of being called multiple times, it will be executed using a single call that will fetch all the relevant data. The new UDF will take an array as a parameter and return an array. For each element in the array it gets as a parameter, it will call the Web Service to get back the result that will be placed in the resulting array (which will have a size that corresponds to the one received as a parameter):

```
[UdfMethod(IsVolatile = true)]
public object[,] GetMultiStockQuote(object[,] symbols)
{
    StockQuote.DelayedStockQuote s =
        new StockQuote.DelayedStockQuote();
```

```
      // Create an array that has n rows (according to what we got as an argument)
      // and 1 column.
      object[,] results = new object[symbols.GetLength(0), 1];

      // Now iterate and call the Web Service- each time with a new value.
      for (int i = 0; i < symbols.GetLength(0); i++)
      {
            results[i, 0] = (double)s.GetQuickQuote(symbols[i, 0].ToString(), "0");
      }

      return results;
}
```

The signature of the method was changed to take an array of objects. Because Excel Services does not support an array of strings as a parameter, an array of object needs to be used.

UDFs use a two-dimensional array instead of jagged arrays. More on that in the UDF reference chapter.

To use this newly created method, the workbook will need to contain an array formula. Array formulas allow Excel users to take a returned range of numbers and place them in a whole range (as opposed to a single cell). Excel then takes care about taking the returned range and numbers and placing them in the correct cells. To use an array formula in Excel, the following steps need to be taken:

1. A range that will contain the result of the UDF needs to be selected.

2. While the range is selected, the appropriate formula needs to be entered in (i.e., `=GetMultiStockQuote(...)`).

3. Instead of pressing Enter to complete editing, Ctrl+Shift+Enter needs to be pressed. The formula will be inserted into the cell and will be decorated by squiggly braces to mark the fact that it's an array formula.

Figure 8.10 shows how usage of the new array function, `GetMultiStockQuote()`, looks in Excel.

Looking at the formula bar, notice that the call is nested inside a pair of braces, the visual cue that lets the user know this is an array formula.

Opening this file on the server again shows the expected results (see Figure 8.11).

Excel Services now makes a single call into the UDF to get all the relevant values instead of multiple calls.

Making It Even Faster — Asynchronous Programming

Generally speaking, Web Service calls that go over the network take very few CPU cycles from the machine making the call. The majority of the time spent on the call is in waiting for the answer to come back. This is doubly true for cases where the server is located outside the local network. If the whole call takes 500 milliseconds, it may be that the CPU will only be engaged for 10 of those milliseconds. Making 100 calls to this service will take roughly 50 seconds, only 1 second of which will be spent utilizing the CPU.

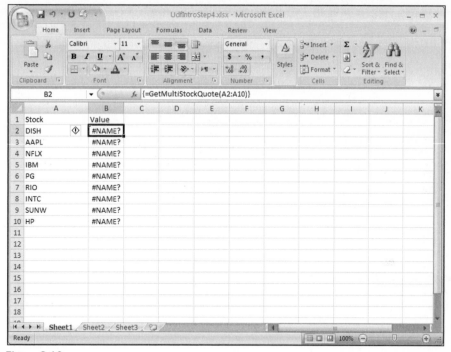

Figure 8.10

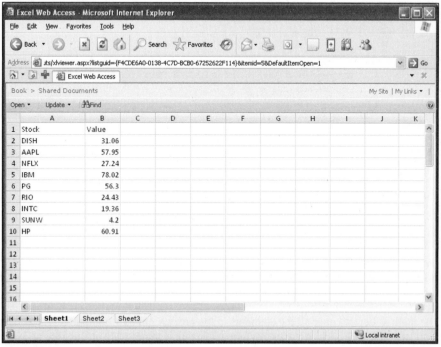

Figure 8.11

Because of this, Web Services are very good candidates for asynchronous calls. In the case above, nine calls are made into the Web Service serially. The following modified UDF makes the calls asynchronously, getting the values back in parallel:

```
[UdfMethod(IsVolatile = true)]
public object[,] GetMultiStockQuote(object[,] symbols)
{
     int count = symbols.GetLength(0);
     object[,] results = new object[count, 1];
     int remaining = count;
     System.Threading.ManualResetEvent ev =
          new System.Threading.ManualResetEvent(false);

     // Iterate and issue async calls for each cell.
     for (int i = 0; i < count; i++)
     {
          StockQuote.DelayedStockQuote s =
               new StockQuote.DelayedStockQuote();

          // Add the event that will be fired when the operation is complete.
          s.GetQuickQuoteCompleted += delegate(object sender,
StockQuote.GetQuickQuoteCompletedEventArgs e)
          {
               int index = (int)e.UserState;

               if (e.Error == null)
               {
                    results[index, 0] = (double)e.Result;
               }
               else
               {
                    results[index, 0] = "Error!";
               }

               int nowRemaining = Interlocked.Decrement(ref remaining);
               if (nowRemaining == 0)
               {
                    ev.Set();
               }
          };

          s.GetQuickQuoteAsync(symbols[i, 0].ToString(), "0", (object)i);
     }

     ev.WaitOne();

     return results;
}
```

This function first needs to prepare the `results` array, which will be used to store the values returning from the call. It also prepares an event that will be signaled when the whole operation is complete.

Next, the method iterates over all the elements in the array it got as a parameter and issues an asynchronous request to the Web Service. An anonymous delegate is attached to each of the asynchronous calls that is made and immediately after that a call is made to GetQuickQuoteAsync() with the appropriate parameters.

The code will now arrive at the last line before returning the value in which ev.WaitOne() is called. Because this code is executing asynchronously, it's probable that this will be reached before any of the calls complete. In any case, the method will wait until the ManualResetEvent object is signaled.

Each of those anonymous delegates will be executed — on a separate thread — when the operation actually completes. Each one of them takes the result received from the asynchronous call and places it in the correct location in the results array. The counter that keeps track of the calls that are still outstanding is then decremented. Last, the delegate checks to see what the value of nowRemaining is. If it equals zero, it means that all the outstanding requests are complete and the event can be signaled.

> *This is done via a call to* Interlocked.Decrement() *so that if two threads will happen to run this code at the same time, they will not modify the value at the same time.*

Signaling the event will cause the UDF function to continue to its end, in which it will return the resulting array to the caller — in this case, Excel Services.

Important Notes about the Faster Version of the UDF

It is important to note the following:

❑ All things being equal, this UDF as it is written will only be twice as fast as the nonasynchronous version. This is due to the fact that the HTTP standard requires clients to only have two concurrent requests to the same server at the same time. This means that, by default, only two calls to the Web Service you are using will be active at any time. There are ways to get around this limitation — see the System.Net.ServicePoint.ConnectionLimit property for more information. (Or check out the ServicePointManager.DefaultConnectionLimit property.)

❑ It is strongly advised that you use some kind of timeout mechanism when running this code. This can be easily achieved by using one of the overloads of the WaitOne() call made on the ManualResetEvent instance. If this is not done and there's some problem with the code, the call may never return, impacting the behavior of the server.

❑ The asynchronous mechanism used in this example leverages the automatically generated Web Service proxy. That proxy, in turn, leverages the .NET thread pool. Taking too many threads from the pool can have an adverse effect on the server. One thing that can be done is to throttle the amount of calls active at any given time. That way, you can still have a faster function, but also not cause the server to starve for threads.

Caching Information

Excel Services enables two levels of caching when executing UDFs. The first is referred to as global caching and allows the developer to cache information across sessions and the other is session-level caching, which allows for caching information for a specific session. Chapter 9 elaborates on these issues. This chapter, however, will show some of the usages of such caching. In this section, a modified version of the GetStockQuote() UDF is shown that caches the quotes allowing for much faster data retrieval.

When a cached quote is 1 minute old, a new value will be queried and returned. This both will allow the developer to minimize the amount of network traffic that the server produces and will make the results return much faster. The disadvantage of using this method is that callers will always have a potentially 1-minute-old result.

To do this, a class is needed that will contain the stock quote and when it was last queried:

```csharp
internal sealed class CachedQuote
{
    private double m_quote;
    private DateTime m_lastQuery = DateTime.MinValue;

    public CachedQuote()
    {
    }

    public double Quote
    {
        get { return m_quote; }
        set
        {
            m_quote = value;
            m_lastQuery = DateTime.UtcNow;
        }
    }

    public TimeSpan Age
    {
        get
        {
            return DateTime.UtcNow - m_lastQuery;
        }
    }
}
```

The class stores the actual value of the quote and the time it was last queried at. It contains two important properties: Quote and Age.

Whenever a value is written into the Quote property, it updates the m_lastQuery field. That field is used to determine the age of the value (how long ago it was queried).

It is important to note that the UtcNow static property of the DateTime structure is being used. This is done so that even if the machine moves to daylight savings time, the method will continue to work properly. Had the Now property been used instead, the code could potentially return the same result for an entire hour when daylight savings time is activated. For even better accuracy, use the Environment.TickCount property or the Stopwatch class.

The UDF class also needs to be modified:

```csharp
[UdfClass]
public class MyUdfClass
{
```

```
        private static TimeSpan MaxAge = TimeSpan.FromMinutes(1);
        private Dictionary<string, CachedQuote> m_quotes =
            new Dictionary<string, CachedQuote>(StringComparer.OrdinalIgnoreCase);
    // ...
```

The read-only `TimeSpan` field contains the maximum age that a quote can reach before it's refreshed. The `Dictionary<>` member will contain all the quotes that have been cached thus far.

> *The* `Dictionary` *instance is being instantiated with a* `StringComparer.OrdinalIgnoreCase` *instance so that all equivalent symbols will be considered the same. Had that not been the case, the symbols "ORCL" and "orcl" would have been considered different and queried multiple times resulting in worse performance.*

The `GetStockQuote()` UDF also needs to be modified:

```
[UdfMethod(IsVolatile = true)]
public double GetStockQuote(string symbol)
{
    CachedQuote quote = null;
    lock (m_quotes)
    {
        if (!m_quotes.TryGetValue(symbol, out quote))
        {
            quote = new CachedQuote();
            m_quotes[symbol] = quote;
        }

    }

    if (quote.Age > MaxAge)
    {
        StockQuote.DelayedStockQuote s =
                new StockQuote.DelayedStockQuote();

        decimal result = s.GetQuickQuote(symbol, "0");
          quote.Quote = (double)result;
    }
    return quote.Quote;
}
```

The first part of the method locks the `m_quotes` field. This is to make sure that the UDF is thread-safe. (Chapter 9 covers thread-safeness in more detail.)

Once the `m_quotes` is safe for usage, a check is made to see if a quote already exists in the cache for the requested symbol. If it does, it will be placed in the `quote` local variable. If one does not exist, the method will create it and place it in the dictionary.

Now that the method has an instance of a `CachedQuote` class, it will check to see if a new query needs to be made. If the `Age` property is larger than the maximum age allowed, the method will go ahead and make the Web Service call to get back the new value, which can then set inside the correct `quote` instance.

The code does not bother with locking the quote *instance. Doing so would allow the method to really only make a single query every minute; however, it would also cause more contention as multiple calls come in at the same time asking for a specific symbol. Since no lock is taken, however, if two callers come at the same exact time, requesting a quote for the same symbol, they will both actually end up making the request.*

Summary

This chapter showed just how easy it is to write UDFs in Excel Services using managed code. The next chapter goes into more detail about the capabilities of UDFs.

9

UDF Reference

Excel Services gives developers the ability to augment the native library of functions that can be used inside Excel formulas. Such augmenting functions are called UDFs (user defined functions) and can be written using any tool that can create .NET 2.0 assemblies.

History

Excel gives developers quite a few ways to extend its available functions in formulas. As new technologies emerged, Excel started taking advantage of them and utilizing them — that explains the jumble of technologies that exist:

❑ Excel macros are probably the oldest way to program in Excel. There are ways to write UDFs with them.

❑ There are ways to call into functions exported inside DLLs. (Only inside macros though. Not inside a regular sheet.)

❑ XLLs are DLLs that are written a certain way. They are considered the most efficient way to add UDFs to Excel.

❑ Functions inside VBA modules can also be used as UDFs inside Excel. Simply having a public function should allow the author of the workbook to use the function inside their formulas.

❑ Automation Servers add-ins can be any COM object that supports IDispatch (and has the "Programmable" key in its CLSID registration). When Excel uses such an Addin, it creates the COM object and makes all the exposed IDispatch functions available for formulas.

❑ Office COM Addins can use IDispatch objects to augment the list of callable functions (very similar to automation addins, but initialized differently).

Over the years, people and companies built more and more infrastructures that allow for a simpler way of writing UDFs. XLLs specifically have quite a few commercial and free libraries out there that will make life easier for UDF writers in one way or another.

The Excel Services UDF mechanism is different than all of these — in Excel Services, managed code with special attributes is used for extending the library of functions.

Excel Services UDFs

The only way to extend the function library of Excel Services is by writing .NET 2.0 managed assemblies. This can be done by using any existing tool that knows how to generate such assemblies — in this book Visual Studio 2005 is used.

Execution of UDFs

It is incredibly important to understand how and when UDFs are executed on the server. As a rule, the server tries to do as little actual work as possible when servicing requests. This means that there's an elaborate mechanism of caching that reduces the need of the server to do complex calculations repeatedly.

This is especially important when discussing UDFs. When two users open the same workbook, Excel Services tests to see if the workbook can be shared between them. (The ability to share a workbook comes down to whether or not, according to administrative settings and the structure of the workbook, the two users should be allowed to see the same information.)

Workbook structural elements that affect the ability to share the workbook are, for example, if the workbook contains any external data sources (such as pivot tables) or not. If it does, it might not be possible to share the workbook because it is possible that the two people can get different results from the external data source.

An example for an administrative setting that controls the ability of the server to share workbooks between users is the Volatile Function Cache Lifetime setting in the Trusted Location configuration of Excel Services. When a workbook is opened, the server checks to see what trusted location it belongs to and then uses that setting to determine how often it should make calls to volatile functions. If that value is set to any value that is larger than zero, Excel Services will share the workbooks between users. However, only the first user to come in and request the workbook will cause a recalculation. The rest of the users who open the workbook for the duration of the volatile function cache lifetime will not actually cause any recalculation to occur on the server — they will all see the same information as the first user.

UDF Requirements

For a user defined function to be accessible to Excel Services, all of the following requirements must be met:

- ❑   The assembly must be created using .NET 2.0.
- ❑   It must be loadable in the architecture the server is running in (x86, x64).

While code written in .NET 2.0 can run on any of these architectures (as long as it was not actively targeted for a specific one), it might be using other DLLs that cannot. For example, if your .NET assembly is importing functions from an x86 native DLL, the assembly will fail to work properly when running under an x64 installation of the server Also note that Excel Services does not support IA64, although .NET 2.0 does.

❑ The class the UDF resides in has to have the following characteristics:

    ❑ It must be public.

    ❑ It must have a public parameterless constructor.

This means the developer can either add a constructor manually or let the compiler create one for them. If the class happens to have a constructor that does take parameters, most compilers will not automatically generate a parameterless one and the developer will have to manually add one.

❑ It must have `UdfClass` attribute applied to it.

❑ It must be creatable — that means it cannot be abstract.

In C# this means it also cannot be static, since a static class is just shorthand for marking a class both abstract and sealed.

❑ The method that is to be a UDF has to have the following characteristics:

    ❑ It must be public.

    ❑ The signature must be supported (more on that when this chapter discusses allowed parameters and return values).

    ❑ It must have `UdfMethod` attribute applied to it.

    ❑ It cannot be abstract.

Only if all these requirements apply to a developed UDF will Excel Services be able to properly load and run it.

The Assembly Loading Process under the Hood

When Excel Services starts up or when the list of available UDFs is modified, the following process takes place for each enabled assembly in the list:

The information in this section is true for the first version of Excel Services. Future versions may be radically different.

1. Excel Services loads the assembly.

2. All the publicly available types in the assembly are iterated and the ones that have `UdfClassAttribute` applied to them are collected.

3. Each class that was collected is then checked for compliance.

4. If the class is compliant, all the public methods in it are iterated and collected.

5. For each method that was collected, the name is checked. If the name already exists, a warning is written to the event log and the method is ignored.

6. The method is added to the list of available methods.

Remember that this also happens whenever Excel Services starts up or whenever it detects that the list of UDFs has changed. This means that administrators can enable and disable UDF assemblies at will and in that way deny access to UDFs without shutting down the server.

Sessions have access to the UDFs that were available when they were created. That means that even if an administrator changed the list of UDFs available during the server's lifetime, users who created sessions before the change will keep using the old list of UDFs.

UDF Classes' Lifetime

Classes that are decorated with UdfClass attribute are instantiated whenever a new session is opened with a workbook from a trusted location that has the Allow User-Defined Functions option turned on.

This instance will be used throughout the life of the session and is bound by it. When a session goes away (due to time out or because it was closed), so do the UDF classes that are used by it. (The UDF classes become *eligible* for collection — the memory may not be relinquished immediately.)

If a UDF class supports the IDisposable interface, Excel Services will make sure it is called before a session dies. It is still advisable to follow the IDisposable pattern and make sure clean up happens in the finalizer as well.

UDF Methods

As discussed in the previous section, before methods can be considered as UDFs, they need to be compliant. This section discusses what method compliancy means.

Other than the fact that the method needs to be public and nonabstract, there is a list of limitations on what can and cannot be in the method signature.

Generally speaking, only the types in the following table are supported by Excel Services — this is called the "Base Supported Type Set."

Supported type	Aliases in .NET languages
System.Boolean	Can use "bool" in C#
System.Byte	Can use "byte" in C#
System.SByte	
System.Int16	Can use "short" in C# Can use "Short" in VB.NET

Supported type	Aliases in .NET languages
System.UInt16	Can use "ushort" in C#
System.Int32	Can use "int" in C# Can use "Integer" in VB.NET
System.UInt32	Can use "uint" in C#
System.Double	Can use "double" in C#
System.Single	Can use "float" in C#
System.String	Can use "string" in C#
System.DateTime	

Excel Services also supports arrays and the object type parameter — however, it supports them in different manners depending on the location in the method signature.

Type Conversion

Excel Services, like Excel, supports only three basic types and two extrapolated types inside cells. The three supported types are string, double-precision numbers, and cell errors. The two extrapolated ones are Boolean and DateTime. UDFs, on the other hand, support many more types. It is very important to understand what types of conversions Excel Services will do before it passes values into a UDF.

The most obvious example of type conversion problems is what to do when a UDF that receives a Double as a parameter is called with a string value. In that case, the UDF will not execute. An error will occur immediately, and Excel Services will show the #VALUE error in the cell containing the UDF. The following table describes what conversions will happen (if at all) when a certain value needs to be passed into a UDF as a parameter. The types Excel supports are on the columns, while the types that are supported by UDFs are on the rows — a checked cell means that a conversion will be attempted.

	Double/DateTime	String	Boolean	Error
System.Byte	✓			
System.SByte	✓			
System.Int16	✓			
System.UInt16	✓			

Continued

	Double/DateTime	String	Boolean	Error
System.Int32	✓			
System.UInt32	✓			
System.Double	✓			
System.Single	✓			
System.String		✓		
System.Boolean			✓	
System.DateTime	✓			
System.Object	✓	✓	✓	

From the table, the following facts arise:

❑ Excel Services does not support the Error data type with UDFs — if a cell contains an error and that cell is used as a parameter to a UDF, the UDF will not be called and the server will return an error for the cell containing the UDF formula.

❑ There is no conversion from a string to a number — if a cell contains the string "1234", Excel Services will not attempt to parse that argument before passing it to the UDF.

❑ Similarly, there's no conversion from a number to a string. If a cell contains a number, and the UDF expects a string, the call will not occur and the cell will contain an error.

❑ Object is the one type that can receive all four supported Excel types — however, it cannot appear by itself as a parameter. Read the section about parameters to understand how to use it.

Return Value

The return value of a UDF may be any of the following:

❑ Any of the Base Supported Type Set (i.e., System.Double).

❑ The System.Object type.

❑ A single- or two-dimensional array with an element type that is of the Base Supported Type Sets (i.e., System.Double[] in C# or System.Double() in VB.NET) or of the Object type (i.e., Object[] or Object[,]).

If the return value is of type Object, the UDF developer needs to make sure that the actual value contained in the Object is of one of the Base Supported Type Set.

Regular Parameters

All method parameters except for those decorated with the `ParamArray` attribute are considered "regular" parameters. These parameters can only be *in* parameters — they may not be `ref` or `out` parameters. The following types are allowed on these:

❑ Any of the Base Supported Type Set.

❑ A single- or two-dimensional array with `object` as the element type.

This means that a parameter of type `object` is not allowed. Neither is a typed array (`System.Double[]`).

When a parameter is of the `object[]` or `object[,]` type, it means that Excel Services can place any value in it — including ranges. In the case of a range, Excel Services will attempt to translate the range passed in into an array (more on that in the section that discusses ranges). However, if the value passed in the parameter is a regular value (not a range), Excel Services will generate an array with a single element in it, which will contain that value.

The following UDF returns the type of the parameter:

```
[UdfMethod]
public string GetTypeOfParameter(object[] param)
{
    return param[0].GetType().ToString();
}
```

Placing an assortment of values in the A column and calling the `GetTypeOfParameter` UDF (in the B column) on each of them produces the results shown in Figure 9-1.

Note how only three types can actually return from Excel Services when `Object[]` is used as a parameter: `Double`, `String`, and `Boolean`. The date value reverts to its numeric form in that case.

ParamArrays

`ParamArrays` are special types of parameters. In the .NET framework, they are used to inform the compiler (such as VB.NET and C#) that the method can be called with an unlimited amount of arguments, and it is then the compiler's job to pack these arguments into an array.

In C#, a method with a `ParamArray` looks like this:

```
public object MethodWithParamArray(int param1, params string[] args)
```

The `params` keyword actually decorates the `args` parameter with a `ParamArray` attribute. In VB.NET this signature would look like:

```
Public Function MethodWithParamArray(param1 As Integer,
        ParamArray args() As String)
```

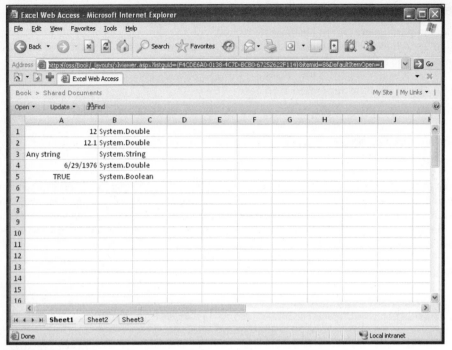

Figure 9-1

When called, it looks like this:

```
MethodWithParamArray(2, "p1", "p2", "p3", "p4", "p5", "p6");
```

When the compilers generate the IL, it actually ends up looking something like this:

```
string[] forParamArray = new string[] { "p1", "p2", "p3", "p4", "p5", "p6" };
MethodWithParamArray(2, forParamArray);
```

When Excel Services encounters a UDF with a `ParamArray` as the last argument, it does much of the same thing — it will create a new array containing the values that will then be passed as the last parameter of the method. In this instance, if `MethodWithParamArray()` was a UDF, it would have been possible to write a cell formula that looks like this:

```
=MethodWithParamArray(0, A1, A2, A3, A4, A5, A6, A7)
```

The method call will succeed only if all the parameters are resolved to be strings. If they are not, the method will not be executed.

The element type of `ParamArray` in Excel Services can be any of the element types allowed on parameters (that is to say, any of the Base Support Type Set and either a single- or two-dimensional arrays of object).

The following are valid signatures that contain `ParamArray`:

```
public int Method1(params double[] paramArray)
public int Method2(params int[] paramArray)
public int Method3(params bool[] paramArray)
public int Method4(params object[][] paramArray)
public int Method5(params object[,][] paramArray)
```

`Method1` and `Method3` are pretty obvious. `Method4` and `Method5` may require further explanation.

`Method4` contains a `ParamArray` that can contain an unlimited amount of `object[]` arguments (these, as discussed before, can be used either for one-dimensional ranges or for single values of any type). An implementation that sums the number of elements in each parameter may look like this:

```
public int Method4(params object[][] paramArray)
{
    int count = 0;
    foreach (object[] param in paramArray)
    {
        count += param.Length;
    }
    return count;
}
```

Each element in the `ParamArray` is in itself an array that contains the passed argument. If this UDF is called from the following formula:

```
=Method4(A1:C1, A2:D2, A3:E3)
```

The result will be 12. The `paramArray` parameter will contain three elements. The first element will correspond to the range A1:C1, which contains three cells (and thus, the `Length` property of the array will be 3). Similarly, the second element will correspond to the range A2:D2, which has four cells and the third to a range that contains five cells.

`Method5` is similar, but it can be used with two-dimensional ranges as well as one-dimensional ones and single values.

Cell Ranges

UDFs can both receive and return cell ranges. These work differently than the Excel Web Services ones. Instead of using jagged arrays, they use straightforward one- or two-dimensional arrays.

One-dimensional arrays correspond to ranges that have a single row and one or more columns. The following UDF, for example, can only receive ranges that do not span more than one row:

```
double SumCells(object[] cells)
```

If this UDF was to be in a formula with the range A1:Z1 as a parameter, the call would go through and the `cells` array would contain the contents of the 26 cells. However, if it was used with the range A1:A26, Excel Services would not even call it, instead placing the error #VALUE in the cell.

To accept ranges such as A1:A26, the UDF needs to be defined as taking a two-dimensional array:

```
double SumCells(object[,] cells)
```

In this case, the array will contain the whole range where the first rank (the first index) stands for row number (zero-based) and the second rank (the second index) stands for the column. In the case of A1:A26, for example, the array will have the size of 1x26 (width x height). To access the cell that stands for A10, the caller should use `cells[9,0]`.

If the range passed in was, say, A1:B3, the *cells* array would have the size of 2x3. To access cell B3 in the range, the caller should use `cells[2,1]`.

UDFs and Interop

UDFs can do anything a .NET library can do. This means that it may load any other managed assembly or managed DLL it may wish to. This is very useful for cases where developers already have libraries that do some of what they need — these libraries can be wrapped and reused by the managed code, drastically reducing development time.

However, as a cinematic wise man once said, with great power comes great responsibility. Using other components inside UDFs can have potential hazardous effects. Developers need to make sure that they fully research the potential problems that can occur in these cases. The next section about thread safety discusses some of the most common cases of problems with interop.

Thread Safety

Excel Service UDFs must be thread-safe. It is very likely that the same UDF will be executed by separate threads at the same time, and not making them safe means the UDF may run into various problems.

If the UDF is a simple calculation that does not use any global resources, it should be safe enough. However, once the UDF starts using any kind of data storage that is not just local variables inside the UDF method, it is liable to be unsafe.

General multithreading programming patterns are beyond the scope of this book; however, the UDFs presented in this book will be developed to be thread-safe.

Thread Safety with Interop

Developers that use external components need to be extra careful about thread safety. While also falling outside the scope of this book, these are the most common issues that will be encountered:

❑ Old libraries that have been designed to work with Excel client may use global resources internally and may be unsafe. Problems that can arise from using such libraries can range from crashes to wrong information being returned to the user. Such libraries should be thoroughly researched before being put into use. One workaround for using such libraries is to protect against any of their functions executing at the same time. This can be easily achieved by using the .NET Monitor class (*lock* keyword in C#).

Synchronizing each and every call may cause prohibitive slowdowns to the system, especially if many users end up using workbooks calling into these UDFs. This solution is greatly discouraged for almost any multiuser scenario of Excel Services.

❑　Most legacy COM libraries written in VB are marked as STA or Apartment threaded. Just like with writing ASP.NET application, this can present some serious problems when developers try to call out into such libraries. At the very least, such libraries may greatly impact the performance of the server. In other cases they may actually cause hangs. Worse, these issues may manifest only when the server is under stress.

> **It is incredibly important to make sure that the libraries a UDF assembly is using are ready for use on a server. Try to stay away from VB6 COM libraries. Research the libraries being used and make sure they are safe.**
>
> **When testing, make sure that your tests consist of calls that are stressing the server and making multiple calls that work with workbooks that are using the UDF so that they get called concurrently.**

Volatility of UDFs

A UDF is said to be volatile if it can return two different results when called with the same exact set of arguments.

Classic examples of volatile built-in Excel functions are the NOW() and RAND() functions. Even when they are called with the same set of arguments, they can still return different values. Excel Services can do a number of optimizations when only nonvolatile functions are used inside workbooks. The existence of a volatile function in a sheet or workbook may cause these optimizations to not occur. Because of that, if a UDF is volatile but is not marked as such, Excel Services may display information that is outdated or just plain wrong.

To mark a UDF as volatile, add IsVolatile=true to the initialization of the UdfMethodAttribute:

```
[UdfMethod(IsVolatile = true)]
public DateTime GetUTCNow()
{
    return DateTime.UtcNow
}
```

Excel Services will make sure that it calls this function as often as allowed by the administrator to make sure that it stays current.

The function will only be called if an actual recalculation occurs on the server. This can happen when a cell changes on a workbook set for auto-recalc or when the workbook is asked to recalculate.

Personal Data UDFs

UDFs are very useful as a tool of bringing external data into a workbook. Sometimes this data can be personal and not sharable between users. An example for that is a UDF that returns the salary of the user who's opening the workbook. If anybody else was to see that salary, I can guarantee that some people would get really mad.

Because of that, Excel Services allows UDFs to be marked as returning personal data. When such a UDF call exists on a workbook, Excel Services will make sure that results from that workbook are not shared among different users. While this may cause a less efficient caching mechanism, it also means that users' privacy is preserved.

Marking a UDF as returning personal data is done by using the `ReturnsPersonalData` property on the `UdfMethod` attribute:

```
[UdfMethod(ReturnsPersonalData = true)]
public double GetSalary()
{
    // ...
}
```

To determine the name of the user that is running the system callers can use the `CurrentPrincipal` static property of the `Thread` class. The `CurrentPrincipal` property has a property called `Identity`, which in turn has a property called `Name`, which will return the name of the user executing the UDF.

> If the UDF is not marked as `ReturnsPersonalData` = true, *the* `CurrentPrincipal` *will contain a generic principal with a user name set to an empty string. This is to protect callers from accidentally using the name of the user when it may cause personal data exposure.*

The example of `GetSalary()` may look like this:

```
[UdfMethod(ReturnsPersonalData = true)]
public double GetSalary()
{
    string userName = Thread.CurrentPrincipal.Identity.Name;
    return CorpInfo.GetSalaryForEmployee(userName);
}
```

In this case, the assembly needs to run with elevated privileges (or at the very least, it needs to have the ability to log in to the corporate database as a user that can see all the information so that it can extract the sensitive salary information). Once logged on with access to the database, it uses the employee ID (deduced from the credentials used to log in to Excel Services) to fetch the information.

Using this mechanism for getting information may not always be possible. It is also potentially less safe because the UDF runs as a sort of superuser that can do whatever it wants with company resources that are usually protected. To solve this problem, Excel Services allows the administrator to set up delegation mode. When delegation mode is turned on in the server, it is possible to impersonate the user that caused the UDF to execute and take action on his or her behalf. In the case of the `GetSalary()` UDF, this means the code does not need to do any security shortcuts to be able to access sensitive information — standard database security can be used to limit what the UDF can access. Turning on delegation cannot be done from the configuration UI and needs to be done through the STSADM command line utility. The following command needs to be executed:

```
stsadm -o set-ecssecurity -ssp <sspname> -accessmodel delegation
```

Once this command is executed on the server, it is possible to use impersonation to take action in the name of the user. To do so, the caller needs to try and cast the thread identity into WindowsIdentity. If the cast is successful, that means it's possible to impersonate by using the Impersonate() method:

```
[UdfMethod(ReturnsPersonalData = true)]
public double GetSalary()
{
    WindowsIdentity wi = Thread.CurrentPrincipal.Identity as WindowsIdentity;
    if (wi == null)
    {
        throw new InvalidOperationException();
    }
    else
    {
        return CorpInfo.GetSalaryForEmployee();
    }
}
```

If the UDF is unable to cast the identity that's set on the thread to WindowsIdentity, it throws an exception (which will cause the system to display #VALUE in the cell). If it's successful, it makes a call into the function that returns the salary. In this version, GetSalaryForEmployee() does not take a user name as a parameter. Instead, it runs *as the user* and thus should have access to whatever information the user has.

Impersonation and Delegation

Using delegation mode brings up the "two-hop" problem. This is the name usually given to the problem where resources can only be used if they are at most one network "hop" away from the user who logged on.

Here's a simple example with one client machine using Internet Explorer, one server machine (Excel Services in this case), and one database machine. The client machine calls into the server machine with a set of credentials. The server machine authenticates the user and knows who he or she is. If the server machine now wants to connect to the database machine with the credentials, it will usually find that it cannot. The reason is that, without extra administrative work, a server cannot connect to a different server as a user without resupplying the full user credentials (usually name and password).

To make this work, one of three things needs to happen:

1. The server machine needs to actively log on as the user into the database machine. This is problematic because it means the server machine needs to know the user's password — something it has no real way to know without sustaining its own database of user names and passwords.

2. The Single Sign On service (SSO) can be employed to figure out the user's password. This is a better solution; however, it requires extra coding on the side of the UDF.

3. Kerberos Constrained Delegation can be used to let Windows pass the token of the user to the third machine (database in the above example). The disadvantage of this method is that it requires some delicate administrative work to enable.

Volatile and ReturnsUserData

These two properties on the UdfMethod attribute are not mutually exclusive. They can be used together. In the example of the GetSalary() UDF, it probably does not make sense to set IsVolatile to true because it is doubtful that the salary changes often enough to matter. However, in other cases it may — for example, a UDF that returns to a broker how much funds are still available in their account probably does needs to be volatile so that it is as accurate as possible. In that case, it is possible to set both properties to true on the UDF:

```
[UdfMethod(ReturnsPersonalData = true, IsVolatile = true)]
public double GetFundsAvailable()
{
    // ...
}
```

Caching Information in UDF Classes

UDF classes that Excel Services recognizes are instantiated once for each new session that is opened. This presents the UDF developer with the ability to cache session specific information in members of the class.

This caching can consist of anything and everything that .NET would allow you to place in class members. As an example, if a UDF is using a .NET library object that is expensive to create, an instance of that object can be saved as a member when the class is constructed and used when calls are made to the UDF:

```
[UdfClass]
class CompanyDataUdf
{
    private SqlConnection m_connection;

    public CompanyDataUdf()
    {
        m_connection = new SqlConnection("...");
    }

    [UdfMethod(IsVolatile = true)]
    public object[,] GetSalesData(DateTime date)
    {
        object[,] result = null;

        lock (m_connection)
        {
            // Code here can use m_connection to get data back from SQL Server.
        }

        return result;
    }
}
```

The code defines an SqlConnection member and uses it in the UDF to communicate with SQL Server.

Important note: With Excel 2007, Microsoft introduced MTR (Multithreaded Recalc). This feature allows Excel 2007 (the client application) to better utilize machines with multiple processors to calculate workbooks. Excel will make use of all CPUs in the system. (That is, it makes use of all of the processors if it can. While most workbooks can be executed in parallel, some are built in such a way where paralleliza-tion is impossible.) This feature did not find its way into Excel Services, but it could be in future service packs or versions. That is why UDFs should always be written in such a way that they are protected from concurrent usage, and which is why m_connection *is protected from concurrent access.*

Static Members

In addition to enabling caching on a per session basis, it is also possible to have serverwide caching by making use of static members in the class.

See Chapter 8 for an example where stock information is globally cached.

User-based Caches

It is sometimes useful to have user-specific caches. While Excel Services does not supply an infrastruc-ture for this, it is very easy to do by using the ReturnsPersonalData property of the UdfMethod attribute.

Taking the previous example (the GetSalary() UDF), it is not unreasonable for UDF developers to want to cache the information so that if the function is used by the same user on multiple sessions or workbooks, that data would not need to be requeried each and every time.

The easiest way to achieve user-based caching is to use a static Dictionary collection keyed off the user name and store the information there. When called, the UDF can use the value returned by Thread.CurrentPrincipal.Identity.Name to get and set values inside the collection.

Cleaning Up Caches

If the cache consists of native objects that need to be cleared as soon as the session goes away, the devel-oper can implement the IDisposable pattern and use that to get rid of such objects.

Since static members live for the duration of the server, clearing up static cache can be somewhat more complex. To do that properly, developers should use some kind of timer mechanism to check when cached items have not been touched for a long time and then clear them.

Farms

Excel Services can run in a farm configuration. In farms, there are multiple machines that are run-ning Excel Services servicing requests that are load balanced among them. It's important to note that there is no mechanism built into Excel Services that allows UDFs to share information across farm machines. In those cases, static members are not enough because every farm machine has its own process running Excel Services — the requests are just load balanced. If sharing information across a farm is needed, the developer will need to use some other solution to do that, such as storing the information in SQL Server.

Loading UDFs on the Server

Chapter 8 contained an explanation about adding UDF DLLs to the server. In the screenshot that showed the configuration screen used to add the UDF, there were two options for Assembly Location. One is called GAC and the other Local file.

The GAC option is used when the UDF DLL is located inside the Global Assembly Cache. In that case, the name used should be the strong name of the assembly. For example:

```
MyUDFAssembly, Version=1.0.0.0, Culture=neutral, PublicKeyToken=21g9bce111e9428c
```

If the assembly represented by the strong name is located in the GAC, it will be loaded and used as a UDF DLL.

There are several ways to find the `PublicKeyToken` of an assembly.

❑   If the assembly is in the GAC, going to `%windir%\assembly` will give a list of all the GACed assemblies. There's a column called Public Key Token there, which can be used.

❑   The `sn.exe` tool (strong name) that ships with the .NET SDK or Visual Studio 2005 can also be used to extract the token. Running the following command with the DLL name, will extract it:

```
SN.EXE -T GacLib.dll
```

The other option, called Local File. is somewhat misleading. Using this option allows administrators to specify an assembly file by its file system location. This also includes files located on the network.

For such files to work properly, the administrator will need to set up the machines to trust the network location for .NET assemblies. This can be done with the .NET Framework 2.0 Configuration application available in Administrative Tools.

The following are examples of valid entries when using this option:

```
c:\udfs\ACME\FinFuncs.dll
\\udfserver\udfs\financial\acme\FinFuncs.dll
```

The latter example (a network path) is especially useful in cases where ECS is in a farm configuration — instead of having to deploy DLLs to the multiple machines on the farm, they can be placed in a central location, which is then referenced by the UDF configuration page.

Updating Assemblies

Excel Services locks the UDF assemblies it uses. This means that while the server is working, loaded UDFs cannot be updated with modified files. This should not be a problem for a production server that gets a new version of an assembly.

If the UDF is used as a local file, the new version can be placed in a separate directory (probably with the version as part of the name) and the UDF settings of Excel Services can be modified to load the new version. If the UDF is installed to the GAC, the strong name contains the version (and the GAC allows different versions of the same assembly to reside side by side).

In both of these cases, when Excel Services notices that there's a new setting, it will go ahead and load the new assembly specified. Since UDF assemblies are loaded into the Excel Services `AppDomain` and because .NET does not allow assemblies to be unloaded, the assembly will keep on being in use for as long as the server is up.

Updating Assemblies during Development

That said, during the development of UDFs, it does not make much sense to have to reversion the assembly and change Excel Services settings.

To have the ability to redeploy the same assembly to the same location, developers need to recycle the Excel Services `AppDomain`. This is obviously not an option in production environments, but it should be harmless in development ones.

There are three ways to recycle the `AppDomain`.

1. Calling IISRESET on the server from the command line or from Start/Run will effectively recycle the whole of IIS, Excel Services included.

2. From the IIS console, it is possible to recycle only the SSP that contains Excel Services. In the Application Pools subtree of the IIS console app, there should be an application pool called `SharedServices1`. (The name may change depending on your installation. `SharedServices1` is the default name.) Right-clicking that and choosing Recycle will make sure that Excel Services unloads, allowing the developer to overwrite UDF assemblies that were locked while Excel Services was running, as shown in Figure 9.2.

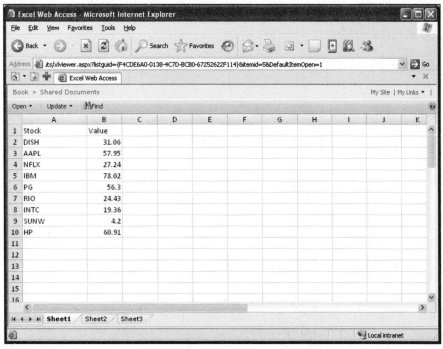

Figure 9-2

3. It is also possible to recycle the application pool from the command line by typing:

```
Iisapp /a SharedServices1 /r
```

When developing UDFs, the cycle is usually to build a version, copy it to the server (or compile it directly to where the server will be looking for it), test it, and recycle the server for the next test.

Troubleshooting UDFs

First time UDF writers run into quite a few "gotchas." They are relatively simple to overcome, and Excel Services gives some very good information about what it is that is going wrong in the Windows event log.

Available from the Administrative Tools folder in the control panel.

#NAME or #VALUE

The first clue to what's wrong with a UDF is when cells calling into the UDF show the #VALUE error or the #NAME error.

If the error shown is #VALUE, it means that Excel Services was probably able to load and recognize the UDF, but either the UDF raised an exception or the parameters passed to it were not valid. There is more about debugging UDFs later in this chapter.

When the error is #NAME, it means that Excel Services was unable to recognize the UDF — either because it could not load the assembly or because of some problem in the UDF methods themselves.

Assembly Load Failure

If the UDF assembly failed to load, the event log will contain an error explaining what went wrong, as shown in Figure 9-3.

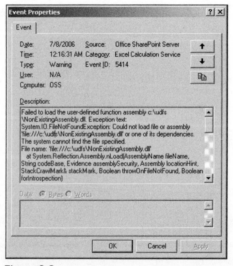

Figure 9-3

The Windows event log entry will start with **"Failed to load the user-defined function assembly"** and will contain the name of the DLL and the error that was encountered.

Assembly load failures can happen due to many reasons. The best way to go around finding them is to use fusion logs to get a detailed list of what it was that went wrong.

> *For more information about fusion, read* `http://msdn2.microsoft.com/en-us/library/` `e74a18c4.aspx` *or just search in* `blogs.msdn.com` *— there are a few excellent articles about it.*

No UDFs in the Assembly

If the assembly loaded properly, it may be that Excel Services was unable to find any UDF methods in it.

If that's the case, the Windows event log will show an error that states: "The user-defined function assembly ProblematicUDFAssembly, Version=1.0.0.0, Culture=neutral, PublicKeyToken=null does not contain any user-defined functions." Of course, the name of the assembly will change based on the actual one being loaded and inspected.

The causes for this problem are usually:

- ❏ The wrong assembly was copied to the server.

    Check the timestamp of the file to make sure that the correct version is there.

- ❏ The class that contains the UDF or the UDF method itself is not public. (From customer experience thus far, this seems to be the number one reason for this problem.)

    Classes containing UDFs must be public and so must the methods. If they are not, Excel Services will not find them.

- ❏ The class that contains the UDF is not decorated with an `UdfClass` attribute or the UDF method itself is not decorated with `UdfMethod` attribute.

The UDF Is Not Compliant

As described at the beginning of this chapter, UDFs have very strict rules about how method signatures should look and about how the class containing the UDF is designed. If a signature is not compliant, Excel Services will ignore the function and not use it. There are various errors that can be displayed in the event log due to noncompliance.

If the class is not compliant, the event log will show a warning saying "A class marked as a UDF class is not supported." The reason for noncompliance will follow as will the name of the assembly.

Noncompliant methods will also appear in the event log. A warning saying "A function marked as a UDF method is not supported." The warning will also contain the name of the method and the reason it is not compliant.

Duplicate Names for UDFs

There is no way to disambiguate UDFs — Excel does not support namespaces. Because of this, UDF names need to be unique in this version of Excel Services. If the server finds a UDF name it has already encountered, it will add an entry to the event log saying "The user-defined function <UDFName> occurs more than once in the list of enabled assemblies. First occurrence . . ." This entry will also supply information about what other class is implementing the UDF with the same name and which one will be used.

Debugging UDFs

When debugging UDFs on the server, there are a few things you need to be aware of. By and large, it's a pretty easy and painless procedure. Excel Services runs inside an IIS worker process. That process is named w3wp.exe.

To debug UDFs that run within the server, you need to attach to the w3wp.exe process using a managed debugger. The only issue is that on most installations there will be multiple w3wp.exe processes running at the same time.

One option is to attach to all of them. That will certainly work but may add some serious "noise" when you are trying to debug a simple UDF. To figure out which one is the process that hosts Excel Services, use the IISApp tool introduced before but this time with only the /a argument:

```
iisapp /a SharedServices1
```

When executed, the output should look like this:

```
The following W3WP.exe processes are serving AppPool: SharedServices1
W3WP.exe PID: 3584
```

To attach with Visual Studio 2005, use Debug/Attach to process option in the menu to bring up the dialog box. When the dialog box comes up, it should show you the list of processes, as shown in Figure 9-4.

Choose the correct w3wp.exe process according to the process ID (PID) returned from running IISApp.

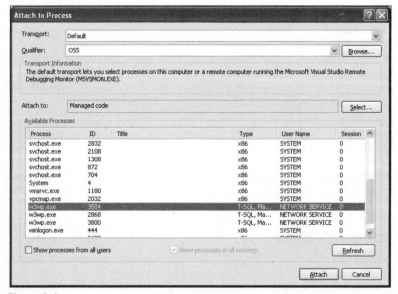

Figure 9-4

Making Sure the Assembly Is Loaded

Once attached, make sure the assembly is actually loaded. To do that, bring up the Modules window by choosing the Debug/Windows/Modules menu option. The list that appears contains all the assemblies/ DLLs that are loaded into the process. Search for the assembly and make sure that its symbols are loaded, as shown in Figure 9-5.

If the UDF assembly is not in the list, it means that Excel Services probably had a problem loading it. Check the event log for more information.

Placing a breakpoint in your UDF code should work now. If it does not, it may be that the source code you are using is out of sync with the binary deployed to the server. When that happens, recompile the code and redeploy it.

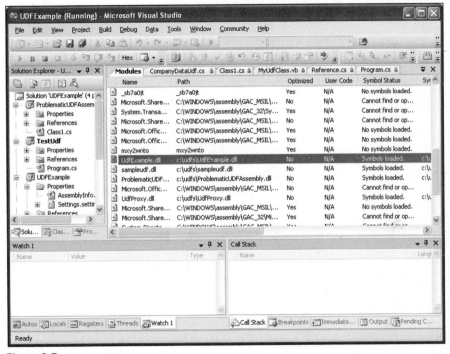

Figure 9-5

Debugging Complex UDFs

When the UDF contains calls to external components such as COM objects or native DLLs, there are a few extra things to do to properly debug it. The following lists some of the issues most commonly encountered when trying to debug such UDFs:

❑ **Breakpoints in native code are not being hit.**

    ❑ Enable native code debugging to be able to break inside native DLLs. Enabling mixed-mode debugging is one way of doing that (by choosing to debug both managed and native code when attaching to a process). Note that on 64-bit machines and when remote debugging, Visual Studio will allow debugging either native code or managed code — but not both at the same time.

❑ The native DLL may not have loaded or the symbols could not be found. Check the Modules window to make sure the DLL was properly loaded and that its symbols were found.

❑ "Just my code" is enabled. Visual Studio 2005 has a feature called "Just my code," which is accessible through the Tools/Options menu, under the Debugging category. When turned on, VS2005 tries to be extra-smart about what code you are actually trying to debug and will not stop on code it thinks you don't own. This is very useful when debugging simple UDFs; however, the more complex the solution is, the more times VS2005 will ignore code you really want it to debug.

❑ **Mixed-mode debugging hangs Visual Studio 2005.**

This problem sometimes occurs when doing mixed-mode debugging (i.e., both managed and native code). If you notice it happening often, there may be an option you can use to alleviate the problem. In the registry, navigate to the key called

```
HKEY_LOCAL_MACHINE\SOFTWARE\Microsoft\Office Server\12.0
```

Once there, add a value called `ExcelServicesDisableExceptionVector` of the type `DWORD`. Set its value to `1`.

This registry setting is undocumented and unsupported. It may go away with future service packs or versions. When done debugging the server, make sure to either delete the registry value or set it to 0. Having this value on a production machine may impact its behavior.

Summary

UDFs allow developers to extend Excel Services in many ways. While the capabilities are not as rich as Excel's, they are enough for a wide variety of solutions. Using some of the tips at the end of the chapter will allow developers to quickly locate and fix common problems.

10

Client Support for Server UDFs

Chapter 8 introduced UDFs on the server. At the beginning of the chapter it was shown how the #NAME error is displayed inside Excel Workbooks. This happens because Excel does not natively support managed UDFs written for the server, which can have a negative impact on people authoring workbooks for the server. Because of this, it is sometimes useful to make server UDFs work on the client.

This chapter discusses two possible ways to add client support to UDFs written for the server. The first way involves adding functionality to the UDF code so that it will be usable on the server. After that, you learn how to develop a generic solution that can be used to utilize server UDFs on the client without any modification to their code. Finally, this chapter will suggest ways to allow UDFs to distinguish when they are executed on the client or on the server.

Modifying UDFs to Run on the Client

Chapter 9 enumerated some of the mechanisms that exist in Excel for augmenting the list of available UDFs. This section will show how to add functionality to a server UDF to make it compliant with one of these mechanisms.

The extensibility point of choice for this will be Automation Servers. These have been around for a few versions now and are very simple to work with. They make use of COM registration for the discovery mechanism. Any COM class that is registered and has the Programmable key will be an automation server usable by Excel. The first time a user types a formula into a cell, Excel will instantiate the automation servers it uses, getting back a pointer to the IDispatch interface supported by the object. Excel will then try to search inside all created automation servers for each UDF that is typed in. When such a UDF is found, Excel will call into it and return the value into the cell.

The server UDF assembly that will be converted to work on the client will comprise two methods that were discussed in Chapter 8: the GetLastWord() UDF and the GetMultiStockQuote() UDF.

Add COM Support to a UDF Assembly

Adding COM support to an assembly is easy. The appropriate attributes are added to the class or methods that need to be exposed to COM clients and .NET will do the rest.

In this example, the class is called `MyUdfClass` and originally looks like this (before modifying it for COM):

The `System.Runtime.InteropServices` *namespace is added here for the COM attributes that will be used from it. The* `Microsoft.Win32` *namespace will be used later to write some entries in the registry using the* `Registry` *class.*

```
using System;
using System.Collections.Generic;
using System.Text;
using System.Runtime.InteropServices;

using Microsoft.Win32;

using Microsoft.Office.Excel.Server.Udf;

namespace UdfWithClientSupport
{
    [UdfClass]
    public class MyUdfClass
    {
        [UdfMethod]
        public string GetLastWord(string phrase)
        {
            int lastSpace = phrase.Trim().LastIndexOf(" ");
            if (lastSpace == -1)
                return phrase;

            string result = phrase.Substring(lastSpace + 1);
            return result;
        }
    }
}
```

Multiple attributes need to be added to tell .NET how this class is to be used through COM. The final class definition becomes:

```
[UdfClass]
[ProgId("UdfWithClientSupport.MyUdfClass")]
[ClassInterface(ClassInterfaceType.AutoDual)]
[Guid(MyUdfClass.Guid)]
[ComVisible(true)]
public class MyUdfClass
{
    public const string Guid = "<Generated GUID goes here>";
    // ...
}
```

The `ProgId` and `Guid` attributes are not strictly needed, but they make the class more predictable. The `ClassInterface` attribute is used to instruct .NET about what type of `IDispatch` implementation is expected. The `ComVisible` attribute implies that this class is exposed via COM.

Excel expects COM servers used for UDFs to support a minimal set of interfaces — namely, `IDispatch` and `ITypeInfo`. Using the `ClassInterfaceType.AutoDispatch` as a parameter to the `ClassInterface` attribute would cause Excel to not recognize the functions that can be called on the object.

Adding the Programmable Key

As explained before, a COM object needs to have the Programmable key for Excel to be able to use a COM object as a UDF.

To do this, the class needs to execute custom code when it is being registered as a COM class. The .NET Framework supplies this functionality by allowing classes to have a method with an attribute called `ComRegisterFunction`. When this attribute is present on a method, .NET will make sure it gets called during the registration process. Similarly, the class will need to delete that key when it's being unregistered:

```
[ComRegisterFunction]
public static void RegistrationMethod(Type type)
{
    // Only add stuff to the registration
    // if it's this class that's being registered.
    if (typeof(MyUdfClass) != type)
    {
        return;
    }

    // Add "Programmable" under our key.
    RegistryKey key = Registry.ClassesRoot.CreateSubKey(
        "CLSID\\{" + Guid + "}\\Programmable");
    key.Close();
}


[ComUnregisterFunction]
public static void UnregisterationMethod(Type type)
{
    // Only add stuff to the registration
    // if it's this class that's being registered.
    if (typeof(MyUdfClass) != type)
    {
        return;
    }

    // Add "Programmable" under our key.
    Registry.ClassesRoot.DeleteSubKey("CLSID\\{" + Guid + "}\\Programmable");
}
```

Now that this class is done, the next step is to register the assembly.

Registering the Assembly

.NET supplies a tool for registering assemblies as COM libraries. The tool is called `RegAsm.exe` and is located deep inside the Windows folder. The following command needs to be executed to register the class:

```
%windir%\Microsoft.NET\Framework\v2.0.50727\RegAsm.exe /codebase
UDFWithClientSupport.dll
```

Executing this command will show a warning but will register the library all the same.

It is not recommended to use the `/codebase` option with assemblies that are not strongly named. For production code, it is highly recommended that developers sign their assemblies.

During development, it is possible to use the Visual Studio 2005 project properties to get the assembly to automatically register.

Using the UDF inside Excel Client

Now that everything is ready, Excel needs to be told to actually use it. This is done by using the Addins section in the Excel Options dialog and clicking Go at its bottom where the combo box displays the "Excel Add-ins" text (see Figure 10-1).

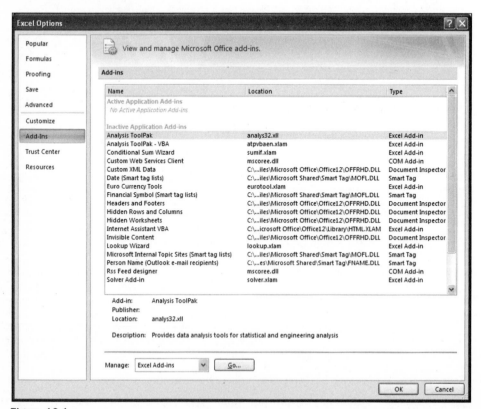

Figure 10-1

144

In the new Excel 2007, the Options dialog is hiding in the well-concealed File menu. The File menu is the circular office button at the top-left side of the Excel app window. Once this menu is opened, the options button is located at its bottom. This should bring up the Addins dialog box. In there, one of the buttons is called Automation and will bring up another dialog box, shown in Figure 10-2, which lists all the available automation servers in the system.

Clicking OK once the UDF automation server is checked will display an error saying that mscoree was not found. This error is ignorable, selecting No will dismiss it.

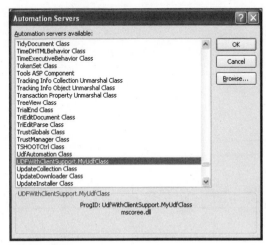

Figure 10-2

Using GetLastWord in a Formula

As shown in Figure 10-3, everything is lined up so that the UDF can be used in Excel.

Adding Client Support for GetMultiStockQuote

While modifying the GetLastWord() UDF to work on the client was relatively easy, the changes needed to make GetMultiStockQuote() work are somewhat more complex.

Excel 2007 does not recognize an object array as a valid parameter, so just calling the method like GetLastWord() does not work. Instead, a new method will be added that will be used by Excel client. This method will not have the UdfMethod attribute — Excel Services will not know about it.

The parameter this new method will receive will be an object instead of the object array that the server method expects. Excel will place one of two values inside this parameter. In cases where the parameter passed is a constant or the result of another UDF, Excel will pass in an object that represents that value.

In the case of values such as doubles or Booleans, the value will be boxed inside the object parameter. In the case of a string, the object will be castable to a string.

When the parameter is a reference to a cell or a range, Excel will pass in a Range COM object. The easiest way to use this object is to reference the Excel 2007 PIA and cast the object and use it.

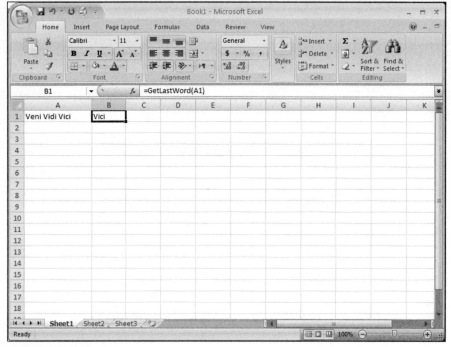

Figure 10-3

PIA stands for Primary Interop Assembly and is a standardized way for software to expose COM interfaces to managed applications.

That way, however, requires that the assembly take a dependency on the Excel 2007 PIA. Instead, it is possible to access the `Range` object using a mechanism similar to reflection. Adding the `ComVisible` attribute set to false to the original `GetMultiStockQuote()` UDF ensures that Excel will not be able to call it:

```
[UdfMethod(IsVolatile = true)]
[ComVisible(false)]
public object[,] GetMultiStockQuote(object[,] symbols)
{
    // ... This code is exactly the same as the one in Chapter 8.
}

public object[,] GetMultiStockQuote(object symbols)
{
    // Get the Value2 property from the object.
    Type type = symbols.GetType();
    object[,] result = null;
    if (type.IsCOMObject)
    {
        object[,] range = (object[,])type.InvokeMember("Value2",
            System.Reflection.BindingFlags.Instance |
```

```
                    System.Reflection.BindingFlags.Public |
                    System.Reflection.BindingFlags.GetProperty,
                null,
                symbols,
                null);
        int rows = range.GetLength(0);
        int columns = range.GetLength(1);
        object[,] param = new object[rows, columns];
        Array.Copy(range, param, rows * columns);
        result = GetMultiStockQuote(param);
    }

    if (result == null)
    {
        result = new object[0, 0];
    }
    return result;
}
```

The new `GetMultiStockQuote()` method first uses the `Invoke()` method on the type to get back the `Value2` property of the `Range` object. This will return an array from the COM API of Excel. Next, it allocates an array of the same size and copies the contents of the fetched array into it. Finally, it sets the resulting array into the local variable that will ultimately be returned to Excel.

There's a seemingly unneeded copy operation in the code — the part that copies the array returned from invoking `Value2` into another managed array. The Excel OM always returns arrays that are 1-based. While .NET languages know how to work with such arrays, it is not the "standard" behavior. If the original `GetMultiStockQuote()` method knew how to handle 1-based arrays, it would be possible to pass the range local variable into the original `GetMultiStockQuote()` method.

Conclusion

Making Excel Services UDFs work on the client is not a hard process. It is pretty simple and requires only a couple of steps per assembly. Some methods, as seen in the `GetMultiStockQuote()` example, may require some extra attention though.

The next section shows a generic solution that will allow server UDFs to work on the client with no modifications. This will keep the UDFs clean and will require significantly less code.

Generic Client UDF Support

The following solution mimics the way server UDFs work by creating a component that acts as a shim between Excel's way of doing UDFs and the server's way of doing it.

There are three parts to this solution. First, there's a simple application that configures what UDF assemblies will be used on the client (similar to the Excel Services UDF configuration page). Second, there's a component that behaves like an automation server that can be added to Excel (called `ClientManagedUdfs`). This component will be written using C++/CLI. Last, there's a component that is responsible for loading the UDF assemblies and invoking them which will be written in C# — its name is `UdfProxy`.

C++/CLI is the new name for Managed C++ or Managed Extensions for C++.

The assembly that loads and invokes the UDF code could have been written as part of the C++/CLI assembly. However, since C++/CLI is still somewhat harder to debug and is actually more verbose than C# in many cases, I usually try to minimize the amount of code written in it.

Figure 10-4 shows the CUDFAutomation addin that is loaded by Excel and is used as any other automation server would be. It exposes an IDispatch interface that is dynamically built on startup. Each method in the IDispatch interface is wired to a method in one of the UDF assemblies the addin is configured to load. When CUDFAutomation detects that a call is made to one of these methods, it does the necessary work to call the correct method with the correct parameters.

Excel calls CUDFAutomation via standard COM interfaces. CUDFAutomation calls into the assembly via managed reflection. The interop occurs inside the implementation of IDispatch.

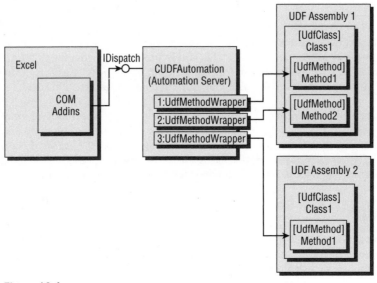

Figure 10-4

Configuration Application

The configuration application contains a single form with a ListView control. It allows the user to add or remove assemblies from the list, as shown in Figure 10-4.

When the configuration application saves the setting, it places it in the following directory:

```
%AppData%\ClientManagedUdf.settings
```

This file contains XML that encapsulates the configuration. For the case depicted in Figure 10-5, the XML will look like this:

```
<?xml version="1.0"?>
<Config xmlns:xsi="http://www.w3.org/2001/XMLSchema-instance"
```

```
xmlns:xsd="http://www.w3.org/2001/XMLSchema">
  <UdfAssemblyCollection>
    <UdfAssembly>
      <Name>C:\Temp\udfs\SampleUdf.dll</Name>
    </UdfAssembly>
    <UdfAssembly>
      <Name>X:\Book\Code
Samples\UDFExample\UDFExample\bin\Debug\UDFExample.dll</Name>
    </UdfAssembly>
  </UdfAssemblyCollection>
</Config>
```

The configuration application uses the classes in the UdfProxy assembly to save this information — the actual logic inside the configurator utility is very simple.

Figure 10-5

UdfProxy

The UdfProxy assembly takes care of loading assemblies, iterating them to find the classes and methods that are actual UDFs. It also takes care of other details such as saving and loading the list of assemblies in the user profile.

Configuration Classes

The names of the assemblies that will be loaded as UDFs are managed by three classes: UdfAssembly, UdfAssemblyCollection, and Config.

UdfAssemblyCollection wraps a List<> instance that contains UdfAssembly instances.

```
public class UdfAssemblyCollection : IEnumerable<UdfAssembly>
{
    private List<UdfAssembly> m_assemblies = new List<UdfAssembly>();
    // ...
}
```

The class exposes some very basic collection members such as Count, GetEnumerator (so it can be used in foreach statements), an indexer and add/remove methods.

`UdfAssembly` contains the name of an assembly that will be searched for viable UDFs:

```
public class UdfAssembly
{
     private string m_name;

     public string Name
     {
          get { return m_name; }
          set { m_name = value; }
     }
}
```

The `Config` classes make use of the `UdfAssemblyCollection` class. It also gives the caller save and load functionality:

```
public class Config
{
     private static Config m_current;
     private UdfAssemblyCollection m_assemblyCollection = new
UdfAssemblyCollection();

     private static string ConfigFileName
     {
          get
          {
               return Path.Combine(
                    Environment.GetFolderPath(
                         Environment.SpecialFolder.ApplicationData),
                    "ClientManagedUdf.settings");
          }
     }

     public static Config Current
     {
          get
          {
               if (m_current == null)
               {
                    m_current = new Config();
                    m_current.Load();
               }
               return m_current;
          }
     }
// ...
```

Use the `Current` property to access the `Config` instance, which checks to see if the configuration instance is already created. If it's not, it will create it.

The `ConfigFileName` property returns the name of the settings file.

This pattern of configuration class will be repeated in the book for client applications.

Loading and saving of the instance is done by using the XmlSerializer class. This class takes care of everything, including the names of the nodes in the XML.

The methods for saving and loading are:

```
private XmlSerializer CreateSerializer()
{
    XmlSerializer s = new XmlSerializer(typeof(Config));
    return s;
}

private void Load()
{
    if (File.Exists(ConfigFileName))
    {
        try
        {
            using (FileStream s = File.Open(ConfigFileName, FileMode.Open))
            {
                m_current = (Config)CreateSerializer().Deserialize(s);
            }
        }
        catch (Exception)
        {
        }
    }

    if (m_current == null)
    {
        m_current = new Config();
    }
}

public void Save()
{
    using (FileStream s = File.Create(ConfigFileName))
    {
        CreateSerializer().Serialize(s, Current);
    }
}
```

The XmlSerializer class created by the CreateSerializer() method takes care of turning the Config instance into XML.

UdfManager Class

The UdfManager class takes care of loading and preparing the actual UDFs for usage. It is the one that will go over the Config instance and load all the assemblies, extract the methods marked with the UdfMethod attribute and build a list of them. Each such method will be wrapped by the UdfMethodWrapper class.

```
public class UdfManager
{
    private StreamWriter m_logWriter;
```

```
        private List<UdfMethodWrapper> m_methodList = new List<UdfMethodWrapper>();
        private Dictionary<string, UdfMethodWrapper> m_methodDictionary =
            new Dictionary<string, UdfMethodWrapper>
                (StringComparer.InvariantCultureIgnoreCase);

        internal List<UdfMethodWrapper> MethodList
        {
            get { return m_methodList; }
        }

        internal Dictionary<string, UdfMethodWrapper> MethodDictionary
        {
            get { return m_methodDictionary; }
        }
        // ...
    }
```

The m_logWriter member is used to write a log file of the loading process — errors and warnings will go there. The log can be found at:

```
%AppData%\ClientManagedUdf.log
```

There are two collection classes used at the same time with UdfManager. Because the solution simulates IDispatch, every method needs to have both a number (a DISPID) and a name. The first collection (m_methodList) will keep an indexed list of the methods while the dictionary (m_methodDictionary) will keep a list keyed by the name of the method.

After creating an instance of the UdfManager class, callers should call the Load() method to have the manager actually load all the UDFs.

```
public void Load()
{
    using (LogWriter = File.CreateText(
        Path.Combine(
            Environment.GetFolderPath(
                Environment.SpecialFolder.LocalApplicationData),
"ClientManagedUdf.log")))
    {
        Log("Loading assemblies...");
        foreach (UdfAssembly udfAssembly in Config.Current.UdfAssemblyCollection)
        {
            try
            {
                LoadFromAssembly(udfAssembly);
            }
            catch (Exception e)
            {
                Log("Error loading assembly '{0}'. Error was: {1}",
                    udfAssembly.Name, e);
            }
        }
    }
```

```
        LogWriter = null;
    }

    private void LoadFromAssembly(UdfAssembly udfAssembly)
    {
        Assembly assembly = Assembly.LoadFrom(udfAssembly.Name);
        LoadTypes(assembly);
    }
```

The Load() method goes through each UdfAssembly in the configuration and tries to load it through
the LoadFromAssembly() method. If the assembly load is successful, the UdfManager class will try to
find all the types that are decorated with the UdfClass attribute:

```
    private void LoadTypes(Assembly assembly)
    {
        Log("Getting types from assembly...");
        Type[] types = assembly.GetTypes();
        Log("Searching through {0} types...", types.Length);
        foreach (Type type in types)
        {
            UdfClassAttribute attribute =
                (UdfClassAttribute)Attribute.GetCustomAttribute(
                    type, typeof(UdfClassAttribute));
            if (attribute != null)
            {
                Log("Found class '{0}' marked as a Udf class.", type.Name);
                LoadMethods(type);
            }
        }
    }
```

Once such a class is located, the LoadMethods() method is called for that type. This method has two
parts. The first one for instantiating the class and the second for getting all the methods out of it:

```
    private void LoadMethods(Type type)
    {
// Create an instance of the class.
        Log("Trying to instantiate the type.");
        object instance = null;
        try
        {
            instance = Activator.CreateInstance(type);
        }
        catch (Exception)
        {
            Log("Unable to instantiate type '{0}'.", type.Name);
            throw;
        }

        // Find methods in the class.
        // ...
    }
```

First, the `Activator` class is used to attempt to create an instance. If for any reason this method fails (in this case, because there is no parameterless constructor, or if constructor throws an exception), loading this UDF class will be considered a failure and a message will be logged.

For each Excel process, there will be instances of the UDF classes. These instances will live for the entire lifetime of the Excel process. This is different from how they work on the server where they get attached to each opened session (and through that, for every opened workbook). For the most part, this is not a big issue because the UDFs don't really have any way of knowing which workbook they are attached to on the server. However, it's worth keeping in mind as in some cases it may lead to differences in behavior.

Once the class itself is instantiated, the code looks for methods that are decorated with the `UdfMethod` attribute:

```
private void LoadMethods(Type type)
{
    // Create an instance of the class.
    // ...

    // Find methods in the class.
    Log("Loading methods from class.");
    MethodInfo[] methodInfos = type.GetMethods();
    foreach (MethodInfo methodInfo in methodInfos)
    {
        UdfMethodAttribute attribute =
            (UdfMethodAttribute)Attribute.GetCustomAttribute(
                methodInfo, typeof(UdfMethodAttribute));
        if (attribute != null)
        {
            Log("Found method '{0}' marked as a Udf method.", methodInfo.Name);
            if (MethodExists(methodInfo.Name))
            {
                Log("A method named '{0}' already exists. " +
                    "Ignoring this one.", methodInfo.Name);
            }
            else
            {
                Log("Adding method to list.");
                UdfMethodWrapper method = new UdfMethodWrapper(
                    methodInfo, methodInfo.Name, instance);
                Add(method);
            }
        }
    }
}

private bool MethodExists(string name)
{
    return MethodDictionary.ContainsKey(name);
}
```

Using reflection, the code uses the `GetMethods()` method to get all the publicly available methods on the class. Each such method is checked against the current list of methods to see if a prior method with the same name already exists (that's what `MethodExists()` returns). If such a method does not exist, the code creates a UdfMethodWrapper class and passes the MethodInfo instance to it. It then adds the newly created UdfMethod to the list of available methods:

```
private void Add(UdfMethodWrapper method)
{
    int index = MethodList.Count;
    method.Index = index;

    MethodList.Add(method);
    MethodDictionary.Add(method.Name, method);
}
```

The Add() method takes the size of the array and uses it as the new index for the method. The index will be needed later when building the dynamic IDispatch interface implementation.

UdfManager also contains methods for getting UdfMethodWrapper instances by their name or index.

UdfMethodWrapper Class

Two jobs are accomplished by the UdfMethodWrapper class. The first is to cache information about the method that is attached to it and the second is the invocation of the method with the proper parameters:

```
public class UdfMethodWrapper
{
    private MethodInfo m_methodInfo;
    private int m_index;
    private string m_name;
    private object m_instance;
    private bool m_hasEllipsis;
    private int m_parameterCount;
    private ParameterInfo[] m_parameters;
    private bool m_isVolatile;
// ...
}
```

The members are used primarily for caching information about the method. All this information is accessible via reflection on the m_methodInfo member, however, since reflection is a relatively slow process, some caching is in order.

In this case, doing this caching shaves roughly 10% off the overhead of executing the method.

The m_instance field points to an instance of the class that contains this UDF method.

```
private void GatherInfo()
{
    // Get the last parameter in the parameter list.
    ParameterInfo[] parameters = MethodInfo.GetParameters();

    m_parameters = parameters;
    m_parameterCount = parameters.Length;

    if (parameters.Length > 0)
```

155

```
        {
            ParameterInfo info = parameters[parameters.Length - 1];
            m_hasEllipsis = Attribute.GetCustomAttribute(info,
typeof(ParamArrayAttribute)) != null;
        }

        UdfMethodAttribute att =
(UdfMethodAttribute)Attribute.GetCustomAttribute(MethodInfo,
typeof(UdfMethodAttribute));
        if (att != null)
        {
            m_isVolatile = att.IsVolatile;
        }
    }
}
```

`GatherInfo()` is called from the constructor and is responsible for caching information about the method. It first takes the parameters and caches them in a member and then checks to see if the last parameter is decorated with the `ParamArray` parameter — if so it means the writer of the UDF expects the method to be called with a varying amount of parameters. Finally, the method checks to see if the method is marked as volatile.

The next step is the invocation method call:

```
public object Invoke(object[] args)
{
    args = AdjustArgs(args);
    object result = MethodInfo.Invoke(m_instance, args);
    return result;
}
```

Using reflection, the method is invoked and the `m_instance` parameter passed in. The `args` local variable is generated by calling the `AdjustArgs()` method which makes sure the arguments passed into the method fit with the ones the method expects.

For example, a method may take an `Int32` as a parameter (`int` in C# and `Integer` in VB.NET). However, Excel cells cannot really contain integers — they only contain doubles. If a double is passed in, it needs to be cast to become an integer. The `AdjustArgs()` method goes over all the parameters and takes care of such conversions.

It also makes sure that the last parameters are packed into an array, which is passed as the last parameter of the method in the case that the method employs the `ParamArray` attribute:

```
private object[] AdjustArgs(object[] args)
{
    object[] realParams = new object[ParameterCount];
    int regularParametersCount = ParameterCount;
    Array paramArray = null;
    ParameterInfo ellipsisParameter = null;

    if (HasEllipsis)
    {
```

```
            regularParametersCount-;
            ellipsisParameter = m_parameters[ParameterCount - 1];
            paramArray = Array.CreateInstance(
                ellipsisParameter.ParameterType.GetElementType(),
                args.Length - regularParametersCount);
            realParams[realParams.Length - 1] = paramArray;
        }

        // Copy/Convert the parameters.
        for (int i = 0; i < regularParametersCount; i++)
        {
            realParams[i] = ConvertParameter(args[i],
                m_parameters[i].ParameterType);
        }

        if (HasEllipsis)
        {
            Type elementType =
                ellipsisParameter.ParameterType.GetElementType();
            for (int i = 0; i < paramArray.Length; i++)
            {
                paramArray.SetValue(
                    ConvertParameter(args[regularParameters + i], elementType),
                    i);
            }
        }

        return realParams;
    }
```

The first part that initializes the local variables creates an array called `realParams`. This will be used to contain the parameters that will be eventually passed to the managed UDF method. The second part (inside the first check for `HasEllipsis`) creates the array that will be passed as the last parameter to the method in the case of a `ParamArray` method. The last two parts go over the parameters and make sure they are converted to the correct values (by calling `ConvertParameter()`).

```
private object ConvertParameter(object value, Type parameterType)
{
    object result = null;
    Type toType = parameterType;
    if (value == null)
    {
        result = GetDefaultValueForType(result, toType);
    }
    else
    {
        Type fromType = value.GetType();

        if (fromType == toType)
        {
            result = value;
        }
        else if (toType == typeof(object[]))
        {
```

```csharp
                if (fromType == typeof(object[,]))
                {
                    throw new InvalidOperationException();
                }

                result = new object[] { value };
            }
            else if (toType == typeof(object[,]))
            {
                if (fromType == typeof(object[]))
                {
                    result = PromoteArrayRank(value, result);
                }
                else
                {
                    result = new object[,] { { value } };
                }
            }
            else
            {
                if (fromType.IsPrimitive &&
                    IsSupportedParameterType(fromType) &&
                    toType.IsPrimitive &&
                    IsSupportedParameterType(toType))
                {
                    result = Convert.ChangeType(value, toType);
                }
                else if (toType == typeof(DateTime) && fromType == typeof(double))
                {
                    result = DateTime.FromOADate((double)value);
                }
            }
        }
    }
    return result;
}
internal static bool IsSupportedParameterType(Type type)
{
    bool result = false;
    if (type.IsPrimitive)
    {
        if (type != typeof(Int64) && type != typeof(UInt64))
        {
            result = true;
        }
    }
    else if (type == typeof(String))
    {
        result = true;
    }
    else if (type == typeof(DateTime))
    {
        result = true;
    }
    return result;
}
```

The `ConvertParameter()` method takes the value that needs to potentially be converted and the type it needs to be converted to (`targetType`). It first makes sure the value that needs to be converted is not null. If it is, it means the code needs to place some kind of default value in the variable — this is taken care of by the `GetDefaultValueForType()` method, which knows, by the type of the parameter, what the default has to be (for example, if the parameter is an integer, and there is an empty cell passed into it, this method will return zero since that's what an empty cell evaluates to).

This method works similarly to how the server does — it returns zero if the parameter is numeric, an empty string if it's a string, and so on, or null otherwise.

Next, the method checks if the types are the same. If they are, it will not do anything to the value and just return it.

If the value is a two-dimensional array but the target type is a one-dimensional array, the function fails because this conversion is not supported on the server. On the other hand, if the value is one-dimensional and the target is two-dimensional, the method will promote the rank of the array by creating a new two-dimensional array and copying the values from the one-dimensional array.

Finally, the code makes sure that the parameter is supported and uses the `Convert.ChangeType()` method to coerce the value that was actually passed in to the one expected by the method. Any errors (such as a `double` source value overflowing a target `Int32` parameter) would throw an exception, which would show an error in the cell (which is the current behavior of the server).

The `DateTime` parameter is somewhat special — when it's a parameter, the `FromOADate()` method is used to generate one out of a `double` (which is the form Excel uses to store dates).

CUdfAutomation

Excel will use the `CUdfAutomation` class to make UDF calls. It is an Active Template Library (ATL) class inside a C++ DLL that supports the common language runtime (CLR) (in other words, a C++/CLI assembly). Using C++/CLI gives this code the unique opportunity to do things that are either very hard for pure managed code to do or are downright impossible. In this case, the code dynamically generates an `IDispatch` interface that is used by Excel to make the appropriate UDF calls.

As with most ATL projects, there are many files that are needed for a successful compilation; however, only two code files are of actual interest and those are the `UdfAutomation.h` and `UdfAutomation.cpp` files. This section will first show the `.h` file, which contains the definition of the class and then the `.cpp` file, which contains the more complex implementation.

The `CUdfAutomation` class itself looks just like a regular ATL class with a few additions:

```
class ATL_NO_VTABLE CUdfAutomation :
    public CComObjectRootEx<CComSingleThreadModel>,
    public CComCoClass<CUdfAutomation, &CLSID_UdfAutomation>,
    public IUdfAutomation,
    public IUdfDispatch,
    public ITypeInfo,
    public IDispatchImpl<AddInDesignerObjects::IDTExtensibility2>
{
    //...
}
```

The interesting part of this class is the inheritance from `IUdfDispatch` and from `IDispatchImpl<AddInDesginerObjects::IDTExtensibility2>`.

The first inherited class is one that is defined at the top of the file and will allow `CUdfAutomation` to implement the dynamically built `IDispatch` interface (the dynamic `IDispatch` interface will have its methods prefixed with `Udf_`.)

> *Because* `IDTExtensibility` *itself inherits from* `IDispatch`, `CUdfAutomation` *cannot just inherit from* `IDispatch` *and call it a day — there needs to be an extra layer there. In this case, the extra layer also changes the names of the methods so that there is no problem with the methods implemented in* `CUdfAutomation` *overriding the methods supplied for* `IDTExtensibility`.

> *Throughout the rest of this section, the term* dispmethods *will be used to describe the "methods" that are exposed by the* `IDispatch` *interface using the* `Invoke` *mechanism.*

`CUdfAutomation` has only two field members — both used to store references to managed instances. Because `CUdfAutomation` is a native class, it needs to store these references via some sort of bridge. In C++/CLI this bridge is implemented by the `gcroot<>` template class:

```
class ATL_NO_VTABLE CUdfAutomation :
    // ...
    private:
    gcroot<UdfProxy::UdfManager^> m_manager;
    gcroot<Excel::Application^> m_app;
```

While `m_manager` will hold a reference to the class that was described before — the one that manages all the UDFs that are loaded, the `m_app` field will hold a reference to the Excel Application object.

The `FinalConstruct()` method of `CUdfAutomation` is called when the class construction is done (when it's created via COM for example). That's where most initialization code should go:

```
HRESULT FinalConstruct()
{
    try
    {
        m_manager = gcnew UdfManager();
        m_manager->Load();
    }
    catch (System::OutOfMemoryException^)
    {
        return E_OUTOFMEMORY;
    }
    catch (System::Exception^)
    {
        return E_FAIL;
    }
    return S_OK;
}
```

In this case, the code creates a new `UdfManager` instance (which was imported from the `UdfProxy` assembly) and loads it.

If you never worked with C++/CLI, the syntax may seem a bit weird. Trust me. It's much better than it was in the first version (Managed C++ in the 2003 release). It just takes a bit of getting used to.

The method also catches exceptions and translates them into errors that the caller of the class will recognize.

IDTExtensibility2 defines five methods, only one of which is utilized in this class — the OnConnection() method. This is called when Excel first creates the automation addin and allows it to properly set up for using Excel.

It should have been possible to forgo implementing IDTExtensibility2 and instead use the Marshal::GetActiveObject() method to get the currently running Excel instance from the ROT (running object table). This approach has two distinct disadvantages. The first one is that it would not have worked as expected when more than one instance of Excel is running. The second is that Excel (and most Office apps for that matter) do not register themselves in the ROT until they lose focus. That means that at least in some cases, the code would not have been able to find the Application object until after the user switched to a different window.

In this case, all the code does is cache the reference to the Application object that Excel exposes so that it can later be used to set the volatility of UDFs:

```
STDMETHOD(OnConnection)(IDispatch * app,
    AddInDesignerObjects::ext_ConnectMode ConnectMode,
    IDispatch * AddInInst,
    SAFEARRAY * * custom )
{
    m_app = (Excel::Application^)
        System::Runtime::InteropServices::Marshal::GetObjectForIUnknown(
            System::IntPtr(app));
    return S_OK;
}
```

Even though this method is only one line long, there are a few things worth noting. IDTExtensiblity2 is implemented natively. This means that the parameters that are passed into it are native, too. In this case, the IDispatch that is passed as the app parameter is a native COM pointer and as such cannot be transparently used by managed code. Since the implementation of the dynamic IDispatch interface will be done mostly in managed C++, the code will need to have a managed wrapper for the COM object representing the Excel application. That's where the call to Marshal::GetObjectForIUnknown() comes in. It takes the IDispatch pointer and turns it into a managed object, which is then cast into an Excel::Application object, which is a managed interop wrapper for the Excel Application COM instance.

The next part is the core implementation of the class that is located inside the UdfAutomation.cpp file. The three most important implementations here are GetFuncDesc(), UDF_GetIDsOfNames(), and UDF_Invoke(). The first method belongs to the ITypeInfo interface, which is used to divine information about various dispmethods. The second method is used by Excel to see if a named dispmethod is supported. The third one is used to invoke the dispmethod.

Theoretically, IDispatch alone should have been enough for achieving the ability to invoke methods. Excel, however, requires both interfaces to be able to do the invocation. The only functionality it really uses from ITypeInfo is metadata about the supported IDispatch methods.

When Excel parses a formula and finds something it does not recognize, but that looks like a UDF call inside a formula, it will go to each of the automation servers registered and call GetIDsOfNames() to see if the server supports the UDF. If it does, the GetIDsOfNames() method returns a dispid (a numeric identifier) that represents the dispmethod corresponding to the name. Later, that dispid will be used to invoke the method:

```
STDMETHODIMP CUdfAutomation::UDF_GetIDsOfNames(
    REFIID riid,
    OLECHAR **rgszNames,
    UINT cNames,
    LCID lcid,
    DISPID *rgdispid)
{
    if (!rgdispid || !rgszNames)
    {
        return E_POINTER;
    }
    HRESULT retResult = S_OK;

    try
    {
        for (UINT i = 0; i < cNames; i++)
        {
            DISPID id;
            int intId = 0;
            UdfMethodWrapper^ method =
                m_manager->UdfMethodFromName(
                    gcnew System::String(rgszNames[i]));
            if (method == nullptr)
            {
                id = DISPID_UNKNOWN;
                retResult = DISP_E_UNKNOWNNAME;
            }
            else
            {
                id = (DISPID)method->Index;
            }
            rgdispid[i] = id;
        }
    }
    catch (System::OutOfMemoryException^)
    {
        return E_OUTOFMEMORY;
    }
    catch (System::Exception^)
    {
        return E_FAIL;
    }
    return S_OK;
}
```

The GetIDsOfNames() method first checks to make sure the out parameter is valid. It then uses the UdfManager instance to fill in the requested information.

The `rgszNames` parameter contains an array of strings — each string representing a name of a disp-method that is being sought.

In Excel, there will only be one dispmethod name request per call to `GetIDsOfNames()`, *but for completeness, this method knows how to handle calls with multiple dispids.*

The out parameter `rgdispid` parameter is an array that needs to be filled with these dispids. `UdfManager.UdfMethodFromName()` is used to get back the method in question. If the name is not located in the `UdfManager` instance, the special value `DISP_E_UNKNOWNNAME` is placed in the array to signify that no such name exists. If a `UdfMethod` instance is located, its index will be used as the `dispid` and placed inside the array.

The `GetFuncDesc()` method is accessible through the `ITypeInfo` interface, which in turn is accessible by calling the `GetTypeInfo()` method of `IDispatch` (in this case, renamed to `UDF_GetTypeInfo()`):

```
STDMETHODIMP CUdfAutomation::UDF_GetTypeInfo(
    UINT itinfo,
    LCID lcid,
    ITypeInfo** pptinfo)
{
    *pptinfo = static_cast<ITypeInfo*>(this);
    (*pptinfo)->AddRef();
    return S_OK;
}
```

The method is very simple. Because the `CUdfAutomation` class implements the `ITypeInfo` interface as well as all the others, all it needs to do is cast itself to that interface and return it (remembering to call `AddRef`).

`GetFuncDesc()` is slightly more involved. Its job is to inform Excel about the dispmethod metadata:

```
STDMETHODIMP CUdfAutomation::GetFuncDesc(
    UINT index,
    ::FUNCDESC **pppfuncdesc)
{
    ::FUNCDESC* pdesc = new ::FUNCDESC();
    if (!pdesc)
        return E_OUTOFMEMORY;

    ZeroMemory(pdesc, sizeof(::FUNCDESC));
    UdfMethodWrapper^ methodInfo;
    try
    {
        methodInfo = m_manager->UdfMethodFromId(index);
    }
    catch (System::Exception^)
    {
        return E_FAIL;
    }

    pdesc->memid = index;
    pdesc->funckind = ::FUNC_DISPATCH;
```

```
        pdesc->invkind = ::INVOKE_FUNC;
        pdesc->callconv = ::CC_STDCALL;
        int paramCount = methodInfo->ParameterCount;
        int optionalCount = 0;
        if (methodInfo->HasEllipsis)
        {
            optionalCount = 200 - paramCount - 1;
            paramCount = 200;
        }
        pdesc->cParams = paramCount;
        pdesc->cParamsOpt = optionalCount;
        *pppfuncdesc = pdesc;
        return S_OK;
}
```

The first part of the method prepares the memory that will be used to return the answer to the caller. That involves allocating an instance of the FUNCDESC structure, which is then filled with the relevant information.

In this case, the relevant information is pretty constant (it is all method calls, all of which use CC_STDCALL, etc.). It's just the number of potential arguments that may change. In this case, the limit will either be the actual amount of parameters a method has (if it does not have a param array) or 200 (an arbitrarily large number of possible arguments) if it does.

The ITypeInfo::GetFuncDesc() method uses an indexed ID for methods rather than DispIds. In the simplistic case presented here, both are one and the same. If you were to elaborate and add extra methods to the IDispatch interface, some fixups of these numbers may be needed.

Because of the unique way in which ITypeInfo works, there's also a method used to delete the allocated FUNCDESC structure:

```
STDMETHODIMP_(void) CUdfAutomation::ReleaseFuncDesc(::FUNCDESC *pfuncdesc)
{
    delete pfuncdesc;
}
```

There are a few more methods on the interface that are needed, namely, GetNames(), GetTypeAttr(), and ReleaseTypeAttr(). These provide more information about the available dispmethods.

The last part of the CUdfAutomation class is the actual Invoke() method (UDF_Invoke() in this case). This method takes the ID of the dispmethod that needs to be executed and an array of the parameters that are to be passed to the method.

The code for UDF_Invoke() looks like this:

```
#pragma managed(push,off)
STDMETHODIMP CUdfAutomation::UDF_Invoke(
                DISPID dispidMember, REFIID riid,
                LCID lcid, WORD wFlags,
                ::DISPPARAMS *pdispparams, VARIANT *pvarResult,
                ::EXCEPINFO *pexcepinfo, UINT *puArgErr)
```

```
{
    return DoInvoke(
        dispidMember, riid,
        lcid, wFlags,
        pdispparams, pvarResult,
        pexcepinfo, puArgErr);
}
#pragma managed(pop)
```

The method simply calls into the `DoInvoke()` method, which takes the same exact set of parameters. The reason for this lies in the two `#pragma` directives wrapping the method. These instruct the C++/CLI compiler to make sure that this `UDF_Invoke()` method is compiled with no managed support. When it in turn calls into the mixed mode `DoInvoke()`, the compiler can do a better job of binding the parameters, shaving a few percentages for the overall time it takes to actually call the `Invoke()` mechanism (from tests performed, a gain of roughly 10% was realized by doing this).

The `DoInvoke()` method contains the actual implementation of invoking the appropriate UDF. It has four stages:

❑ Initialization

❑ Excel `Range` to array transformation for those parameters that need it

❑ Native to managed transformation for all parameters

❑ Calling the UDF method, returning to Excel the value that was returned from the managed UDF and doing some cleanup

This section will show the method using these four stages:

```
HRESULT CUdfAutomation::DoInvoke(
            DISPID dispidMember, REFIID riid,
            LCID lcid, WORD wFlags,
            ::DISPPARAMS *pdispparams, VARIANT *pvarResult,
            ::EXCEPINFO *pexcepinfo, UINT *puArgErr)
{
    // Stage 1
    if (!pdispparams || !pvarResult)
    {
        return E_POINTER;
    }
    if (pdispparams->cNamedArgs > 0)
    {
        return E_FAIL;
    }

    int paramCount = pdispparams->cArgs;
    VARIANT* params = new VARIANT[paramCount];
    bool* owned = new bool[paramCount];

    for (int i = 0; i < paramCount; i++)
    {
        VariantInit(&params[i]);
        owned[i] = false;
```

```
        }
        HRESULT hr;
        // Stage 2
        // ...
        // Stage 3
        // ...
        // Stage 4
        // ...
}
```

The method prepares a secondary VARIANT array that will contain the parameters passed into the DoInvoke() method (inside the DISPPARAMS array.) These parameters may contain Excel Range objects, and these are not consumable by a server UDF. The method also prepares a bool array, which will be used during cleanup. Finally, this stage zeroes out the memory in these arrays.

The second stage looks for Excel Range objects among the passed in parameters and turns them into arrays instead:

```
HRESULT CUdfAutomation::DoInvoke(
            DISPID dispidMember, REFIID riid,
            LCID lcid, WORD wFlags,
            ::DISPPARAMS *pdispparams, VARIANT *pvarResult,
            ::EXCEPINFO *pexcepinfo, UINT *puArgErr)
{
    // Stage 1
    // ...
    // Stage 2
    try
    {
        // Go over the list of arguments and transform the
        // IDispatch type to be the Value2 property value.
        for (int i = 0; i < paramCount; i++)
        {
            VARIANT* current = &pdispparams->rgvarg[i];
            if (current->vt == VT_DISPATCH)
            {
                VARIANT* pNewVariant = &params[i];
                IDispatch* piDisp = current->pdispVal;

                ::DISPPARAMS invokeParams = {0};
                hr = piDisp->Invoke(0, IID_NULL,
                    0, DISPATCH_PROPERTYGET,
                    &invokeParams, pNewVariant,
                    NULL, NULL);
                if (FAILED(hr))
                {
                    throw gcnew System::InvalidOperationException();
                }
                owned[i] = true;
            }
            else
            {
```

```
                          params[i] = *current;
                }
        }

        // Stage 3
        // ...
        // Stage 4
        // ...
    }
    // ...
    return S_OK;
}
```

Each dispmethod parameter is examined (inside the dispparams array) to see if its type is VT_DISPATCH. When that's the case, it means that Excel has passed in a VARIANT containing a reference to the Excel object model Range object. Since this code is only interested in the array of values contained inside that range, it will execute the default property on these Range objects to get back the array of data by calling Invoke() on the IDispatch pointer. The array value is placed inside the pNewVariant pointer (which actually resides inside the allocated array of VARIANT objects we allocated). When a range is retrieved, the code also sets an entry in the owned array to true, to signify that this VARIANT will need to be freed when the method is done. If the type of the parameter is not VT_DISPATCH, the code simply bit-copies the VARIANT into the array. Because the owned array will have false for that element, it will not be freed.

Each of these parameters now needs to be transformed to its managed equivalent so that the managed UDF will be able to comprehend it:

```
HRESULT CUdfAutomation::DoInvoke(
            DISPID dispidMember, REFIID riid,
            LCID lcid, WORD wFlags,
            ::DISPPARAMS *pdispparams, VARIANT *pvarResult,
            ::EXCEPINFO *pexcepinfo, UINT *puArgErr)
{
    // Stage 1
    // ...
    // Stage 2
    try
    {
        // ...
        // Stage 3
        array<System::Object^>^ params =
            GetObjectsForVariants(params, pdispparams->cArgs);

        // Reverse the array.
        array::Reverse(params);

        // Stage 4
        // ...
    }
    // ...
    return S_OK;
}
```

First, the method calls into the `GetObjectsForVariants()` method to get back a managed `Object` array (that's the funky `array<System::Object^>^` thingamajig). Because the original parameters passed to the `UDF_Invoke()` method are in reverse order, they also need to be straightened out to the correct order before being passed into the managed code.

This reverse order has nothing to do with UDFs or Excel. It's just how `IDispatch` is designed. This is probably due to the fact that, historically, when parameters have been passed on the stack to regular functions, parameters have been reversed, and this simulates that for (almost) no good reason.

At the end of stage 3, the `params` local variable will contain correctly ordered managed references to the values passed by Excel into the UDF:

```
HRESULT CUdfAutomation::DoInvoke(
            DISPID dispidMember, REFIID riid,
            LCID lcid, WORD wFlags,
            ::DISPPARAMS *pdispparams, VARIANT *pvarResult,
            ::EXCEPINFO *pexcepinfo, UINT *puArgErr)
{
    // Stage 1
    // ...
    // Stage 2
    try
    {
        // Stage 3
        // ...
        // Stage 4
        UdfMethodWrapper^ method = m_manager->UdfMethodFromId(dispidMember);

        // Set method to be volatile if needed.
        if (method->IsVolatile)
        {
            m_app->Volatile(System::Type::Missing);
        }
        System::Object^ resultObject = method->Invoke(params);
        Marshal::GetNativeVariantForObject(
            resultObject, System::IntPtr(pvarResult));
    }
    catch (System::OutOfMemoryException^)
    {
        return E_OUTOFMEMORY;
    }
    catch (System::Exception^)
    {
        return E_FAIL;
    }
    finally
    {
        for (int i = 0; i < paramCount; i++)
        {
            if (owned[i])
```

```
                {
                    VariantClear(&params[i]);
                }
            }
        delete[] params;
        delete[] owned;
    }
    return S_OK;
}
```

This last stage actually makes the call. It retrieves the UdfMethodWrapper instance from the UdfManager and checks if the method is volatile. If it is, it makes sure to call the Excel Application object and notify it that the method is volatile. The UdfMethodWrapper.Invoke() method is then called, with the params local variable passed as a parameter.

This is how volatility works in Excel. While running, UDFs need to make sure they call the Volatile method on the Application object. Excel detects that and marks them as volatile. Of course, a UDF has a return value. This value gets assigned to the resultObject managed reference, which is then transformed to its native equivalent and placed in a VARIANT so that it can be returned to Excel.

Finally, the code makes sure it cleans up after itself, clearing what VARIANT instances were allocated and deleting the allocated arrays.

There are four more methods in the UdfAutomation.cpp file responsible for transforming managed values to native ones and vice versa. These functions are pretty long and are beyond the scope of this book. Debugging them, though, should help you understand their functionality. The methods are:

❑　GetObjectsForVariants() — Called from UDF_Invoke(), this method is used to take an array of VARIANT structures and transform them into an array of Object instances.

❑　GetObjectForNonArrayVariant() — Used by GetObjectForVariant() as a helper method for transforming simple types of VARIANTs into their Object equivalents.

❑　GetObjectForVariant() — Transforms a single VARIANT into an equivalent Object instance. Does this for arrays as well.

❑　GetVariantForObject() — Used for the result of the UDF call — transforms an Object instance into a VARIANT that is consumable by Excel.

Final Steps

To complete the project, the UdfProxy class needs to be strong-named and placed in the GAC so that it can be used by the UdfAutomation object. If it were not placed in the GAC, it would have to be placed in the Excel 2007 directory.

The UdfAutomation DLL needs to be registered in the system, using the regsvr32.exe utility. That will ensure that Excel can find it in the list of automation servers.

Improvements

The following improvements can be made to the project, but are outside the scope of this book:

❑ **Easier configuration**

It is possible to move the logic of the configuration utility into Excel itself by adding a ribbon button that will bring up the dialog box. Once that's done, UdfProxy can be modified to dynamically add or remove UDF assemblies without having to reboot Excel.

❑ **Setup**

A deployment program can be made that takes care of placing the files in the correct location, doing the necessary registration and configuring Excel to automatically load the addin.

❑ **Detecting client**

Sometimes it might be useful to have different behavior in the same UDF class based on whether or not it's running on the client. There are two ways of doing this. The first involves checking for the name of the process running the UDF. (See the System.Diagnostics.Process class for more information on how to do that.) If it's Excel.exe that means it's the client. Otherwise, it probably means it's the server.

The name of the process for the server will be w3wp.exe; however, do not check for that as it may change in the future. Instead, if the name is not Excel.exe, assume that it's the server running the UDF.

The second, more correct, way of doing this would be to add a base class inside the UdfProxy assembly. That class will have a property named IsClient, which will return true in the case where it's being executed by Excel. Instead of checking the process name though, this property is set when the UdfManager class instantiates the UDF class. It can easily cast the produced object to the base class and if the cast is successful, set that property to true.

Other Generic Solutions

The solution described here is by no means the only one or even the best one. There are at least two more solutions — each with its advantages and disadvantages.

The first uses a similar outlook on the problem but uses a generic XLL instead of a generic COM automation server. This has the advantage of potentially performing better than the one described here.

Actually, it may have much better performance than the automation addin, since it can take advantage of the Multithreaded Recalc engine — something automation addins cannot do in this version.

The disadvantage is that it is significantly more complex — XLLs are not as simple to use as automation addins and would require such things as custom code for pushing parameters onto the stack and handling the XLOPER structures in the XLL SDK.

The second possible solution is to use code generation to automatically create assemblies that look like the one described at the beginning of this chapter (instead of adding code to the existing UDF assembly, though, these assemblies would instantiate them and call into them from methods accessible through an automation server). The main advantage is that there is no need for any configuration — these assemblies can be individually used by the regular Excel mechanisms. The disadvantage is that they will probably perform worse than the solution presented here (due to the fact that COM interop, for the most part, is much slower than C++/CLI interop).

Summary

Regrettably, Excel Services UDFs do not work on the client. This chapter shows how to work around that limitation in two different ways. Both ways have their advantages and disadvantages — at the end of the day, it is up to the person deploying the solution to decide which way is best for them.

Part IV: Excel Web Access

Chapter 11: Using Excel Web Access

Using Excel Web Access

Excel Web Access (EWA) allows users to view workbooks in a Web browser using plain HTML and ECMA script (JavaScript). The EWA is a Web Part that can be hosted inside a SharePoint Web Part page or inside any ASPX page hosted inside of SharePoint. For the first version of the server, the programmability options of the EWA are very limited. This chapter discusses ways to use the workbook rather than program it. The examples show how to develop a Web Part that supports part to part communication to allow Web Part page designers to write more elaborate pages.

EWA Usage

The easiest way to get started with EWA is to use SharePoint Web Part pages. Most pages that are automatically generated by SharePoint are Web Part pages and as such can be used to host EWA. In addition, SharePoint allows users to create Web Part pages inside document libraries. Creating a new Web Part page is done by using the Create menu item on the Site Actions menu inside a SharePoint site. Choosing this menu item navigates the caller to the Create web page, which presents a large number of choices to the user. Clicking on Web Part page will take you to the page that allows for the creation of Web Parts, as shown in Figure 11-1.

In this example, a page called `MyExcelViewer.aspx` is created on the server. It will have a very simple layout (just a single zone to drop Web Parts in).

At the bottom of the form, there is also a combo box that allows users to specify in which folder this page is to be created. In this example, the new ASPX page will be located in the Shared Documents document library.

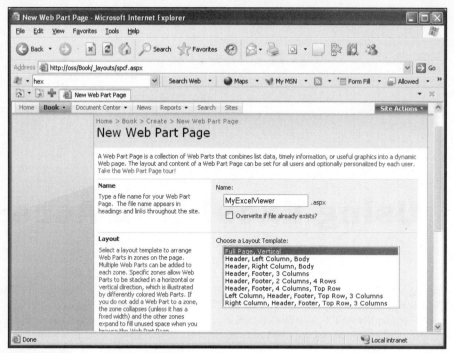

Figure 11-1

Once the Create button is clicked, SharePoint generates the new page and navigates to it. The page should be in editing mode by default. If it's not, it's always possible to go into edit mode by using the Site Actions menu and choosing Edit page.

In Edit mode, it is possible to add Web Parts to the page. The next step, shown in Figure 11.2 will add an Excel Web Access Web Part to the page. This is done by clicking the Add a Web Part button inside the zone. (If there are multiple zones, each one will have an Add a Web Part button.)

Selecting the Excel Web Access Web Part and clicking on the Add button will place the Web Part in the location chosen by the user.

SharePoint stores the ASPX page and its contents inside the content database.

Note that multiple Web Parts can be selected at the same time and added en masse to the page. SharePoint also supports the gallery option of adding pages as it did in previous versions. This new Add Web Parts dialog box, however, greatly simplifies the process.

Once the Web Part is added, the page should look like the one shown in Figure 11-3.

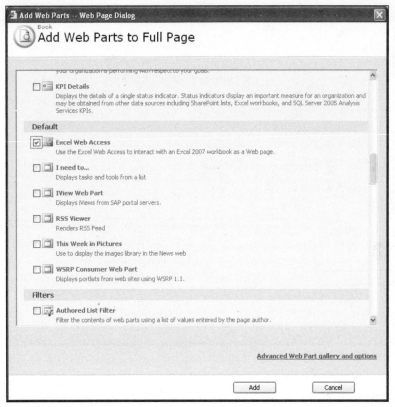

Figure 11-2

Setting up the Web Part can be achieved either by clicking on the helpful Click here to open the tool pane link or by clicking on the dropdown button at the top-right (top-left in right-to-left languages) area of the Web Part and choosing Modify Shared Web Part.

Web Part Properties

Once the tool pane is opened, it will present the user with various options for customizing the Web Part, as shown in Figure 11-4. This section describes the various customizations that are possible and explains what goes on under the hood.

EWA has three categories of properties, each governing a different aspect of the Web Part behavior. All of these properties are available programmatically to developers who embed the control in their solutions.

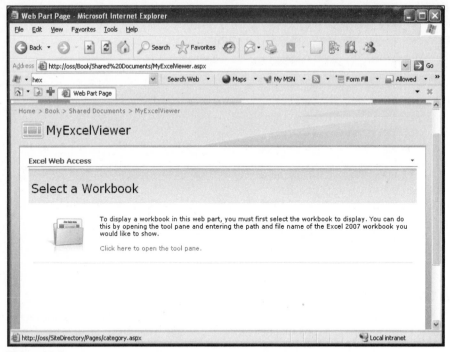

Figure 11-3

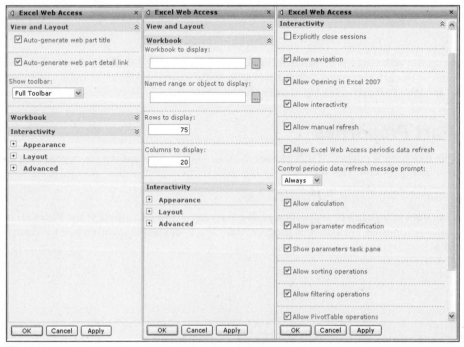

Figure 11-4

View and Layout Category

The View and Layout category controls the way the Web Part looks to the user. The Auto-generate Web Part title property controls the text that appears at the top of the Web Part. When checked, it will be set up automatically to display the name of the workbook.

The Auto-generate Web Part detail link option controls the URI that the title links to (when clicked). When auto-generate is turned on, clicking on the title of the Web Part will allow you to navigate to the XLViewer page (a web page containing only EWA).

The last property in the View and Layout category controls the functionality of the toolbar. There are three options here — the first, called Full Toolbar, displays all the available options to the user, including the ability to recalculate and refresh the workbook. The second option, Summary Toolbar, contains only very rudimentary functionality such as opening in the workbook in Excel and refreshing a selected connection. The last option, None, will hide the toolbar completely.

Hiding the toolbar completely is used when the Web Part page designer wants to have a seamless integration between Excel workbook portions and the page. It is especially useful when the workbook is in Named object view and shows a well formatted grid or chart.

Workbook Category

This section of the tool allows the user to modify what EWA shows to the user. The Workbook to display property is a link to the workbook that needs to be shown inside the web page. This can be in any form that is supported by Excel Services (a URL pointing to an HTTP resource or a network path).

The property called Named range or object to display allows the user to switch EWA to the named object view (NOV) mode. Typing a name of a range, PivotTable, or chart into this property will cause EWA to display only that specific object.

The two properties Rows to display and Columns to display define the amount of data shown to the user at any given moment. The smaller these numbers are, the quicker EWA will load (and the less information it will show).

Interactivity Category

The last category has many options available for modifying what interactivity will be available for the user. Two of these are "master" options, which will control the availability of other options, namely, Allow Navigation and Allow Interactivity.

Part to Part Communication

Part to part (P2P) communication is a SharePoint infrastructure feature that allows users to build Web Part pages that are actual applications. The idea behind part to part is that each Web Part can be either a consumer or a provider of connections (or both). Each such connection point supports a specific interface. The SharePoint infrastructure lets users decide which connections they want to make between the parts. It also takes care of reconciling potentially incompatible interfaces by using transformers.

As an example, take a regular document library Web Part. It can be used as a part to part provider of information (it will provide the selected row in the list) and it supports the Row interface of part to part (because it can provide a whole row of information). On a Web Part page, this Web Part can be combined with any other Web Part that can consume fields or rows. The Image Web Part, for example, can consume field connections. Because a transformer from a row connection to field connection exists, page designers can connect the two Web Parts to get an image viewer application (where the user clicks on items in the document library and sees them in the image viewer).

EWA can consume part to part providers in three ways. First, the workbook URL can be taken from any field provider (such as a document library). The second is the named object, which is also taken from a field provider (such as a SharePoint list). Last, the parameters of a workbook can be set by using filter providers.

Workbook Connection

To set up a part to part connection between an EWA and a document library, the Web Part page designer needs to first make sure both components are on the page. The designer can then use the EWA dropdown and choose the Connections menu option, followed by the Get Workbook URL from… option, as shown in Figure 11-5.

Once selected, the two Web Parts (the Sales Library at the right side of the page and the EWA on the left) will be connected. When a workbook is selected in the "Sales Library," the whole page will be refreshed and the EWA will show the selected workbook, as shown in Figure 11-6.

Named Object Connection

Similarly to connecting the workbook property to another Web Part, it is possible to use part to part connections to control what object is shown inside the EWA. Instead of choosing the Get Workbook URL From… menu option, though, the page designer chooses the Get Named Object from… option.

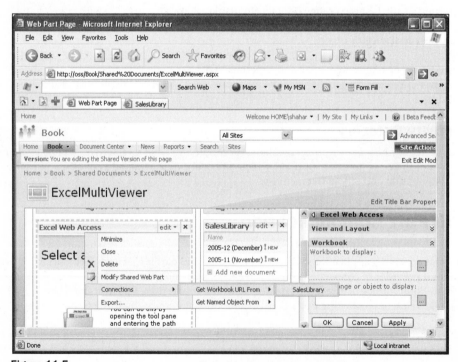

Figure 11-5

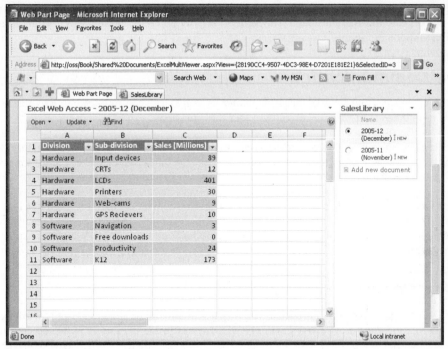

Figure 11-6

Connecting both workbook and named object is not advisable because there is no real control over which connection will happen first. Doing so may work when first designing the page; however, it may stop working when the page is copied over to another site or when it's restored from backup.

Filter Connections

It is possible to use part to part connections with parameters that are defined inside a workbook. SharePoint Portal Server has an extensive library of filtering components that give Web Part page designers many tools they can use to create dashboard applications.

Inside EWA

Because the workbook can potentially take a long time to load, the EWA has been designed in such a way that it does not interfere with the rest of the page when it loads or refreshes. The actual Web Part that is used by SharePoint does not really have any workbook-rendering logic in it. Instead, it hosts an IFrame HTML element that loads a SharePoint ASPX page that does the actual rendering.

This could also be achieved by using AJAX, however, at the time the project was starting, AJAX was still not mature enough and so the IFrame method was employed instead.

For the purpose of this book, the term *outer EWA* will refer to the publicly used Web Part — the one that ends up being on the Web Part page. The term *inner EWA* will refer to the Web Part that is used to do the actual workbook rendering.

Frame Communication

Due to the nature of the EWA Web Part, the outer EWA needs to communicate to the inner EWA the information it needs in order to correctly render the workbook.

To do this, the outer EWA contains scripts that fill the `IFrame` element with an HTML form that is then submitted to the page containing the inner EWA. Once the inner EWA receives the information, it takes the necessary measures to open the workbook and render the information that is returned from it.

One of the unfortunate side effects of this is that it is impossible for the rendering page to know the SessionID that is being used to communicate with the workbook. This can present some interesting challenges when developers want to generate an application that uses EWA (a later chapter will show how this can still be achieved).

Session Cookie

One of the nice features EWA supports is the way it remembers the session a user is working on. Even when navigating away from a Web Part page and then returning to it, users will keep getting back the same session they were working on (provided that it has not timed out). This is achieved by maintaining a session cookie per Web Part.

> *EWA makes sure to retire cookies when a certain limit is reached. If it did not do that, the request header would become too big for IIS to handle, making the site unresponsive. Because of this adaptability, the amount of EWA sessions that can be maintained is governed by the amount of information in the HTTP header.*

> *While it's possible to modify the cookie to achieve some capabilities that are otherwise impossible, developers are strongly advised against doing so. It is highly doubtful that the next version of Excel Services will employ the same mechanism. Any code written to take advantage of the cookie is very likely to stop working with the next release of Excel Services.*

Summary

The Excel Web Access Web Part allows users and developers to create pages that show Excel workbooks without resorting to any ActiveX or Object Linking and Embedding (OLE) solutions. Because the page generated is dynamic HTML (DHTML), it can be consumed by any of the supported browsers with no requirements of installing extra software. While the book concentrates on UDF and Excel Web Services solutions, you will find some examples that use the EWA.

Part V: Reusable Excel Web Services Projects

12

Utilizing Web
Services in UDFs

As long as they've been around, Web Services have functioned like Distributed Component Object Model (DCOM) and Common Object Request Broker Architecture (CORBA), but without their advanced features and without inspiring the fear usually associated with those technologies. Also, Web Services actually work most of the time.

To this point, this book has discussed Web Services in two ways. The first was when it introduced Excel Web Services—the interface that allows callers to use Excel Services programmatically. The second was when it introduced UDFs—one of the examples showed how to consume Web Services inside Excel Services.

This chapter will show how to build a component that can automatically generate Excel Services UDFs such as those described in Chapter 8. For the sake of completion, the code on the book's web site will also contain an implementation for generating such UDFs so that they are usable in Excel 2007.

The main part of the project will be a library that takes care of the assembly generation. The second part will show a simple WinForms application written using the library (the UI application will not be shown in detail, just the idea behind it).

Library Component

The name of the assembly containing the library component will be `Pes.WebServiceUdf.Library.DLL`. ("Pes" stands for Professional Excel Services.) The namespace will be called `Pes.WebServiceUdf.Library`.

The library component contains a `UdfDefinition` class that is responsible for taking a WSDL of a Web Service and transforming it into a UDF library usable by Excel Services, Excel 2007, or both.

UdfDefinition also has a list of all the methods available within the Web Service, allowing callers to pick and choose which methods will be available and what their names will be.

Once the definition of the UDF is decided upon, the library users call into UdfDefinition.Generate(), which returns a GeneratedResult instance. That instance can be used to generate the assembly or get source code in any supported .NET language.

> This project relies heavily on the System.CodeDom namespace for creating code trees that can then be transformed into assemblies. This sort of code tends to be verbose and potentially hard to follow. For that reason, for each part of the Pes.WebServiceUdf.Library that generates code, the book will also show an example of what the generated code will look like.

How It Works

The UdfDefinition class uses CLR classes to generate a code DOM for a WSDL supplied by the caller. This code will be similar to that used by Visual Studio 2005 when it generates Web Service references (by using the Add Web Reference option in the IDE). Unlike VS2005, however, the library takes the code DOM and looks into its structure to understand what methods exist and what their structure is. The library then exposes the list of methods and allows the developer to modify which ones will be available in the UDF.

> Code DOM stands for Code Document Object Model. It is the .NET object representation of source code. Other tools in the CLR know how to take a code DOM tree and turn it into actual source code (which can then be compiled).

When generating the UDF, the library uses the proxy that was created as a blueprint of how the UDF methods need to look. It modifies the signatures if appropriate and adds calls that may be needed for the UDFs to work properly, adding new code DOM elements to the namespace that contains the proxy class that will be used as the UDF classes.

About Code Generation

The .NET framework provides some very impressive tools for generating code from code. Examples of places where this is used can be found throughout the .NET development process. Some serialization mechanisms will generate code on the fly when they need to save or load a class from a stream. VS2005 uses code generation when it builds up proxy files for Web Services. Regular expressions can potentially build code on the fly to generate compiled versions of themselves. Most of the classes having to do with code generation are located in the System.CodeDom namespace.

Each element in a program is represented by an object from that namespace—these can then be assembled into a tree, which can then be used to generate binary assemblies or actual source code. For example, to create a class code element called MyClass inside a namespace code element called MyNamespace, you would write the following code:

```
// Generating code
CodeNamespace ns = new CodeNamespace("MyNamespace");
CodeTypeDecleration type = new CodeTypeDecleration("MyClass");
ns.Types.Add(type);
```

The type variable will hold an instance of what will be recognized as being a class. That class was added into the ns variable, which represents a namespace. If C# code was to be generated from this, it would look like this:

```
// Generated code
namespace MyNamespace
{
    class MyClass
    {
    }
}
```

Similarly, code elements such as calls, casts, and conditions can be generated as well.

The code presented in this chapter will do both code tree building (for generating the actual code) and code tree traversing (to check what methods are actually available).

WebServiceMethodCollection and WebServiceMethod Classes

The WebServiceMethodCollection and WebServiceMethod classes are used to traverse the list of web methods inside an imported Web Service. The collection inherits from the List<WebServiceMethod> class and adds no functionality beyond that:

```
namespace Pes.WebServiceUdf.Library
{
    public class WebServiceMethodCollection : List<WebServiceMethod>
    {
        internal WebServiceMethodCollection()
        {

        }
    }
}
```

Each WebServiceMethod, on the other hand, contains information about how the generated code looks and what it should contain:

```
namespace Pes.WebServiceUdf.Library
{
    public class WebServiceMethod
    {
        private CodeMemberMethod m_method;
        private WebServiceParameterCollection m_parameters;
        private bool m_included = true;
        private string m_name;
        private bool m_supported;


        internal WebServiceMethod(CodeMemberMethod method)
        {
```

```
                m_method = method;
                Name = method.Name;
            }
        }
        // ...
    }
```

The `MemberMethod` property returns an instance of the `CodeMemberMethod` class, which represents a method in the generated proxy code (this is the code that was generated from the WSDL).

`Name` represents the name of the UDF. In some cases, it may be necessary for Excel Services or Excel to have a UDF called by a name different from the one under which the Web Service's provider published it. This can happen when a Web Service method happens to have a name of an already existing Excel internal function (Sum, Rand, and so on). It can also happen when two Web Services are needed that happen to have the same name.

The `IsSupported` property is set by the infrastructure when this class is first initialized, depending on the generated method parameters (see the `UdfDefinition.IsMethodSupported` method later in this chapter). When a method is not supported, it cannot be included as part of the generated UDF.

The `Included` property is used to specify whether or not a UDF method will even be generated. In some cases, users of the library may decide that a given Web Service method is not really needed. When this property is changed to false, the `UdfDefiniton` class will make sure that these methods are not present in the generated UDF classes.

```
public bool IsSupported
{
    get { return m_supported; }
    internal set { m_supported = value; }
}

public bool Included
{
    get
    {
        if (!IsSupported)
        {
            return false;
        }
        return m_included;
    }

    set
    {
        if (value && !IsSupported)
        {
            throw new InvalidOperationException(
                "Unsupported methods cannot be included.");
        }
        m_included = value;
    }
}
```

There is also a property called `Parameters`, which returns a `WebServiceParameterCollection` instance used to traverse the list of parameters the method has. This list is generated on the fly when the `Parameters` property is first accessed.

WebServiceParameter and WebServiceParameterCollection Classes

These two classes are used as thin wrappers to the code DOM classes representing parameters (`CodeParameterDeclerationExpression`). See the "Summary" section at the end of this chapter about "possible improvements" for potential reasons for usage of these parameters.

UdfDefinition Class

The `UdfDefinition` class, shown by the following code, is the one instantiated by the user of the library to start the process of creating the UDF assembly (or source code):

```
using System;
using System.Collections.Generic;
using System.Text;
using System.Net;
using System.IO;
using System.Web.Services.Description;
using System.CodeDom;
using System.Web.Services.Protocols;

namespace Pes.WebServiceUdf.Library
{
    public class UdfDefinition
    {
        private string m_namespace = "Pes.GeneratedWebService";
        private WebServiceMethodCollection m_methodCollection =
            new WebServiceMethodCollection();
        private GeneratedResult m_baseResult;
        private SupportedProducts m_supportedProducts;
        private ServiceDescription m_description;

        private ServiceDescription Description
        {
            get { return m_description; }
            set { m_description = value; }
        }

        public SupportedProducts SupportedProducts
        {
            get { return m_supportedProducts; }
            set { m_supportedProducts = value; }
        }

        private GeneratedResult BaseResult
        {
            get { return m_baseResult; }
```

```
                    set { m_baseResult = value; }
            }

            public string NamespaceName
            {
                    get { return m_namespace; }
                    set
                    {
                            ThrowIfLoaded();
                            m_namespace = value;
                    }
            }

            public WebServiceMethodCollection MethodCollection
            {
                    get { return m_methodCollection; }
            }

            // …
    }
}
```

The MethodCollection property contains the list of methods available in the Web Service.
NamespaceName contains the name of the namespace that will contain the classes of the
generated assembly.

SupportedProducts is an enumeration that specifies which UDFs are requested by the user library:

```
[Flags]
public enum SupportedProducts
{
    Excel = 0x01,
    ExcelServices = 0x02
}
```

As explained at the beginning of this chapter, the library knows how to generate UDFs for both Excel
and Excel Services. Setting this property to SupportedProducts.Excel | SupportedProducts
.ExcelServices will produce a UDF assembly containing both.

BaseResult holds a reference to a GeneratedResult instance, which is used for understanding the
structure of the proxy class.

The Description property points to a ServiceDescription instance, which is a CLR object representing a parsed WSDL. This object is used to create the GeneratedResult instances.

Once a UdfDefinition class has been instantiated and its NamespaceName property modified, callers
need to call the Load() method with a candidate WSDL URI:

```
public void Load(string uri)
{
    if (BaseResult != null)
    {
```

```
                    throw new InvalidOperationException(
                    "This operation is not available once the Load() method has been
        called");
            }

            // Get the description from the WSDL.
            Description = CreateDescription(uri);

            // Create the importer.
            ServiceDescriptionImporter importer = CreateImporter(Description);

            BaseResult = new GeneratedResult(this);
            BaseResult.Import(importer);
            try
            {
                BuildMethodTable();
            }
            catch
            {
                BaseResult = null;
                throw;
            }
        }
```

The first step uses the `CreateDescription()` method to load the WSDL and create a `Service-Description` instance based on it. Next, a `GeneratedResult` instance is created and initialized (by using the `GeneratedResult.Import()` method, discussed later in this chapter).

The final part of this method, shown in the following listing, uses the `BuildMethodTable` method to populate the `WebServiceMethodCollection` property. Once that part is done successfully, the class can be used to generate UDF assemblies and source code.

```
private ServiceDescription CreateDescription(string uri)
{
    ServiceDescription result = null;
    try
    {
        WebRequest request = WebRequest.Create(uri);

        using (WebResponse response = request.GetResponse())
        using (Stream s = response.GetResponseStream())
        {
            result = ServiceDescription.Read(s);
        }
    }
    catch (Exception e)
    {
        throw new CannotLoadWsdlException(
            "Could not load WSDL or parse it.",
            e);
    }
    return result;
}
```

The CLR gives developers access to the `ServiceDescription` class, which can be used to generate Web Service proxy code. The `WebRequest` class is used to get the WSDL stream from the supplied URI—this guarantees that whatever the URI form is (file location, HTTP location, or anything else supported by .NET), the correct action is taken and a stream is produced (into the stream local variable).

> `CannotLoadWsdlException` *and* `CompilationErrorException` *are both defined in the project. They both inherit from* `WebServicesUdfException`.

```
private ServiceDescriptionImporter CreateImporter(
    ServiceDescription description)
{
    ServiceDescriptionImporter importer =
        new ServiceDescriptionImporter();
    importer.AddServiceDescription(description, null, null);
    importer.ProtocolName = "Soap";
    importer.Style = ServiceDescriptionImportStyle.Client;
    importer.CodeGenerationOptions =
        System.Xml.Serialization.CodeGenerationOptions.None;
    return importer;
}
```

The `ServiceDescriptionImporter` class is used to transform a `ServiceDescription` instance into a code DOM tree. The `ServiceDescriptionImporter.Style` property is used to specify that proxy code is required (as opposed to server code, which the importer can also generate). The `ServiceDescriptionImporter.CodeGenerationOptions` is used to specify that only the standard methods are required (this property allows developers to specify that they also want asynchronous methods).

The `BuildMethodTable()` method gets the `CodeTypeDeclaration` from the `BaseResult` instance and traverses the list of `CodeMemberMethod` objects it contains, collecting all those that look like proxy methods. Each `CodeTypeMember` in the iteration is tested to see if it's a method.

The attributes of each method are then examined, looking for one that marks this method as a proxy method. Because there is no built-in mechanism for finding an attribute definition by name, the `Utils.FindAttribute()` is used as a helper method for doing that.

> *The CLR supports two SOAP call mechanisms—XML formatted using an XML Schema Definition (XSD) schema and one using the SOAP for the remote procedure call (RPC) part of the SOAP specifications. Methods marked with the* `SoapDocumentMethod` *attribute will use the XSD-formatted messages, while those marked with the* `SoapRpcMethod` *attribute will use the RPC method.*

Once a proxy method is recognized, it is added to the method collection:

```
private void BuildMethodTable()
{
    // Get the proxy type decleration.
    CodeTypeDeclaration proxyType = BaseResult.ProxyType;

    // Iterate all the methods that are proxy methods.
    foreach (CodeTypeMember member in proxyType.Members)
```

```
        {
            CodeMemberMethod method = member as CodeMemberMethod;
            if (method != null)
            {
                // We have a method, check its attributes to see if it's
                // a proxy method.
                if (Utils.FindAttribute(method,
                        typeof(SoapDocumentMethodAttribute).FullName) != null ||
                    Utils.FindAttribute(method,
                        typeof(SoapRpcMethodAttribute).FullName) != null)
                {
                    WebServiceMethod webServiceMethod =
                        new WebServiceMethod(method);
                    MethodCollection.Add(webServiceMethod);
                }
            }
        }

    ExcludeIncompatibleMethods();
}
```

The last step of building the method table happens in the `ExcludeIncompatibleMethods` method. It iterates over the exposed methods and makes sure they are properly marked as unsupported if their parameters do not work well with Excel Services or Excel.

```
private void ExcludeIncompatibleMethods()
{
    foreach (WebServiceMethod method in Methods)
    {
        method.Supported = IsMethodSupported(method);
    }
}

private bool IsMethodSupported(WebServiceMethod method)
{
    // Check the parameters of the method and return value
    // to see if they are compatible.
    bool supported = IsCompatibleType(method.MemberMethod.ReturnType);
    if (supported)
    {
        // Check all the parameters.
        foreach (WebServiceParameter param in method.Parameters)
        {
            supported = IsCompatibleParameter(param);
            if (!supported)
            {
                break;
            }
        }
    }
    return supported;
}
```

The `ExcludeIncompatibleMethods()` method iterates through all the methods in the table and checks with each one if it's supported by using the `IsMethodSupported()` call.

`IsMethodSupported()` checks the return value and each parameter against a list of supported types by using the `IsCompatibleType()` and `IsCompatibleParameter()` methods respectively:

```
private bool IsCompatibleParameter(WebServiceParameter param)
{
    if (param.Parameter.Direction != FieldDirection.In)
        return false;
    return IsCompatibleType(param.Parameter.Type);
}

private bool IsCompatibleType(CodeTypeReference codeTypeReference)
{
    Type type = Type.GetType(codeTypeReference.BaseType, false);
    return IsCompatibleType(type, codeTypeReference.ArrayRank);
}

private bool IsCompatibleType(Type type, int arrayRank)
{
    if (type == null)
    {
        return false;
    }

    bool compatible =
        type == typeof(Int32) ||
        type == typeof(UInt32) ||
        type == typeof(Int16) ||
        type == typeof(UInt16) ||
        type == typeof(Byte) ||
        type == typeof(SByte) ||
        type == typeof(Double) ||
        type == typeof(Single) ||
        type == typeof(Boolean) ||
        type == typeof(String) ||
        type == typeof(Object);

    compatible &= arrayRank == 0;
    return compatible;
}
```

`IsCompatibleParameter()` takes a `WebServiceParameter` instance and checks if it is compatible first by making sure the direction of the parameter is supported and then by checking if its type is compatible. Only in parameters are supported by UDFs and so only those are allowed.

`IsCompatibleType()` has two overloads, the interesting one taking the `Type` class as a parameter, which is checked against all the supported types (as well as making sure that it's not an array).

Note that object is treated as a supported type. For Excel Services UDFs, extra code will be generated for translating the really supported object array parameter into a regular object parameter.

The `Generate()` method is what users of the library will finally use when everything has been set up. It returns a `GeneratedResult` instance, which can then be used for getting back a binary assembly or textual source code.

```
public GeneratedResult Generate()
{
    // Create the result set.
    GeneratedResult result = new GeneratedResult(this);
    result.Import(CreateImporter(Description));

    // Now generate the appropriate extra classes.
    result.GenerateWrapperClasses();
    return result;
}
```

GeneratedResult Class

Calls to the `UdfDefinition.Generate()` method return an instance of the `GeneratedResult` class. When returned, this class already contains the code DOM tree that represents the UDFs the developer is interested in.

`GeneratedResult` is also used for discovering what methods are exposed by a given Web Service. The class contains an internal constructor so that it can only be created by the `UdfDefinition` class. `Proxy-FieldName` contains the member name that will be used in the UDF classes to hold a reference to the Web Service proxy (that's the code that was originally generated by the `ServiceDescriptionImporter`). The declaration of the proxy is stored inside the `m_proxyType` field.

```
using System;
using System.Collections.Generic;
using System.Text;
using System.CodeDom;
using System.Web.Services.Description;
using System.Web.Services.Protocols;
using System.IO;
using System.CodeDom.Compiler;

using Microsoft.Office.Excel.Server.Udf;

using Pes.WebServiceUdf.Library.Helpers;

namespace Pes.WebServiceUdf.Library
{
    public class GeneratedResult
    {
        internal const string ProxyFieldName = "m_proxy";

        private CodeCompileUnit m_compileUnit;
        private CodeTypeDeclaration m_proxyType;
        private UdfDefinition m_udfDefinition;
        private CompilerParameters m_compilerParameters =
            new CompilerParameters();
```

```
                internal GeneratedResult()
                {


                }
                internal CodeNamespace Namespace
                {
                     get
                     {
                          return CompileUnit.Namespaces[0];
                     }
                }

   // ...
   }
```

CodeCompileUnit is a container for the namespace that contains all the classes that are generated by the project. CompilerParameters will be used for collecting the assembly references needed by the UDF (see the GenerateWrapperClasses() method for more information).

Since there's only one namespace in the generated code, the Namespace property can just return the first one available inside the CodeCompileUnit.

As described in the UdfDefinition.Generate() method, the first step when instantiating the GeneratedResult class is to call the Import() method, as shown in the following code.

```
   internal void Import(ServiceDescriptionImporter importer)
   {
        CodeNamespace ns = new CodeNamespace(UdfDefinition.NamespaceName);
        CodeCompileUnit cu = new CodeCompileUnit();

        cu.Namespaces.Add(ns);

        // Import the proxy into the namespace.
        ServiceDescriptionImportWarnings warnings = importer.Import(ns, cu);

        // Build method table out of code dom.
        m_compileUnit = cu;
   }
```

The method prepares the CodeCompileUnit instance and adds a namespace to it. It then uses the ServiceDescriptionImporter.Import() method to generate a proxy for the Web Service.

The next method to be called is GenerateWrapperClasses():

```
   internal void GenerateWrapperClasses()
   {
        CompilerParameters.ReferencedAssemblies.Add("System.Web.Services.dll");
        CompilerParameters.ReferencedAssemblies.Add("System.dll");

        ModifyProxyClass();

        if ((UdfDefinition.SupportedProducts & SupportedProducts.ExcelServices) ==
```

```
                    SupportedProducts.ExcelServices)
        {
            ProcessHelper(new Helpers.ExcelServicesHelper());
        }

        if ((UdfDefinition.SupportedProducts & SupportedProducts.Excel) ==
            SupportedProducts.Excel)
        {
            ProcessHelper(new Helpers.ExcelHelper());
        }
    }
```

The first stage for generating the wrappers is to add the default references to the `CompilerParameter` property (`System.dll` is needed by practically any .NET program, and `System.Web.Services.dll` is needed because the imported code uses classes from that assembly).

The call to `ModifyProxyClass()` adds some lines of code to the proxy to make sure that it runs under the correct credentials.

The last part of the method checks what supported products are required and uses the `ProcessHelper()` method to generate them.

The hierarchy for the helper classes contains three classes that will be discussed shortly. In essence, the helper classes know how to generate a wrapper. For each product (Excel or Excel Services), there's a helper class that knows how to add code elements to the code DOM so that it has the code needed for implementing the UDF. The two helper classes both inherit from the `Helper` class, and they reside inside the `Pes.WebServiceUdf.Library.Helpers` namespace.

The `ModifyProxyClass` method adds a line of code to the constructor of the generated proxy:

```
private void ModifyProxyClass()
{
    CodeTypeDeclaration proxy = ProxyType;
    foreach (CodeTypeMember m in proxy.Members)
    {
        if (m is CodeConstructor)
        {
            // Add the credentials code to the ctor.
            CodeStatement s = new CodeAssignStatement(
                new CodeFieldReferenceExpression(
                    new CodeThisReferenceExpression(), "Credentials"),
                new CodeFieldReferenceExpression(
                    new CodeTypeReferenceExpression(
                        new CodeTypeReference(
                        typeof(System.Net.CredentialCache))),
                        "DefaultCredentials"));
            CodeConstructor ctor = (CodeConstructor)m;
            ctor.Statements.Add(s);
            break;
        }
    }
}
```

The code finds the constructor of the proxy class and adds the following line to it:

```
// Generated code added to the proxy constructor
this.Credentials = System.Net.CredentialCache.DefaultCredentials;
```

The `CodeStatement` variable s holds the entire generated statement. Since that statement is an assignment statement, the `CodeAssignStatement` class is used.

The constructor overload takes two parameters—the left and right parts of the assignment. The left side is the `this.Credentials` portion of the expression; the left is the `DefaultCredentials` property.

To create the `this.Credentials` code fragment, a `CodeFieldReferenceExpression` instance is instantiated and passed the `CodeThisReferenceExpression` (which corresponds to `this` reference in C# or `Self` in VB.NET) and the string "Credentials", which is the name of the property.

The right side of the assignment statement also uses a `CodeFieldReferenceExpression` code element instantiated with a `CodeTypeRefernece` that's passed the `System.Net.CredentialCache` type (which will generate code corresponding to that type) and the string "DefaultCredentials", which will create a call to that static property.

Finally, the statement is added to the constructor.

As you can see, explaining code DOM code is quite a verbose endeavor. To avoid that, the generated code will always be shown with the code that's generating it and only with a short explanation as to what it's supposed to do.

The `ProcessHelper()` method calls into the supplied `Helper` class, letting it modify the code DOM as it needs:

```
private void ProcessHelper(Helper helper)
{
    helper.Result = this;
    helper.GenerateWrapper();
}
```

Once the developer gets back a `GeneratedResult` instance, it can use it to retrieve a binary assembly or source code. The two overloads of the `GenerateAssembly()` method produce a binary assembly that can be used in Excel or Excel Services without compilation:

```
public void GetAssembly(string fileName)
{
    CompilerParameters.OutputAssembly = fileName;
    CompilerParameters.GenerateInMemory = false;

    CodeDomProvider provider = CodeDomProvider.CreateProvider("CSharp");

    CompilerResults compilerResults =
        provider.CompileAssemblyFromDom(CompilerParameters, CompileUnit);

    if (compilerResults.Errors.HasErrors)
    {
        throw new CompilationErrorException(compilerResults);
```

```
    }

}

public byte[] GetAssembly()
{
    byte[] result = null;

    string fileName = Path.GetTempFileName();
    GetAssembly(fileName);
    try
    {
        using (FileStream stream = File.OpenRead(fileName))
        {
            byte[] buffer = new byte[stream.Length];
            stream.Read(buffer, 0, buffer.Length);
            result = buffer;
        }
    }
    finally
    {
        try
        {
            File.Delete(fileName);
        }
        catch
        {
        }
    }

    return result;
}
```

The first overload creates a physical file on disk. To do that, it first creates a C# `CodeDomProvider` (it could have done the same thing with a VB.NET provider). The `CodeDomProvider` is then used to produce an assembly on disk (by calling the `CodeDomProvider.CompileAssemblyFromDom` method). Once the call returns, the code checks for any compilation errors that occurred and reports them to the caller by throwing a `CompilationErrorException` exception.

In .NET, compilation units cannot be compiled to produce binaries. Instead, they first need to be represented by a .NET language (C# in this case) and only then compiled into an assembly.

The second overload returns a byte array of the binary that was generated. The code uses the `GetAssembly()` overload that writes a file to generate a temporary file on disk. It then reads the file and returns the buffer to the caller.

On top of generating binary assemblies, the library also knows how to generate source code in any of the languages supported by .NET:

```
public string GetSourceCode(string codeProvider)
{
    string result = "";
    MemoryStream s = new MemoryStream();
```

```
        StreamWriter w = new StreamWriter(s);
        CodeDomProvider provider = CodeDomProvider.CreateProvider(codeProvider);

        provider.GenerateCodeFromCompileUnit(CompileUnit, w, new
CodeGeneratorOptions());
        w.Flush();
        s.Seek(0, SeekOrigin.Begin);
        StreamReader r = new StreamReader(s);
        result = r.ReadToEnd();
        return result;
    }

    public string GetCSharpSourceCode()
    {
        return GetSourceCode("csharp");
    }

    public string GetVBCode()
    {
        return GetSourceCode("vb");
    }
```

The `GetSourceCode()` method takes a code provider name and creates an instance of it. It then uses the `GenerateCodeFromCompileUnit()` method to write the source code into the pre-prepared memory stream, which is then converted into a string and returned to the caller.

The `GetCSharpSourceCode()` and `GetVBCode()` methods are shortcuts to the `GetSourceCode()` methods.

Helper Class

The `Helper` class, shown in the following code, is an abstract class that gives some base functionality shared by both the Excel Services UDF generator and the Excel UDF generator.

It is responsible for the following:

- ❑ Generate a skeleton for the class that will be the UDF class.
- ❑ Create a field that will point to the proxy and create a constructor that will instantiate the proxy.
- ❑ For each method that is included in the UDF, it generates a skeleton method in the UDF class that calls into the proxy field and passes the parameters through.

```
using System;
using System.Collections.Generic;
using System.Text;
using System.CodeDom;

namespace Pes.WebServiceUdf.Library.Helpers
{
    internal abstract class Helper
    {
        private GeneratedResult m_result;
        private CodeTypeDeclaration m_wrapperType;
```

```
            private CodeConstructor m_ctor;
            // ...
        }
    }
```

The m_result field points back to the GeneratedResult instance that is executing the helper. The m_wrapperType field will contain the CodeTypeDecleration instance of the wrapper class. m_ctor will contain the code element representing the constructor of the class.

As seen previously, when the GeneratedResult.ProcessHelper() method is called, it initializes and then calls the GenerateWrapper() method on the helper class:

```
internal virtual void GenerateWrapper()
{
    WrapperType =
        new CodeTypeDeclaration(
            WrapperPrefix + Result.ProxyType.Name);

    WrapperType.Attributes = MemberAttributes.Public | MemberAttributes.Final;

    AddProxyUseCode();

    foreach (WebServiceMethod exposedMethod in
        Result.UdfDefinition.MethodCollection)
    {
        if (exposedMethod.Included)
        {
            CodeMemberMethod method =
                CreateProxyCallingMethod(exposedMethod);

            WrapperType.Members.Add(method);
        }
    }

    ModifyCompilerParameters();
    Result.Namespace.Types.Add(WrapperType);
}
```

This method creates the CodeTypeDeclaration instance that will represent the class. The name of the class is determined by whatever the abstract WrapperPrefix property returns combined with the name of the proxy. The class is then made public and the code that instantiates and uses the proxy is added by calling AddProxyUseCode(). The methods specified in UdfDefinition are then iterated and for each one that's included, a skeleton is created by calling the virtual method CreateProxyCallingMethod(). Finally, the helper class gives its derived classes a chance to modify the compiler parameters and the newly created class is added to the namespace via a call to the Result.Namespace.Types.Add() method.

The code generated from this method (without the inner methods that it calls) will look like this:

```
// Generated code
public class ExcelServices_TemperatureConvertService
{
}
```

(In this case, the `WrapperPrefix` property returns `ExcelServices_`, and the name of the proxy class is `TemperatureConvertService`).

`AddProxyUseCode()`, as described, adds a field and an instantiation of that field in a constructor:

```
protected virtual void AddProxyUseCode()
{
    // Add the field.
    CodeMemberField proxyField = new CodeMemberField(
        new CodeTypeReference(Result.ProxyType.Name),
GeneratedResult.ProxyFieldName);

    WrapperType.Members.Add(proxyField);

    // Add the constructor.
    Ctor = new CodeConstructor();
    CodeStatement s = new CodeAssignStatement(
        new CodeFieldReferenceExpression(
            new CodeThisReferenceExpression(),
            GeneratedResult.ProxyFieldName),
        new CodeObjectCreateExpression(
        Result.ProxyType.Name));
    Ctor.Attributes = MemberAttributes.Public;
    Ctor.Statements.Add(s);
    WrapperType.Members.Add(Ctor);
}
```

The code generated from this will look like this:

```
private TemperatureConvertService m_proxy;

public ExcelServices_TemperatureConvertService() {
    this.m_proxy = new TemperatureConvertService();
}
```

Next in the `GenerateWrapper()` method comes the iteration that creates the methods by using the `CreateProxyCallingMethod()` method, which is too verbose for presenting in a book. The signature, though, is important (because it's going to be overriden in the derived classes):

```
protected virtual CodeMemberMethod CreateProxyCallingMethod(
    WebServiceMethod exposedMethod)
{
    // ...
}
```

These are the steps the method goes through:

1. It first creates a new instance of `CodeMemberMethod` and sets its return value to be the same as the one of the proxy method it calls into.

2. Then, it goes through the parameters of the proxy method and replicates them, creating the same parameters (name and type) and adds them to the method's `Parameters` collection.

3. Last, it creates a `CodeMethodReturnStatement` returning a `CodeMethodInvokeExpression` that calls into the `m_proxy` field with the appropriate parameters.

A skeleton method created by this call looks like this:

```
// Generated code
public virtual float CelsiusTOFahrenheit(float temp)
{
    return this.m_proxy.CelsiusTOFahrenheit(temp);
}
```

ExcelServicesHelper Class

The `ExcelServicesHelper` class inherits from the `Helper` class and adds the functionality needed for an Excel Services UDF:

```
using System;
using System.Collections.Generic;
using System.Text;
using System.CodeDom;
using System.Reflection;

using Microsoft.Office.Excel.Server.Udf;

namespace Pes.WebServiceUdf.Library.Helpers
{
    class ExcelServicesHelper : Helper
    {
        private const string UdfAssemblyName =
            "Microsoft.Office.Excel.Server.Udf,
Version=12.0.0.0,Culture=neutral, PublicKeyToken=71e9bce111e9429c";

        protected override string WrapperPrefix
        {
            get { return "ExcelServices_"; }
        }
        // ...
    }
}
```

The constant `UdfAssemblyName` contains the strong name of the UDF assembly. It will be needed later when the code will need to add the `UdfClass` and `UdfMethod` attributes to the generated code.

The `WrapperPrefix` property will be used as shown previously to generate the name of the class containing the UDF.

The `GenerateWrapper()` method is also overridden in this class:

```
internal override void GenerateWrapper()
{
    base.GenerateWrapper();
    WrapperType.CustomAttributes.Add(
        new CodeAttributeDeclaration(
            new CodeTypeReference(
                typeof(UdfClassAttribute))));
}
```

The method first calls the `Helper.GenerateWrapper()` method and then modifies the generated type (which is accessed via the `WrapperType` property), adding the `UdfClass` attribute to it.

```
// Generated code
[Microsoft.Office.Excel.Server.Udf.UdfClassAttribute()]
public class ExcelServices_TemperatureConvertService
{
    //...
}
```

A second method that is overridden is `CreateProxyCallingMethod()`. As described before, it is called for each method that is included in the UDF, creating a skeleton method calling the appropriate proxy method:

```
protected override CodeMemberMethod CreateProxyCallingMethod(
    WebServiceMethod exposedMethod)
{
    CodeMemberMethod method =
        base.CreateProxyCallingMethod(exposedMethod);

    method.CustomAttributes.Add(
        new CodeAttributeDeclaration(
            new CodeTypeReference(typeof(UdfMethodAttribute))));

    ModifyParameters(method);
    return method;
}
```

After calling the `CreateProxyCallingMethod()` on the base class, the result is further modified to add the `UdfMethod` attribute to it, as shown in the following code, making sure that it is recognized by Excel Services as a valid UDF.

```
// Generated code
[Microsoft.Office.Excel.Server.Udf.UdfMethodAttribute()]
public virtual float CelsiusTOFahrenheit(float temp)
{
    return this.m_proxy.CelsiusTOFahrenheit(temp);
}
```

The last stage calls `ModifyParameters()` to check if any of the parameters of the method need some special processing:

```
private void ModifyParameters(CodeMemberMethod method)
{
    // The statement in the method is the one calling the proxy.
    CodeMethodReturnStatement returnStatement =
        (CodeMethodReturnStatement)
            method.Statements[method.Statements.Count - 1];

    // Get the method call that is returned.
    CodeMethodInvokeExpression invocation =
        (CodeMethodInvokeExpression)returnStatement.Expression;

    for (int i = 0; i < method.Parameters.Count; i++)
    {
        CodeParameterDeclarationExpression param =
            method.Parameters[i];
        CodeStatement statement =
            ModifyParameter(i, param, invocation);
        if (statement != null)
        {
            method.Statements.Insert(0, statement);
        }
    }
}
```

This method finds the return statement in the method call (the last statement) and grabs the expression returned (the proxy called) from it. This will be needed if any of the parameters need to be modified.

Next, the method iterates over the parameters of the generated method, calling `ModifyParameter()` on each of them. In some cases (shown in the following code), `ModifyParameter()` may return a statement that needs to be added to the method—in those cases, the method calls the `method.Statements.Insert()` method to add them at the beginning of the generated method.

```
private CodeStatement ModifyParameter(
    int index,
    CodeParameterDeclarationExpression param,
    CodeMethodInvokeExpression invocation)
{
    CodeStatement statement = null;
    if (param.Type.BaseType == typeof(object).FullName)
    {
        string variable = "_" + param.Name;
        param.Type = new CodeTypeReference(typeof(object[]));
        CodeArrayCreateExpression arrayCreation =
            new CodeArrayCreateExpression(
                typeof(object[]),
                1);
        arrayCreation.Initializers.Add(
            new CodeArgumentReferenceExpression(param.Name));

        statement = new CodeVariableDeclarationStatement(
                new CodeTypeReference(typeof(object[])),
                variable,
                arrayCreation);
```

```
                invocation.Parameters[index] =
                        new CodeVariableReferenceExpression(variable);
        }
        return statement;
    }
```

`ModifyParameter()` inspects the `CodeParameterDeclarationExpression` with which it is supplied to see if it is of type `Object`. Because object types are not directly supported by UDFs (only object arrays are), this needs to be rectified by changing the type to one Excel Services will recognize. In this case, if the parameters type is object, the code will generate a local variable that will contain an object array containing the original object. On top of that, the return statement will be modified to take the local variable instead of just passing the original parameter through:

```
// Generated code
[Microsoft.Office.Excel.Server.Udf.UdfMethodAttribute()]
public double GetStockQuote(object symbol) {
    object[] _symbol = new object[] {
            symbol};
    return this.m_proxy.HelloWorld(_symbol);
}
```

Finally, the `ExcelServicesHelper` class also overrides the `ModifyCompilerParameters()` method and adds the `Microsoft.Office.Excel.Server.Udf.dll` assembly as a reference to the assembly:

```
protected override void ModifyCompilerParameters()
{
    base.ModifyCompilerParameters();

    // Find the location of the UDF assembly.
    string location = typeof(UdfClassAttribute).Assembly.Location;
    Result.CompilerParameters.ReferencedAssemblies.Add(location);
}
```

The first stage is to locate the assembly on disk—to do that, the library finds the currently loaded assembly by using the `UdfClassAttribute` type. It then adds that to the `ReferencedAssemblies` collection that the `CompilerParameters` class exposes.

ExcelHelper Class

On top of creating Excel Services UDFs out of Web Services, the library also knows how to generate Excel UDFs. Generating those UDFs is done by the `ExcelHelper` class, which, much like the `ExcelServicesHelper` class just discussed, goes through the list of methods and creates an appropriate wrapper class with the appropriate methods in it.

These are some of the things `ExcelHelper` does:

❑ It adds attributes to the class, making it visible for interop with COM, and it automatically creates a guest user ID (GUID) and a `ProgId` for it.

❑ For each method that takes object as a parameter, code is added to check if the type is a COM object and then invoke the default property to get to the actual value inside it. It then uses the same mechanism of replacing the parameters in the return statement with the returned result.

❑   A COM registration method will be added so that when the assembly is registered, the Programmable key will automatically be added to the registry.

The generated C# UDF for Excel will look like this:

```
[ComVisibleAttribute(true)]
[GuidAttribute("8ffea70c-02a4-4526-987b-2eec4ccf9f9d")]
[ProgIdAttribute("WebServicesWrapper.Excel_TemperatureConvertService")]
[ClassInterfaceAttribute(ClassInterfaceType.AutoDual)]
public class Excel_TemperatureConvertService
{
    private TemperatureConvertService m_proxy;

    public Excel_TemperatureConvertService()
    {
        this.m_proxy = new TemperatureConvertService();
    }

    public float CelsiusTOFahrenheit(float temp)
    {
        return this.m_proxy.CelsiusTOFahrenheit(temp);
    }

    [System.Runtime.InteropServices.ComRegisterFunctionAttribute()]
    public static void @__RegisterComServer(System.Type type)
    {
        if ((typeof(Excel_TemperatureConvertService) != type))
        {
            return;
        }
        Microsoft.Win32.RegistryKey key =
            Microsoft.Win32.Registry.ClassesRoot.CreateSubKey(
            "CLSID\\{8ffea70c-02a4-4526-987b-2eec4ccf9f9d}\\Programmable");
        key.Close();
    }

    private object @__TranslateObjectToValue2(object o)
    {
        try {
            if (o.GetType().IsCOMObject) {
                o = o.GetType().InvokeMember(
                    "",
                    System.Reflection.BindingFlags.Public
                    | System.Reflection.BindingFlags.Instance
                    | System.Reflection.BindingFlags.GetProperty,
                    null,
                    o,
                    null);
            }
        }
        catch (System.Exception ) {
```

```
        }
        return o;
    }
}
```

In VB.NET the generated code will look like this:

```
<.ComVisibleAttribute(True), _
  GuidAttribute("ae252819-f209-434e-b7b7-05e1e448c2c9"), _
  ProgIdAttribute("WebServicesWrapper.Excel_TemperatureConvertService"), _
  ClassInterfaceAttribute(ClassInterfaceType.AutoDual)> _
Public Class Excel_TemperatureConvertService

    Private m_proxy As TemperatureConvertService

    Public Sub New()
        MyBase.New()
        Me.m_proxy = New TemperatureConvertService
    End Sub

    Public Function CelsiusTOFahrenheit(ByVal temp As Single) As Single
        Return Me.m_proxy.CelsiusTOFahrenheit(temp)
    End Function


    <System.Runtime.InteropServices.ComRegisterFunctionAttribute()> _
    Public Shared Sub __RegisterComServer(ByVal type As System.Type)
        If (GetType(Excel_TemperatureConvertService) <> type) Then
            Return
        End If
        Dim key As Microsoft.Win32.RegistryKey = _
            Microsoft.Win32.Registry.ClassesRoot.CreateSubKey _
            ("CLSID\{ae252819-f209-434e-b7b7-05e1e448c2c9}\Programmable")
        key.Close()
    End Sub

    Private Function __TranslateObjectToValue2(ByVal o As Object) As Object
        Try
            If o.GetType.IsCOMObject Then
                o = o.GetType.InvokeMember( _
                "", _
                BindingFlags.[Public] Or BindingFlags.Instance _
                Or BindingFlags.GetProperty, _
                Nothing, _
                o, _
                Nothing)
            End If
        Catch __exception As System.Exception
        End Try
        Return o
    End Function
End Class
```

UI Component

On the web site there is also a WinForms application that gives access to the library. This section shows how to use the application and concentrates specifically on the code that uses the `UdfDefinition` class to generate the assemblies/UDF source code.

The main form of the application, shown in Figure 12-1, has a text box at the top allowing users to enter the URI containing the Web Service WSDL—once entered, the user can click the "go" arrow, which will show in the list view all the methods that are exported by the Web Service.

Once all the desired methods have been selected (unsupported methods appear in gray), users can select the options they want.

In this example, an Excel Services binary (compiled assembly) UDF is requested. It is also possible to check both Excel Client and Excel Services.

> When selecting both client and server UDFs, the deployment of the assembly becomes slightly more complex. Because an Excel Services UDF needs the `Microsoft.Office.Excel.Server.Udf.dll` assembly, it will not work unless that assembly is present on the loading system. In most cases, that will not be the case by default because it's usually only installed with an Office Server installation.

Checking and unchecking items in the list view will change the `Included` property of the `WebService-Method` instances in the `UdfDefinition.WebServiceMethodCollection` property. Similarly, renaming a method will modify the `WebServiceMethod.Name` properties of those instances.

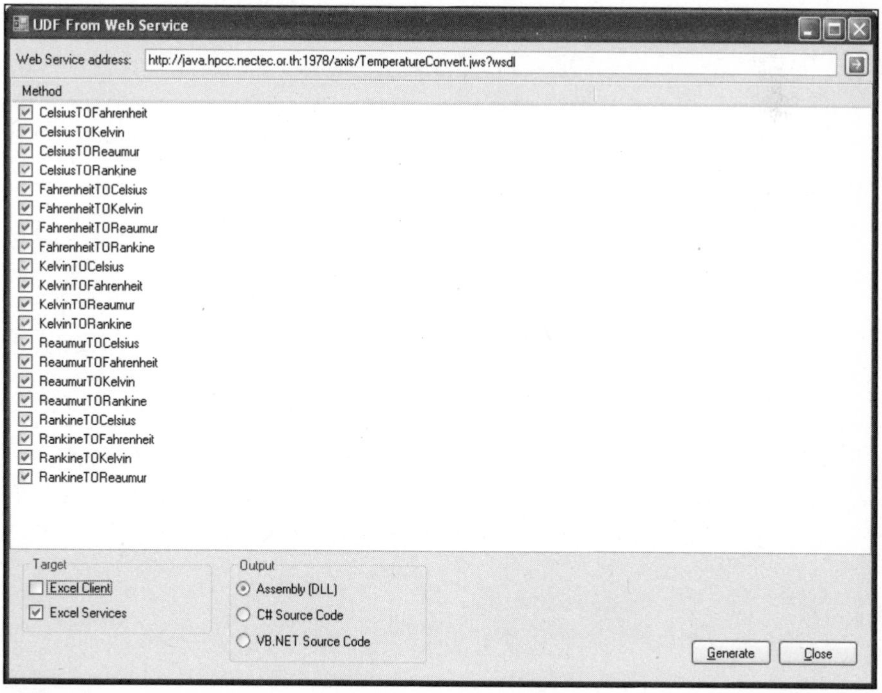

Figure 12-1

Clicking the Generate button will bring up a Save as dialog box, allowing the user to save the requested output.

```csharp
private void generateButton_Click(object sender, EventArgs e)
{
    UdfDefinition.SupportedProducts = 0;
    if (excelTargetCheckbox.Checked)
    {
        UdfDefinition.SupportedProducts |= SupportedProducts.Excel;
    }

    if (excelServicesTargetCheckbox.Checked)
    {
        UdfDefinition.SupportedProducts |= SupportedProducts.ExcelServices;
    }
    GeneratedResult generatedResult = UdfDefinition.Generate();
    string filter = "";
    if (assemblyOutputRadioButton.Checked)
    {
        filter = "Assemblies (*.dll)|*.dll";
    }
    else if (csharpOutputRadioButton.Checked)
    {
        filter = "C# files (*.cs)|*.cs";
    }
    else if (vbnetOutputRadioButton.Checked)
    {
        filter = "VB.NET files (*.vb)|*.vb";
    }
    saveFileDialog.Filter = filter;
    DialogResult result = saveFileDialog.ShowDialog(this);
    if (result != DialogResult.OK)
    {
        return;
    }
    string saveString = "";
    if (assemblyOutputRadioButton.Checked)
    {
        generatedResult.GetAssembly(saveFileDialog.FileName);
    }
    else if (csharpOutputRadioButton.Checked)
    {
        saveString = generatedResult.GetCSharpSourceCode();
    }
    else if (vbnetOutputRadioButton.Checked)
    {
        saveString = generatedResult.GetVBCode();
    }
    if (!String.IsNullOrEmpty(saveString))
    {
        using (StreamWriter writer =
            File.CreateText(saveFileDialog.FileName))
```

```
        {
            writer.Write(saveString);
        }
    }
}
```

The first phase of the method examines the `excelTargetCheckbox` and `exclServicesTarget-Checkbox` checkboxes and uses them to figure out what flags to turn on in the `UdfDefinition.SupportedProducts` enumeration (`UdfDefiniton` is a property that returns a private member. The member is initialized with a new instance of `UdfDefinition` when the user chooses a new Web Service in the text box).

The code then calls the `UdfDefinition.Generate()` method to create the `GeneratedResult` instance that will be used to produced the required output.

Once that is done, the radio buttons relating to the output type (`assemblyOutputRadioButton`, `csharpOutputRadioButton`, or `vbnetOutputRadioButton`) are inspected to determine the filter text that will be used in the Save as dialog box. After the user clicks OK in that dialog, the system again uses the radio buttons to determine which method to call to generate the appropriate output.

Summary

This solution allows administrators to very easily create wrapper UDFs for Web Services. On top of that, because it is possible to generate C# and VB.NET code, it is also very easy to use this component as a stepping stone to a more elaborate solution by adding code to the automatically generated classes.

The solution is by no means complete. Here's a list of a few features that did not make the cut for this example and may be an interesting exercise to add:

❑ **Renaming parameters** is something the current code does not let the developer do. Adding this functionality should be easy enough—one just needs to follow the way the `WebServiceMethod.Name` property is used.

❑ The current implementation only knows how to handle single-valued parameters and return values in Web Services. It may be interesting to also support Web Services that return jagged arrays so that callers can use them in **array functions**.

❑ The **DateTime type** is not supported currently. It may be useful to add support for it.

❑ There is no reason why the code could not import **multiple Web Services** into the same assembly—that could decrease the amount of assemblies deployed in an organization.

❑ The library code does minimal **error checking** on the produced code. It would be good to add support for rudimentary checks before trying to generate code. Checks such as duplicate method names and potential parameter name collisions should be easy to add.

13

Custom Web Services

Excel Services provides a good set of APIs to modify and manage workbooks. When using these APIs, though, the developer ends up working with Excel primitives. Namely, workbooks, sheets, cells, and named ranges. While this is not overly complex, it can be made even easier and more abstract.

This chapter will demonstrate how to develop a solution that will allow users (who are not software developers) with access to an Excel workbook and Excel Services to create a custom Web Service that does not require any Excel Web Services knowledge to use. On top of that, the project developed in the previous chapter will be utilized to bring everything back into Excel client, showing one way of doing Excel/Excel Services integration.

Since there is quite a bit of code in this solution, this chapter will only touch on some of the more important pieces.

Overview

As discussed in previous chapters, one of the great uses of Excel Services is to let Excel users build complex models using their favorite tool and then utilize that model in a programmatic manner in an application. The Custom Web Services solution presented in this chapter takes this a step further by allowing Excel users to generate Web Services that look nothing like Excel Web Services, but still make use of them. This makes the model much cleaner and easier to use. Developers get a set of web methods with names that make sense and parameters that make sense, which they can use with no further training. Furthermore, if at some point it is decided to move the model away from Excel Services, it is always possible to rewrite that simple set of web methods and run them in whatever fashion is needed.

The solution uses an Excel addin and a web application to create dynamic Web Services that wrap the Excel Web Services APIs and does all the appropriate calls. Calls into the custom Web Service then cause sessions to be opened against Excel Services, values to be set into workbooks, and cells to be read back and returned to the user.

To illustrate, take a simplistic auto insurance model. It takes the number of accidents a potential client has had in the past 10 years, their age, and the car price. The result of the model is the insurance premium. Using Excel Web Services, the analyst who creates the model tells the developer all the information they need to know to make this work — the name and location of the workbook, the named ranges corresponding to age, accidents, and the car price. The analyst also tells the developer what cell to get the final monthly payment from. Once the developer has all that information, they can use Excel Web Services to easily set values into the workbook and get the payment back, integrating it into their application.

Contrast this to using custom Web Services. The analyst, inside Excel, uses an addin to define a web method called `GetCarInsurancePayment`. The ranges corresponding to the data that is needed are defined as parameters with appropriate names and the return value is also specified. The analyst then publishes the new Web Service. The WSDL link can then be sent to the developer who can import the service and immediately utilize the easily understandable method. When the model needs to be updated, all the analyst needs to do is to resave the file with the new model and the Web Service will immediately be updated

Usage Example

This example will use the insurance model described above. Figure 13.1 shows what the model looks like.

As always, the model is kept very simple so that it does not interfere with the rest of the explanation.

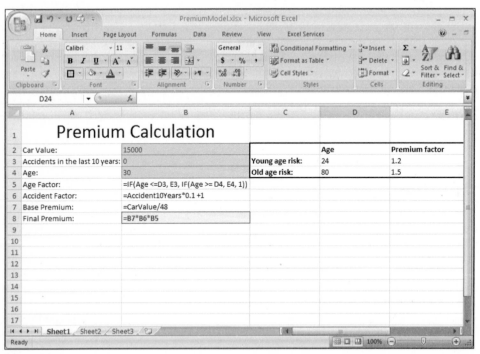

Figure 13-1

The model takes the car's value, the number of accidents, and the driver's age. It then calculates how the age affects the premium (from the table on the right side of the model) and how the accidents affect the premium. Finally, it calculates the base premium (which is based on the car's price) and multiplies it by the other factors.

If this model was given to a developer, the model designer would have had to explain that there are three cells that need to be modified and that the result comes from a fourth cell.

With the Custom Web Services solution, the workbook designer (or anybody else who wants to make the model easily available) uses the ribbon to switch to the Excel Services tab and activate the workbook functions pane, as shown in Figure 13.2.

Once the task pane is open, the user needs to click the Create button. Doing this will add the needed information into the workbook so that it can support the Web Service methods.

The metadata about the available web methods is embedded within the workbook. This guarantees that even if the workbook is copied around, that information will always be available for its users.

When Create is clicked, the user is presented with editable information about the Web Service that will be published out of the workbook, as shown in Figure 13.3.

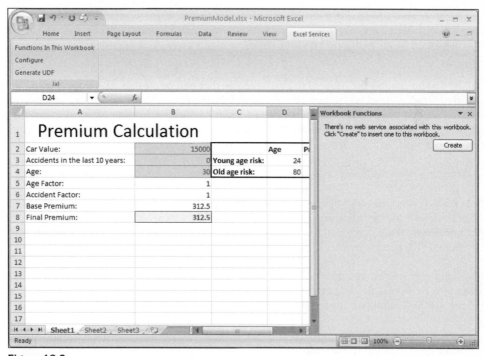

Figure 13-2

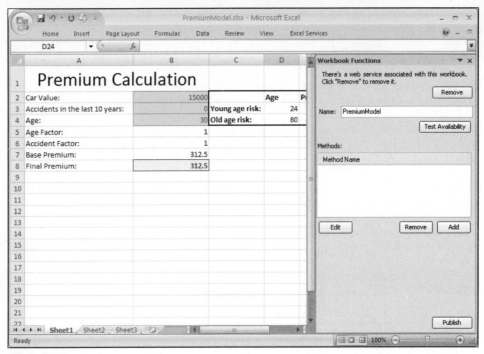

Figure 13-3

The first text box shows the name of the Web Service that will be created. Developers using the model through this mechanism will recognize it through this name. The Test Availability button allows the user to make sure that the workbook is on the server and is responsive. In essence, what the addin does is to make an `OpenWorkbook` and `CloseWorkbook` call on the currently opened file to see if it's on the server and is accessible.

If the file is saved locally or to a location that is not trusted by Excel Services, this call will fail.

There are two ways to work with the task pane. The first is to manually add methods by using the Add button under the Methods list. The user can then control exactly what the name of the method is and what parameters it has. On top of that, the user can add a description to the method which will be visible with most WSDL parsing tools.

The second way is to let the addin automatically deduce the name of the method and the names of the parameters. To do this, the user can multi-select the cells that are to participate (by Ctrl-clicking the cells). Clicking Add will automatically build a method according to the following rules:

❏ If the cell contains a formula, it will be used as the return value of the web method (i.e., it will be the value that will be returned to the caller from the web method).

❏ Cells that do not contain formulas will be used as parameters.

❏   If a cell corresponds to a parameter, the parameter will be named after an Excel named range that corresponds to that single cell (if such a named range exists).

❏   If a cell corresponds to the return value, the method will be named after the Excel named range that corresponds to that single cell, prepended by the string "Get".

In this case, if the user Ctrl-clicks cells B2, B3, B4, and B8 and then clicks the Add button, the web method shown in Figure 13.4 is created.

After clicking "Add" the task pane shows the web method it has deduced. In this example, the name of the method came out as GetFinalPremium automatically (since the only cell with a formula from the selected cells was the one called FinalPremium). The addin was also able to recognize the three parameters, and it named them according to the named ranges they correspond to (CarValue, Accident10Years, and Age).

By selecting the newly created method and clicking Edit, the user sees that the model designer also added a description to the FinalPremium named range — that description was copied over to the metadata of the Web Service method. Notice how the Return value field contains the name of the cell that corresponds to the final premium count (FinalPremium). Changing this to any other Excel reference (Sheet1!A1 for example) will change the whole model to return a different value. Users have the choice of clicking inside the Excel sheet to choose the cell they want as the return value.

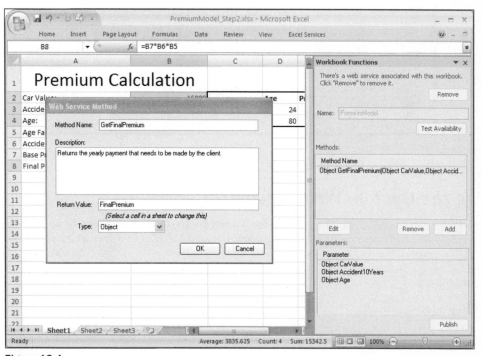

Figure 13-4

Similarly, editing the definition of a parameter will show the cell to which that parameter corresponds. In the above example, editing the `CarValue` parameter shows the user the cell that will be set to the value passed in.

Clicking the Publish button will send the definition of the Web Service to the server and make it available there for consumption as a custom Web Service, as shown in Figure 13.5.

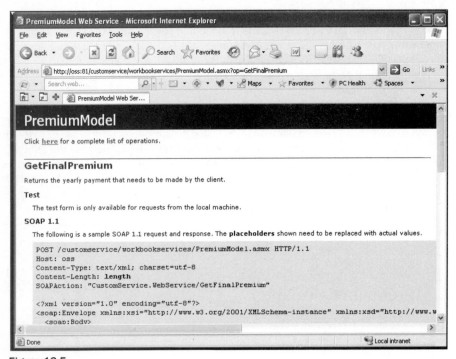

Figure 13-5

Using the Custom Web Service

This Web Service is now usable by any tool that knows how to call Web Services. As an example, the following console application will calculate the premium for a 23-year-old driver who had 2 accidents in the past 10 years and whose car cost $6000:

```
class Program
{
    static void Main(string[] args)
    {
        PremiumModel model = new PremiumModel();
        model.Credentials =
            System.Net.CredentialCache.DefaultCredentials;

        double payment =
            (double)model.GetFinalPremium(6000, 2, 23);
```

```
            System.Console.WriteLine("Premium cost is {0}", payment);
    }
}
```

The call for checking the premium is a single line of code. Consider the amount of code (and worse, knowledge) that is required from developers who were to use the workbook directly.

The code also looks much more readable — the method calls are "typed," there is less of a chance of missing important parameters or of misunderstanding what the model does.

This is what happens behind the scenes when `GetFinalPremium()` is called:

1. The Custom Service server receives the request with the three parameter values.

2. The Custom Service server then opens the appropriate workbook using Excel Web Services (in this case `PremiumModel.xlsx` — note how the developer does not need to know this detail).

3. Once that's done, the Custom Service server makes three calls to `SetCellA1()` to set the three parameters into their correct cells.

4. Finally, the Custom Service server calls the `GetCellA1()` method to retrieve the cell that is the result of the model, returning it to the caller.

Updating the Model

If the analyst updates the model to divide the total cost of the car by 36 instead of by 48, all he or she has to do is resave the actual Excel workbook back into SharePoint with the updated model, and the software, using the Web Service, will immediately be able to take advantage of the new model.

More Type Safety

As can be seen in Figure 13-4, it is possible for the author of the Web Service to also modify the types of the parameters or return value. This gives even better type safety for callers.

Generating UDFs

Finally, the Custom Service solution also gives easy access to the library presented in the previous chapter to create Excel UDFs out of Web Services. Clicking the Generate UDF button brings up a dialog box, shown in Figure 13.6, containing the published custom Web Services.

This completes the circle of pushing calculations results from server to client. The generated UDF can now be used inside Excel as part of larger models that will now be partly calculated on Excel Services!

Topology

It is important to understand how this solution works. The diagram shown in Figure 13.7 illustrates one possible topology.

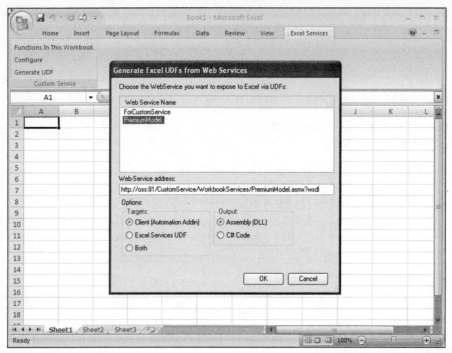

Figure 13-6

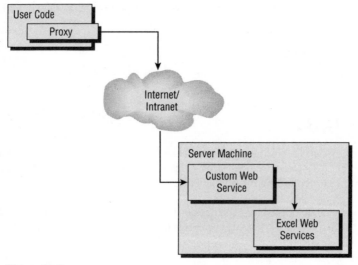

Figure 13-7

The user calls into the custom Web Service, which in turn calls into Excel Web Services. Note how both the Custom Web Service and Excel Web Services both reside on the same machine. This is necessary due to the two-hop problem. Placing the Custom Web Service and Excel Web Services on separate machines is feasible but will either require the solution to use some kind of preset credentials to access the Web Services or, alternately, enable constrained Kerberos delegation.

Coding the Solution

As was explained at the top, this book is not long enough to contain the whole implementation of this solution. Instead, choice sections of code from all three projects will be shown, describing how things work on the server and in the Excel addin.

Solution Structure

The solution is built out of three projects — a library, a web application, and an Excel addin.

Library

Namespace: `Pes.CustomWebService.Library`.

The library is a C# DLL project, which contains a set of classes that are used as the blueprint for a Web Service definition. It is used by both the web application and Excel addin.

The classes are serialized to XML and are either saved (when the addin needs to store information inside the Excel workbook) or transferred to the Web Service for publishing. This simplifies the communication between the web application and the addin, although it requires that the XML that is sent back and forth be compatible.

ExcelAddin

Namespace: `Pes.CustomWebService.ExcelAddin`.

Another C# DLL project, this one compiles to an assembly that exposes COM interfaces via .NET COM interop. The addin registers itself and starts up when Excel boots.

The addin allows the user to design a Web Service on top of a workbook. The designer is exposed as a task pane. The addin also lets the user do a few other things such as generating UDFs usable in Excel client from the custom Web Services (more on that later).

Web Application

Namespace: None.

The web application has a dual role in the solution. The first is handling requests made by users to publish Web Services or discover them. The second is as the container of the published Web Services.

Library

Defining Web Services in the solution is done by a set of classes used both by the web application and by the Excel addin. The classes are straightforward. The only additions they have on top of very simple properties for storing data is a set of events and a mechanism for recognizing when a subtree has changed. Figure 13-8 shows the structure of the classes used to define the Web Service.

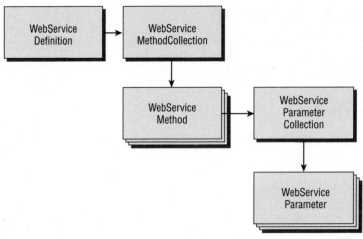

Figure 13-8

Two sample classes will be shown in this chapter — the WebServiceDefinition class, shown in the following listing, which is the top-level object for defining a Web Service, and the WebServiceParameter class, which is used to define a single parameter (or return value) in a web method. The rest of the classes follow a very similar structure.

```
public class WebServiceDefinition : DirtyClass
{
    private string m_name;
    private WebServiceMethodCollection m_methodCollection;
    private string m_workbookUrl;
    private string m_excelServiceUrl;

    public event EventHandler ExcelServiceUrlChanged;
    public event EventHandler WorkbookUrlChanged;
    public event EventHandler NameChanged;

    public WebServiceDefinition()
    {
        MethodCollection = new WebServiceMethodCollection();
    }

    private void FireNameChanged()
    {
        if (NameChanged != null)
```

```
            {
                NameChanged(this, EventArgs.Empty);
            }
        }

        public string Name
        {
            get { return m_name; }
            set
            {
                if (m_name == value)
                {
                    return;
                }
                m_name = value;
                FireNameChanged();
                SetDirty();
            }
        }
        // ...
}
```

The class stores the service URL, the workbook URL, and the name. In this snippet, the code for the Name property is shown. Note that the class is inheriting from DirtyClass — this allows for a hierarchical notification mechanism when data members change — most classes in the hierarchy inherit the same class and that allows a class that is at a lower level in the hierarchy to "dirty" the rest of the structure, notifying whoever is listening to the top-level class that a change has been made. This is important later on when the code needs to know whether or not the definition of the Web Service has been changed and needs to be saved back into disk.

The WebServiceParameter is very similar to the WebServiceDefinition class:

```
public class WebServiceParameter : DirtyClass
{
    private string m_name;
    private WebServiceParameterType m_type;
    private string m_sheetName;
    private string m_range;
    private string m_description;
    // ...
}
```

The information differs — parameters have a name, type, the sheet name from which the parameter comes and the range (either a name or an Excel A1 type reference). There's also a description for annotating the parameter.

Excel Addin

The Excel addin is written as a C# library that exposes COM interop for Excel to consume. The project itself contains a lot of UI and as such has quite a bit of code in it.

The Connect Class

The entry point that allows Excel to actually load the addin is the `Connect` object that implements the needed interfaces:

```
[ComVisible(true)]
[GuidAttribute("BA3EC2A2-96FA-4561-8B4B-4AA8AF81942A"),
ProgId(Constants.ConnectProgId)]
public class Connect :
IDTExtensibility2,
Core.ICustomTaskPaneConsumer,
Core.IRibbonExtensibility
{
    // ...
}
```

The addin supports `IDTExtensibility2` so that it can get the application object of Excel. It implements `ICustomTaskPaneConsumer` so that it can add the task pane to the Excel UI. Finally, it implements the `IRibbonExtensibility` interface for tighter integration with the new Excel toolbar UI.

```
public void OnConnection(object application,
    ext_ConnectMode connectMode,
    object addInInst,
    ref System.Array custom)
{
    m_excelApp = (Excel.Application)application;

    Core.COMAddIn myComAddin = (Core.COMAddIn)addInInst;
    myComAddin.Object = this;
}

public void CTPFactoryAvailable(Core.ICTPFactory factory)
{
    m_webServiceTaskPane =
        factory.CreateCTP(
            Constants.WebServiceControlProgId,
            "Workbook Functions",
            Type.Missing);
    m_webServiceControl =
        (WebServicePaneControl)this.m_webServiceTaskPane.ContentControl;
    m_webServiceControl.Connect = this;
}

public string GetCustomUI(string RibbonID)
{
    Assembly asm = Assembly.GetExecutingAssembly();
    Stream stream = asm.GetManifestResourceStream(
        "Pes.CustomWebService.ExcelAddin.Resources.RibbonInfo.xml");
    return new StreamReader(stream).ReadToEnd();
}
```

The `OnConnection()` method takes care to store the application object as a member. That way, later, the addin will be able to call back into Excel. The `CTPFactoryAvailable` method calls into the `CreateCTP()`

method on the factory. That in turn instructs Excel to create the ActiveX control represented by the `progId` that is passed in.

> *Again, the magic of .NET takes care of all our misery. The user control represented by the `progId` gets exposed as a COM ActiveX control by the framework interop support.*

Finally, the ribbon integration method `GetCustomUI()` uses the XML resource embedded inside the assembly to return the definition of how the ribbon should look.

> *The ribbon XML namespace is* `http://schemas.microsoft.com/office/2006/01/customui`. *Excel (and most office applications) will use the information inside the XML to extend the ribbon. In this case, the code will be adding a new tab called Excel Services. Under that tab, it will add a group called Custom Service. Finally, three buttons are added for the functionality that was shown before. Within the XML, each button has a method name associated with it. That function will be sought in the* `Connect` *class and used to execute code whenever the associated ribbon button is clicked.*

```xml
<customUI xmlns="http://schemas.microsoft.com/office/2006/01/customui">
  <ribbon>
    <tabs>
      <tab id="workbookFunctions" label="Excel Services">
        <group id="customServiceGroup" label="Custom Service">
          <button id="webServicePane" label="Functions In This Workbook"
onAction="WebServicePane_Click" />
          <button id="configCustomService" label="Configure"
onAction="ConfigCustomService_Click" />
          <button id="generateCustomServiceUdf" label="Generate UDF"
onAction="GenerateUdf_Click" />
        </group>
      </tab>
    </tabs>
  </ribbon>
</customUI>
```

The task pane containing the Web Service is shown when the webServicePane button is clicked:

```csharp
public void WebServicePane_Click(Core.IRibbonControl control)
{
    WebServiceTaskPane.Visible = !WebServiceTaskPane.Visible;
    if (WebServiceTaskPane.Visible)
    {
        if (m_firstShow)
        {
            m_firstShow = false;
            if (!Config.ConfigurationExists)
            {
                ConfigForm.ShowModalDialog(GetExcelHwnd());
            }
        }
        WebServiceControl.AttachToWorkbook(ExcelApp.ActiveWorkbook);
    }
}
```

When the user asks for the task pane, the addin checks to see if it is properly configured. If it is not, it will show the configuration dialog box.

The method then attaches to the currently opened workbook (this is the client-side workbook). Since there is a single task pane, it needs to reattach itself to the workbook whenever the active workbook changes in the UI.

Web Service Metadata

Excel 2007 introduced extensible elements in workbooks called Custom XML parts. These are customizable XML fragments that can be stored as part of a workbook for use by third-party applications. In the case of the Custom Service solution, information about the attached Web Service will be stored in there — in essence, its XML representation.

The following methods are executed when the task pane attaches to a workbook that is activated. If the workbook already contains a Web Service representation, the task pane will show the definition. If the addin does not find a definition, it will show the Create button described at the beginning of this chapter. First, the support methods (located on the `WebServicePaneControl` class) that give access to the XML parts:

```
private Core.CustomXMLPart GetWebServiceXmlPart()
{
Core.CustomXMLParts parts =
        Workbook.CustomXMLParts.
            SelectByNamespace(Constants.BaseXmlNamespace);
    if (parts == null || parts.Count == 0)
    {
        return null;
    }

    return parts[1]; // Excel is 1 based
}
private bool HasWebService
{
    get
    {
        if (Workbook == null)
        {
            return false;
        }

        Core.CustomXMLPart xmlPart = GetWebServiceXmlPart();
        return xmlPart != null;
    }
}
```

The `GetWebServiceXmlPart()` method tries to retrieve the appropriate XML from the XML part store inside the workbook. It uses the `Workbook` property of the class to call into the custom XML part collection and retrieve the appropriate part. Excel retrieves custom XML parts by using the namespace that is associated with the XML. In the case of this solution, the `Constants.BaseXmlNamespace` constant (defined inside the `Constants` class in the project) represents that. `HasWebService` is a support method that returns `true` if the workbook contains the Web Service definition XML part.

Next is the code that determines what to display on the task pane — either the Create button or the definition of the Web Service:

```
internal void AttachToWorkbook(Excel.Workbook workbook)
{
    KillDefinitionControl();

    string top = Resources.Strings.TitleNoWorkbook;
    string buttonText = "";
    bool buttonVisible = workbook != null;
    bool showPanel = false;
    bool publishVisible = false;
    m_workbook = workbook;


    if (Workbook != null)
    {
        if (HasWebService)
        {
            // Get the XML part and set it.
            top = Strings.TitleWebServiceAvailable;
            buttonText = Strings.RemoveWebServiceButton;
            showPanel = true;
            CreateDefinitionControl();
            publishVisible = true;
        }
        else
        {
            // We dont have a Web service definition in here.
            top = Strings.TitleNoWebServiceAvailable;
            buttonText = Strings.CreateWebServiceButton;
        }
    }
    topLabel.Text = top;
    createRemoveButton.Text = buttonText;
    createRemoveButton.Visible = buttonVisible;
    webServicePanel.Visible = showPanel;
    publishButton.Visible = publishVisible;
}
```

This piece of code gets called whenever the active workbook changes. The first step after clearing the state of the pane (by calling `KillDefinitionControl()`) and initializing all local variables is to check if the workbook contains a definition inside it using the support methods. If it does, the various variables are changed to reflect that in the UI. A call is also made to `CreateDefinitionControl()`, which will take the XML and use it to populate the UI.

Web Service Definition UI

The Web Service definition UI is standard UI programming in WinForms. The control creates lists according to its state. The web method list (encapsulated in the `MethodListView` control) is bound to the web method collection class (`WebServiceMethodCollection`) and listens to changes, which it uses to refresh its contents. Similarly, the `ParameterListView` control gets shown whenever a method is selected and is bound to the parameters of that list.

Users can manually add or edit methods and parameters to the Web Service. Doing so brings up the appropriate floating windows that describe the element. With this window, users can manually edit information about the element. They can also click on a cell inside the sheet to modify the referenced cell. The addin will try to figure out the best way to describe the cell. The following code attaches to the selection change event in Excel so that it knows that the user selected something. In this example, the code for parameter editing is shown:

```csharp
private void ParameterEditorForm_Load(object sender, EventArgs e)
{
    AttachEvents(true);
    Connect.WebServiceControl.Enabled = false;
}
private void AttachEvents(bool attach)
{
    if (attach)
    {
        Connect.ExcelApp.WorkbookDeactivate +=
            new Excel.AppEvents_WorkbookDeactivateEventHandler(
                ExcelApp_WorkbookDeactivate);
        Connect.ExcelApp.SheetSelectionChange +=
            new Excel.AppEvents_SheetSelectionChangeEventHandler(
                ExcelApp_SheetSelectionChange);
    }
    else
    {
        Connect.ExcelApp.WorkbookDeactivate -=
            new Excel.AppEvents_WorkbookDeactivateEventHandler(
                ExcelApp_WorkbookDeactivate);
        Connect.ExcelApp.SheetSelectionChange -=
            new Excel.AppEvents_SheetSelectionChangeEventHandler(
                ExcelApp_SheetSelectionChange);
    }
}
```

In the `ParameterEditorForm_Load` method (which is attached to the `Load` event of the form), the code calls the `AttachEvents()` helper method. The helper method is responsible for connecting to various events inside Excel. In this case, the events that are being connected to are the `WorkbookDeactivate` event (which occurs when the workbook goes out of focus) and the `SheetSelectionChange` event (which occurs when the selection on the sheet changes).

In this case, the code that will run when the workbook goes out of focus will make sure to close the window (since the task pane will no longer be showing the old workbook's attached Web Service information).

The method can also be called to detach events from Excel. It is an important step — not doing this may cause an inadvertant memory leak or potentially unexpected behavior.

When the selection changes however, the `ExcelApp_SheetSelectionChange` method is called:

```csharp
void ExcelApp_SheetSelectionChange(
    object Sh,
    Microsoft.Office.Interop.Excel.Range Target)
```

```
{
    string sheet = "";
    string range = "";
    Utils.GetRangeInfo(Target, out sheet, out range);
    rangeTextBox.Text =
        WebServiceParameter.GetRangeString(sheet, range);
}
```

The method first calls the utility method `GetRangeInfo()`, which takes a range and tries to find the best way to express it. Once that is determined, the text box that contains the range string is updated — the `GetRangeString()` method is used to transform the two parts of the range into one string.

The following method is defined inside the `Utils` static class in the project. Its job is to find the best representation for a range. For this solution, this means using the name of a named range if there is such a name that represents the cell. Otherwise, it will give the A1 representation of the cell:

```
internal static void GetRangeInfo(
    Excel.Range excelRange,
    out string sheet,
    out string range)
{
    range = "";
    sheet = "";
    Excel.Workbook workbook =
        (Excel.Workbook)excelRange.Worksheet.Parent;
    foreach (Excel.Name name in workbook.Names)
    {
        if (Utils.GetRangeString(name.RefersToRange) ==
          Utils.GetRangeString(excelRange))
        {
            range = name.Name;
            break;
        }
    }

    if (String.IsNullOrEmpty(range))
    {
        range = excelRange.get_AddressLocal(
          false,
          false,
          Excel.XlReferenceStyle.xlA1,
          System.Type.Missing,
          System.Type.Missing);
        sheet = excelRange.Worksheet.Name;
    }
}
```

The method iterates over all named ranges in the workbook. For each one, it checks if the range it represents is the one that was actually selected by the user. This is done by taking the `RefersToRange` property of the named range object and comparing it to the one that was passed into the method. The `GetRangeString()` is used to properly format the string into an Excel line reference (i.e., `Sheet1!A1`).

Automatically Adding a Method

As shown before, the addin also knows how to automatically generate a Web Service when the user selects multiple cells and clicks the Add button. The logic was explained earlier in this chapter — if a cell does not contain a formula, it is assumed that it acts as a parameter; otherwise, it is assumed that it is a return value.

Web Application

The web application portion of the solution is responsible for generating the custom Web Services that will serve the users of the solution.

There is one nondynamically generated Web Service in it called `Manager` — within it the developer can find two methods — one for creating a new Web Service and one for enumerating the available ones.

The Generated Web Service

ASP.NET makes life very easy with this project. Because it will compile and run code that is deployed to the server, all the web application needs to do is generate the appropriate ASMX file and place it in an accessible location — when that ASMX is accessed by a user, ASP.NET will compile it and execute it.

The following snippet shows the ASMX file generated in the `PremiumModel` example in this chapter:

The code has been modified to fit in the confines of the book. The generated code is much more verbose, containing fully qualified names and less line breaks.

```
<%@ WebService Language="C#" Class="CustomService.WebService.PremiumModel"%>
namespace CustomService.WebService {
    using System;

    [WebService(Namespace="CustomService.WebService")]
    [WebServiceBinding(
        ConformsTo=
            System.Web.Services.WsiProfiles.BasicProfile1_1)]
    public class PremiumModel : WorkbookInvokerWebService {

        [WebMethod(
            Description=
                "Returns the yearly payment.")]
        public virtual object GetFinalPremium(object CarValue,
            object Accident10Years,
            object Age) {
            WorkbookLocationInfo[] parameters =
                new WorkbookLocationInfo[] {
                    new WorkbookLocationInfo(
                        "",
                        "CarValue",
                        CarValue),
                    new WorkbookLocationInfo(
                        "",
                        "Accident10Years",
```

```
                     Accident10Years),
                new WorkbookLocationInfo(
                    "",
                    "Age",
                    Age)};
         object result = this.InvokeWorkbook(
             "http://oss/_Vti_bin/ExcelService.asmx",
             "http://oss/book/shared documents/PremiumModel.xlsx",
             parameters,
             new WorkbookLocationInfo("", "FinalPremium"));
         return result;
      }
   }
}
```

As opposed to Web Services classes Visual Studio generates, the ASMX files generated by the Custom Service solution does not use the code behind pattern. This simplifies the mechanism, allowing the solution to generate a single file that does all the work.

The first line in the ASMX tells ASP.NET which class will be servicing this Web Service.

The solution generates a class that inherits from the `InvokerWebService` class. This class is part of the web application and it is there to simplify the generated code. Inside the generated class, a method is generated to correspond to the single web method that the user defined using the addin. That method creates an array of `WorkbookLocationInfo` classes, which it initializes with information about each of the parameters.

Finally, the method calls into the `InvokeWorkbook()` method with the `WorkbookLocationInfo` array, the information about the location of Excel Web Services and the location of the workbook. It also passes in information about the location of the result it wants — also inside a `WorkbookLocationInfo` instance.

InvokerWebService Class

The `InvokerWebService` class is used as a helper to simplify the code that is generated. It contains a single method, which can be used to execute a set of operations against Excel Web Services:

```
public object InvokeWorkbook(
    string server,
    string workbook,
    WorkbookLocationInfo[] infos,
    WorkbookLocationInfo returnInfo)
{
ExcelServices e =
      new ExcelServices(ExcelServicesType.Soap, server);
    using (Session s = e.Open(workbook))
    {
            foreach (WorkbookLocationInfo info in infos)
            {
                s.SetCellA1(info.SheetName,
                    info.Name,
                    info.Value);
```

```
        }
        object o = s.GetCellA1(
                returnInfo.SheetName,
                returnInfo.Name,
                false);
        return o;
    }
}
```

The method creates an instance of the `ExcelServices` class described in Chapter 7 — it initializes it with the server name.

The method then opens a new session against the workbook. Each of the `WorkbookLocationInfo` instances inside the `infos` array is then used inside a loop with calls to the `SetCellA1()` method.

Finally, the method calls into `GetCellA1()` to get back the result, which is then returned to the user.

Code for Generating the Web Service

To generate the Web Service code, the solution employs code DOM (much like the UDF Web Service solution in the previous chapter). The entire code for generating the Web Service is located inside the `WebServiceGenerator.cs` file.

The following static method is called when a new Web Service is required:

```
public static void GenerateWebService(
    WebServiceDefinition def)
{
    const string WebServicePrefix =
        "<%@ WebService Language=\"C#\" Class=\"{0}.{1}\"%>";

    WebServiceGenerator g =
        new WebServiceGenerator(def);

    string fileName = Path.Combine(
        Config.DynamicServiceLocation,
        g.ClassName + ".asmx");
    if (!Directory.Exists(Config.DynamicServiceLocation))
    {
        Directory.CreateDirectory(Config.DynamicServiceLocation);
    }

    using (StreamWriter writer = File.CreateText(fileName))
    {
        writer.WriteLine(
            String.Format(
                WebServicePrefix,
                g.AssemblyNamespace,
                g.ClassName));
        g.Generate(writer);
    }
}
```

The first part of this static method creates a new instance of the `WebServiceGenerator` class. It initializes it with the Web Service definition it got.

Next, the method makes sure the directory housing the Web Services files exists. Then it creates the ASMX file inside that directory and writes the first line — the ASP.NET directive enclosed in `"<%@ %>"`.

Finally, the code goes and writes the C# code into the file by using the `Generate()` method.

The code for generating the C# code is even simpler than the one presented in the previous chapter to generate UDFs. It generates the code DOM much like that in Chapter 12 did for UDFs, but instead of generating methods that call into a Web Service, it generates a Web Service.

Enumerating Web Services

The second method on the Manager Web Service allows callers to check which Web Services are available for usage (this is used by the Generate UDF option in the addin to display a list of available services).

For this, the method iterates of the contents of the folder that contains the dynamic Web Services files and constructs a URL that can be used by the caller.

```
[WebMethod]
public PublishedWebService[] GetWebServices()
{
    List<PublishedWebService> list =
        new List<PublishedWebService>();

    string[] files = Directory.GetFiles(
        Config.DynamicServiceLocation,
        "*.asmx");
    foreach (string file in files)
    {
        PublishedWebService p = new PublishedWebService();

        p.Name = Path.GetFileNameWithoutExtension(file);
        string appPath =
            HttpContext.Current.Request.Url.GetLeftPart(
                UriPartial.Authority) +
            HttpContext.Current.Request.ApplicationPath;
        string link =
            appPath + "/" + Config.ServicesFolder + "/" +
            p.Name + ".asmx?wsdl";
        p.Url = link;
        list.Add(p);
    }

    return list.ToArray();
}
```

The `HttpContext` is used to figure out what URL the caller used to get to the Web Service (since the user had to issue a request in the Web Service to invoke the `GetWebServices()` method). From that it is possible to deduce the whole URL for each of the custom Web Services.

Summary

While this solution illustrates just how powerful the combination of custom Web Services and Excel Services can be, it is by no means complete. There are many more features that could be added to make this even better and more usable.

❑ The solution currently only knows how to handle single cells as parameters and returned values. It could be interesting to allow it to take/return arrays (multi-cell ranges).

❑ Generating UDFs from the Web Services is an all-or-nothing deal. It will generate a UDF that will contain all of the exported methods. It could be useful to allow users to pick and choose (much as the application written in the previous chapter does).

❑ In the section discussing topology, it is suggested to use this solution on the same server that houses Excel Web Services (the Web front end [WFE]). For large deployments that may have more than one WFE, this stops being feasible. The only alternative then is to enable some sort of delegation or mirror the dynamic Web Services across the farm.

❑ While generating custom Web Services has its own appeal, it is also possible to generate stand-alone assemblies that will be usable by callers who want a custom way of calling the Excel model. This has the added value of avoiding the topologies issues (since the calls will be made directly from the client machine without having to pass through another web application), however, it means more code to distribute and maintain.

❑ Currently, each web method can only return a single value (as the return value of the web method). It is possible to allow it to return multiple values (by using out parameters).

❑ The solution ignores issues such as version control and conflicting services. For large-scale deployments, developers may want to consider adding code to add these features.

14

RSS over Excel Services

The previous chapter showed how any user can create custom Web Services by employing Excel Services as the "programming engine" behind the scenes. That's a very compelling scenario that can give nondevelopers the ability to create models that are easily consumed by developers who may not have any knowledge about Excel Services.

This chapter takes the same idea and pushes it even further. Instead of creating Web Services that require the consumer to be a developer, it provides an RSS interface to workbooks published in Excel Services, allowing any user who has an RSS reader to consume information from Excel Services in a form which is not necessarily the original workbook form.

And in this day and age, what user doesn't have an RSS reader? Some high-end refrigerators even come with RSS readers built in.

Overview

RSS (Really Simple Syndication) has become a ubiquitous way of sharing information and logic. Many tools exist for consuming it, and people have grown used to seeing the little orange icon that will allow them to add more feeds to their favorite reader making it even more cluttered then before.

The idea behind the RSS over Excel Services solution is to allow people to consume information inside a workbook and aggregating it with other information streams, allowing users to see textual derivations of the workbook instead of the tabular form.

Just as with the custom Web Services, the user does not even need to know that the feed is coming from Excel Services. It can be made to look just like any other feed.

Readers will notice that the solution looks very much like the custom Web Services solution presented in Chapter 13. It also consists of a web application server that services requests and an Excel addin to facilitate authoring.

What Is RSS

RSS is a file format that is based on XML. Each RSS feed file contains some basic information describing the feed itself and a number of child nodes, each describing one "item." The textual contents of the item are completely arbitrary, which is one of the reasons RSS has been so successful and is used in so many places. RSS items may also contain other elements such as enclosures (basically, attached files) and other metadata about the item itself.

The following XML shows a very simple RSS feed:

```xml
<?xml version="1.0" encoding="utf-8"?>
<rss version="2.0">
  <channel>
    <title>Example of an RSS feed</title>
    <description>
      This feed is an example of how rss feeds look
    </description>
    <item>
      <title>Example 1</title>
      <description>
        Any text can exist here.
      </description>
      <link>http://example/example1.html</link>
      <pubDate>10/22/2006 4:15:07 PM</pubDate>
    </item>
    <item>
      <title>Example 2</title>
      <description>
        Any text can exist here too.
      </description>
      <link>http://example/example2.html</link>
      <pubDate>10/22/2006 6:15:07 PM</pubDate>
    </item>
  </channel>
</rss>
```

This feed consists of two items — "Example 1" and "Example 2."

The description element can contain encoded HTML text — most modern RSS readers know how to handle such tags and will show the user the rendered text in HTML form.

Usage Example

To show one way of using the RSS solution, this chapter will use a simple workbook containing information about a collection of books available for sale. The amount of data is kept small so that the example will remain manageable.

The workbook contains three sheets. The first sheet contains a table showing what books are available for purchase, their price, and the number sold. It also contains a pie chart that shows how the various quantities of sold books are distributed. The second sheet contains information about special pricing. The last sheet contains information that will help with the RSS feed later on.

The workbook is published with named objects in it. Figure 14-1 shows how the workbook looks when opened in the browser:

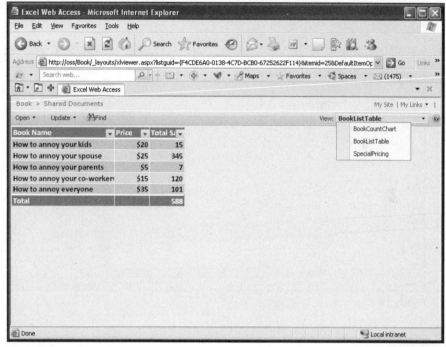

Figure 14-1

Starting a New RSS Feed

The workbook's authors want the users to also be able to consume the information in their RSS readers. To do that, the authors will use Excel to open the workbook and use the Excel RSS Server addin to show the RSS feed authoring pane. When the pane appears on a workbook that does not contain a feed definition in it; it shows a button that allows the user to create one. Figure 14-2 shows what Excel looks like after the button has been clicked:

The RSS feed pane consists of three parts:

❑ The Name text box contains the proposed name for the feed. This will be displayed for users connecting to the feed and is used to uniquely identify a feed on the server.

❑ The list on the pane contains all the feed items that can be produced from this Excel workbook. Users can add or remove items to or from the list or clear it.

❑ The bottom part shows how the feed will look when consumed — however, instead of using the server to get information, it uses the workbook as it is loaded inside Excel.

The next step is to create a new item inside the feed.

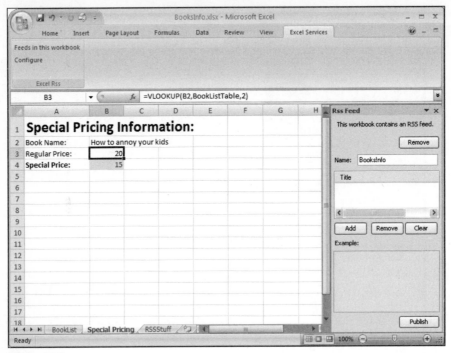

Figure 14-2

Adding an Item

Figure 14-3 shows the dialog box that comes up when the Add button is clicked. This dialog allows the user to define the RSS feed.

The dialog box that comes up allows the author to define exactly how the item will look. The various Insert buttons will add a reference to the currently selected cell to the field with which they are associated.

In this example, the title of the item is set to be:

```
Special pricing is available for "{Special Pricing!B2}"!
```

This will instruct the RSS server to place cell B2 from the "Special Pricing" sheet into the title of the feed. Similarly, the Description field contains the following string:

```
There is special pricing available for the book: "{Special Pricing!B2}". It can now
be purchased for ${Special Pricing!B4} instead of the usual ${Special Pricing!B3}.
```

In this case, three cells will be placed in the appropriate locations inside the description.

Publishing the Feed

Clicking the Publish button at the bottom of the RSS Feed pane will publish the feed to the server (see Figure 14-4).

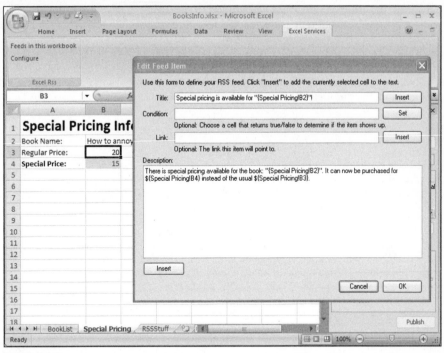

Figure 14-3

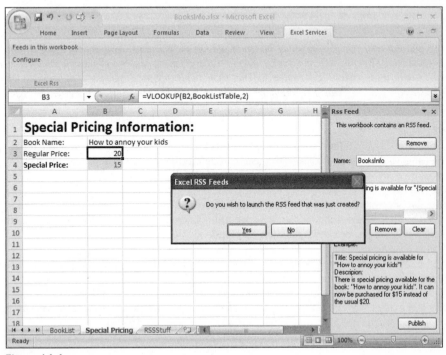

Figure 14-4

Once published, the addin gives the user the option to see what the feed looks like. If Yes is clicked, the addin will launch the link that represents the RSS feed. In this case, the link will look like this:

```
http://oss:81/ExcelRssServer/RssFeed.aspx?feed=BooksInfo
```

This link points to the server side of the solution, which knows how to serve RSS requests. When navigating to that location, the produced XML will look like this:

```
<?xml version="1.0" encoding="utf-8"?>
<rss version="2.0">
  <channel>
    <title>BooksInfo</title>
    <link>http://oss/book/shared documents/BooksInfo.xlsx</link>
    <description>Rss produced from Excel Services</description>
    <copyright />
    <item>
      <title>Special pricing is available for "How to annoy your kids"!</title>
      <description>There is special pricing available for the book: "How to annoy
your kids". It can now be purchased for $15 instead of the usual $20.</description>
      <link>http://oss/book/shared documents/BooksInfo.xlsx</link>
      <pubDate>10/22/2006 10:21:26 PM</pubDate>
    </item>
  </channel>
</rss>
```

The RSS feed contains only one item, describing the fact that there is currently special pricing on a specified book. The description goes further and explains the actual price that is given.

Figure 14-5 shows what the feed looks like when used inside an RSS reader (Outlook 2007 in this case).

Note: Diligent readers will notice that the <pubDate> in the RSS feed changes with every refresh. This is because the RSS server does not track changes — every request causes a whole new RSS feed to be created. Luckily, most modern RSS readers will not show items that are duplicates of others from the same feed. The <pubDate> element is optional — if needed, it can be removed from the generated XML.

Adding Formatting

Items in RSS feeds can contain encoded HTML. It is possible to leverage this to make the displayed feeds more pleasing to the eye. In this case, the feed can be modified to be in a larger font and green if the discount is more than 50%.

There are two steps to doing this — the first is to have Excel do all the calculation needed to both figure out if the discount is more than 50% and the second is to create the needed formatting information inside Excel cells so that it can be used inside the RSS feed.

Figure 14-6 shows the first step, which involves adding the following calculations to the RSSStuff sheet.

The RSSStuff sheet exists to remove noise from the normal sheets of the workbook, making sure that users who are not interested in the RSS feed that's inside the workbook do not need to see information that have to do with it. To make it even less intrusive, the sheet can be hidden.

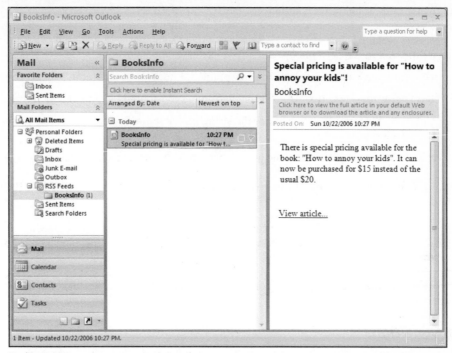

Figure 14-5

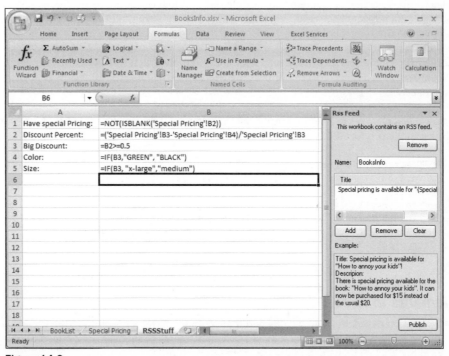

Figure 14-6

The following formulas have been added:

❑ **Have special pricing** — This checks to see if there's an item with a special price. It will be used a little later in the example.

❑ **Discount percent** — Calculates the size of the discount and used in the "Big Discount" formula.

❑ **Big Discount** — Returns "True" if the discount is considered big and "False" if not.

❑ **Color** — This formula will produce the string BLACK if the discount is not considered big and GREEN if it does.

❑ **Size** — Determines the size of the text — "medium" if not a big discount and "x-large" otherwise.

Once this information is available, it can be used inside the RSS feed item to specify HTML tags. The new item description field will now be:

```
<div style="font-size:{RSSStuff!B5};color:{RSSStuff!B4}">There is special pricing
available for the book: "{Special Pricing!B2}". It can now be purchased for
${Special Pricing!B4} instead of the usual ${Special Pricing!B3}.</div>
```

If the workbook author places a 50% or more discount in the special pricing sheet, the text will appear in large green letters.

Adding Conditions

Another interesting scenario is the availability of items in the feeds. Sometimes a feed item should not be sent to the user. The RSS publishing mechanism has the "Condition" part of each item to enforce this. This field needs to contain a reference to a single cell — if that cell contains the Boolean value of FALSE, the item will not appear in the feed. Any other value (empty, string, numeric, or TRUE) will make the feed item show up in the final feed.

Figure 14-7 shows the special pricing feed item and guarantees that it should only appear if there is indeed an item with a special price. For this, the RSS author will use cell B1 that was added to the RSSStuff sheet:

If the workbook changes to have an empty cell in the name of the product that has the discount, it would not appear in the produced RSS feed:

```
<?xml version="1.0" encoding="utf-8"?>
<rss version="2.0">
  <channel>
    <title>BooksInfo</title>
    <link>http://oss/book/shared documents/BooksInfo.xlsx</link>
    <description>Rss produced from Excel Services</description>
    <copyright />
  </channel>
</rss>
```

Link Elements in Feeds

Each RSS item has a link that can be attached to it. With the Excel RSS solution, the RSS server will automatically place a link to the workbook inside that element, allowing users of the feed to navigate directly to the workbook when they are looking for more information.

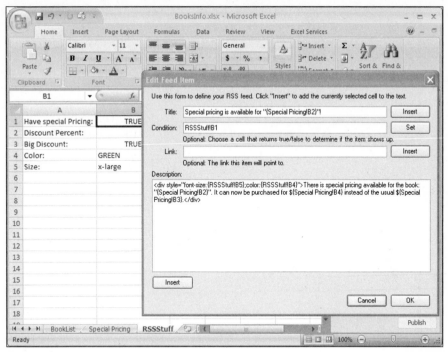

Figure 14-7

It is, however, possible to override the link to be something else decided by the author. For example, in this case the author may want the user of the feed to see the actual Excel table when clicking on the link associated with the feed. To do that, all the author needs to do is change the empty link text box to point to the desired address.

The XLViewer.aspx page, which is used to show an EWA in full screen, can take a "range" parameter in its query string that will determine the object that will be shown when it executes. In this case, the link will be:

```
http://oss/book/_layouts/xlviewer.aspx?id=http://oss/book/shared%20documents/BooksI
nfo.xlsx&DefaultItemOpen=1&Cookie=3&range=SpecialPricing
```

The id and range parameters are the important ones — they will guarantee that the desired workbook and range are displayed to the user. After clicking the link in the RSS item, the page shown in Figure 14-8 displays in the browser.

Of course, the link can point to more active parts of the workbook such as PivotTables, allowing the user to do more interactivity and understand more about the workbook.

The link does not necessarily need to point to the workbook either — it can be any link. For example:

```
http://shopping.msn.com/noresults/shp/?text={Special Pricing!B2}
```

In this case, the link will bring the user to a shopping site with the item as the search criteria.

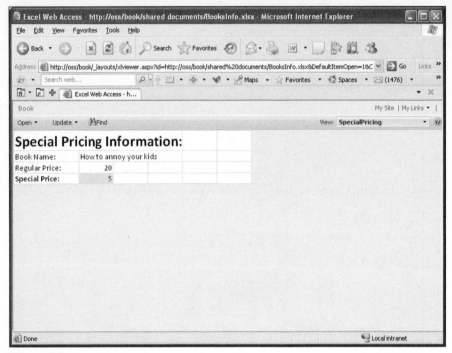

Figure 14-8

Feed of Feeds

Finally, the RSS server also knows how to publish its list of feeds, updating it as new feeds are published. To see the list, the user can register to the following RSS feed:

```
http://servername/ExcelRssServer/rssfeed.aspx
```

The result will contain a list of all the feeds that are available:

```
<?xml version="1.0" encoding="utf-8"?>
<rss version="2.0">
  <channel>
    <title>Feeds available from Excel</title>
    <description>A list of RSS feeds produced from Excel Services</description>
    <copyright>Professional Excel Services book</copyright>
    <item>
      <title>BooksInfo</title>
      <description />
      <link>http://oss:81/ExcelRssServer/RssFeed.aspx?feed=BooksInfo</link>
      <pubDate>10/22/2006 11:50:52 PM</pubDate>
    </item>
  </channel>
</rss>
```

Coding the Solution

The solution is very similar to the one described in the custom Web Services chapter.

Solution Structure

The solution is constructed out of three parts — a library, an Excel addin, and a server.

Library

Namespace: `Pes.ExcelRss.Library`.

This library contains the classes that define a feed. It also contains the mechanism that translates textual workbook locations to actual data (used by both the addin and the server).

Works similarly to the custom Web Service library.

ExcelAddin

Namespace: `Pes.ExcelRss.ExcelAddin`.

COM interop C# project that supplies the RSS authoring task pane.

Web Application

Namespace: None.

The web application supplies the service for publishing the RSS feeds and an ASPX page that returns the live feeds.

Library

The library contains the classes that represent a feed.

FeedDescription Class

This class contains information about the feed that will be needed to properly render the RSS XML:

- ❑ **Name** — This acts as the title of the feed and is also the name that uniquely identifies the feed.
- ❑ **Workbook URL** — All feed items are connected to the same workbook in a feed.
- ❑ **Excel Services URL** — The location of the Excel Services server that will be used to open the workbook (usually in the form of `http://server/_vti_bin/ExcelService.asmx`).

The class also has a collection of `FeedItem` instances.

IItemInfoProvider Interface

This interface is used by the `FeedItem` class to turn the various textual templates into actual text, replacing the Excel references inline in the text into their corresponding values:

```
public interface IItemInfoProvider
{
    string GetInfo(string range);
}
```

The `GetInfo()` method takes an Excel-style reference and returns the string value of that item.

This interface will be implemented both by the addin and the server. The addin will implement a version that reads information from the Excel 2007 workbook, while the server will implement one that returns information from an Excel Services connection.

FeedItem Class

Each feed item has a `FeedItem` instance representing it, containing most of the information. Some fields are optional and will potentially have defaults applied by the server if not present:

❑ **Title.** Represents the template for the title of the item. Can contain inline references to cells.

❑ **Description.** The template for the description of the item; it can also contain inline references to cells.

❑ **Condition.** Determines if an item will be generated. If not empty, needs to contain an Excel-style reference to a cell. If that cell contains a Boolean `FALSE`, the item will not be shown.

❑ **Link.** The template for the link of the item. If not present, the server will put a link to the workbook in the item.

The `FeedItem` class also contains facilities to get the processed title, description, and link (i.e., including the actual data behind the inline Excel references).

The methods that translate the template into actual text looks like this:

```
private string FillString(IItemInfoProvider provider, string template)
{
    StringBuilder b = new StringBuilder();
    while (!String.IsNullOrEmpty(template))
    {
        template = GenerateNextPart(provider, template, b);
    }
    return b.ToString();
}

private string GenerateNextPart(
    IItemInfoProvider provider,
    string template,
    StringBuilder b)
{
    string part = "";
    int newTemplatePos = 0;
    if (template[0] == '{')
```

```
    {
        newTemplatePos = template.IndexOf('}') + 1;
        part = template.Substring(1, template.IndexOf('}') - 1);
        part = provider.GetInfo(part);
    }
    else
    {
        newTemplatePos = template.IndexOf("{");
        if (newTemplatePos == -1)
        {
            part = template;
        }
        else
        {
            part = template.Substring(0, newTemplatePos);
        }

    }
    b.Append(part);
    if (newTemplatePos >= template.Length || newTemplatePos == -1)
    {
        template = "";
    }
    else
    {
        template = template.Substring(newTemplatePos);
    }
    return template;
}
```

The `FillString()` method gets called with a provider and a template string. The method then keeps calling the `GenerateNextPart()` until the template string has been completely processed.

`GenerateNextPart()` tries to figure out what the string it has starts with — a template token (the references wrapped in braces) or pure text. If it's text, it simply lops it off and returns it. If it's a template token, it cleans it up, passes it into the `IItemInfoProvider` instance and concatenates the returned string.

Each of the properties (`Title`, `Description`, and `Link`) has a corresponding method that will return the processed text:

```
public string GetFilledTitle(IItemInfoProvider provider)
{
    return FillString(provider, Title);
}
```

Excel Addin

The Excel addin presents the user with a panel for authoring RSS feeds. Most of the code for handling the custom task pane and the custom XML parts is copied from the custom service code.

Copying code is bad — I know. However, the projects already have quite a bit of componentization as it is, and I decided against creating a whole custom task pane framework just for two projects.

The most interesting part in the addin is the code that inserts tokens into the textual templates and the code that creates the sample RSS result.

Inserting Tokens into the Text

The dialog box that allows the user to edit a feed item contains multiple Insert buttons. These buttons execute the following code:

```
private void InsertCell(TextBox target)
{
    if (Workbook == null)
        return;

    Excel.Range selection = Workbook.Application.ActiveCell;
    string sheet;
    string range;

    Utils.GetRangeInfo(selection, out sheet, out range);
    if (!String.IsNullOrEmpty(sheet))
    {
        range = String.Format("{0}!{1}", sheet, range);
    }
    target.SelectedText = "{" + range + "}";
}
```

The `InsertCell()` method takes the currently active cell in the workbook and uses the `Utils.Get-RangeInfo()` method (also copied from the custom Web Services project) to figure how best to reference the cell. It then uses the `SelectedText` property of the text box to add the text at the caret position.

Generating Sample RSS Items

In the RSS authoring pane, the user can see a preview of the RSS item that will be generated from the authored RSS item.

The title and description strings are created by calling into a class that implements the `IItemInfoProvider` interface:

```
class ExcelClientInfoProvider : IItemInfoProvider
{
    private Excel.Workbook m_workbook;

    public ExcelClientInfoProvider(Excel.Workbook workbook)
    {
        Workbook = workbook;
    }

    public Excel.Workbook Workbook
    {
        get { return m_workbook; }
        set { m_workbook = value; }
    }

    public string GetInfo(string rangeString)
    {
```

```
            int index = rangeString.IndexOf('!');
            Excel.Range range = null;
            if (index == -1)
            {
                foreach (Excel.Name name in Workbook.Names)
                {
                    if (name.Name.Equals(
                        rangeString,
                        StringComparison.OrdinalIgnoreCase) &&
                        name.RefersToRange != null)
                    {
                        range = name.RefersToRange;
                        break;
                    }
                }
            }
            else
            {
                string sheetString = rangeString.Substring(0, index);
                rangeString = rangeString.Substring(index + 1);
                Excel.Worksheet sheet =
                    (Excel.Worksheet)Workbook.Sheets[sheetString];
                range = sheet.Cells.get_Range(rangeString, Type.Missing);
            }
            string result = "#ERROR!";
            if (range != null)
            {
                result = range.Value2.ToString();
            }
            return result;
        }
    }
```

The class gets instantiated with the workbook that is being used as the source for the RSS feed. The implementation of the interface method checks to see if the range string contains the sheet delimiter (exclamation mark).

In the case where it does not exist, the system iterates over the names in the workbook — if it finds one that corresponds to the range name, it will use the `Range` object it refers to (as returned by the `Name.RefersToRange` property). If, however, the range is in the form of `Sheet!Cell`, the method uses the `Sheets` collection to find the appropriate sheet and then uses the cell reference to get the corresponding string.

Publishing to the Server

When the author of a feed is ready to publish, he presses the Publish button on the task pane. This executes the following code, which communicates with the Excel RSS server:

```
private void publishButton_Click(object sender, EventArgs e)
{
    try
    {
        ExcelRssService.Service s =
            new Pes.ExcelRss.ExcelAddin.ExcelRssService.Service();
```

```
            s.Credentials = System.Net.CredentialCache.DefaultCredentials;
            s.Url = Config.Current.RssServerUrl;
            FeedDescription.WorkbookUrl = Workbook.FullName;
            FeedDescription.ExcelServicesUrl = Config.Current.ExcelServiceUrl;
            string rssLink = s.Publish(FeedDescription.ToXml());
            DialogResult result = ShowMessageBox(
                Resources.Strings.LaunchRssLinkQuestion,
                MessageBoxIcon.Question,
                MessageBoxButtons.YesNo);
            if (result == DialogResult.Yes)
            {
                Process.Start(rssLink);
            }

        }
        catch (SoapException ex)
        {
            ErrorForm.Show(this, ex);
        }
        catch (WebException ex)
        {
            ErrorForm.Show(
                this,
                Resources.Strings.CouldNotConnectToRssServer,
                ex.ToString());
        }
        catch (Exception ex)
        {
            ErrorForm.Show(
                this,
                Resources.Strings.UnknownError,
                ex.ToString());
        }
    }
```

The first step is to instantiate the `ExcelRssService.Service` class (an imported Web Service proxy) and set it up. The addin then makes sure that the `FeedDescription` instance the user has been working on contains the most recently configured Excel Services URL and the URL of the workbook that is being edited.

Once the `FeedDescription` is ready, it is serialized to XML via the `ToXml()` method and passed to the `Publish()` method of the proxy. The resulting string is the URL for accessing the feed. After showing a prompt to the user, the addin starts the feed URL causing the default browser to show it.

RSS Server

The RSS server contains two user entry points — the first is the `Service.asmx` file that contains the Web Service that is used to publish the RSS feed. The second is `RssFeed.aspx`, which is used to get back the available RSS feeds.

The server maintains the available RSS feeds both in memory and on disk. When a new RSS feed is published, the server adds it into its memory-stored list but also saves the list back to disk so that the feed will not be lost when the application recycles. The RSS feeds are stored in memory as a simple hash table and are accessible through the `RssManager` class, which also takes care of all the locking and file management.

Service.asmx Web Service

Callers that want to publish a new RSS feed (or to update an existing one) need to use the `Service.asmx` Web Service in the web application. The service exposes a single web method:

```
[WebMethod]
public string Publish(string xml)
{
    FeedDescription description = FeedDescription.FromXml(xml);
    RssManager.Current.AddFeed(description);
    return Utils.GetFeedLink(description);
}
```

The `Publish()` method takes an XML string representing a `FeedDescription` (from the Library module) and turns it into a `FeedDescription` instance. It then uses the `RssManager` class to update the feed on the server.

RssFeed.aspx Page

The `RssFeed.aspx` page (implemented by the `RssFeed` class) knows how to service two types of requests.

When the page is accessed without the `feed` query parameter, it will return the "feed of feeds," which will contain all the RSS feeds available on the server:

```
http://server/ExcelRssServer/RssFeed.aspx
```

However, if the `feed` query parameter is available, the page will try to find the feed and return it to the caller:

```
http://server/ExcelRssServer/RssFeed?feed=MyFeed
```

This section will show how a specific RSS feed is rendered.

```
protected void Page_Load(object sender, EventArgs e)
{
    string name = Request.QueryString["feed"];

    if (!String.IsNullOrEmpty(name))
    {
        FeedDescription description = RssManager.Current.GetFeed(name);
        if (description != null)
        {
            FillRss(description);
        }
    }
    else
    {
        FillRssFeedOfFeeds();
    }
}
```

The first step in the `Page_Load()` event is to check which type of feed is wanted. Once determined, the appropriate method is called. In the case of an Excel Services feed, the page uses the `RssManager` class to get at the `FeedDescription` instance, which represents the actual feed.

```
private XmlTextWriter StartFeed()
{
    Response.Clear();

    Response.ContentType = "text/xml";

    XmlTextWriter reader = new XmlTextWriter(Response.OutputStream,
Encoding.UTF8);

    reader.WriteStartDocument();
    return reader;
}
private void FillRss(FeedDescription description)
{
    XmlTextWriter reader = StartFeed();

    // The mandatory rss tag
    reader.WriteStartElement("rss");
    reader.WriteAttributeString("version", "2.0");

    // The channel tag contains RSS feed details
    reader.WriteStartElement("channel");
    reader.WriteElementString("title", description.Name);
    reader.WriteElementString("link", description.WorkbookUrl);
    reader.WriteElementString("description", "Rss produced from Excel Services");
    reader.WriteElementString("copyright", "");

    ExcelServices service = new ExcelServices(
        ExcelServicesType.Soap,
        description.ExcelServicesUrl);
    using (Session session = service.Open(description.WorkbookUrl))
    {
        foreach (FeedItem item in description.FeedItemCollection)
        {
            WriteRssItemInfo(reader, item, session, description);
        }
    }

    //closing the elements
    reader.WriteEndDocument(); // rss
    reader.Flush();
    reader.Close();
    Response.End();
}
```

The `StartFeed()` method prepares the page to display an RSS feed. It clears the response ASP.NET automatically adds in and resets it with the appropriate information such as the type of the response (`text/xml` in this case). It also creates an XML stream that will be used to write the contents of the RSS feed.

The `FillRss()` method takes the `FeedDescription` instance and uses it to produce the RSS XML. After adding the top level element of the RSS feed, it adds the `<channel>` element and fills all the appropriate child elements such as `<title>`, `<link>`, and so on.

The next step is to add all the appropriate items into the `<channel>` element. However, before doing that the workbook needs to be opened on Excel Services. For each item in the feed, `FillRss()` calls the `WriteRssItemInfo()` method with the created session:

```
public void WriteRssItemInfo(
    XmlTextWriter reader,
    FeedItem item,
    Session session,
    FeedDescription feed)
{
    object condition = null;

    if (!String.IsNullOrEmpty(item.Condition))
    {
        condition = session.GetCellA1(item.Condition);
    }

    if ((condition is bool && (bool)condition) ||
        !(condition is bool)
        || condition == null)
    {
        ExcelServicesInfoProvider provider =
            new ExcelServicesInfoProvider(session);

        reader.WriteStartElement("item");
        reader.WriteElementString(
            "title",
            item.GetFilledTitle(provider));

        reader.WriteElementString(
            "description",
            item.GetFilledDescription(provider));

        string link = feed.WorkbookUrl;
        if (!String.IsNullOrEmpty(item.Link))
        {
            link = item.GetFilledLink(provider);
        }

        reader.WriteElementString("link", link);
        reader.WriteElementString("pubDate", DateTime.Now.ToString());
        reader.WriteEndElement(); // item
    }
}
```

The first step of the operation is to figure out if the item needs to be visible at this time in the feed. This is done by using the `Condition` property of the `FeedItem` and executing it to get the value that's in the cell. The returned value is then checked. Only if it's FALSE will the feed item be unavailable.

Once it is determined that the feed is needed, the information is read from it using the `ExcelServices-InfoProvider` class that implements the `IItemInfoProvider` interface from the library. If the `Link` property of the item is empty, the system places the workbook link there instead.

ExcelServicesInfoProvider

This class implements the `IItemInfoProvider` interface for getting information needed to fill the RSS textual portions.

```
public class ExcelServicesInfoProvider : IItemInfoProvider
{
    private Session m_session;
    public ExcelServicesInfoProvider(Session session)
    {
        m_session = session;
    }

    public string GetInfo(string range)
    {
        int index = range.IndexOf('!');
        string sheet = "";
        if (index >= 0)
        {
            sheet = range.Substring(0, index);
            range = range.Substring(index + 1);
        }
        object result = m_session.GetCellA1(
            sheet,
            range,
            true);
        string resultString = "";
        if (result != null)
        {
            resultString = result.ToString();
        }
        return resultString;
    }
}
```

The class is instantiated with an open session. `GetInfo()` can then be used to get information from the workbook. If the range contains a "!" character, the range is parsed and the sheet name placed in a different variable. The `Session.GetCellA1()` method is then called and the result returned to the caller.

RssManager Class

The `RssManager` class is used by the two entry points to handle the RSS feeds in the server. The class defines a hash table (`Dictionary<>` class), which it uses to store the feed descriptions in memory. In parallel, it also stores the feed description to disk (under the name of `RssFeeds.info` under the root of the application) so that they will be available next time the process recycles. The class manages its own singleton instance in the Current property:

```
public class RssManager
{
    private FeedCollection m_feedCollection;
    private object m_lock = new object();

    private static RssManager m_current = new RssManager();

    public RssManager()
    {
    }


    public static RssManager Current
    {
        get { return m_current; }
        set { m_current = value; }
    }

    private FeedCollection FeedCollection
    {
        get { return m_feedCollection; }
    }

// ...
}
```

The m_current static field contains the singleton instance. The m_feedCollection field contains a reference to the in-memory feed collection. The m_lock field contains an instance that will be used to serialize access to the m_feedCollection instance.

The ReadIfNeeded() method is called before each access to the feed collection in the class — it makes sure to read the collection of feeds from disk, if it has not yet been read. If the file does not exist, it creates an empty FeedCollection instance:

```
private void ReadIfNeeded()
{
    if (m_feedCollection == null)
    {
        if (File.Exists(FeedFileName))
        {
            XmlSerializer s = CreateSerializer();
            using (Stream stream = File.OpenRead(FeedFileName))
            {
                m_feedCollection = (FeedCollection)s.Deserialize(stream);
            }
        }
```

```
        else
        {
            m_feedCollection = new FeedCollection();
        }
    }
}
```

The `Publish()` web method of the Web Service calls `RssManager.AddFeed()`. This method goes through the following steps:

1. Call `ReadIfNeeded()` to make sure that the RSS feeds are loaded into memory.

2. Add (or overwrite) the supplied feed in the collection.

3. Save the feeds description back into disk (this makes sure that the feeds are properly persisted).

These operations all happen inside a lock — this guarantees that multiple users accessing the feeds at the same time will not be able to corrupt the state of the application.

> *While having a simple lock can make the process slower, for most scenarios this should be fine. However, if this turns out to be a problem for a specific scenario, there are some solutions for this, all of them probably making the solution more complex to code.*

```
public void AddFeed(FeedDescription description)
{
    description.UpdateDate = DateTime.Now;
    lock (m_lock)
    {
        ReadIfNeeded();
        FeedCollection.Add(description);
        XmlSerializer s = CreateSerializer();
        using (Stream stream = File.Create(FeedFileName))
        {
            s.Serialize(stream, FeedCollection);
        }
    }
}
```

Feeds requested by users through the `RssFeed.aspx` page ultimately make a call into the `RssManager.GetFeed()` method. While also protected by the lock, this method issues no I/O calls (except for the initial call):

```
public FeedDescription GetFeed(string name)
{
    lock (m_lock)
    {
        ReadIfNeeded();
        return FeedCollection[name];
    }
}
```

Summary

Authoring RSS feeds through Excel Services is another way of giving Excel users the power to do more with their data without having to know how to write code. While this solution can be augmented to make it even more useful, it can be used as is for small deployments of Excel Services.

More ideas for this solution:

❑ **Multi-cell ranges.** The current solution only knows how to return single-cell values into the RSS strings. It may be useful, for the `<description>` element of the RSS feed at least, to be able to get back multi-cell ranges of data.

❑ **Sample viewer.** The text box that shows the result of the feed in the task pane could be changed to use Internet Explorer to display the values, resulting in a WYSIWYG representation of the feed result.

❑ **Enclosures.** RSS feeds support the notion of enclosures — these are simply links that some RSS readers know how to download as they download the RSS feed. This could be used in conjunction with workbooks to allow the RSS reader to download the actual workbook that produced the feed. See Chapter 17 for more information about Dynamic Workbook Links for other potential features.

❑ **Storing feeds in a database.** For larger installation, it may be more scalable to store feed definitions inside a database. This would allow farm solutions to function properly. It can also make busier solutions more efficient.

❑ **Error handling.** The solution is light on error handling. This ranges from allowing users to generate faulty templates to potential issues when accessing a problematic workbook. More work can be done to make the application more robust.

❑ **Encoding of "{".** The curly braces character is used for tokens inside text. It is impossible with the current solution to actually have these in a feed. To enable that, the developer will need to add some kind of encoding (the .NET encoding of double braces should work properly).

❑ **Overwriting.** There is no protection against overwriting other feeds.

❑ **Parameters.** Some feeds may be defined with parameters that will be passed in the query string of the feed and passed into the workbook by way of `SetCellA1()` calls. This can make for more elaborate and customizable feeds. For an example of this, see Chapter 17, which uses a similar mechanism to generate modified workbooks

❑ **Safer save.** When saving feeds to disk, it would have been safer to save to a temporary file first and then, only when successful, delete the original feeds file and rename the newly created file.

❑ **Management.** There is no feed management in the solution right now. Feeds cannot be deleted from any sort of UI — the only way to do this is to edit the XML manually and recycle the application. A simple Web form or two could allow administrators to manage the feeds.

❑ **More metadata.** Feed information could contain more metadata for management purposes. Information such as the feed's author could be very useful for some scenarios.

15

Excel Services as an RTD Server

RTD (Real Time Data) was first introduced with Excel 2002, allowing organizations to get fast-updating information into workbooks without Excel users having to manually update the data. Since the mechanism uses a simple in-process COM object with very little overhead to get the data, it was possible for Excel to get updates hundreds of times a second.

RTD can also be used with DCOM to execute objects in a remote location. The overhead, when compared to database queries for example, is still relatively small in that case.

According to Microsoft documentation, a "Pentium III 500 MHz processor with 128mb of RAM" can have 200 updates a second on a single value. One can just imagine how many updates tomorrow's multicore machines will be able to achieve in a second!

Instead of the pull model employed by other external data sources such as databases and UDFs, RTD servers were based on a push model. ("push model" was the "Web 2.0" of the late 1990s.) While with databases, the client needed to call out and ask for an update, push models told the client when an update was available, allowing it to ask for the value then and there.

Server is used here in the sense of a server component — not a server machine. Through this chapter, these servers will be referred to as "COM servers" or "RTD servers" to reduce confusion.

There are many scenarios for RTD in Excel. For the most part, organizations have been using them when there's need to keep an eye on changing data and act according to how worksheet models change because of that.

This chapter discusses an Excel client addin that will let users bring Real Time Data from Excel Services to the client. The scenarios for using Excel Services as an RTD server are very similar to the classic RTD scenarios. This solution allows the callers to have a model calculate on Excel Services and then get the values back from it in real time.

Overview

Excel's RTD architecture is based on COM. For an RTD function to work on the client, an RTD server needs to be available. RTD servers are identified by their COM `ProgIds`. When Excel encounters an RTD function it will look up to see if a COM object with that `ProgId` has already been created. If it has, Excel will reuse it; otherwise, it will instantiate and initialize it. The RTD function on the client is called in this manner:

```
=RTD(ProgId, RemoteServer, Topic1[,Topic2, Topic3, …])
```

The `ProgId` represents the COM object that will be created. The `RemoteServer` parameter enables the user to instruct Excel to create the object on a potentially different machine in the network. The `Topic` parameters functionality depends entirely on the RTD server — they are passed to the RTD server and are used to determine the information that's required by the user.

The Excel Services RTD solution works by having a COM RTD object that knows how to call into Excel Services and fetch back values. These values are then pushed into Excel. The RTD object also monitors each value for changes — values that change more often will be queried more often, resulting in more updates overall.

With this version of Excel Services, the RTD server cannot be a true "push model." After all, Excel Services keeps getting polled for new values — it is just the connection between the RTD server and Excel that is of a push nature.

Use

After installing the RTD server on the machine, the Excel user simply needs to place a call to the appropriate RTD function in a cell. The following table describes what each topic parameter means for the RTD server.

Topic Parameter	Meaning
1	The URL of the Excel Services server. For example: `http://oss/_vti_bin/ExcelService.asmx`
2	The URL of the workbook to open. For example: `http//oss/Shared Documents/RTDSource.xlsx`
3	The cell to fetch. For example: `Sheet1!A1` or `TotalSales` (if `TotalSales` is a named range)

A workbook containing an RTD connection to the Company Sales workbook, reading values from the `TotalSales` named range will look like Figure 15-1.

The RTD call passes the `ProgId` of the RTD server, which is "pes.excelservicesrtd". It omits the second parameter since the RTD server is executed on the local machine.

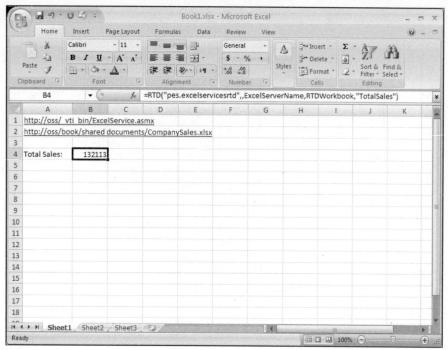

Figure 15-1

"Server" is an unfortunately overloaded technical term here. Throughout the chapter, the term "RTD server" will be used for COM objects supporting the RTD interface. "Excel Services" will be used to refer to the software this book is about. The word "server" will be used sparingly and only to refer to a physical machine running any type of server software.

The third parameter is the URL of Excel Services, represented here by the `ExcelServerName` named range, which references A1. The fourth parameter is the URL of the workbook, represented here by the `RTDWorkbook` named range, which references A2. The final parameter is the string `TotalSales`, which is the *server side* range that contains the desired value.

Each time the value on the target workbook is changed, it will also change on the client sheet.

The rate at which Excel will check for updates on the RTD servers in the sheet is dependant on an Excel-wide setting. By default, that value is 2 seconds. To modify the minimum update interval, users can call into the `Application.RTD.ThrottleInterval` property and set it to whatever interval they wish. The value is represented in milliseconds. The easiest way of doing this is via the immediate window in the VBA development environment of Excel, shown in Figure 15-2.

After this change, Excel will allow RTD data to be updated up to 10 times a second.

Of course, how many times a second the information actually gets updated depends on how often the actual topic changes, how much RTD is present on the workbook, and how fast the machine running Excel is.

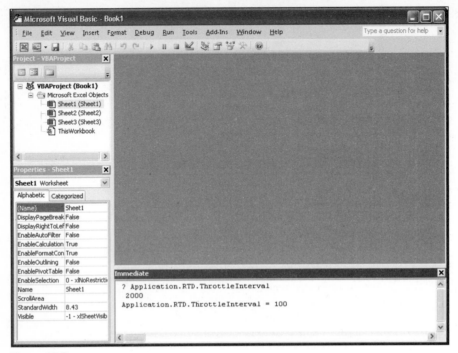

Figure 15-2

Coding the Solution

The solution consists of a single project called `Pes.ClientSideRtd` that implements a COM object using .NET's COM interop mechanisms. The COM object makes calls into Excel Services to get the appropriate values.

How RTD Works on the Client

Excel creates RTD servers as needed and then uses the `IRTDServer` interface to communicate with them. For each unique RTD call on the worksheet, Excel creates a new topic, which is used to identify that call. When the RTD server detects that there's new information available for it, it makes a call to Excel telling it that new data is available. Excel then calls back to the RTD server (when it's ready) asking for that information and places it in the appropriate location.

About Topics

Sadly, the term "topic" is overloaded in the world of RTD servers — it means two things. Each of the custom parameters passed into the RTD function is called topic. "Topic" is also the term used to identify a *set* of unique custom parameters. To avoid confusion, the custom parameters will be called "topic parameters."

As an example, take a workbook that contains the following three formulas in cells A1 through A3:

```
=RTD("RTD.Server",,"A","B")
=RTD("RTD.Server",,"A","C","D")
=RTD("RTD.Server",,"A","B")
```

The first and third calls each take two topic parameters. The second call takes three topic parameters. Excel will create two topics from these calls. One to serve the first and third cells, which share one unique set of topic parameters ("A", "B") and another to serve the second cell which uses another unique set of topic parameters ("A", "C", "D").

Startup and Shutdown

When an RTD server is first instantiated, the `IRTDServer.ServerStart()` method is called by Excel. The method takes a callback object, which can be used to notify Excel that new information is available.

When shutting down an RTD server, Excel calls the `IRTDServer.ServerTerminate()` method.

Creating and Deleting Topics

As explained, a new topic is created when a new unique set of topic parameters is discovered in RTD functions. Excel calls `IRTDServer.ConnectData()` for notification on the creation of a new topic. Each topic is arbitrarily assigned a unique ID, which is passed in with the call, along with the topic parameters. The RTD server is expected to keep track of its topics and be aware of any new data arriving from them.

When a topic is no longer needed, a call to `IRTDServer.DisconnectData()` is made with the appropriate topic ID.

Pushing Back Data

When Excel detects that new data is ready on a given RTD server, it makes a call to `IRTDServer.RefreshData()`. That function returns an array containing all the topics that have new data in them, allowing Excel to update the sheet.

ClientSideRtd

There are only two classes in the project, one containing the COM object that implements the RTD server and called, appropriately, `RtdServer`. The other is a helper class that helps with the querying and tracking of a single topic.

The base namespace for the project is `Pes.ClientSideRtd`. The assembly references the Excel interop assembly so that it can implement the appropriate interfaces.

RtdServer Class

`RtdServer` will be the COM server that will service Excel Services RTD requests. The definition of the class marks it as a COM object with the "Pes.ExcelServicesRtd" `ProgId`.

The class also contains a reference to the callback interface used to notify Excel that new data is available and a collection of `Topic` instances contained with a `Dictionary<>` class, keyed off the topic ID Excel assigns:

```
using System;
using System.Collections.Generic;
using System.Text;
using System.Runtime.InteropServices;

using Excel = Microsoft.Office.Interop.Excel;

namespace Pes.ClientSideRtd
{
    [ComVisible(true)]
    [ProgId("Pes.ExcelServicesRtd")]
    [Guid("84AA86A4-3985-49ec-AF8C-CB4670E39EBC")]
    public class RtdServer : Excel.IRtdServer
    {
        private Dictionary<int, Topic> m_topics = new Dictionary<int, Topic>();
        private Excel.IRTDUpdateEvent m_callback;

        public RtdServer()
        {
        }
        internal Dictionary<int, Topic> Topics
        {
            get { return m_topics; }
            set { m_topics = value; }
        }
        internal Excel.IRTDUpdateEvent Callback
        {
            get { return m_callback; }
        }
        // ...
    }
}
```

The next part of the class is the implementation of the `IRtdServer` interface methods. The first two methods are the ones called when the RTD server starts up and shuts down.

When starting up, the RTD server stores the supplied callback in a member (`m_callback`). Shutting down is a somewhat more involved process — the RTD server makes sure that all `Topic` instances it knows of are disposed and cleared away:

```
public int ServerStart(Excel.IRTDUpdateEvent CallbackObject)
{
    m_callback = CallbackObject;
    return 1;
}

public void ServerTerminate()
{
    lock (m_lock)
```

```
        {
                foreach (Topic topic in Topics.Values)
                {
                        topic.Dispose();
                }
                Topics.Clear();
        }
}
```

Once the RTD server is started, Excel can start making calls for creating new topics via the `ConnectData()` method:

```
public object ConnectData(int TopicID, ref Array Strings, ref bool GetNewValues)
{
    if (Strings.Length < 3)
    {
        throw new COMException(
            "Strings parameter does not contain enough values.",
            HResults.E_FAIL);
    }
    string server = (string)Strings.GetValue(0);
    string workbook = (string)Strings.GetValue(1);
    string range = (string)Strings.GetValue(2);
    Topic topic = new Topic(this, TopicID, server, workbook, range);

    Topic existingTopic;
    if (Topics.TryGetValue(TopicID, out existingTopic))
    {
        existingTopic.Dispose();
        Topics.Remove(TopicID);
    }
    Topics.Add(TopicID, topic);

    topic.CauseValueUpdate();

    return topic.LastValue;
}
```

The first stage makes sure there are enough arguments passed for the topic to be created. The RTD server then instantiates the `Topic` class with the appropriate arguments, including the passed-in `TopicID` argument, which will uniquely identify the topic with Excel.

Next, the RTD server makes sure to clear any existing topics if they exist. Finally, the RTD server adds the newly created `Topic` instance to the dictionary and makes sure it is updated, returning the `Topic.LastValue` property, which will contain the result from the server call.

> *Note: The* Topic *class is "self-containing" in that it will query Excel Services independently and make the appropriate calls to Excel that new values are available. It is described in length in the next section.*

The `DisconnectData()` method of the `IRTDServer` interface disposes of the appropriate `Topic` instance and removes it from the collection (similarly to what the `ConnectData()` method does before adding the new topic).

The final important method in this class is the `RefreshData()` method, which is called by Excel when it is ready for the next batch of data from the RTD server. This method goes over the list of topics, collecting all the ones that have been updated since the last `RefreshData()` call and returns it to Excel in the form of an array:

```
public Array RefreshData(ref int TopicCount)
{
    // Count how many dirty topics we have.
    List<Topic> dirtyTopics = new List<Topic>();
    foreach (Topic topic in Topics.Values)
    {
        if (topic.IsDirty)
        {
            dirtyTopics.Add(topic);
        }
    }

    object[,] updatedValues = new object[2, dirtyTopics.Count];
    TopicCount = dirtyTopics.Count;

    for (int i = 0; i < dirtyTopics.Count; i++)
    {
        Topic topic = dirtyTopics[i];
        topic.ResetDirty();
        updatedValues[0, i] = topic.TopicId;
        updatedValues[1, i] = topic.LastValue;
    }

    return updatedValues;
}
```

The first part makes a pass over all the `Topic` instances attached to the RTD server and checks which ones are dirty. These topics are added to a list, which is then again processed and transferred into an array structure Excel recognizes.

The returned array is a two-dimensional VARIANT array in which each row contains the topic ID in the first index and the new value for that topic ID in the second one. (COM Interop will translate an object array into a VARIANT array.) In this case, the code creates an array with a number of rows that corresponds to the "dirty" topics found.

When Excel receives the array from the `RefreshData()` method, it will iterate over it, finding the cells corresponding to a given topic and updating it with the new piece of data.

Topic Class

The `Topic` class represents a single topic communicating with Excel Services, getting back data. Each topic is self-regulating and self-contained — it is responsible for all communication and takes care of the entire process of connecting to Excel Services, getting back information and then updating it as needed.

Topics are self-regulating in that they will make sure they do not overly stress the server if not needed. Each topic tracks how often the value it gets back changes. The less often a value changes, the less often it is going to be fetched. On the other hand, if it is detected that a value changes very often, queries will be made more often to try and get the newer values.

The class itself has quite a few members that are needed so that it will be able to properly connect, reconnect, and get information from the server:

```csharp
private class Topic : IDisposable
{
    private const int InitialInterval = 1000;
    private const int MinInterval = 50;
    private const int MaxInterval = 5000;

    private Session m_session;
    private System.Timers.Timer m_timer = new
System.Timers.Timer(InitialInterval);
    private string m_excelServicesUrl;
    private string m_workbookName;
    private string m_sheet;
    private string m_range;
    private int m_topicId;
    private bool m_dirty;
    private bool m_disposed;
    private RtdServer m_server;
    private object m_lock = new object();
    private object m_lastValue;

    internal Topic(
        RtdServer server,
        int topicId,
        string excelServicesUrl,
        string workbook,
        string range)
    {
        m_excelServicesUrl = excelServicesUrl;
        m_server = server;
        WorkbookName = workbook;
        int separatorIndex = range.IndexOf('!');
        string sheet = "";
        if (separatorIndex >= 1)
        {
            sheet = range.Substring(0, separatorIndex);
            range = range.Substring(separatorIndex + 1);
        }
        Sheet = sheet;
        Range = range;
        TopicId = topicId;
        m_timer.Elapsed += new ElapsedEventHandler(Timer_Elapsed);
        m_timer.Enabled = true;
    }
    // ...
}
```

The following table describes the function of each of the fields:

Field/Constant	Usage
InitialInterval	This is the initial polling interval, which a topic will use to query the server.
MinInterval	When a value changes very often, the self-regulation mechanism of a topic will make queries occur more and more often. This constant is the absolute minimum interval between queries.
MaxInterval	The counterpart of MinInterval — queries will not be issued in intervals larger than this number.
m_session	Holds a Session object that is connected to Excel Services. This will be used to communicate with Excel Services.
m_timer	A .NET Timer object that is used to initiate queries to Excel Services.
m_excelServicesUrl	The URL of Excel Services (i.e., http://server/_vti_bin/ ExcelServices.asmx)
m_workbookName	The URL of the workbook that is to be queried (i.e., http://server/ Shared Documents/RTDSource.xlsx)
m_sheet/m_range	Contains the sheet name and range name to be queried. m_sheet may be empty if it is a named range that is being requested.
m_topicId	The topic ID that was assigned by Excel.
m_dirty	Set to true when the Topic has a new value in it that has not yet been reported to Excel.
m_disposed	Set to true when the Topic has been disposed.
m_server	References the RtdServer class.
m_lock	Used by the class to serialize access to some of the internal structures. Since the instance may be disposed on one thread while it is still working on another, it is important to protect from using resources at the same time from two different threads.

The Topic constructor intializes the member variables with the arguments it is passed. It also creates a new Timer instance and immediately puts it to work, calling the Timer_Elapsed() method when each interval elapses:

```
void Timer_Elapsed(object sender, ElapsedEventArgs e)
{
    m_timer.Enabled = false;
```

```
        try
        {
            double timeout = m_timer.Interval;
            if (CauseValueUpdate())
            {
                timeout = Math.Max(timeout / 2, MinInterval);
            }
            else
            {
                timeout = Math.Min(timeout * 2, MaxInterval);
            }
            if (!IsDisposed)
            {
                m_timer.Interval = timeout;
            }
        }
        finally
        {
            if (!IsDisposed)
            {
                m_timer.Enabled = true;
            }
        }
    }
```

Each time the `Timer_Elapsed()` method is called, it checks to see if there's a new value in the server by calling the `CauseValueUpdate()` method. If a new value exists, the timeout interval is changed to be half the current value. Otherwise, the value is set to be twice what it used to be.

`CauseValueUpdate()` is the method that actually makes the Excel Services call and checks to see if there's a new value. First, it checks to see if the `Topic` has been disposed of — making sure to return immediately. If the `Topic` is still alive, the method checks to see if it needs to create a new `Session` object. If one already exists, the method recalculates the workbook (allowing new values to be available on the server). The method then calls the `GetCellA1()` method on the `Session` object and sets that value in the `newValue` local variable.

Finally, the method calls the `SetLastValue()` method (shown next in this section) with the new value:

```
internal bool CauseValueUpdate()
{
    lock (m_lock)
    {
        if (IsDisposed)
        {
            NukeTimer();
            return false;
        }
        object newValue = LastValue;
        try
        {
            if (Session == null)
            {
                ExcelServices s = new ExcelServices(
```

```
                            ExcelServicesType.Soap,
                            ExcelServicesUrl);
                Session = s.Open(WorkbookName);
            }
            else
            {
                Session.CalculateWorkbook(CalculateType.Recalculate);
            }
            newValue = Session.GetCellA1(Sheet, Range, false);
        }
        catch (SoapException)
        {
            Session = null;
        }
        catch (WebException)
        {
            Session = null;
        }
        return SetLastValue(newValue);
    }
}
```

When there's any kind of `SoapException` or `WebException` *coming out of the request, the Topic instance makes sure it resets the* `Session` *object. This guarantees that the next time an update is attempted, the RTD server does not try to use a potentially nonfunctional session, but tries from scratch. That in turn allows the RTD server to recover from dropped sessions or restarting servers.*

`SetLastValue()` takes care of checking if the value is actually new and notifying Excel that new information is available:

```
private bool SetLastValue(object value)
{
    bool needToUpdate = false;
    if (value == null)
    {
        if (m_lastValue != null)
        {
            needToUpdate = true;
        }
    }
    else if (!value.Equals(m_lastValue))
    {
        needToUpdate = true;
    }

    if (needToUpdate)
    {
        m_lastValue = value;
        ValueUpdated();
    }
    return needToUpdate;
}
```

```
private void ValueUpdated()
{
    SetDirty();
    if (Server != null && Server.Callback != null)
    {
        Server.Callback.UpdateNotify();
    }
}
```

Note: The call to `Server.Callback.UpdateNotify()` *does not immediately cause the values to be retrieved from the* `Topic`. *The frequency in which this happens is dependent on Excel itself. Calling that method lets Excel know that new values are available and that it can call to get them at its leisure.*

Summary

The Excel Services client RTD solution is an excellent solution for scenarios where potentially fast-updating models can be calculated on the server and their results are useful on the client. Using this solution is another example of how users can get great features from Excel Services without doing any development work. This can be especially interesting when used in conjunction with volatile server-side UDFs that execute code for the caller.

More ideas for this solution:

❑ **Writing to the server workbook.** It can sometimes be useful to write data into cells in the workbook that is opened in Excel Services prior to actually reading values from it. These values can be passed into the other topic parameters in the RTD function. It is important to remember to store them in the `Topic` class so that they can be reused whenever the RTD server needs to make another connection to Excel Services due to the session timing out or the server restarting.

❑ **Refreshing.** Another interesting scenario that is not covered in this chapter is one where the Excel Services workbook contains external data such as PivotTables or sheet data. Either by using periodic refresh or by making an explicit call to `Session.Refresh()`, the RTD server can get updated data from the database that is connected to the Excel Services loaded workbook.

❑ **Reload of workbook.** Currently, the RTD server only reloads workbooks when it loses the session on Excel Services. It may be useful to have the ability to pass some kind of flag that tells the RTD server to reopen the workbook every so often so that if there's a new workbook saved to the server, it will be loaded.

❑ **Share workbooks.** Each topic has its own session opened against an Excel Services workbook. Theoretically, a potential optimization here would be to allow the topics to share sessions among themselves. This, however, would require a more elaborate locking mechanism that will guarantee that two topics don't query the same session at the same time.

❑ **RTD Server Layer.** RTD can cause a lot of traffic on Excel Services. In some cases, it may be useful to have an extra layer of abstraction that is used by callers to get values from Excel Services. The new layer will return data to the user based on the topic parameters but will dramatically reduce the number of actual Excel Services calls that are made because it will cache return values.

❑ **Fine tune update intervals.** Currently, the update interval (the rate at which the server is called for new data) is only dependant on how often its data changes. It may be useful to take other variables into account such as how often Excel actually calls for updates.

16

Real Time Data UDF

The previous chapter discussed RTD (Real Time Data) in depth and showed a way of creating an RTD server that uses Excel Services as the source of its data. This chapter is also related to RTD, but from a different angle.

Since Excel Services does not natively support RTD, and since there are solutions out there that use RTD to bring data into workbooks, it seemed like a good idea to add pseudo-support of RTD to the server.

It is important to understand what this solution is not before going into what it is.

The solution does not magically give Excel Services the ability to have true Real Time Data feeds into the sheet and actively cause refreshes in workbooks that are then updated automatically on the browser. While it may be possible to come close to such a solution, it is outside of the scope of this chapter to do so.

What this chapter does offer is a way of leveraging existing RTD servers and using them to get information into server calculated workbooks without rewriting the code that gets the information.

At the end of the day, it is highly recommended that users rewrite the RTD servers as UDFs for consumption on the server. That's the only way to guarantee smooth server operation.

Overview

The idea behind this solution is to produce an Excel Services UDF that simulates the RTD framework that Excel has and then allow workbooks to call it just like calling any other UDF. The UDF will need to maintain the infrastructure running and organized so that the RTD servers will keep on functioning properly.

It is important to have prior knowledge of how RTD works (or read the previous chapter, which goes into depth about how to write an RTD server) before carrying on with this chapter.

Use

The RTD UDF exposes two methods — one for shared Real Time Data feeds and one for private ones. Because the solution contains an implementation of the RTD infrastructure, it's possible to have two flavors of the function.

The shared version of the UDF is the more efficient one. It holds a single copy of the RTD infrastructure and shares results between all users. The private version gives each session its own version of the infra-structure, with its own instance of the RTD servers. While less efficient (and potentially less stable — see "Dangers of Using RTD Servers in Excel Services" later in this chapter), this version, in some cases, will return data that is more in line with what the RTD server would have returned on the client.

The two UDFs are called `SharedServerRtd()` and `PrivateServerRtd()`, and they are used similarly to how the client-side RTD is used, as shown in Figure 16-1.

> *Both versions lack the second parameter representing the remote machine on which to execute the RTD server. This feature is not supported by the solution.*

The signature for both methods is identical — the first parameter is the `progId` that represents the COM object that needs to be created. The rest of the parameters are strings that act as the topic parameters in the regular Excel RTD function.

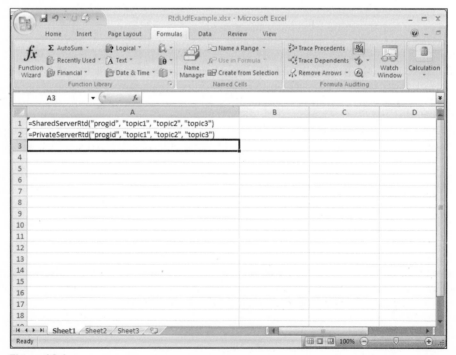

Figure 16-1

Making RTD Work on Both Client and Server

It is possible to make a workbook that will work with RTD both on the client and on the server. Since the Excel RTD function is simply not recognized on the server, using the IFERROR function of Excel allows the workbook author to have a simple formula that will work on both environments:

```
=IFERROR(RTD("progid", , "topic1", "topic2"), SharedServerRtd("progid","topic1",
"topic2"))
```

In Excel Services, the call to RTD() will be evaluated to the #NAME error. This will prompt the second argument to be evaluated and returned to the user. In this way, the workbook will work seamlessly whether it is running in Excel or in Excel Services.

How It Works

As was mentioned already, using RTD servers in Excel Services is merely a way of leveraging the code rather than really adding RT capabilities to Excel Services. This is how the solution works:

The infrastructure maintains a list of all created RTD objects — each one receiving its own callback (the IRTDUpdate interface) for notification when there is new information. When a site receives a call saying that new information is available, it does not immediately call into the RTD server for the new information. Instead, it marks the RTD server site as dirty and bides its time.

When a UDF is called on the server (due to a recalculation request or due to a new session being opened), that's when the infrastructure will make a call into the RTD server asking for the updated information. In that way, it is guaranteed that there is less stress on the server machine — since the data is not really needed until a request is made for it by a user, there's no reason to actually query for it.

When a topic is no longer used by Excel, in the original RTD infrastructure, it takes care to shut it down (via the DisconnectData() method on the IRtdServer interface). Because the UDFs have no way of knowing if an RTD topic is no longer used, there's a cleanup process that happens periodically looking for topics that have not been used for a while. These topics get disconnected and cleaned up.

Dangers of Using RTD in Excel Services

RTD servers are COM objects that have been written and tested for a very specific environment, namely, the Excel client. There are a few associated dangers in using RTD servers on Excel Services, which are very important to understand:

1. RTD servers are usually built to deliver maximum performance. The problem is that "maximum performance" means different things when applied to a server environment and when applied to a client environment. An RTD server might make some assumptions about its behavior based on the fact that it's running on a client machine. Such assumptions can be potentially harmful for a server environment. Specifically, RTD servers expect to serve a single user at a given time on a machine. When executed in Excel Services, they need to serve a potential multitude of users.

2. As explained in an earlier chapter, COM objects have their own thread models and their own rules about how to run in a process. These rules may sometimes be at odds with the way Excel Services runs. While most COM objects should run fine in this respect, some may have problems adjusting and may cause crashes or even deadlocks.

3. The private version of the RTD UDF can potentially create multiple instances of the same RTD server. Some RTD servers may have global state, which can potentially make them corruptible in such situations.

The reason it's "potentially" and not definite is that the COM thread models that may protect this state in one manner or another. Still, this is not something that should be relied upon.

4. Finally, due to the nature of RTD servers, users may see a degradation of performance directly proportional to the number of server instances active in the system. Most RTD servers will execute on the same thread, causing calls to be serialized and requests to return later to their users.

5. Some RTD servers may try to access the executable they are running in and execute Excel API calls. These servers will probably completely fail to run in the context of Excel Services.

It is incredibly important to test, retest, and test again solutions that use RTD servers in Excel Services, to make absolutely sure that no bad behavior is detected. This includes testing with a much stressed server with multiple users concurrently running the various RTD servers.

Testing with only a single user on a nonproduction box may result in a false sense of security.

Coding the Solution

The solution comprises a single project that contains a class that exports the UDFs that Excel Services will use. There are also multiple internal classes that simulate the RTD infrastructure of Excel.

A single instance of the infrastructure is used in the `SharedServerRtd()` UDF, while the `Private-ServerRtd()` UDF will cause a new instance to be created for each newly opened session. Figure 16-2 shows a diagram of the simulated RTD infrastructure.

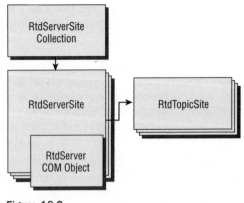

Figure 16-2

The `RtdServerSiteCollection` class is the class that manages a single infrastructure instance. It maintains an `RtdServerSite` instance for each created RTD server COM object. Each `RtdServerSite` also maintains a list of `RtdTopicSite` instances, each corresponding to a single topic.

RtdUdf Project

The base namespace for this project is `Pes.RtdUdf`. It references the Excel PIA so that it can use the relevant RTD interfaces. It also references the `Microsoft.Office.Excel.Server.Udf` assembly so that it can use the UDF attributes.

TopicKey

`TopicKey` instances identify a topic by the set of topic parameters used to call the RTD functionality. Because it is used as a key in a hash table, it needs to properly override the `Equals()` and `GetHashCode()` methods.

The class maintains a list of strings, which are the topic parameters used when calling the RTD UDFs:

```
private class TopicKey
{
    private string[] m_strings;

    internal TopicKey(string[] strings)
    {
        m_strings = strings;
    }
    // ...
}
```

The `Equals()` method compares all strings of both `TopicKey` instances and returns true only if they are identical:

```
public override bool Equals(object obj)
{
    TopicKey callId = obj as TopicKey;
    if (callId == null)
    {
        return false;
    }

    if (callId.m_strings.Length != m_strings.Length)
    {
        return false;
    }

    for (int i = 0; i < m_strings.Length; i++)
    {
        if (m_strings[i] != callId.m_strings[i])
        {
            return false;
        }
```

```
    }

        return true;
    }
```

Finally, the GetHashCode() method combines the hash codes of all the strings into one hash code:

If it is expected that RTD servers will get passed multiple strings that are all the same, it may be more efficient to combine the strings' hash codes in a manner different from a straight XOR.

```
public override int GetHashCode()
{
    int hash = 0;
    foreach (string s in m_strings)
    {
        hash ^= s.GetHashCode();
    }

    return hash;
}
```

RtdServerSiteCollection Class

The root of the infrastructure, this class maintains a list of RtdServerSite instances in a synchronized manner:

```
private sealed class RtdServerSiteCollection : IDisposable
{
    private Dictionary<string, RtdServerSite> m_servers;
    private object m_lock = new object();

    internal RtdServerSiteCollection()
    {
        m_servers = new Dictionary<string,RtdServerSite>(
            StringComparer.InvariantCultureIgnoreCase);
    }
    // ...
}
```

The m_servers field holds a hash table of all the available sites. The m_lock field is used to synchronize access to the collection.

The one important method in RtdServerSiteCollection is the one that serves up RtdServerSite instances:

```
internal RtdServerSite GetServer(string progId)
{
    lock (m_lock)
    {
        RtdServerSite site;
        if (!m_servers.TryGetValue(progId, out site))
```

```
            {
                site = new RtdServerSite(progId);
                m_servers.Add(progId, site);
            }
            return site;
        }
    }
```

Inside the lock, the collection looks up the progId. If it already exists, the appropriate site instance is returned. Otherwise, the call creates a new one and returns it.

There is also a Dispose() method in the class, which iterates over all the sites and disposes each of them.

RtdServerSite Class

This class tracks instances of RTD servers in the system:

```
[ComVisible(true)]
public sealed class RtdServerSite : Excel.IRTDUpdateEvent, IDisposable
{
    private static readonly TimeSpan TopicTimeout = TimeSpan.FromSeconds(30);

    private Excel.IRtdServer m_server;
    private int m_heartbeat = 200;
    private bool m_needUpdate;
    private List<TopicSite> m_topicsByIndex = new List<TopicSite>();
    private Dictionary<TopicId, TopicSite> m_topicsByTopicKey =
    new Dictionary<TopicId, TopicSite>();
    private object m_lock = new object();
    private Timer m_timer;

    public RtdServerSite(string progId)
    {
        Type type = Type.GetTypeFromProgID(progId);
        m_server = (Excel.IRtdServer)Activator.CreateInstance(type);
        m_server.ServerStart(this);

        m_timer = new Timer();
        m_timer.Interval = TopicTimeout.TotalMilliseconds / 2;
        m_timer.Enabled = true;
        m_timer.Elapsed += new ElapsedEventHandler(Timer_Elapsed);
    }
    //...
}
```

The following table describes what each of the fields is used for.

Field/Constant	Usage
TopicTimeout	The amount of time it takes an unused topic to timeout and get closed.
m_server	Reference to the RTD server COM object.

Continued

Field/Constant	Usage
m_heartbeat	A dummy value used by the system to simulate the HeartbeatInterval property of the IRtdUpdateEvents interface. Not really used.
m_topicsByIndex	A list of topics. The location of the topic corresponds to its numeric topic ID (not to be confused with its TopicKey, which just identifies it as a unique topic and does not necessarily have any connection to the numeric ID it has).
m_topicsByTopicKey	A hash table of the topics keyed off a TopicKey instance.
m_lock	Used to protect access to the various members in the class.
m_timer	Used for periodically cleaning up the various topics.

Before a new topic can be connected to an RTD server, it needs to be identified and its TopicSite instance properly stored. Creating a TopicKey class is not a problem because the list of strings is available when the topic is first requested. The topic ID, however, requires a bit more attention. These are arbitrary numbers that gives the solution the freedom of allocating them as it sees fit. It cannot, however, give two topics the same ID. That's what the m_topicsByIndex list is used for. Each topic ID corresponds to a location in that list. When a topic is removed, its entry in the list gets nullified and can be reused. Finding an empty index is done by UnsafeGetFreeIndex():

"Unsafe" in the context of this method simply means that it's not doing any locks and thus is not thread-safe. It needs to be called from within a locked context.

```
private int UnsafeGetFreeIndex()
{
    for (int i = 0; i < m_topicsByIndex.Count; i++)
    {
        if (m_topicsByIndex[i] == null)
        {
            return i;
        }
    }

    m_topicsByIndex.Add(null);
    return m_topicsByIndex.Count - 1;
}
```

The method first searches for any null in the list. If it finds one, it returns that index. If not, it adds a new item and returns that one.

When a topic is needed by the infrastructure, it calls the GetTopic() method. This method will return the topic if it already exists or will create a new one if not:

```
internal TopicSite GetTopic(string[] topicParams)
{
    lock (m_lock)
    {
```

```
        DoUpdate();
        TopicKey key = new TopicKey(topicParams);
        TopicSite site;
        if (!m_topicsByTopicKey.TryGetValue(key, out site))
        {
            int newIndex = UnsafeGetFreeIndex();
            site = new TopicSite(key, newIndex);
            bool getNewValues = true;
            Array array = (Array)topicParams;
            object result = m_server.ConnectData(
                newIndex,
                ref array,
                ref getNewValues);
            site.Value = result;
            m_topicsByTopicKey.Add(key, site);
            m_topicsByIndex[newIndex] = site;
        }

        return site;
    }
}
```

The method first tries to find the topic using a `TopicKey` instance. If it fails, it creates a new `TopicSite` and makes sure to call the RTD server's `ConnectData()` method with the appropriate arguments so that it knows a new data channel is needed. The site is then added to both collections and is ready for usage.

The method also calls `DoUpdate()` method. If any topics need updating, this method will make sure they will call the RTD server and retrieve the new pieces of data:

```
private void DoUpdate()
{
    if (m_needUpdate)
    {
        lock (m_lock)
        {
            if (!m_needUpdate)
            {
                return;
            }

            int count = 0;
            Array array = m_server.RefreshData(ref count);
            if (array.Rank != 2)
            {
                throw new InvalidOperationException(
                    "Unrecognized array");
            }
            // How many topics we really have
            int topicCount = array.GetLength(1);
            int dim0Base = array.GetLowerBound(0);
            int dim1Base = array.GetLowerBound(1);
            for (int i = 0; i < topicCount; i++)
            {
                int index = Convert.ToInt32(
```

```
                    array.GetValue(dim0Base + 0, dim1Base + i));
                object o = array.GetValue(dim0Base + 1, dim1Base + i);
                if (index >= 0 &&
                    index < m_topicsByIndex.Count &&
                    m_topicsByIndex[index] != null)
                {
                    m_topicsByIndex[index].Value = o;
                }
            }
            m_needUpdate = false;
        }
    }
}
```

The first step in this method first checks if there is real need for an update. If there isn't (meaning that no RTD server has called with updated data since the last time this method was called), it simply returns.

Next, the method calls the IRtdServer.RefreshData() method, which causes the RTD server to return all the new data. The method then takes the returned array and deconstructs it to figure out which topic IDs are being updated. These are then used to find the corresponding TopicSite instances (by using the m_topicsByIndex collection) and update them with the new values.

The m_needUpdate field is modified when the RTD server notifies the RtdServerSite instance that it has new data via the IRtdUpdateEvent interface:

```
public void UpdateNotify()
{
    m_needUpdate = true;
}
```

The last interesting method of this class is the one responsible for cleaning up the sites. It gets called by the timer every 15 seconds, and it looks to see if it can find topics that haven't been used for the past 30 seconds; if it can, it will clear them away.

The "cutoff" time is calculated by reducing the topic timeout constant from the current date. The topics are then iterated through and cleaned up if they are old enough:

```
private void CleanTopics()
{
    lock (m_lock)
    {
        DateTime cutOff = DateTime.Now - TopicTimeout;

        for (int i = 0; i < m_topicsByIndex.Count; i++)
        {
            TopicSite site = m_topicsByIndex[i];
            if (site != null)
            {
                if (site.LastUpdated < cutOff)
                {
                    m_topicsByIndex[i] = null;
                    m_topicsByTopicKey.Remove(site.TopicKey);
```

```
                              m_server.DisconnectData(site.Index);
                    }
                }
            }
        }
    }
```

The method also takes care to call the `IRtdServer.DisconnectData()` method to make sure that the RTD server no longer looks for updates for that site.

TopicSite

The `TopicSite` class tracks down specific topics. It stores the last time the topic was updated, the last value that was returned, and the key and ID of the topic:

```
private class TopicSite
{
    private int m_index;
    private TopicKey m_topicKey;
    private object m_value;
    private DateTime m_lastUpdated;

    public TopicSite(TopicKey id, int index)
    {
        m_index = index;
        m_topicKey = id;
    }

    internal DateTime LastUpdated
    {
        get { return m_lastUpdated; }
    }

    internal object Value
    {
        get { return m_value; }
        set
        {
            m_value = value;
            m_lastUpdated = DateTime.Now;
        }
    }

    internal TopicKey TopicKey
    {
        get { return m_topicKey; }
    }

    internal int Index
    {
        get { return m_index; }
    }
}
```

Every time a new value is set into the `Value` property of the `TopicSite` instance, it changes the `m_lastUpdated` timestamp so that the topic is not prematurely cleaned up.

ServerRtdUdf Class

Finally, everything comes together inside the `ServerRtdUdf` class, which exposes the actual UDFs used by Excel Services:

```
[UdfClass]
public class ServerRtdUdf : IDisposable
{
    private static RtdServerSiteCollection m_sharedServers =
        new RtdServerSiteCollection();
    private RtdServerSiteCollection m_sessionServers = new
RtdServerSiteCollection();

    private static RtdServerSiteCollection SharedServers
    {
        get { return m_sharedServers; }
    }

    private RtdServerSiteCollection SessionServers
    {
        get { return m_sessionServers; }
    }
    // ...
}
```

There are two fields in the class, both of the same type. The `m_sharedServers` field holds a copy of the infrastructure that will be shared by all users on Excel Services, and `m_sessionServers` holds a copy of the infrastructure that will be used only inside a session and not be shared.

Each of the two defined UDFs call the `ServerRtd()` private method, which takes care of issuing the appropriate requests on the `RtdServerSiteCollection` instance. The simpler of the two is the `ShareServerRtd()` UDF:

```
[UdfMethod(IsVolatile=true)]
public static object SharedServerRtd(string progId, params string[] args)
{
    return ServerRtd(SharedServers, progId, args);
}
```

The method calls into the `ServerRtd()` helper. That method uses the `progId` argument to find the appropriate `RtdServerSite` instance (using the `GetServer()` method). It then finds the appropriate `TopicSite` instance by calling the `GetTopic()` method. Finally, it returns the `Value` property of the `TopicSite`, which contains the most up-to-date value:

```
private static object ServerRtd(
    RtdServerSiteCollection servers,
    string progId,
    string[] args)
{
```

```
    RtdServerSite server = servers.GetServer(progId);

    TopicSite topic = server.GetTopic(args);

    return topic.Value;
}
```

The `PrivateServerRtd()` method is somewhat more involved. It will only work in delegation mode — it tries to impersonate the user, and if that results in a failure, the UDF will not run:

```
[UdfMethod(IsVolatile = true, ReturnsPersonalInformation = true)]
public object PrivateServerRtd(string progId, params string[] args)
{
    WindowsIdentity id = Thread.CurrentPrincipal.Identity as WindowsIdentity;
    if (id == null)
    {
        throw new InvalidOperationException("Must execute in delegation mode.");
    }
    using (WindowsImpersonationContext context = id.Impersonate())
    {
        return ServerRtd(SessionServers, progId, args);
    }
}
```

Summary

Excel Services was not designed to use Real Time Data the way Excel can. Using this UDF, it is still possible to leverage existing RTD servers to at least get the data into Excel Services workbooks.

Great care should be taken before using *any* code that is potentially not meant to work on the server.

More ideas for this solution:

❑ **Out-of-proc isolation.** It should be a relatively easy task to move the actual execution of the various RTD services into their own process. This grants isolation from Excel Services (which translates into better Excel Services reliability) and lets the RTD run in a process that it owns (translating into better RTD server reliability). The interface is relatively simple and should translate well to interprocess communication. If this approach is taken, though, it can probably be useful to remove support for the private RTD functionality, since it would mean opening too many processes in the system.

❑ **Trusted RTD servers.** It would be a good idea to allow the solution to have a configuration list of "allowed" progIds to minimize the potential attack vector of running unprotected code on the server. The solution as presented in this chapter allows attackers who can upload workbooks to the server to create COM objects that are potentially harmful.

17

Directly Parameterized Workbooks

Before Excel Services, one scenario for running Excel client on the server was to prepare workbooks out of templates on the server and make those available to users.

With some help, Excel Services can be used in a similar manner, allowing modified workbooks to be downloaded to the client (either as a file via the Save As dialog box or directly into Excel) without actually creating physical files on the server or running Excel on the server.

Overview

This chapter discusses a partial solution to allow administrators and developers to create links that can be sent via email that create modified and up to date Excel files on the fly (in the memory of the server) and lets users download them.

Use

Chapter 13 introduced an insurance model to explain the usefulness of creating custom Web services over Excel. In this chapter, the same workbook will be used — this time in a scenario where the insurance salesperson wants to send a quote to a client. The idea behind this is that the insurance salesperson wants to let the customer use Excel to view the nicely formatted workbook containing the proposal inside Excel.

Figure 17-1 shows the modified insurance model (this time, for user consumption).

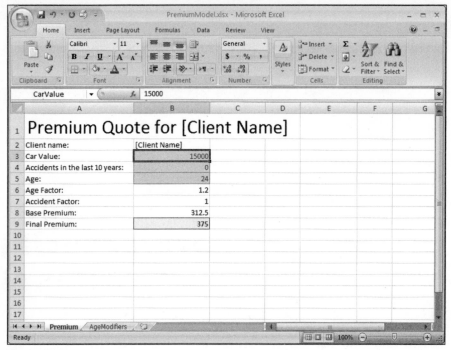

Figure 17-1

This workbook has gone through a few minor changes to make it more readable by clients. The table of age modifiers was moved to a different sheet, and the caption of the workbook displays the name of the client.

The insurance salesperson can now generate a link that will be sent to the client for usage. That link will include all of the information needed to modify the workbook to reflect the information about the user.

The link is relatively long — it does not necessarily need to be written by hand but can be produced by a simple Web application:

```
http://server/CustomWorkbooks/ExcelWorkbook.aspx?_wb=http://server/shared%20documen
ts/PremiumModel.xlsx&ClientName=Eti%20Prish&CarValue=7000&Age=24&Accident10Years=0
```

Deconstructing the Link

The link is built of the parts described n the following table.

Link part	Meaning
http://server/CustomWorkbooks/ ExcelWorkbook.aspx	This is the Web application that will be shown later in this chapter.
_wb=http://...	The _wb parameter is used by the application to figure out which workbook to use as a template.

Link part	Meaning
ClientName=Eti%20Prish	When this parameter is encountered by the application as it parses the request, it instructs it to place the value "Eti Prish" inside the named range called ClientName. (In encoded URL strings, the space is replaced by the %20 encoded sequence.)
CarValue=7000&Age=24&Accident1 0Years	Similar to the ClientName parameter. Will be used to set the relevant named ranges in the workbook. It would have also been possible to pass Excel-style ranges such as Sheet1!B5 instead.

When this link is clicked in an email message or on a web page, it will bring up Excel with the workbook shown in Figure 17-2.

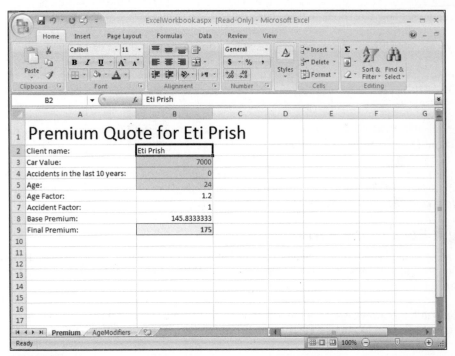

Figure 17-2

What Exactly Happened Here?

The Web application received the request with all the parameters. It used the _wb parameter in an OpenWorkbook() call to Excel Services to open the appropriate workbook. It then iterated over the other parameters and used each one in a SetCell() call to place their values in the workbook. Once that was done, the solution called the GetWorkbook() method to get back the binary workbook. That workbook was then sent back through the HTTP response and opened by Excel, showing the modified Excel workbook.

Protecting Data

Of course, the insurance salesperson probably does not want the user to be able to see the calculations that happen behind the scenes to reach the results. Because of that, the solution allows the link creator to decide what method will be used to get the workbook from the server. In this case, the salesperson can use the `_typ` parameter to require the application to send back a snapshot of the Excel workbook:

```
http://server/CustomWorkbooks/ExcelWorkbook.aspx?_wb=http://server/shared%20
documents/PremiumModel.xlsx&ClientName=Eti%20Prish&CarValue=7000&Age=24&Accident
10Years=0&_typ=snap
```

When the workbook opens up in Excel with this URL, it will not show any of the formulas present in the workbook — just a snapshot of the data.

Another possibility with this solution is to get back a "Published Items" snapshot of the workbook. In that case, Excel Services takes all the published items and puts each of them on its own sheet (no formulas) and sends that new workbook to the caller.

In this case, the URL for the request will have the "pub" value for the `_typ` parameter:

```
http://server/CustomWorkbooks/ExcelWorkbook.aspx?_wb=http://server/shared%20
documents/PremiumModel.xlsx&ClientName=Eti%20Prish&CarValue=7000&Age=24&Accident
10Years=0&_typ=pub
```

When opened in Excel, the result is a single sheet (shown in Figure 17-3) containing only the information that should be interesting to the user.

This is not by itself a security measure against users gaining access to the formulas in the workbook. Consider using the "View only right" option of SharePoint document libraries to prevent certain users from accessing sensitive information inside a workbook.

Taking It Back to the Server

Instead of using the workbook inside Excel 2007, it is also possible to make EWA load the workbook — placing the full link in the Workbook `Url` property of EWA will make the workbook open on the server, parameterized.

To allow this, the administrator of the server needs to remember to add the `CustomWorkbook` Web application to the Trusted locations configuration list so that Excel Services will allow files to be loaded from it.

> A word of caution: Such custom workbooks on the server gain absolutely no benefits from optimizations. Due to the nature of the application, each new workbook will be treated as a completely new entity and be loaded accordingly. This means that server load can increase dramatically if used in such a manner.

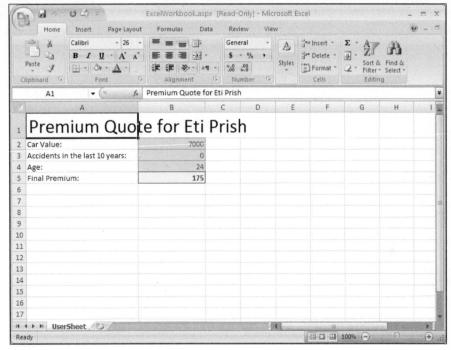

Figure 17-3

Coding the Solution

The solution consists of a single web project containing a single ASPX page. The page uses the same "trick" used in Chapter 14 when the RSS project had to send an XML RSS feed back to the client.

CustomWorkbooks Project

The project is a Web site application with a single helper static class in it, used to store various string constants. The actual processing occurs on the `ExcelWorkbook.aspx` web page, which is using the `ExcelWorkbook` class for code-behind.

Constants Class

The constants class contains all of the strings used in the query string by the application:

```
public static class Constants
{
    public const string WorkbookQuery = "_wb";
    public const string ServerQuery = "_server";
    public const string RecalcQuery = "_rec";
    public const string RefreshQuery = "_ref";
    public const string WorkbookTypeQuery = "_typ";
```

```
        public const string WorkbookTypeFull = "full";
        public const string WorkbookTypeSnapshot = "snap";
        public const string WorkbookTypePublished = "pub";
    }
```

ExcelWorkbook Class (ExcelWorkbook.aspx)

The code-behind class for the `ExcelWorkbook.aspx` page contains all the logic needed for querying and returning the modified workbooks to the callers.

The code entry point is at the `Page_Load()` method, which is tied to `Load` event of the page:

The pages that ASP.NET creates by default hook up events automatically by using reflection. There's no need to make the event hooking calls.

```
protected void Page_Load(object sender, EventArgs e)
{
    string workbookUrl = Request.QueryString[Constants.WorkbookQuery];
    string server = Request.QueryString[Constants.ServerQuery];
    if (String.IsNullOrEmpty(server))
    {
        server = String.Format(
            "http://{0}/_vti_bin/ExcelService.asmx",
            Environment.MachineName);
    }
    RenderWorkbook(workbookUrl, server);
}
```

For each request, the page tries to find the workbook and server parameters. If there is no server parameter, the method guesses at the server name by using the default SharePoint installation location.

This logic for figuring the name of the server is not perfect. Depending on deployment type, it may fail to produce a valid server name. Another option for doing this is to use a configuration option to specify the default server name.

The `RenderWorkbook()` method is responsible for interfacing with Excel Services and opening the workbook, modifying it and writing the result to the HTTP stream that is returned to the caller:

```
private void RenderWorkbook(string workbookUrl, string server)
{
    bool recalc = Request.QueryString[Constants.RecalcQuery] != null;
    bool refresh = Request.QueryString[Constants.RefreshQuery] != null;
    string type = Request.QueryString[Constants.WorkbookTypeQuery];

    ExcelServices service = new ExcelServices(ExcelServicesType.Automatic,
server);
    byte[] buffer = null;
    using (Session session = service.Open(workbookUrl))
    {
        ModifyWorkbook(session);

        if (refresh)
```

```
            {
                session.Refresh();
            }
            if (recalc)
            {
                session.CalculateWorkbook();
            }

            buffer = GetWorkbook(session, type);
        }

        // Read the workbok information.
        Response.Clear();
        Response.AddHeader("LAST-MODIFIED", DateTime.Now.ToString("r"));
        Response.Charset = "";
        Response.ContentType =
            "application/vnd.openxmlformats-officedocument.spreadsheetml.sheet";
        Response.OutputStream.Write(buffer, 0, buffer.Length);
        Response.End();
    }
```

This method first takes from the query string some of the other information it needs, such as whether or not the workbook needs to be recalculated and/or refreshed. It also takes the value that represents the type of workbook the caller expects to get back (more on that in the section that discusses the GetWorkbook() method).

Once all the information is available, the method creates an ExcelServices class instance and a Session instance from it. That session is used in the ModifyWorkbook() method, which makes sure to update all the appropriate cells. Then, as needed, the session is refreshed and recalculated and then the workbook binary representation is retrieved from the server.

Finally, the Response object is modified to return the Excel workbook back to the caller instead of the standard HTML that it usually returns. The Response instance is first cleared, then the appropriate headers are placed in it. The AddHeader() call adds the "LAST-MODIFIED" header to the HTTP response. Excel Services will fail to load the file if this header is missing. The ContentType property specifies the mime type that will be used to activate the downloaded contents. In this case, the mime type corresponds to the new XLSX format.

The last action on the Response object is to take the buffer that was received from the workbook and place it in the stream by using the OutputStream.Write() method.

The ModifyWorkbook() method that was mentioned iterates the query string parameters received in the request and uses the SetCellA1() method to modify the workbook:

```
private void ModifyWorkbook(Session session)
{
    foreach (string key in Request.QueryString.Keys)
    {
        if (!key.StartsWith("_"))
        {
            string value = Request[key];
            string range = key;
```

```
                string sheet = "";
                int index = range.IndexOf('!');
                if (index >= 0)
                {
                        sheet = range.Substring(0, index);
                        range = range.Substring(index + 1);
                }

                session.SetCellA1(sheet, range, value);
        }
    }
}
```

The `Keys` collection of the `QueryString` object is iterated through and each key examined. If the key starts with an underscore, it is ignored (as it is assumed to be part of the hard-coded parameters).

In the cases where the key is expected to be a range name, the method uses the `SetCellA1()` method on the session to modify the cell after parsing the range name.

The `GetWorkbook()` method uses the `Session` instance to get back the binary representation of the workbook. Depending on what the parameters are, it may request the workbook in one of a few ways:

```
private static byte[] GetWorkbook(Session session,string type)
{
    byte[] buffer = null;
    WorkbookType?[] types = new WorkbookType?[2] { null, null };
    if (String.IsNullOrEmpty(type))
    {
        types[0] = WorkbookType.FullWorkbook;
        types[1] = WorkbookType.FullSnapshot;
    }
    else if (type.Equals(
        Constants.WorkbookTypeFull,
        StringComparison.OrdinalIgnoreCase))
    {
        types[0] = WorkbookType.FullWorkbook;
    }
    else if (type.Equals(
        Constants.WorkbookTypeSnapshot,
        StringComparison.OrdinalIgnoreCase))
    {
        types[0] = WorkbookType.FullSnapshot;
    }
    else if (type.Equals(
        Constants.WorkbookTypePublished,
        StringComparison.OrdinalIgnoreCase))
    {
        types[0] = WorkbookType.PublishedItemsSnapshot;
    }

    foreach (WorkbookType? tryType in types)
    {
        if (tryType.HasValue)
```

```
        {
            try
            {
                buffer = session.GetWorkbook(tryType.Value).RawData;
                break;
            }
            catch (SoapException)
            {
            }
        }
    }

    return buffer;
}
```

The first `if-else` chain in the method checks to see what type is requested — this will determine the contents of the `types` array. For each of the strings "full", "snap", or "pub", the `WorkbookType` enum requested from the server will be `FullWorkbook`, `FullSnapshot`, or `PublishedItemSnapshot`, respectively. If no parameter is specified, the array will contain two values — `FullWorkbook` and `FullSnapshot`.

The `types` array is then iterated through, and each of the `WorkbookType` values is passed to the server. The first call to succeed is returned.

When the type of workbook wanted is present on the query string of the URL, the solution will only try to fetch that specific type. If that results in a failure, nothing is returned to the user. If, on the other hand, the URL does not specify the type of workbook required, the system will first try `FullWorkbook` and, failing that, `FullSnapshot`.

Summary

This chapter shows one way of creating workbooks on the fly. The usage can range from auto-generating whole libraries of workbooks that differ only by a few parameters or, alternately, by allowing people to dynamically access workbooks with parameters modified according to their needs, without actually having to modify the workbook.

18

SQL Tables and SharePoint Lists

While Excel Services does not support relational query tables out of the box, it is possible to add a UDF that will make some of the functionality available.

With query tables in Excel, it is possible to bring massive amounts of data in raw form directly into the grid. This is different from having the data as part of a PivotTable, which is supported in Excel Services but requires extra steps of postprocessing.

Overview

The idea is to create a UDF that can return data from relational sources in the form of an array so that it can be returned into a range. The final UDF project will have both a UDF that does native SQL Server querying and one that uses any OLE DB relational source. Since both are really similar, this chapter only shows the SQL Server one.

Incidentally, this lack of support for query tables also means no support for SharePoint lists inside Excel Services. Another UDF shown in this chapter solves this problem, while at the same time adding writeback abilities as well.

> **Important!!! The UDFs prefixed with** `Private` **in this chapter allow impersonated data access from Excel workbooks to SQL Server or other OLE DB sources. This can open up vulnerabilities in your system. In a worst-case scenario, malicious workbooks can cause databases to be corrupted or potentially even execute malicious code on database servers. It is imperative that the examples shown in this chapter are only used with trusted workbooks. At the end of the chapter, in the "Extras" section, there are a few ideas that can help UDF authors write safer versions of these methods. Using the "Shared" versions of these methods should be safe as long as the system is properly configured (databases are properly guarded by access control, for example).**

Use

This section shows a few examples of where database queries can be used. It also shows some of the extended capabilities of UDFs such as caching and gives some ideas for advanced usage such as dynamic parameters for WHERE clauses.

All examples use SQL Server as the relational database source and the sample AdventureWorks database for data. Another UDF available inside the module allows for querying any OLE DB provider.

Shared and Private Flavors

The UDF used to access the database throughout these examples is PrivateSqlServerQuery. This ensures that the query will be made while the UDF is impersonating the user opening the workbook and thus behave as if the user issued the query (see Chapter 9 for more information). Things to keep in mind when using this method:

❏ When this method is used, the amount of sharing done between users is reduced — on systems with no interactivity, this can negatively impact performance.

On deployments that expect a lot of workbook interactivity this privatization would probably happen anyway, so the only impact should be the time it takes to execute the query.

❏ This method will fail if Excel Services is not properly configured. The server has to allow delegation as an access method for it to work.

❏ Different results may return from different calls due to the fact that they are executed under different user accounts.

While PrivateSqlServerQuery() is useful in most cases, sometimes it's not really needed and the potentially more efficient SharedSqlServerQuery() UDF can be used. This flavor does not impersonate the user, so it can be shared across users, producing a potentially more efficient system.

When caching is used with shared version of the UDF, even more performance gains can be realized. Caching is discussed a little later in this chapter.

It is important to note, however, that when the shared flavor of the UDF is used, the connection string needs to contain the credentials used to access the database (or, alternatively, the database needs to allow access to anonymous users).

Both UDFs have the same signature — everything described below can be used with both flavors of the UDF.

Basic Example — Getting to the Data

The first example shows how to bring data from a relational source into an Excel Services workbook. On a separate sheet from the rest of the workbook, the author placed some information about the wanted table. In this case, the data will contain information about the connection string and about the SQL statement that needs to be executed.

In this case, the connection string will be:

```
Data Source=OSS\SQLEXPRESS;Initial Catalog=AdventureWorks;Integrated Security=True
```

And the SQL statement:

```
Select Product.ProductID, Product.Name, Product.ProductNumber from
Production.Product
```

The cells containing these strings are named `Conn_AdventureWorks` and `SQL_Products` (respectively). They can then be used in the following array UDF to get back relational data from an SQL server:

```
{=PrivateSqlServerQuery(Conn_AdventureWorks, SQL_Products)}
```

Figure 18-1 shows the result, when viewed in the EWA.

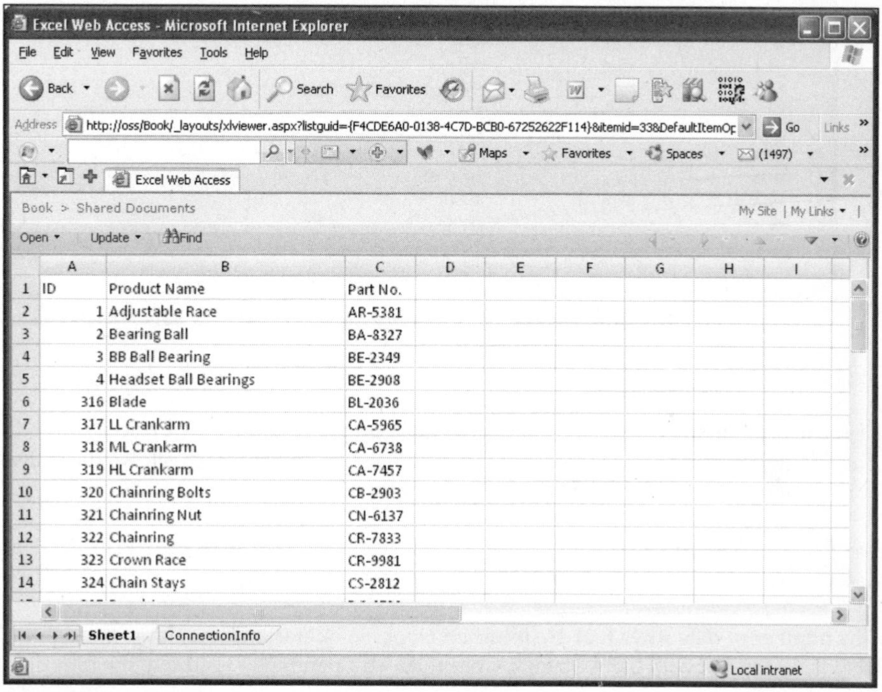

Figure 18-1

Less Data — the "#N/A" Problem

When an array function returns less data than the range it is in, Excel Services places the "#N/A" error in the area for which it does not have information.

This problem can surface if the SQL statement inside the `SQL_Products` cell changes so that it returns less information:

```
Select Product.ProductID, Product.Name, Product.ProductNumber from
Production.Product WHERE Product.Name Like '%Bearing%'
```

Figure 18-2 shows the results after the UDF has been executed. In this case, the call returns only three rows, resulting in a lot of "#N/A" errors in the cells.

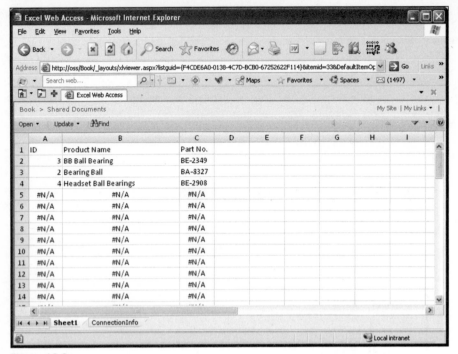

Figure 18-2

Because the list contains fewer items than the range is prepared for, Excel Services shows the "#N/A" error. For this reason, the UDF also contains an optional parameter, which allows the caller to select the minimum amount of rows that can be returned from the UDF.

Excel Services UDFs do not actually support optional parameters. Instead, this specific UDF uses a `ParamArray` *at the end of its parameter list. This serves a similar role.*

When the number of data rows that are returned from the operation is not large enough to fill that range, the UDF will fill the rest with blank strings. Once that extra parameter is added, the formula looks like this:

```
{=PrivateSqlServerQuery(Conn_AdventureWorks, SQL_Products, ROWS(DataTableArea))}
```

The name of the range into which the array function is called is `DataTableArea`. Calling the `ROWS()` Excel function on that range returns the amount of rows in it. When executed, the UDF will make sure it returns at least that number of rows, as shown in Figure 18-3.

Adding Parameters to the Query

Of course, this being Excel, the query that is executed against the relational server can be produced by any Excel formula. This gives authors the freedom of creating SQL statements that return different data based on user input.

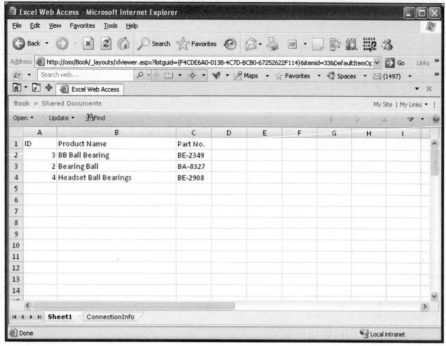

Figure 18-3

For the next example, the string representing the SQL statement is changed to include the contents of a different cell on the sheet:

```
=CONCATENATE("Select Product.ProductID, Product.Name, Product.ProductNumber from
Production.Product WHERE Product.Name Like '%", ProductSearch,"%'")
```

The formula will produce a SELECT statement, which uses the named range ProductSearch in the WHERE clause to only return those rows that has that string in them. If the workbook is saved with [ProductSearchParameter] inside the ProductSearch cell, the resulting text will be:

```
Select Product.ProductID, Product.Name, Product.ProductNumber from
Production.Product WHERE Product.Name Like '%[ProductSearchParameter]%'
```

The last step the author needs to do is to publish the workbook to a SharePoint document library with the ProductSearch named range exposed as a parameter. When opened in EWA, the parameter pane will show, giving users the ability to define what data they want to see (as shown in Figure 18-4).

Caching Data

In the previous examples, each time the workbook is calculated, the UDF is executed and the query is issued. While useful in some scenarios, it can also be a relatively costly way of getting data back from the server.

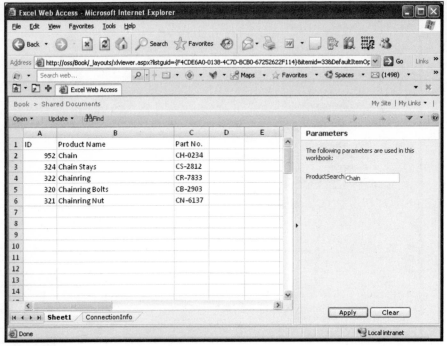

Figure 18-4

The UDFs allow the author to choose a name for each query. Results of queries that have names are always cached by the system, allowing for speedier retrieval on each calculation.

The name of the query is passed in the fourth parameter:

```
{=PrivateSqlServerQuery(Conn_AdventureWorks, SQL_Products, ROWS(DataTableArea),
"QueryName")}
```

By default, the UDF will cache queries for 60 seconds — requests coming after that time is up will cause a query to occur again. To override this setting, it is possible to pass as the fifth parameter the lifetime of the cached query:

```
{=PrivateSqlServerQuery(Conn_AdventureWorks, SQL_Products, ROWS(DataTableArea),
"QueryName", 300)}
```

In the case above, the query cache will be cleared every 5 minutes, allowing new data to flow in.

There are two levels of caching — one for private tables and one for shared tables. These caches are not related or connected. When a named cache item is created by using the private flavor of the UDF, that name can still be used in the shared flavor and will be isolated.

OLE DB Providers

Similarly to the SQL Server–querying UDFs, there are two UDFs that query OLE DB data sources. The methods have the same exact signatures as the SQL server ones:

```
PrivateOleDBQuery(connectionString, sql[, minRows[, queryName[, cacheTimeout]]])
SharedOleDBQuery(connectionString, sql[, minRows[, queryName[, cacheTimeout]]])
```

The connection string has to contain more information than the one in the SQL Server version, though:

```
Provider=SQLOLEDB;Data Source=OSS\SQLEXPRESS;Integrated Security=SSPI;Initial
Catalog=AdventureWorks
```

Getting Data from SharePoint Lists

SharePoint lists are a great location in which to save data. With this solution, it is possible to get data from such a list and display it in a workbook.

The list used in this example contains a SharePoint list of quotes prepared for various people (as shown in Figure 18-5).

A workbook author (perhaps an analyst in the insurance company) wants to take the list and see how low each quote will be after an applied discount. Figure 18-6 shows the result after using the UDF to fetch the data into a range in Excel; the analyst can add a column containing the calculation.

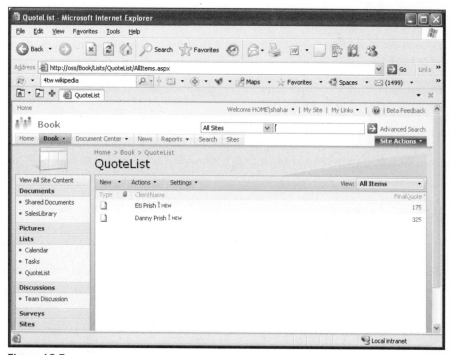

Figure 18-5

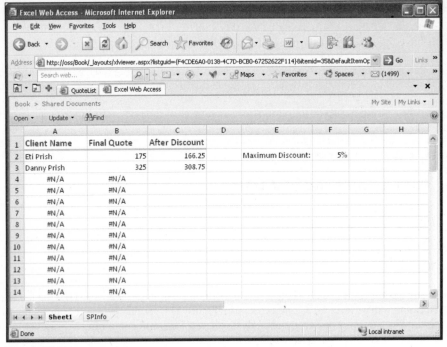

Figure 18-6

The C column in this workbook is actually calculated, based on the corresponding B column and on the discount in cell F2.

The UDF call that returns the SharePoint data contains a reference to the server, the list name and to a list of columns that need to be fetched:

```
=PrivateGetSharePointList(SPSite, SPWeb, ListName, FieldList)
```

In this case, each of the names passed to the UDF is a named range inside the workbook, as shown in the following table.

Named Range	Contents	
SPSite	"http://oss"	The SharePoint site.
SPWeb	"book"	The Web name inside the site that contains the list.
ListName	"QuoteList"	The name of the list in SharePoint.
FieldList	A multi-cell range containing the strings "ClientName" and "FinalQuote".	Can contain more field names; each one will cause another column to exist in the return array.

Like the relational data retrieval UDFs described before, the SharePoint list retrieval methods also have an extra parameter specifying the minimum size the list should be to get rid of the "#NA" errors in the cells.

Writing Data Back to SharePoint

The solution also exposes functionality that will allow the caller to write data back into SharePoint lists. The UDF that does this is called `WriteToSharePointList()` and has the following signature:

```
WriteBackToSharePointList(siteName, webName, listName, findRowField, findRowValue,
writeBackInfo)
```

The first three parameters are the same as the ones passed to the `PrivateGetSharePointList()` UDF. The `findRowField` and `findRowValue` parameters will be used to find a specific row in the list — the UDF will search for the first row where the column with the name `findRowField` equals to the values inside the `findRowValue` parameter.

Once the row is found, the UDF uses the cells inside `writeBackInfo` parameter to set data back into the list. Each cell in the range passed into `writeBackInfo` needs to contain a string in the following form:

```
fieldName = newValue
```

Each such pair is parsed and the left side (`fieldName` in this case) is sought inside the found SharePoint item. Once found, the value of that field is modified to the right side (`newValue` in this case).

Placing a call to this UDF in the PremiumModel workbook that was shown in previous chapters will allow the list seen in the previous section to update automatically when an insurance agent changes values in the workbook (as shown in Figure 18-7).

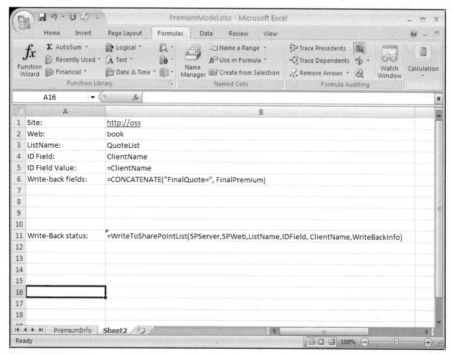

Figure 18-7

The call to `WriteToSharePointList()` passes the first three parameters identifying the lists. Next the named ranges, `IDField` and `ClientName` are passed in (the first corresponding to the SharePoint column name that houses the name of the client and the second corresponding to the name of the client as specified in the workbook). Finally, the named range `WriteBackInfo` is passed in — containing a single cell (B6 in this case). This cell will contain the string "FinalQuote=####" where #### is the final premium as calculated by the workbook.

For clarification, in this case, if the name of the client is "Danny Prish" and the final quote is $125, the call will look like this:

```
=WriteToSharePointList("http://oss", "book", "QuoteList", "ClientName", "Danny
Prish", { "FinalQuote=125" })
```

Once executed, the UDF will go through the list shown in the previous section, find the name "Danny Prish" in the ClientName column and set the FinalQuote column to be 125.

Coding the Solution

All the functionality presented in this chapter is implemented in a single C# library project, exposing the various UDF classes.

While nothing prevents all the code from residing inside the same class, the solution exposes three — one for SQL Server data, one for OLE DB data, and one for the SharePoint UDFs.

Pes.DataUdfs Project

On top of the three classes, this project also contains some support classes for caching and for functionality that is shared across the OLE DB and SQL Server UDF classes.

CachedTableCollection Class

This class implements a collection of `CachedTable` instances in the system. The implementation is based on a hash table but contains only a single method, called `GetTableByName()`, which, on top of returning a `CachedTable` instance by its name if it exists, will also add a new `CachedTable` instance if it does not. The method also returns a new instance of the `CachedTable` class if the name requested is empty. (As explained earlier in the chapter, empty names tell the UDFs not to cache results at all.)

The class also takes care of protecting itself against concurrent usage using a simple .NET lock:

```
public class CachedTableCollection
{
    private Dictionary<string, CachedTable> m_tables =
        new Dictionary<string, CachedTable>(StringComparer.OrdinalIgnoreCase);
    private object m_lock = new object();

    public CachedTable GetTableByName(string name)
    {
        lock (m_lock)
        {
```

```
                CachedTable result = null;
                if (String.IsNullOrEmpty(name))
                {
                     result = new CachedTable("");
                }
                else if (!m_tables.TryGetValue(name, out result))
                {
                     result = new CachedTable(name);
                     m_tables[name] = result;
                }
                return result;
          }
     }
}
```

CachedTable Class

Each named cache references an instance of a CachedTable class. This class contains a reference to a System.Data.DataTable class (which is what the various relational data access modules return).

As implemented now, it would have been more efficient for the CachedTable class to store a reference to the object array produced from the DataTable. However, like most projects, this one is just a starting point for a potentially more elaborate one. Some of the potential functionality that can be added to the project later on may rely on the metadata being there.

```
public class CachedTable
{
     private DataTable m_table;
     private string m_name;
     private DateTime m_lastUpdate = DateTime.MinValue;

     public CachedTable(string name)
     {
          Name = name;
     }
     // ...
}
```

Since caches have a preset lifetime after which they expire, The NeedsUpdate() method is used to figure out if the cache is still viable:

```
public bool NeedsUpdate(int updateFrequency)
{
     bool result;
     if (DataTable == null)
     {
          result = true;
     }
     else if (updateFrequency == Constants.NeverUpdate)
     {
          result = false;
     }
     else
```

```
        {
            result = DateTime.Now - TimeSpan.FromSeconds(updateFrequency) >
                LastUpdate;
        }
        return result;
    }
```

In this case, the `m_dataTable` member is first checked (via the `DataTable` property) to see if it exists. If it does, the `CachedTable` instance checks to see if the update frequency is set such that the cache never ages. Finally, the actual age of the item is checked against the update frequency, and if it is too old, the method returns `true`, meaning that the item needs to be updated.

DatabaseUdfHelper Class

The `DatabaseUdfHelper` class is used as a base class for both the `SqlServerUdfs` class and the `OLE DB Udfs` one — it supplies some functionality that is common to both.

The class contains a single instance (nonstatic) member, which holds a `CachedTableCollection` instance used for the cached tables. This instance is used by the UDFs to store the caches accessed via the private flavors of the methods (`PrivateSqlServerQuery()` and `PrivateOLE DB Query()`). For the shared flavors of the UDFs, the class also contains an abstract property for accessing the shared cache. (Since the shared cache table is implemented as a static field in the derived class, it cannot otherwise be accessible to the base class.)

```
public abstract class DatabaseUdfHelper
{
    private CachedTableCollection m_privateTables = new CachedTableCollection();

    protected CachedTableCollection PrivateTables
    {
        get { return m_privateTables; }
        set { m_privateTables = value; }
    }

    protected abstract CachedTableCollection SharedTables
    {
        get;
        set;
    }
// ...
}
```

The method responsible for querying and handling the cache is called `QueryServer()`.

```
protected object[,] QueryServer(
    CachedTableCollection tables,
    string connectionString,
    string sql,
    object[][] extras)
{
    int minRows = Constants.NoRowLimitation;
    string name = null;
    int interval = 60; // 1 minute = 60 seconds
```

```
        InterpretParameters(extras, ref minRows, ref name, ref interval);

    try
    {
        CachedTable cachedTable = tables.GetTableByName(name);

        if (cachedTable.NeedsUpdate(interval))
        {
            DataTable table = GetDataTable(connectionString, sql);
            cachedTable.DataTable = table;
        }

        object[,] result = TableToArray(cachedTable.DataTable, minRows);
        return result;

    }
    catch (Exception e)
    {
        return new object[2, 2] { { e.ToString(), "" }, { "", "" } };
    }
}
```

The first step in the method is to interpret the parameter array passed in from the UDFs. The `InterpretParameters()` method takes the first three items in the array and transforms them (if they exist) to the minimum rows the caller wants, the name of the cached table and the update interval (in that order).

Then, an instance of the `CachedTable` class is retrieved from the appropriate collection. It is then tested to see if it needs updating. If it does, the abstract `GetDataTable()` method retrieves the table, which is then turned into an object array and returned to the caller.

The `GetDataTable()` method above returns an empty `CachedTable` instance if the name is empty or null. In those cases, the call to `NeedsUpdate()` will always return true, causing calls not specifying a name to always issue a database request.

If an exception occurs, it is returned as a 2x1 array to the caller. Had the result been returned in a 1x1 array, it would have been tiled on the entire range. This way, only a single string will appear in the table.

The signature of the abstract method for querying data takes a connection string and an SQL statement, and it returns a `DataTable`.

```
protected abstract DataTable GetDataTable(string connectionString, string sql);
```

Both derving classes will implement this method with the appropriate querying functionality.

The following two methods are called by the UDF methods exposed in the derived classes:

```
protected object[,] SharedQuery(
    string connectionString,
    string sql,
    params object[][] extras)
{
```

```
        return QueryServer(SharedTables, connectionString, sql, extras);
}

protected object[,] PrivateQuery(
     string connectionString,
     string sql,
     params object[][] extras)
{
     WindowsIdentity id =
         Thread.CurrentPrincipal.Identity as WindowsIdentity;
     if (id == null)
     {
         throw new InvalidOperationException(
             "Cannot run if cannot impersonate");
     }

     using (WindowsImpersonationContext context =
         id.Impersonate())
     {
         return QueryServer(PrivateTables, connectionString, sql, extras);
     }
}
```

SharedQuery() and PrivateQuery() both call the QueryServer() helper method with the relevant CachedTableCollection instance. PrivateQuery() also impersonates the user before calling the method to guarantee that the call will be made under the correct account.

SqlServerUdfs Class

Inheriting from the DatabaseUdfHelper class, this class has very little actual work to do. It implements the two abstract methods on the base class, one for returning the shared instance of the CachedTableCollection class and the method for querying the data:

```
[UdfClass]
public class SqlServerUdfs : DatabaseUdfHelper
{
     private static CachedTableCollection m_sharedTables = new
CachedTableCollection();

     protected override CachedTableCollection  SharedTables
     {
         get { return m_sharedTables; }
         set { m_sharedTables = value; }
     }

     protected override DataTable GetDataTable(string connectionString, string sql)
     {
         using (SqlConnection connection = new SqlConnection(connectionString))
         using (SqlCommand command = new SqlCommand())
         {
             connection.Open();
             command.Connection = connection;
             command.CommandType = CommandType.Text;
             command.CommandText = sql;
```

```
                        using (SqlDataReader reader = command.ExecuteReader())
                        {
                                DataTable table = new DataTable();
                                table.Load(reader);
                                return table;
                        }
                }
        }
        // ...
}
```

GetDataTable() opens an SqlConnection instance and an SqlCommand instance against the connection string that is passed in.

The command's properties are set and then it is executed, producing an SqlDataReader instance, which is used to produce a DataTable that is then returned to the caller (the DataBaseUdfHelper.Query-Server() method).

The two UDF methods make calls into the DataBaseUdfHelper support methods:

```
[UdfMethod(IsVolatile = true)]
public object[,] PrivateSqlServerQuery(
     string connectionString,
     string sql,
     params object[][] extras)
{

     return PrivateQuery(connectionString, sql, extras);

}

[UdfMethod(IsVolatile = true)]
public object[,] SharedSqlServerQuery(
     string connectionString,
     string sql,
     params object[][] extras)
{

     return SharedQuery(connectionString, sql, extras);
}
```

OleDbUdfs Class

This class is very similar to the SQL Server one — instead of using the System.Data.SqlClient namespace for data access, though, it uses System.Data.OleDb (and its appropriate connection and command classes).

SharePointUdfs Class

Implementing the SharePoint functionality described above, this class contains two UDF methods and is using the Microsoft.SharePoint namespace for interacting with the SharePoint server:

```
[UdfClass]
public class SharePointUdfs
```

```
{
    // ...
}
```

The `PrivateGetSharePointList()` UDF impersonates the user, similarly to the way the `Database-UdfHelper.PrivateQuery()` method does and calls into the `GetSPListData()` method:

This solution only includes the private flavor of this method. See the Extras section for more information.

```
[UdfMethod(IsVolatile = true)]
public object[,] PrivateGetSharePointList(
    string siteName,
    string webName,
    string listName,
    object[,] fields,
    params object[][] extras)
{
    WindowsIdentity wi = Thread.CurrentPrincipal.Identity as WindowsIdentity;

    if (wi == null)
    {
        throw new InvalidOperationException(
            "Cannot get private information if cannot impersonate");
    }

    using (WindowsImpersonationContext context = wi.Impersonate())
    {
        return GetSPListData(siteName, webName, listName, fields, extras);
    }
}
```

`GetSPListData()` finds the appropriate list in SharePoint and then figures out which fields are needed inside it. It then calls into `GetArrayFromList()` and returns the object array representing the requested list data.

```
private object[,] GetSPListData(
    string siteName,
    string webName,
    string listName,
    object[,] fields,
    object[][] extras)
{
    int minRecords = 2;
    if (extras.Length >= 1)
    {
        minRecords = Convert.ToInt32(extras[0][0]);
    }

    using (SPSite site = new SPSite(siteName))
    {
        SPWeb web = site.AllWebs[webName];
        SPList list = web.Lists[listName];
        Guid[] fieldGuids = GetFieldGuidArray(fields, list);
```

```
            object[,] result = GetArrayFromList(minRecords, list, fieldGuids);
            return result;
    }
}
```

The SharePoint site is first opened by using the SPSite object. The SharePoint list is then accessed by using the indexer on the Lists property of the appropriate SPWeb instance.

The GetFieldGuidArray() method takes field names (also called column names) contained in the fields parameter (which can contain a multi-cell range) and looks for them inside the SharePoint list:

```
private static Guid[] GetFieldGuidArray(object[,] fields, SPList list)
{
    SPFieldCollection fieldCollection = list.Fields;
    List<Guid> fieldIdList = new List<Guid>();

    foreach (object fieldName in fields)
    {
        if (fieldName is string)
        {
            fieldIdList.Add(fieldCollection[(string)fieldName].Id);
        }
    }

    Guid[] fieldGuids = fieldIdList.ToArray();
    return fieldGuids;
}
```

Once GetSPListData() has the list of GUIDs of each of the requested fields, it calls into the GetArray-FromList() method:

```
private static object[,] GetArrayFromList(
    int minRecords,
    SPList list,
    Guid[] fieldGuids)
{
    int recordCount = Math.Max(minRecords, list.ItemCount);
    object[,] result = new object[recordCount, fieldGuids.Length];

    for (int i = 0; i < recordCount; i++)
    {
        if (i < list.ItemCount)
        {
            SPListItem item = list.Items[i];
            for (int j = 0; j < fieldGuids.Length; j++)
            {
                result[i, j] = item[fieldGuids[j]];
            }
        }
        else
        {
            for (int j = 0; j < fieldGuids.Length; j++)
            {
```

```
                          result[i, j] = "";
                    }
              }

        }
        return result;
}
```

Each item in the list is retrieved and then, for each field in the `fieldGuids` parameter, the method finds the appropriate field in the item and adds it to the appropriate location in the returned array.

The `minRecords` parameter is also used in the method as it was in the SQL server data retrieval UDFs so that the caller can determine how many "empty" rows are wanted at the end of the array to avoid the #N/A error.

The last UDF for this chapter writes data back into a SharePoint list. Much like the previous method, it impersonates the user and calls into a helper method — `WriteToSharePointList()` in this case:

```
[UdfMethod]
public string PrivateWriteToSharePointList(
        string siteName,
        string webName,
        string listName,
        string findRowField,
        object[] findRowValue,
        object[,] writeBackInfo)
{
        // Impersonate and call WriteToSharePointList().
}
```

The method that does the writing first looks for the appropriate item in the list (by using the `findRowField` and the `findRowValue` parameters). Once found, it modifies it by using the `WriteValues()` method:

```
private string WriteToSharePointList(
        string siteName,
        string webName,
        string listName,
        string findRowField,
        object[] findRowValue,
        object[,] writeBackInfo)
{
        string result = "#SUCCESS";
        using (SPSite site = new SPSite(siteName))
        {
              SPList list = site.AllWebs[webName].Lists[listName];

              SPItem item = FindItem(list, findRowField, findRowValue[0]);

              if (item == null)
              {
                    return "#SPITEM_NOTFOUND";
              }
```

```
            if (!WriteValues(item, writeBackInfo))
            {
                result = "#SOME_ERRORS";
            }
        }
    }
    return result;
}
```

The strings that this method returns are "status" strings. They are not really errors.

The FindItem() method iterates over the list, looking at the findRowField column, searching for contents that equal the first item in the findRowValue array:

```
private SPItem FindItem(SPList list, string findRowField, object findRowValue)
{
    // Get the column id.
    SPField field = list.Fields[findRowField];
    System.Collections.IComparer comparer = null;

    switch (field.Type)
    {
        case SPFieldType.Number:
            findRowValue = Convert.ToDouble(findRowValue);
            comparer = System.Collections.Comparer.DefaultInvariant;
            break;
        default:
            findRowValue = findRowValue.ToString();
            comparer = StringComparer.OrdinalIgnoreCase;
            break;
    }

    for (int i = 0; i < list.ItemCount; i++)
    {
        SPItem item = list.Items[i];
        if (comparer.Compare(findRowValue, item[findRowField]) == 0)
        {
            return item;
        }
    }
    return null;
}
```

The first step in the method is to make sure the type of the findRowValue parameter is appropriate to the field that is being searched. The code also initializes an IComparer instance to do the actual comparing of the value.

The list is then iterated and each item is checked to see if its findRowField column equals the coerced findRowValue parameter. If a comparison returns 0 (zero), it has been successful and the item is returned to the caller. If an item is not found, null is returned instead.

The WriteValues() method is called by WriteToSharePointList() method if an appropriate item is found:

```
private bool WriteValues(SPItem item, object[,] writeBackInfo)
{
    bool cleanSuccess = true;
    foreach (object o in writeBackInfo)
    {
        string info = o as string;
        if (info == null)
            continue;

        string[] splat = info.Split(Seperator, 2);
        if (splat.Length != 2)
            continue;

        try
        {
            item[splat[0].Trim()] = splat[1].Trim();
        }
        catch
        {
            cleanSuccess = false;
        }
    }
    item.Update();
    return cleanSuccess;
}
```

WriteValues() takes each string contained in the writeBackInfo array and parses it — each one has to be in the form of "X=Y" where X is the name of the field and Y is the new content that needs to be written into it.

If the parsing is successful, the method tries writing the data into the item at the appropriate field. If one of the calls for setting data into a field fails, the method changes its return value to false, indicating some potential problems.

As a final step, the method calls the item.Update() method, which guarantees that the data is written back into the SharePoint list.

Summary

This solution touched on three major areas that lack proper support in Excel Services. While the solution is not perfect, it answers some of the needs that people may run into when they want to integrate Excel Services with relational databases or with SharePoint lists.

On top of that, the solution can also be integrated with SharePoint by writing data back to it. This can be very helpful in some cases where tracking scenarios need to be baked directly into Excel Services.

More ideas for this solution:

❑ **Flexible access to tables.** Cached tables can be accessed using a row/field coordinate system instead of as a whole range of data. This can be especially useful when authors want to have more granular access to the queried data. Specifically, this can allow authors to have data tables with filters and sorting.

❑ **Allow only stored procedures to run.** Allowing arbitrary SQL to run can be dangerous with the private flavors of the UDFs. Limiting these UDFs to only running stored procedures can alleviate some of the potential dangers. For more security, it is also required that the UDFs be configurable so that they only run certain stored procedures against certain databases. Only under these circumstances should administrators enable usage of the private UDFs on trusted workbooks.

❑ **Paging.** Some scenarios may gain from allowing paging of the data. In those cases, the author of the UDF can allow more parameters that govern the first page and page sizes, returning less data to the sheet. When combined with workbook parameters (in EWA), this can give the work-book user more control over which portions of the data should be visible.

❑ **Shared SharePoint calls.** The UDFs do not contain shared flavor for the UDFs that access SharePoint lists. Allowing those would probably require extra parameters for proper user authentication to happen.

❑ **SQL-aware caching.** The caching mechanism built into the SQL Server UDFs and into the OLE DB UDFs does not take into account the SQL used to get the data. This means that if the SQL statement is modified, but the timeout interval has not yet passed, no requerying will occur. Checking for changes in the SQL statement as part of the decision on whether or not to issue a requery would solve this problem.

❑ **Clean up.** The caching mechanism for the UDFs does not perform any cleanup on the cached data. This is less of an issue with the private caches, since those will be cleared when the session times out or is closed. For the shared caches though, this can result in large amounts of allocated memory that is never cleaned up. A timer mechanism that keeps polling the cache and clearing unneeded items would solve this problem.

❑ **Different columns.** It can be useful to allow the relational data UDFs to select which columns are needed from a cached query. This will allow a single cached query to be used as a source for multiple targets on the workbook.

19

External Workbook References

One of the features that Excel supports and Excel Services does not is the External Workbook Reference feature. This allows an Excel workbook to reference cells in another workbook. The behavior of this feature depends on a number of things, described below in the "Overview" section.

The solution shown in this chapter brings some of the capabilities of this feature to the server. It also adds some capabilities that the Excel feature does not contain.

Overview

One of three things may occur when a target workbook is opened in Excel (the referencing workbook will be called the "target workbook" and the referenced workbook the "source workbook"):

❑ **Scenario 1**: The source workbook does not exist. Excel will use the last cell value that was fetched (the last values are stored in the target workbook).

❑ **Scenario 2**: The source workbook exists, but is not opened in Excel. The source workbook file will be opened and the referenced cell read and placed into the target workbook.

❑ **Scenario 3**: The source workbook is opened in Excel. The target workbook and source workbook get calculated together, each being part of the other's calculation chain.

Figure 19-1 shows Book1 and Book2:

In Figure 19-1, two workbooks are shown. Book1 is used as a source to Book2 (A2 in Book2 is referencing A1 in Book1). Book2 is also used as a source to Book1 (A3 in Book1 is referencing A2 in Book2).

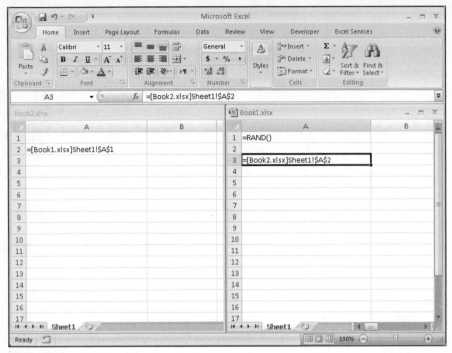

Figure 19-1

Following the rules described above, one of the following things will happen:

❑ **Scenario 1**: Book2 does not exist. Excel will remember the last value read from it (the random number it referenced the last time it was opened) and display that (showing different values in A1 and A3 of Book1).

❑ **Scenario 2**: Book2 does exist, but is not opened in Excel. Excel will open the file itself (but will not calculate it) and take the value it was saved with (showing different values in A1 and A3).

❑ **Scenario 3**: Book2 is opened in Excel. Excel will calculate both workbooks at the same time, showing the same value in A1 and A3 of Book1. Book2 will also show the same value in its A2.

The solution proposed for Excel Services works differently. None of the scenarios actually fit the server environment:

❑ **Scenario 1**: If a workbook does not exist, the solution will return an error. The ability to store information for later retrieval in a cell is beyond UDFs in the first version of Excel Services.

By using a database it is possible to store the last value of the cell and use it when a workbook that is being referenced does not exist. However, even if that method is used, there is still a potential security problem. Since Excel Services is a protected multiuser environment, if the same exact mechanism was to be used as it is used in Excel, there would be a potential data disclosure problem with this method. The database solution would also entail storing which user got the value and making sure that different users don't get values they are not allowed to see.

❑ **Scenario 2**: Since each session a user works in is roughly equivalent to an instance of Excel running, and since it is impossible to open more than one workbook inside a single session, Scenario 2 seems to be the closest one to what can be done on the server. However, there are two potential problems with it. The first is that some users may not have access to the actual file contents of the referenced workbook (if, for example, they have view-only rights). This will make it impossible for the solution to read the static value stored in the workbook. The second issue is similar to the one in Scenario 1 — allowing the reading of values from the workbook may result in information disclosure.

❑ **Scenario 3**: As explained in Scenario 2 — it is impossible to open two workbooks in the same session. For that reason, Scenario 3 is impossible to implement as well.

The solution proposed is a combination of Scenario 2 and Scenario 3. When an external workbook is referenced, it will be opened in its own session and (potentially) calculated.

This solution ends up calculating the workbook as Scenario 3 does, but it does so in isolation, which is similar to how Scenario 2 works.

Note: This UDF provides functionality that is somewhat similar to what the custom Web Services solution did in Chapter 13. There are a few differences though.

1. Using this UDF requires very little administrator work — the only thing needed is for the UDF to be registered on the server. The custom Web Services solution requires a dedicated Web application running on a server.

2. The session manipulation UDFs (the ones prefixed with `PrivateSession_`) allow a much more elaborate way of working against sessions. Instead of just writing values and getting back results (which is what the custom Web Service does), it allows for iterative modifications of a workbook on the server and returning the results of those modifications to the calling workbook.

3. The custom Web Services solution provides a way of completely abstracting Excel Services out of the picture — developers or users using those Web Services don't even know they are working against an Excel Workbook.

4. Custom Web Services users also get an annotated programming interface that explains exactly what parameters are available for each method. Users of the External Workbook References UDFs need to know the structure of the workbook to be able to make use of it.

Use

The UDF library exposes two families of functions. The first contains a single function that behaves in a one-off manner whereby a workbook is opened and read, and cells are returned. The second contains multiple functions allowing callers to write "Excel programs" that interact with a server workbook.

Getting Data out of Workbooks Quickly

Figure 19-2 shows a risk analysis workbook that shows the authors how their risk factors compare to the national average. Since the risk factor table used already exists in an external workbook (the PremiumModel workbook, which was used in some of the previous chapters), the authors will get the data from there.

The workbook contains an array formula on the right side, which retrieves data from PremiumModel workbook. The formula reads:

```
=PrivateGetWorkbookRange(ExcelServer, PrermiumWorkbook, "AgeRiskTable")
```

`ExcelServer` is a named range that references a cell containing the name of the server that's being used (in this case, `http://oss/_vti_bin/ExcelService.asmx`). `PremiumWorkbook` is also a named range, containing the full URL of the workbook (in this case, `http://oss/book/shared documents/PremiumModel.xlsx`).

When displayed on the server, the workbook will show the data from the premium model and use it to calculate the risk (as shown in Figure 19-3).

The conditional formatting alerts the user of the workbook as to which of their companies risk factors are below national average.

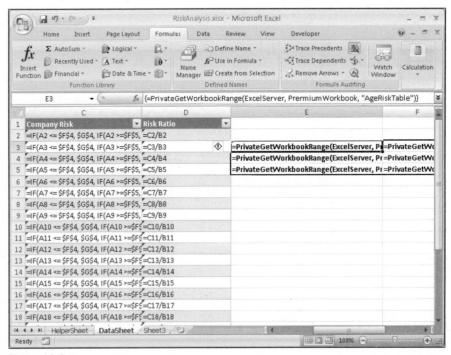

Figure 19-2

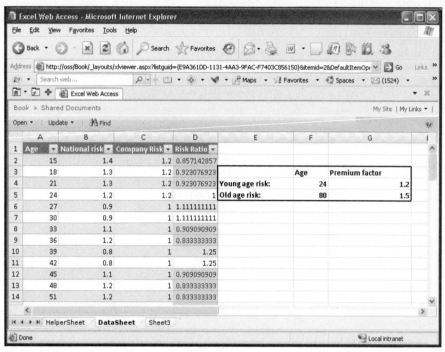

Figure 19-3

Setting Values to the Workbook

The risk table, as seen in Figure 19-2, contains a calculation in the third column that uses the age table to calculate the risk. The calculation is:

```
=IF(A3 <= $F$4, $G$4, IF(A3 >=$F$5, $G$5, 1))
```

Note that this formula is very similar to the formula that's already inside the premium model. The logic is being duplicated. With this solution, these issues can be resolved by using some of the extra parameters available on the `PrivateGetWorkbookRange()` method, as shown in Figure 19-4.

In this workbook, the age risk table has been removed and instead the caller now uses the following formula in the "Company Risk" column:

```
=PrivateGetWorkbookRange(ExcelServer, PrermiumWorkbook,"AgeFactor", Table1[[#This
Row],[AgeSetCommand]])
```

The first two arguments are the same as before. The third one requests a different named range, though — the `AgeFactor` named range. There is also a fourth argument that is being passed — `Table1[[#ThisRow], [AgeSetCommand]]`. This uses structured references to take the value from the AgeSetCommand column. The column contains a string telling the UDF which cells should be set to what values in the source workbook before the resulting cells are read.

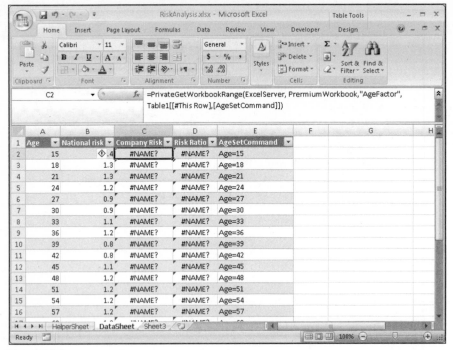

Figure 19-4

If this were the real risk analysis workbook, this column would probably have been hidden.

In this case, the UDF will do the following operations:

1. Use the server passed in the first argument to open the workbook passed in the second argument.

2. Use the fourth argument to figure out what cells need to be set (in this case for each row, the named range Age gets set to the value inside the "Age" column). This argument can contain a range of cells containing values in the form of "XXX=YYY" where XXX is the cell to set and YYY is the value.

3. From the source workbook that was opened and modified, take the cell or range passed in by the third argument and return that to the user.

4. Close the workbook.

Session manipulation through Excel

The method shown before has a pretty steep overhead. With each row in the table, a workbook is opened, modified, and closed. It would have been much more efficient to open the workbook once, make changes for each row, extracting the calculated value each time, and only then close the workbook.

To do this, the solution provides a special set of UDFs, which resembles the functionality exposed by Excel Web Services.

Figure 19-5 shows a workbook that produces the same result but in less time.

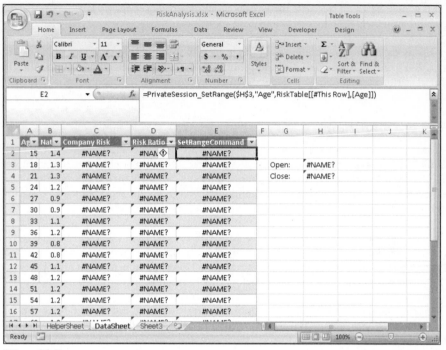

Figure 19-5

The following list shows what each cell contains:

```
H3: =PrivateSession_Open(ExcelServer, PremiumWorkbook)
H4: =PrivateSession_Close(H3,RiskTable)
SetRangeCommand column: =PrivateSession_SetRange($H$3,"Age",RiskTable[[#This
Row],[Age]])
CompanyRisk column: = =PrivateSession_GetRange(RiskTable[[#This
Row],[SetRangeCommand]],"AgeFactor",FALSE)
```

The formula in H3 opens up a workbook and returns a Session ID. All the other formulas use H3 as their first parameter — this means that Excel Services will need to calculate it first, before it calculates the other formulas referencing it, which guarantees that the workbook will be opened on the server.

Inside H4 there's a call to a UDF that will close the workbook. The second parameter to the `Private-Session_Close()` method is the name of the risk table. This guarantees that Excel will only call this method after it has evaluated the entire table and thus after it has finished reading all the values from the session.

The SetRange column contains a call to the UDF that sets values inside the workbook. It takes the session as the first argument, the range that needs to be set as the second (the named range "Age" in the source workbook `PremiumModel.xlsx`) and the value that needs to be set (the number inside the "Age" column on the target workbook — the one shown in the screen shot).

Finally, the CompanyRisk column contains a call to the UDF that extracts values from the workbook. It takes the result of the SetRange column as a parameter (since all action UDFs in this family return the session ID), making Excel calculate the workbook in the correct order (first the set range operation will execute and then the get range operation).

Using this method for manipulating the workbook will make half the number of calls to the server, reducing the overall time by half the amount of time the calls' overhead takes. In reality, the actual amount of performance increase is dependent on how complex the calculation is. The more complex and time-consuming the calculation, the less time you will save with this method.

Using Other Operations

The following example shows a workbook that helps an insurance agent track a list of her clients. Each row in the list displays all the relevant information (car price, age, accidents). The workbook uses that information (and the external workbook PremiumModel) to calculate the yearly price of the premium. Since the agent buys the premium for a potentially lower price, the workbook also contains information about the lowest price for which they can actually offer the premium.

Each row requires its own calculation — the three values need to be placed inside the cells in the external workbook and a single cell gets read. In this case, though, the PremiumModel workbook does not automatically calculate when the workbook changes. This in turn means that after placing all three values, the workbook needs to be calculated before the real results are extracted (as shown in Figure 19-6).

The calls to opening and closing the workbooks are the same as in the previous example, as is the one for retrieving the premium — the same tricks are used to make sure that the cells are calculated at the right moment.

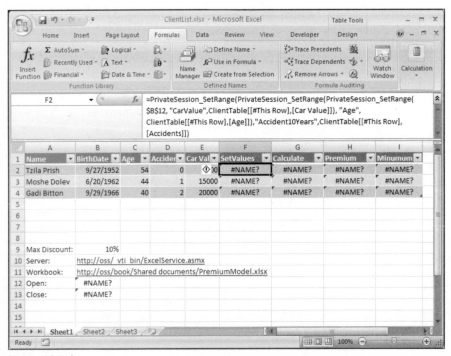

Figure 19-6

The SetValues column sets all three values into the Premium model. The formula used for that is:

```
=PrivateSession_SetRange(PrivateSession_SetRange(PrivateSession_SetRange($B$12,
"CarValue",ClientTable[[#This Row],[Car Value]]), "Age", ClientTable[[#This
Row],[Age]]),"Accident10Years",ClientTable[[#This Row],[Accidents]])
```

There are three calls nested here, all to `PrivateSession_SetRange()`. Since each such call just returns the session ID, they can be nested in such a manner. For the two outermost calls, the first argument that is passed is the nested `PrivateSession_SetRange()` call. The innermost one uses the result of the `PrivateSession_Open()` UDF (located in B12).

The Calculate column contains a call that will cause the session to recalculate the workbook:

```
=PrivateSession_Calculate(ClientTable[[#This Row],[SetValues]])
```

Again, the call uses a reference to the SetValues column as the first argument, making sure it gets called only after the values are set into the workbook. Finally, the Premium column contains a call to the UDF that will return the result from the FinalPremium cell in the PremiumModel workbook:

```
=PrivateSession_GetRange(ClientTable[[#This Row],[Calculate]], "FinalPremium")
```

This call uses the result of the Calculate column to make sure that things happen in order.

Figure 19-7 shows the workbook that contains all the relevant information.

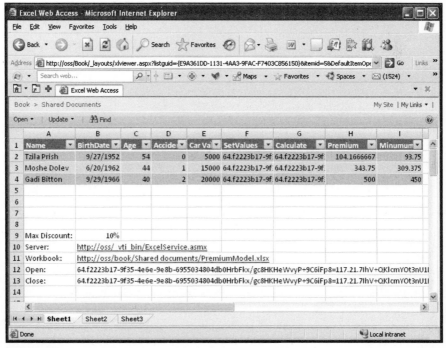

Figure 19-7

As before, the two columns "SetValues" and "Calculate" would be hidden in a standard implementation. The information about the workbook to open and results of the `Open/Close` workbook calls would probably be located in a different sheet.

Coding the Solution

The solution is a single C# library project. It implements all the various UDFs in a single class called `Udfs`.

Pes.DataUdfs Project

On top of the `Udfs` class, this project also contains a `Utils` class for handling the transformation between jagged arrays and two-dimensional arrays.

Udfs Class

This is implemented as a standard class that has the `UdfClass` attribute applied to it:

```
using System;
using System.Collections.Generic;
using System.Text;
using System.Security.Principal;
using System.Threading;

using Microsoft.Office.Excel.Server.Udf;

using ExcelServicesLibrary;

namespace Pes.ExternalWorkbookUdfs
{
    [UdfClass]
    public class Udfs
    {
        private readonly List<string> EmptyStrings = new List<string>();
        private readonly char[] Separator = new char[] { '=' };

        private delegate object ImpersonationCall();
        private delegate object CreateErrorCall(Exception e);

        private Dictionary<string, Session> m_sessions =
            new Dictionary<string, Session>();
        private object m_lock = new object();
        // ...
    }
}
```

The two delegates will be explained later in length. The dictionary contains a hash table of each of the opened sessions. The `m_lock` field is used to synchronize access to the dictionary.

All the UDF methods in this class impersonate the user — for this reason, there is a helper method that does the impersonation. That method also takes care of returning an appropriate error object:

```
private object RunImpersonated(ImpersonationCall call, CreateErrorCall errorCall)
{
    try
    {
        WindowsIdentity wid =
            Thread.CurrentPrincipal.Identity as WindowsIdentity;

        if (wid == null)
        {
            throw new InvalidOperationException
                ("Cannot impersonate user.");
        }

        using (WindowsImpersonationContext context =
            wid.Impersonate())
        {
            return call();
        }
    }
    catch (Exception e)
    {
        return errorCall(e);
    }
}
```

The method takes two delegates (defined in the class). The first is the code that needs to be called. The second is used to turn an exception that occurs into a return value that is valid for the method.

The first stage makes sure that the method can impersonate the user (by casting to WindowsIdentity). Next, it impersonates the user and calls into the call delegate. If an exception is raised, the method uses the errorCall delegate reference to turn it into something that's valid to return to the caller.

The next UDF uses this method to run impersonated:

```
[UdfMethod(IsVolatile = true, ReturnsPersonalInformation = true)]
public object[,] PrivateGetWorkbookRange(
    string server,
    string workbookUrl,
    string range,
    params object[][,] extras)
{
    ImpersonationCall call = delegate()
    {
        return GetWorkbookRange(server, workbookUrl, range, extras);
    };

    return (object[,])RunImpersonated(call, CreateArrayError);
}
```

The first stage creates an anonymous delegate that fits the `ImpersonationCall` signature (stored inside the `call` local variable). That delegate calls into the `GetWorkbooRange()` private method, passing the arguments through. The method then gets executed by the `RunImpersonated()` helper method and the return value cast into an object array (`CreateArrayError()` will be explained later).

The real work of opening the workbook and working against it is done inside `GetWorkbookRange()`:

```
private object[,] GetWorkbookRange(
    string server,
    string workbookUrl,
    string range,
    object[][,] extras)
{
    List<string> rangeSetCommand = EmptyStrings;
    bool recalc = false;
    bool formatted = false;

    if (extras.Length >= 1)
    {
        rangeSetCommand = GatherStringsFromRange(extras[0]);
    }
    if (extras.Length >= 2)
    {
        formatted = (bool)extras[1][0,0];
    }
    if (extras.Length >= 3)
    {
        recalc = (bool)extras[2][0,0];
    }

    ExcelServices service = new ExcelServices(ExcelServicesType.Soap, server);
    using (Session session = service.Open(workbookUrl))
    {
        SetValuesInWorkbook(rangeSetCommand, session);

        if (recalc)
        {
            session.CalculateWorkbook();
        }

        string sheet = "";
        ParseRange(ref range, ref sheet);
        object[,] result = Utils.JaggedToTwoDimensional(
            session.GetRangeA1(sheet, range, formatted).RawData);
        return result;
    }
}
```

The first part of the method uses the argument passed inside extras and figures from it the "optional" arguments passed into the method. The first optional parameter is the range of strings used to set values into cells in the workbook — this is done by the `GatherStringsFromRange()` method. The second is used to determine if the result is wanted in its formatted form or not. The last determines if the workbook needs to be recalculated after the cells are set.

The second part opens a session on the server, using the `ExcelServices` class. The `SetValuesIn-Workbook()` method is then called to set all the appropriate values inside the source workbook (before extracting the wanted values). The workbook is then recalculated if needed.

Finally, the UDF calls into Excel Services, requesting the needed range. Since the result resides within a jagged array, it needs to be transformed into a two-dimensional array (by using the `Utils.JaggedToTwo-Dimensional()` static method).

```csharp
private List<string> GatherStringsFromRange(object[,] range)
{
    List<string> result = new List<string>();
    foreach (object obj in range)
    {
        if (obj is string)
        {
            result.Add((string)obj);
        }
    }
    return result;
}
```

This method gathers the "Range=Value" strings from the input range — if the range contains a cell that is not a string, it is ignored.

The following two methods are used to parse range names (the Excel form of `Sheet!Range` and named ranges) and to parse out the "Range=Value" strings:

```csharp
private static void ParseRange(ref string range, ref string sheet)
{
    int index = range.IndexOf('!');
    if (index >= 0)
    {
        sheet = range.Substring(0, index);
        range = range.Substring(index + 1);
    }
}
private bool ParseRangeSetCommand(
    string command,
    out string sheet,
    out string range,
    out string value)
{
    sheet = "";
    range = "";
    value = "";

    string[] splat = command.Split(Separator, 2);
    if (splat.Length != 2)
    {
        return false;
    }
```

```
        range = splat[0];
        value = splat[1];

        ParseRange(ref sheet, ref range);

        return true;
    }
```

The first method parses a range string. This method parses out either a straight named range or a range in the form of "Sheet!Range". The second method takes a string in the form of "Range=Value" and parses it out to the sheet (which may be empty), the range name, and the value to set.

The method that takes a collection of "Range=Value" strings and calls into the session looks like this:

```
private void SetValuesInWorkbook(
    List<string> rangeSetCommand,
    Session session)
{
    foreach (string command in rangeSetCommand)
    {
        string setSheet;
        string setRange;
        string setValue;
        if (ParseRangeSetCommand(
            command,
            out setSheet,
            out setRange,
            out setValue))
        {
            session.SetCellA1(setSheet, setRange, setValue);
        }
    }
}
```

The method takes the list of "Range=Value" strings and parses them, calling SetCellA1() on each of the pairs.

The next two methods are used by the various UDFs in this class to return proper errors. Each of them returns a representation of an Exception instance nestled inside a different type:

```
private object CreateStringError(Exception e)
{
    return e.ToString();
}

private object CreateArrayError(Exception e)
{
    return new object[,] { { e.ToString(), "" }, { "", "" } };
}
```

The first one (CreateStringError()) returns an Exception string representation as a string instance. The second one returns the same string inside a two-by-two two-dimensional array with empty string "padding" the rest of elements. `CreateStringError()` will be used in conjunction with the `RunImpersonated()` method by the various UDFs that return strings. In this case, the returned string will report what the problem was, giving the author a clue as to what went wrong.

This is especially useful when developing the UDF. Developers may wish to write to the event log instead of simply outputting the error to the workbook. This will also remove the need for the `CreateErrorCall()` *delegate.*

The `CreateArrayError()` is used for the same purpose but with methods that return object arrays. The reason for the padding is so that Excel does not "tile" the result over large ranges, but displays the single error string at the top-leftmost cell.

There are six UDFs available for manipulating sessions inside an Excel workbook:

UDF Method	Purpose
PrivateSession_Open	Opens a workbook on the server. Returns a string representing the Session ID. Calls `Session_Open()`
PrivateSession_Close	Closes a workbook on the server. Returns the string "#SUCCESS". Calls `Session_Close()`
PrivateSession_GetRange	Returns a two-dimensional array of data from the session. Calls `Session_GetRange()`
PrivateSession_SetRange	Sets a two-dimensional array of data into the source workbook. Returns the Session ID string that was passed in as the first argument. Calls `Session_SetRange()`
PrivateSession_Calculate	Calculates the workbook. Returns the Session ID string that was passed in as the first argument. Calls `Session_Calculate()`
PrivateSession_Refresh	Refreshes all data sources inside the workbook. Returns the Session ID string that was passed in as the first argument. Calls `Session_Refresh()`

All UDFs that return the Session ID they get right back to the user can be chained like the ones in the workbook shown in Figure 19-6.

The UDFs follow a very similar pattern in their design. They all use the `RunImpersonated()` method to call an anonymous method that in turn calls a regular method that does the actual work (just like the `PrivateGetWorkbookRange()` UDF). For example, the `PrivateSession_Open()` method makes a call to `Session_Open()`:

```
[UdfMethod(IsVolatile = true, ReturnsPersonalInformation = true)]
public string PrivateSession_Open(string server, string workbookUrl)
```

```
{
        ImpersonationCall call = delegate()
        {
            return Session_Open(server, workbookUrl);
        };

        return (string)RunImpersonated(call, CreateStringError);
}
```

In this method, as opposed to the `PrivateGetWorkbookRange()` *method, the* `RunImpersonated()` *method is called with the* `CreateStringError` *delegate rather than the* `CreateArrayError` `delegate`*. This is done so that the error is properly returned to the caller. Using the incorrect method would cause an* `InvalidCastException` *to be thrown when the method tries to cast the result to its return value type.*

All the session manipulating UDFs look pretty much the same. The only difference is that some of them take a parameter array when they don't really need it. For example, the `PrivateSession_Refresh()` method takes a parameter array called `extras`, which is never used in the UDF:

```
[UdfMethod(IsVolatile = true, ReturnsPersonalInformation = true)]
public string PrivateSession_Refresh(
        string sessionId,
        params object[][,] extras)
{
        ImpersonationCall call = delegate()
        {
            return Session_Refresh(sessionId);
        };
        return (string)RunImpersonated(call, CreateStringError);
}
```

This allows authors to pass extra ranges into the UDF, allowing them to artificially force Excel to call the UDFs in a certain order.

An author that wishes for the `PrivateSession_Refresh()` method to be called in the middle of a sequence of `PrivateSession_GetRange()` calls needs to first make sure the calls that need to happen before the `PrivateSession_Refresh()` call are passed as extra arguments to the method (i.e., =PrivateSession_Refresh(SessionIdNamedRange, Sheet1!A1, Sheet1!A2), where Sheet1!A1 and Sheet1!A2 contain the calls to `PrivateSession_GetRange()`). The author then needs to make sure the cell containing the `PrivateSession_Refresh()` call is passed as an extra argument to the formulas that contain `PrivateSession_GetRange()` that need to run after the refresh operation.

The `Session_Open()` method takes a server and a workbook and opens up a new session. The `Session` instance is then stored inside the hash table and the ID is returned to the user.

```
private string Session_Open(string server, string workbookUrl)
{
        ExcelServices service = new ExcelServices(ExcelServicesType.Soap, server);
        Session session = service.Open(workbookUrl);
        lock (m_lock)
```

```
    {
            m_sessions[session.SessionId] = session;
    }
    return session.SessionId;
}
```

This method could be written without actually resorting to saving elements inside a hash table. Doing so would require callers to pass in the server name every time they call the UDF. Using the dictionary simplifies the usage of the UDFs.

```
private string Session_Close(string sessionId)
{
    Session session = GetSession(sessionId);
    lock (m_lock)
    {
        try
        {
            m_sessions.Remove(session.SessionId);
        }
        catch
        {
        }
    }
    session.Close();
    return "#SUCCESS";
}
```

`Session_Close()` makes a call into Excel Services, closing the appropriate session ID and removing the session from the internal hash table.

The `GetSession()` method returns the session saved in the hash table or throws an error if it does not exist:

```
private Session GetSession(string sessionId)
{
    lock (m_lock)
    {
        Session session;
        if (!m_sessions.TryGetValue(sessionId, out session))
        {
            throw new InvalidOperationException("Session does not exist.");
        }
        return session;
    }
}
```

The `Session_SetRange()` method uses the `ParseRange()` method described earlier to get the name of the sheet (if any) and the range. It then calls into `Session.SetRangeA1()`, placing the range that is passed into the source workbook.

```
private string Session_SetRange(
    string sessionId,
    string range,
```

```
         object[,] rangeToSet)
{
    Session session = GetSession(sessionId);

    string sheet = "";
    ParseRange(ref range, ref sheet);

    session.SetRangeA1(sheet, range, rangeToSet);
    return sessionId;
}
```

The UDFs for refreshing and recalculating a workbook call into the appropriate methods in the `Session` instance:

```
public string Session_Refresh(string sessionId)
{
    Session session = GetSession(sessionId);

    session.Refresh();
    return sessionId;
}

public string Session_Calculate(string sessionId)
{
    Session session = GetSession(sessionId);

    session.CalculateWorkbook();
    return sessionId;
}
```

The last method in the list is `Session_GetRange()`, which retrieves a range from an opened session:

```
private  object[,] Session_GetRange(
    string sessionId,
    string range,
    object[][,] extras)
{
    bool formatted = false;
    if (extras.Length >= 1)
    {
        formatted = (bool)extras[0][0, 0];
    }

    Session session = GetSession(sessionId);

    string sheet = "";
    ParseRange(ref range, ref sheet);
    object[,] result = Utils.JaggedToTwoDimensional(
        session.GetRangeA1(sheet, range, formatted).RawData);
    return result;
}
```

The first "optional" parameter in the UDF is a Boolean specifying whether or not the returned range should be formatted. The UDF then finds the appropriate session and gets the requested range from it. It uses the `Utils.JaggedToTwoDimensional()` method to transform the array returned to something that is consumable by the Excel Services UDF infrastructure.

Utils Class

This class contains the method that transforms a jagged array retrieved from a call to Excel Services into the two-dimensional array used for ranges in the Excel Services UDF infrastructure:

```csharp
using System;
using System.Collections.Generic;
using System.Text;

namespace Pes.ExternalWorkbookUdfs
{
    Private static class Utils
    {
        internal static object[,] JaggedToTwoDimensional(object[] source)
        {
            int rows = source.Length;
            int cols = ((object[])source[0]).Length;

            object[,] target = new object[rows, cols];
            for (int row = 0; row < rows; row++)
            {
                object[] currentRow = (object[])source[row];
                for (int col = 0; col < cols; col++)
                {
                    target[row, col] = currentRow[col];
                }
            }

            return target;
        }
    }
}
```

Each row in the jagged array is enumerated and its content copied to the appropriate location in the target array.

Summary

This solution allows authors to integrate workbooks in ways that are not inherently supported by Excel Services. Workbooks can be leveraged both as sources of information and as ad hoc models.

Some of the features that Excel supports cannot be achieved on the server. However, other features (such as incrementally updating models and using them to get calculated information back to the target workbook) are impossible to do in Excel client.

Like most UDFs presented in this book, this one also has its uses on the client, allowing it to leverage generic workbooks that are located on the server to offload some of the processing that takes place on the client.

More ideas for this solution:

❑ **Error handling.** As with most solutions in this book, error handling can be spotty at places to reduce the amount of code that's actually being written. The solution could be made more robust if some failures were ignored rather than returning errors.

❑ **Better refresh/recalc resolution.** The UDFs for refreshing and recalculating workbooks happen over the entire workbook. If relevant, parameters can be added to allow these methods to refresh or recalculate only a portion of the workbook.

20

Excel Services Workflows

With SharePoint 2007, Microsoft introduced workflow into SharePoint Services. The workflow is based on the Windows Workflow Foundation (WWF) included in .NET 3.0, adding some of its own capabilities to it.

Workflow allows SharePoint managers to cause various operations to run when certain events happen in the system. Events are either items changing or being added to lists and a manual invocation of a workflow. There are also many operations (or activities) defined in the system that can be used when the event occurs. This can be as simple as adding a task to the site or running custom .NET code.

The solution introduced in this chapter contains two workflows. One for calculating workbooks saved to a document library so that the author does not need to calculate them on his machine. The second workflow saves a series of generated snapshots of a document library for consumption by users.

Overview

The overview shows how to use both workflows described in this solution. Since workflow is a new feature in SharePoint, this section will show the whole sequence that needs to be done step by step.

The first example will show how to create a document library that automatically recalculates the workbooks that are stored within it. The second example will again dip into the PremiumModel workbook to show how to create a document library that generates workbook snapshots into another library.

Use

The first example will require a document library to which authors will save their calculation-heavy workbooks. For this example, the library will be called "AutomaticRecalcLibrary." From that library, the SharePoint contributor can go into the "Document Library Settings" menu item under the "Settings" dropdown, as shown in Figure 20-1.

Once inside the document library settings, under the "Permissions and Management" section, the contributor can find the "Workflow settings" options, which will allow him or her to add a workflow process (see Figure 20-2) to the document library. (If there is already workflow present on the document library, this option allows the contributor to either edit it or add a new one.)

First, the user makes a selection inside the workflow template (in this case the choice was "Workbook Background Calculation"). The workflow then needs to be named (in this case, "AutoCalc").

Figure 20-3 shows the bottom of the form where other options are available:

The Task List option allows users to set where tasks that are derived from running the workflow are written. The History List allows users to choose an alternative list where the history of all that transpired in the workflow goes. Finally, checking "Start this workflow when a new item is created" and the "Start this workflow when an item is changed" will cause the newly created workflow to be issued whenever anything changes inside the document library.

Clicking OK will apply the workflow to the document library. Any additions or changes will now kick off the workflow process that was defined.

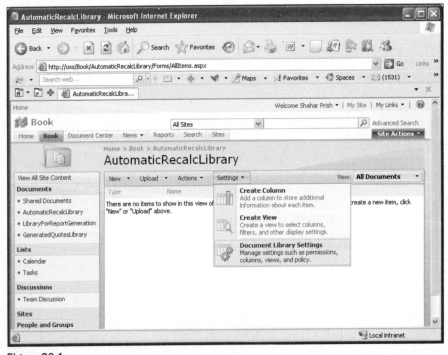

Figure 20-1

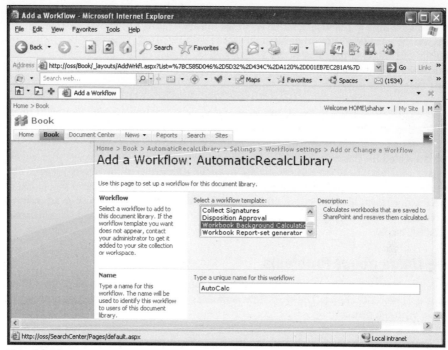

Figure 20-2

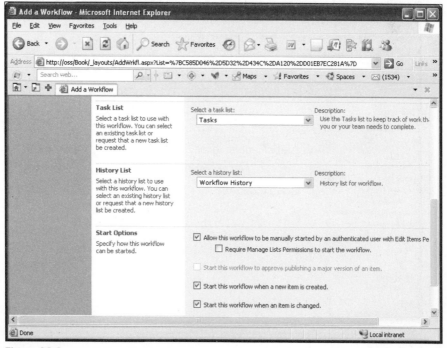

Figure 20-3

Once this is set up, the next step is to make use of the document library. In this case, a complex workbook that takes a long time to calculate gets saved to the library. Figure 20-4 shows the document library and the fact that the workflow is in progress.

Looking at the newly created AutoCalc column in the document library will show the status of the currently active workflow.

When the workflow finishes doing its job, it creates a new workbook in the document library that has the _Calculate postfix appended (as shown in Figure 20-5).

The newly created file has as its Modified By property set to System Account — those are the credentials under which the workflow runs. If the user goes to the properties of the newly created file, he sees a property called __IgnoreCalc set to true — this allows the workflow to ignore this workbook when it's saved to the document library (without this property, the process would continue ad infinitum — each newly created workbook would spawn a new workflow process, which would in turn cause another one to be created, etc.).

Notifying Users about Problems

In the previous section, when the document library was prepared for use with the workflow process, there was a "Task List" choice. The workflow is aware of this choice and can use it for adding tasks that have to do with the process.

Figure 20-6 shows a new workbook is uploaded to the SharePoint site — this one containing a query table. When finished, the workflow for this workbook will display a generic error string.

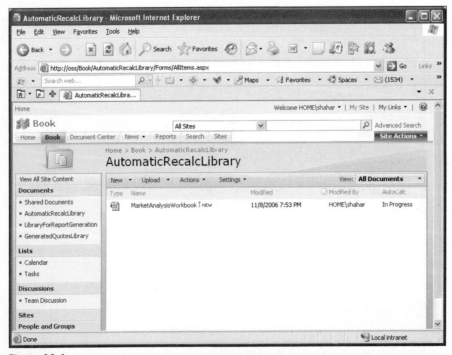

Figure 20-4

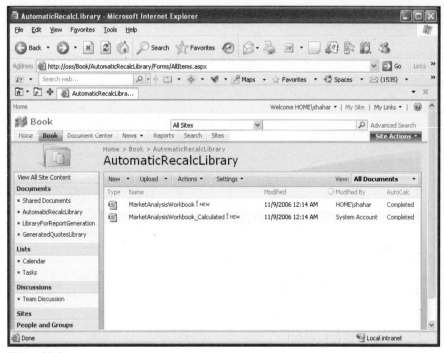

Figure 20-5

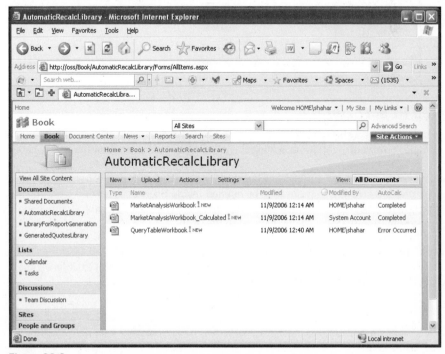

Figure 20-6

The user who saved the workbook can then go to the SharePoint task list — it will contain, among other things, errors arriving from the workflow. Figure 20-7 shows the task that was produced in this instance.

The task contains complete information about the problem — including the workbook URL and the verbose error that has occurred. Similar tasks get created from other errors as well. Workbooks that fail to calculate, that are corrupt, or that returned a generic error will add a task to the list.

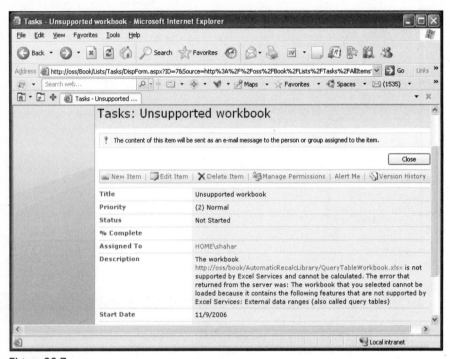

Figure 20-7

Generated Report Library

The second type of workflow this solution shows is one that is capable of generating multiple workbooks from a single "template" workbook, saving them to a dedicated document library.

Going back to the solution described in Chapter 17, one of the examples shown was a link that automatically generates a workbook that can then be opened inside Excel or Excel Services. The link contained named ranges that were set to values and would then use the GetWorkbook() functionality to get a binary representation that was then streamed to the user.

This workflow employs a similar solution, only it does it automatically and creates ready-made workbook snapshots for immediate consumption. In cases where the process of calculating the workbook is a lengthy operation, this can greatly reduce processing time on the server.

There are two prerequisites for this solution. The first is in the document library, which must contain a special column called "ReportLibraryTarget." This column is used during the workflow operation to figure out where the workbooks need to be saved.

The second is the information used to generate the multiple workbooks. The data could, conceptually, come from any source — XML files, databases, and so on.

In this example, the data is actually embedded inside Excel, allowing the workbook to be "self-contained" and not require extra files or information. The workbook needs to contain a named range called __ReportData (that's double underscore and the string ReportData), which will be used to generate all the workbooks.

The workbook this example (shown in Figure 20-8) uses is a modified version of the PremiumModel.xlsx workbook that has been used throughout the book. This one has had a sheet added to it, containing the table of required reports:

The named range __ReportData is a two-dimensional table where the first column represents the postfix string that will be added to the workbook file name when saved to the document library. All the other columns contain names of ranges in Excel that will be populated using the data inside the table.

In this example, the first row in the table will cause the creation of a file called PremiumModel_GadiBitton.xlsx. Before being saved, each of the named ranges ClientName, CarValue, Accident10Years, and Age will be set to "Gadi Bitton", 20,000, 2, and 40 accordingly.

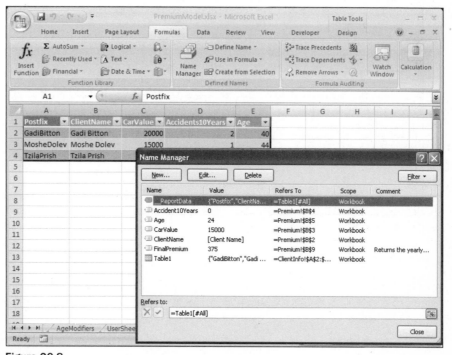

Figure 20-8

345

Once the prerequisites are in place, the next step is to set up the workflow on the document library. This is done in the same way as the previous example. This time the name of the workflow template selected in the list box is "Workbook report-set generator."

The document library in this example has been set up so that the ReportLibraryTarget column is mandatory. This causes Excel to prompt for that field when saving the workbook to the library (as shown at the top of Figure 20-9).

Once the user types in the target document library and the file is saved, the workflow will open the workbook, get the range containing the report generation data, and go over each row, creating the appropriate workbook for each row. The resulting list can be seen in Figure 20-10.

As the solution is set up, each of the generated workbooks is the "Published Items" snapshot of the workbook — making sure that these are purely static workbooks for potential user consumption.

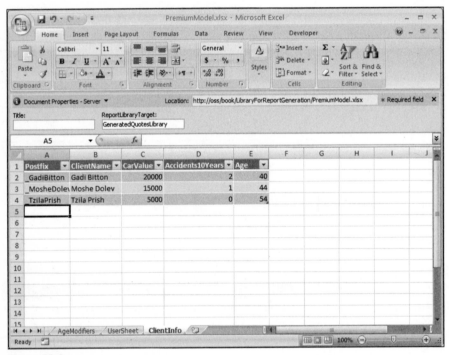

Figure 20-9

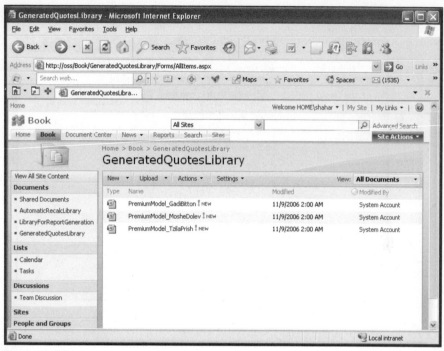

Figure 20-10

Coding the Solution

The solution is based on a Workflow template inside Visual Studio that has been modified to work with SharePoint workflows.

Pes.ExcelWorkflows Project

Since this is not a trivial library project, this section will go through the tasks needed to create it.

The first stage involves using the .NET 3.0 Workflow SDK to create a Workflow library in C#. Figure 20-11 shows the New Project dialog box with the Sequential Workflow Library template selected.

The next stage is to set up Visual Studio so that it can use the SharePoint workflow extensions. For this, the following assemblies need to be added to the list of references assemblies in the project:

❑   Microsoft.Office.Workflow.Tasks

❑   Microsoft.SharePoint

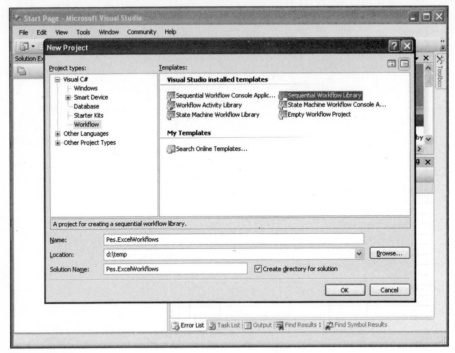

Figure 20-11

❑ `Microsoft.SharePoint.Library`

❑ `Microsoft.SharePoint.WorkflowActions`

❑ `ExcelServicesLibrary` (not needed for workflow, but will be used to access Excel Services)

Once it is added to the list of references, the toolbox needs to be updated. To do that, right-click the toolbox and select the Choose Items option. Select Microsoft.SharePoint.WorkflowActions, and click the OK button — the toolbox should now have a list of items that the assembly exports.

The next few sections explain how to code the class responsible for the workflow shown at the beginning of the chapter (the calculation workflow). That class makes use of a few support classes (`Helper`, `TaskException`, and `DontFailException`), which will be shown immediately after. After that, the chapter will show the second workflow (the report library workflow).

CalculationWorkflow Class

By default, the project template adds a workflow called `Workflow1.cs` to the project. Rename this file to `CalculationWorkflow.cs` (allowing the environment to rename the class as well). This class contains the sequence of activities that happen when a workflow is activated. The UI allows the developer to graphically design what the workflow looks like. In both workflows shown here, the workflow will be very simplistic, comprising a single activity — the one executed when the workflow starts up.

Double-clicking on the `CalculationWorkflow.cs` file will bring up the workflow designer. To the middle of the sequence, the toolbox item called `OnWorkflowActivated` needs to be added, as shown in Figure 20-12.

The activity should be renamed to `onWorkflowActivated` (removing the "1" from it). Once all that is done, the next step is to set up the activity to invoke code that needs to execute.

First, the class needs to contain a reference to an instance that will include the information describing what the workflow is about. This information is managed by the `SPWorkflowActivationProperties` class. Adding that field to the workflow class will make it look like this:

```
namespace Pes.ExcelWorkflows
{
    public sealed partial class CalculationWorkflow: SequentialWorkflowActivity
    {
        // ...
        public SPWorkflowActivationProperties m_workflowProperties =
            new SPWorkflowActivationProperties();
        // ...
    }
}
```

Once this is done, the properties of the activity that was added to the workflow sequence can be edited. The following table shows the values that need to be set inside each of the properties.

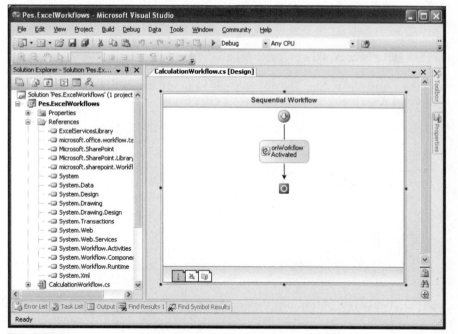

Figure 20-12

*Some of the properties have their own properties. The property grid of Visual Studio will display a "+"
sign for some properties that represent instances of objects that themselves have properties, allowing to
further edit the items.*

Property	Value	Meaning
CorrelationToken	excelCalculationWorkflow	Used to identify the workflow.
CorrelationToken. OwnerActivityName	CalculationWorkflow	The name of the class representing the workflow.
Invoked	OnWorkflowStarted	The event that will cause this workflow to execute.
WorkflowProperties	Activity=CalculationWorkflow, Path=m_workflowProperties	This allows the workflow to bind the workflow properties that are supplied by the infrastructure to the member that was defined in the code. Setting this property is done by clicking the "…" near the property value, and choosing the field (m_workflowProperties in this case) from the UI.

Once these properties are set (Figure 20-13), the method pointed to from the EventName property needs
to be created. This can be added either manually or by selecting the property and choosing the Generate
Handlers link at the bottom of the property page.

The class is now ready for coding. The first step will be to add the code that will execute when the workflow is activated. The class contains the following extra fields:

```
public sealed partial class CalculationWorkflow: SequentialWorkflowActivity
{
    private const string IgnoreCalcField = "__IgnoreCalc";

    private  Helper m_helper;
    public SPWorkflowActivationProperties m_workflowProperties =
        new SPWorkflowActivationProperties();

    public CalculationWorkflow()
    {
        InitializeComponent();
}
```

The m_helper class (accessible through the Helper property) contains a reference to an instance of the
Helper class that will be described later in this chapter. It wraps the SPWorkflowActivationProperties
instance and adds some utility functionality on top of it. The Helper class also provides logging support.

The m_workbookData and m_session (which is accessible through the Session property) fields will
hold transient instances used by some of the methods in the class.

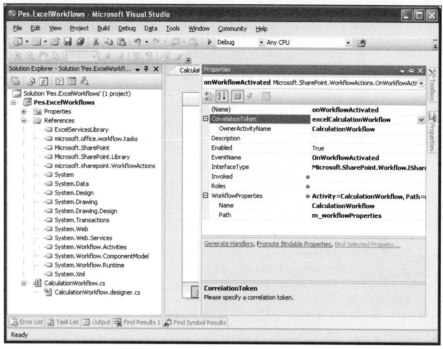

Figure 20-13

Some of the strings in this solution reside inside a resource file called Strings. Using the type-safe resource management capabilities of Visual Studio 2005, the system uses the generated Strings *class to get access to the strings. The names of the strings are self-explanatory.*

When the workflow starts, the OnWorkflowStart() method gets executed by the infrastructure. It takes care to log some information and execute the OperateOnWorkbook() method, which does the actual work of calculating the workbook and saving it.

```
private void OnWorkflowStarted(object sender, ExternalDataEventArgs e)
{
    m_helper = new Helper(m_workflowProperties);
    Helper.WriteToLog("Starting calculation workflow operation.");
    try
    {
        OperateOnWorkbook();
    }
    catch (TaskException ex)
    {
        Helper.AddTask(ex);
        throw;
    }
    catch (DontFailException ex)
    {
        Helper.WriteToLog(Strings.LogNonFatalException, ex);
    }
    catch (Exception ex)
```

```
        {
            Helper.WriteToLog(Strings.LogOuterException, ex);
            throw;
        }
        Helper.WriteToLog("Completed calculation workflow operation.");
    }
```

The first stage of the method makes sure that the m_helper instance is properly initialized. The method wraps the call to OperateOnWorkbook() with a try/catchblock. Depending on the type of error that occurs, the system will do one of three things. If a TaskException (defined later in the chapter) is caught, a task is added to the SharePoint site using the Helper class AddTask() method. If the exception that was caught was the DontFailException (also defined later in this chapter), the workflow returns normally with no error code. This catch clause is useful when the file that was uploaded to the document library is not an Excel workbook that can be loaded by Excel Services. In those cases, the workflow should just complete quietly and do nothing about the file. As a last resort, the generic Exception class is also caught and the information logged to the log file.

The OperateOnWorkbook() method first makes sure that the document library that contains the document is properly configured. It then checks to make sure that the file that was changed or added needs to be calculated by calling the CheckIfUpdateNeeded() method. Once it was determined that the workbook needs to be calculated, the method opens up a new session against Excel Services, recalculates the workbook and saves the result back into the document library:

```
private void OperateOnWorkbook()
{
    ValidateListSettings();

    Helper.WriteToLog("Opening workbook '{0}' on server '{1}'",
        Helper.Workbook,
        Helper.ExcelServices);

    if (!CheckIfUpdateNeeded())
    {
        Helper.WriteToLog("Workbook does not need to be loaded");
        return;
    }

    using (Session session = Helper.CreateWorkbookSession())
    {
        RecalculateWorkbook(session);
        WorkbookData data = GetWorkbookData(session);
        byte[] workbookData = data.RawData;
        SaveToDocumentLibrary(workbookData);
    }
}
```

The next few pages will go through each of the methods called here and explain how they work.

The Helper.CreateWorkbookSession() call in the middle of OperateOnWorkbook tries to open the workbook on the server and checks any failures that occur to decide what path to take with the workbook. It will be explained in length in the next section.

`ValidateListSettings()` makes sure that the document library that contains the files is properly configured and has the appropriate fields. In this case, this method adds the "__IgnoreCalc" field to the list if it does not exist there.

Since the workflow operation will save a new file into the document library, it is important to know which files need to be recalculated and which do not. In this case, when the workflow will save the newly calculated workbook to the library, it will make sure it sets the __IgnoreCalc field to "true" so that the newly (and already calculated workbook) does not get recalculated again.

```
private void ValidateListSettings()
{
    try
    {
        SPList list = Helper.Properties.List;
        if (!list.Fields.ContainsField(IgnoreCalcField))
        {
            string name = list.Fields.Add(
                IgnoreCalcField,
                SPFieldType.Boolean,
                false);
            SPField field = list.Fields[name];
            field.Hidden = true;
            field.Update();
        }
    }
    catch
    {
        Helper.WriteToLog(Strings.LogFieldAdditionFailed, IgnoreCalcField);
        throw;
    }
}
```

First, the method takes the fields off the `SPList` instance and checks if one by the name of "__IgnoreCalc" (which is the string contained in the `IgnoreCalcField` constant) is one of them. If it does not exist, a call is made to the `Add()` method on the `SPFieldCollection` class to try and add the field. The `Hidden` property of the field is also turned on to make sure that users won't be able to see or access it.

The `CheckIfUpdateNeeded()` method uses the item instance to check and see if the file needs to be recalculated. It does this by checking the "__IgnoreCalc" field and seeing if it's false:

```
private bool CheckIfUpdateNeeded()
{
    SPListItem item = Helper.Item;
    object ignoreObject = item[IgnoreCalcField];
    return ignoreObject == null ||
        !((bool)ignoreObject);
}
```

The `RecalculateWorkbook()` method uses the created session to call the `CalculateWorkbook()` method. On any sort of `SoapException` failure, the method will add a task that explains to the author that the calculation failed. `GetWorkbookData()` is similar — it tries to get the binary workbook representation from Excel Services and returns it.

```
private void RecalculateWorkbook()
{
    try
    {
        Session.CalculateWorkbook();
    }
    catch (SoapException ex)
    {
        Helper.WriteToLog(
            "Was unable to calculate workbook. Error was:{0}", ex);
        string message = String.Format(
            Strings.CalculationFailedDescription,
            Helper.Workboook,
            ex.Message);
        throw new TaskException(
            Strings.CalculationFailedTitle,
            message,
            ex);
    }
}
private WorkbookData GetWorkbookData()
{
    WorkbookData data = null;
    Helper.WriteToLog("Getting workbook binary data.");
    try
    {
        data = Session.GetWorkbook(WorkbookType.FullWorkbook);
    }
    catch (SoapException ex)
    {
        Helper.WriteToLog("Unable to get the workbook. Error was: {0}", ex);
        string message = String.Format(Strings.GetWorkbookFailedDescription,
            Helper.Workboook,
            ex.Message);
        throw new TaskException(
            Strings.GetWorkbookFailedTitle,
            message,
            ex);
    }
    return data;
}
```

Finally, the method that saves the workbook back to SharePoint; SaveToDocumentLibrary() is called. It generates a new file name (postfixed with the _Calculated string) and creates the file in the document library, writing the data retrieved from the session into it. It also sets the "__IgnoreCalc" field to true so that the file will not be processed by the workflow again.

```
private void SaveToDocumentLibrary()
{
    SPListItem item = Helper.Item;
    try
    {
        SPFile calculatedFile =
            Helper.FindOrAddFile(
```

```
                    Helper.GetPostfixedWorkbookName("_Calculated"));
        SPListItem calcItem = calculatedFile.Item;
        calcItem[IgnoreCalcField] = true;
        calcItem.Update();

        Helper.WriteToLog("Trying to save...");
        calculatedFile.SaveBinary(m_workbookData);
    }
    catch (Exception ex)
    {
        Helper.WriteToLog(
            "Tried saving back to library. Failed with error: {0}",
            ex);
        throw;
    }
}
```

The `Helper.FindOrAddFile()` method makes sure that a new file is created if it does not exist. The `SPFile.SaveBinary()` method is used to persist the file into the SharePoint document library.

Helper Class

The `Helper` class supplies utility functionality and helper methods to the project. It wraps the `SPWorkflowActivationProperties` class.

```
[Serializable]
public class Helper
{
    private SPWorkflowActivationProperties  m_properties;

    public Helper(SPWorkflowActivationProperties properties)
    {
        m_properties = properties;
    }
    // ...
}
```

The first method in the `Helper` class opens the workbook that is the subject of the workflow inside Excel Services. The `try/catch` block checks for some of the possible errors that an Excel Services server can return. Depending on the error that occurred, the system may throw different types of exceptions. If the `WorkbookUnsupported` error occurs, the call creates a new `TaskException` instance and fills it with information that will help the author understand what the problem was. (The `Message` property of a `SoapException` thrown because of unsupported features inside the workbook contains a text message that explains what the unsupported feature is.) If the file is considered corrupt, the call checks to see what the extension is. If it's not one of the two supported by Excel Services, the method will gracefully ignore the workbook, throwing a `DontFailException`. On all the other errors that may come back from Excel Services, the workflow will add a task that contains a generic error message.

```
internal Session CreateWorkbookSession()
{
    ExcelServices service = new ExcelServices(
        ExcelServicesType.Soap,
```

```
            ExcelServices);
        Session session = null;
        try
        {
            session = service.Open(Workboook);
        }
        catch (SoapException soapEx)
        {
            if (soapEx.SubCode.Code.Name == "WorkbookNotSupported")
            {
                string message =
                    String.Format(Strings.UnsupportedWorkbookDescription,
                    Workboook,
                    soapEx.Message);
                throw new TaskException(
                    Strings.UnsupportedWorkbookTitle,
                    message,
                    soapEx);

            }
            else if (soapEx.SubCode.Code.Name == "FileCorrupt")
            {
                string ext = Path.GetExtension(Workboook);
                if (ext.Equals(".xlsx", StringComparison.OrdinalIgnoreCase) ||
                    ext.Equals(".xlsb", StringComparison.OrdinalIgnoreCase))
                {
                    string message =
                        String.Format(Strings.CorruptWorkbookDescription,
                        Workboook);
                    throw new TaskException(
                        Strings.CorruptWorkbookTitle,
                        message,
                        soapEx);
                }
                else
                {
                    throw new DontFailException();
                }
            }
            else
            {
                string message = String.Format(
                    Strings.UnknownOpenErrorDescription,
                    Workboook,
                    soapEx.Message);
                throw new TaskException(
                    Strings.UnknownOpenErrorTitle,
                    message,
                    soapEx);

            }
        }
        return session;
    }
}
```

The `TaskException` instances that are thrown will cause the `OnWorkflowStarted()` method to add tasks to the task list and assign them to the user who authored the workbook.

Another method provided by the `Helper` class is `AddTask()`, which takes a `TaskException` instance and creates a SharePoint task out of it:

```
public void AddTask(TaskException ex)
{
    WriteToLog("Adding task to {0}.", Properties.TaskList);
    SPListItem task = Properties.TaskList.Items.Add();
    task["Title"] = ex.Title;
    task["Assigned To"] = Properties.OriginatorUser;
    task["Description"] = ex.Message;
    task.Update();
}
```

The method adds a new `SPListItem` instance to the task list object (the `TaskList` property of the `SPWorkflowActivationProperties` instance is determined by the configuration form shown at the beginning of the chapter).

The method that returns a workbook that is postfixed with another string uses some string manipulations to figure out the name of the file and its extension, which it then puts back together with the postfix:

```
public string GetPostfixedWorkbookName(string postfix)
{
    string url = Item.File.Url;
    string noExt = url.Substring(0, url.LastIndexOf('.'));
    string ext = Path.GetExtension(url);
    string workbook = String.Format(
        "{0}{1}{2}",
        noExt,
        postfix,
        ext);
    return workbook;
}
```

The following two propeties also do some string manipulations — the first to return the full URL of the item that the `SPWorkflowActivationProperties` holds on to, and the second to return the URL for Excel Web Services:

```
public string Workboook
{
    get
    {
        string workbook = Properties.Web.Url + "/" + Properties.Item.Url;
        return workbook;
    }
}

public string ExcelServices
{
    get
```

```
        {
                string server = Properties.Web.Url + "/_vti_bin/ExcelService.asmx";
                return server;
        }
    }
```

The method that does logging uses the `File.AppendAllText()` static method to append text to a file inside the temporary Windows directory:

```
public static void WriteToLog(string format, params object[] args)
{
        string fileName = Path.GetTempPath();
        fileName = Path.Combine(fileName, "WFLog.txt");
        string text = String.Format(format, args);
        string final = String.Format("{0}:{1}\r\n", DateTime.Now, text);
        File.AppendAllText(fileName, final);
}
```

The method also prepends the date and time to each line in the log.

The last method in the `Helper` class is the one that returns an `SPFile` instance by either finding it inside SharePoint or by creating it if it does not exist:

```
internal SPFile FindOrAddFile(string url)
{
        SPWeb web = Properties.Web;
        SPFile file = web.GetFile(url);
        if (file == null)
        {
                web.Files.Add(url, new byte[] { 4 }, true);
        }
        return file;
}
```

DontFailException Class

When parts of the workflow want to bail out without showing an error to the user, they will throw a `DontFailException` instance. See the `CalculationWorkflow.OnWorkflowStarted()` method for the way to use it.

Since there's no information that's really needed when this exception is thrown, it has no settable properties in its constructor.

```
namespace Pes.ExcelWorkflows
{

        [global::System.Serializable]
        public class DontFailException : Exception
        {
                public DontFailException() { }
                protected DontFailException(
                    System.Runtime.Serialization.SerializationInfo info,
```

```
                          System.Runtime.Serialization.StreamingContext context)
                      : base(info, context) { }
         }
    }
```

TaskException Class

When a method needs to fail and add a task for the user who changed or added the file, it throws this exception. The exception is initialized with the information needed to create the task:

```
namespace Pes.ExcelWorkflows
{

    [global::System.Serializable]
    public class TaskException : Exception
    {
        private string m_title;

        public TaskException() { }

        public TaskException(string title, string message) :
            this(title, message, null) { }

        public TaskException(
            string title,
            string message,
            Exception inner) :
                base(message, inner)
        {
            m_title = title;
        }

        protected TaskException(
          System.Runtime.Serialization.SerializationInfo info,
          System.Runtime.Serialization.StreamingContext context)
            : base(info, context) { }

        public string Title
        {
            get { return m_title; }
        }

    }
}
```

The `Message` property of the task will be copied to the `Description` field in the task.

`Helper.AddTask()` is the method used to take this class and transform it into a task in the task list.

ReportGeneratorWorkflow Class

This workflow is somewhat similar to the one described at the beginning of this section. Instead of saving a workbook to the same document library, it uses a range inside the workbook to generate multiple workbooks into a different report library. To create the class, the developer should follow the same steps outlined in the creation of the `CalculationWorkflow` class.

```
namespace Pes.ExcelWorkflows
{
    public sealed partial class ReportGeneratorWorkflow:
SequentialWorkflowActivity
    {
        private const string ReportLibraryTarget = "ReportLibraryTarget";
        private const string ReportMergeRangeName = "__ReportData";
        public SPWorkflowActivationProperties m_workflowProperties =
            new SPWorkflowActivationProperties();
        private Helper m_helper;
        private string m_targetLibraryName;

        public ReportGeneratorWorkflow()
        {
            InitializeComponent();
        }
        // ...
    }
}
```

The class defines a constant called `ReportLibraryTarget`, which is the name of the field that will be used to figure out where the generated reports need to be saved. It also defines `ReportMergeRangeName`, which is the range that contains the table that contains the various values that need to be set into the workbook before it is saved to the generated report library. `m_targetLibraryName` will store the contents of the field that is used to determine where the generated reports need to go to.

The `OnWorkflowStarted()` method, which is executed when the workflow starts, is virtually identical to the one in the `CalculationWorkflow` class. It also calls a method called `OperateOnWorkbook()`. This method does the heavy lifting of generating all the workbooks:

```
private void OperateOnWorkbook()
{
    ExtractTargetLibrary();

    Helper.WriteToLog(
        "Opening workbook '{0}' on server '{1}'",
        Helper.Workbook,
        Helper.ExcelServices);

    using (Session session = Helper.CreateWorkbookSession())
    {
        RangeResult result = ExtractReportMergeRange(session);

        List<string> columns = ExtractColumnNames(result);

        GenerateWorkbooksFromRange(session, result, columns);
    }
}
```

The first step extracts the target library from the document library. Then, the method creates a session and tries to extract the range that contains the information needed to generate the workbooks. Once the method has that range, it extracts the various columns from it and passes all that information into the GenerateWorkbooksFromRanges() method. At the end, the method attempts to dispose of the instance stored inside the session local variable.

ExtractTargetLibrary() figures out what the target library is. It first tries to find the appropriate field in the list (ReportLibraryTarget). If it is not found, a task is created explaining the problem to the user and the workflow fails. If the field is found, the workflow takes its contents and sets it inside the m_targetLibraryName member.

```
private void ExtractTargetLibrary()
{
    object targetLibraryObject = Helper.Item[ReportLibraryTarget];
    if (targetLibraryObject == null || !(targetLibraryObject is string))
    {
        Helper.WriteToLog("Could not figure out target library from item.");
        string message = String.Format(
            Strings.NoTargetLibraryDescription,
            Helper.Workbook);
        TaskException taskEx = new TaskException(
            Strings.NoTargetLibraryTitle,
            message);
        throw taskEx;
    }

    m_targetLibraryName = ((string)targetLibraryObject).Trim();
    if (!m_targetLibraryName.EndsWith("/"))
    {
        m_targetLibraryName += "/";
    }
    Helper.WriteToLog("Target library is: {0}", m_targetLibraryName);
}
```

ExtractReportMergeRange() calls into the opened session, asking for the __ReportData named range. If the range does not exist, the workflow fails and a task is added, explaining that that field is needed for reports to be properly generated.

```
private RangeResult ExtractReportMergeRange(Session session)
{
    try
    {
        RangeResult result = session.GetRangeA1(ReportMergeRangeName);
        return result;
    }
    catch (SoapException soapEx)
    {
        string message = String.Format(
            Strings.ReportMergeRangeNotFoundDescription,
            Helper.Workbook,
```

```
                         soapEx.Message);
            TaskException taskEx = new TaskException(
                Strings.ReportMergeRangeNotFoundTitle,
                message,
                soapEx);
            throw taskEx;
        }
    }
```

`ExtractColumnNames()` is the method responsible for getting the header of the range retrieved by `ExtractReportMergeRange()` and turning it into a list that can then be used by the workflow to determine what ranges need to be set in the workbook:

```
private List<string> ExtractColumnNames(RangeResult rangeResult)
{
    List<string> columns = new List<string>();
    Row row = rangeResult.RowCollection[0];
    foreach (object col in row.CellCollection)
    {
        if (!(col is string))
        {
            string message = String.Format(
                Strings.ReportMergeRangeInvalidDescription,
                Helper.Workbook,
                "Column header was not a string");
            TaskException taskEx = new TaskException(
                Strings.ReportMergeRangeInvalidTitle,
                message);
            throw taskEx;
        }
        columns.Add((string)col);
    }
    return columns;
}
```

The `GenerateWorkbookFromRange()` is responsible for setting the ranges into the workbook and calling the `SaveWorkbook()` method (described later in this section) to place the generated report back in a document library. The method goes over each of the rows in the range returned from the `ExtractReportMergeRange()` and sets their contents (the cells) back into the workbook into the appropriate named range.

Because this workflow can be a potentially long operation, the workflow knows how to recover from failures that may occur when calling into Excel Services. When such an error occurs, the workflow will retry up to five times to recreate the session. Once all five retries fail, the workflow will error out, adding a task to the user explaining what happened. While not all error cases are covered, the most common ones are.

```
private Session GenerateWorkbooksFromRange(Session session, RangeResult result,
List<string> columns)
{
    const int MaxRetries = 5;
```

```
for (int rowIndex = 1; rowIndex < result.RowCollection.Count; rowIndex++)
{
    int retryCount = 0;
    bool success = false;
    while (!success)
    {
        try
        {
            if (session == null)
            {
                try
                {
                    session = Helper.CreateWorkbookSession();
                }
                catch (Exception ex)
                {
                    throw new RetryException(ex);
                }
            }

            Row row = result.RowCollection[rowIndex];
            string postfix = (string)row[0];
            Helper.WriteToLog(
                "Preparing workbook for postfix '{0}'",
                postfix);
            for (int colIndex = 1;
                colIndex < columns.Count;
                colIndex++)
            {
                object value = row[colIndex];
                string namedRange = columns[colIndex];
                Helper.WriteToLog(
                    "Setting '{0}' to '{1}'.",
                    columns[colIndex],
                    value);
                SetCellInWorkbook(session, namedRange, value);
            }
            SaveWorkbok(postfix, session);
            success = true;
        }
        catch (RetryException ex)
        {
            Helper.WriteToLog(
                "Got RetryException - retry #{0}. Error was:{1}",
                retryCount,
                ex);
            if (retryCount == MaxRetries - 1)
            {
                string message = String.Format(
                    Strings.MaxRetriesDescription,
                    Helper.Workbook,
                    ex.InnerException);
                TaskException taskEx = new TaskException(
                    Strings.MaxRetriesTitle,
```

```
                                  message,
                                  ex.InnerException);
                          throw;
                      }
                      session = null;
                      Thread.Sleep(20000);
                      retryCount++;
                  }
              }
          }
      return session;
  }
```

The method iterates over all the rows in the returned range. Each row is then iterated and all the values are used with the appropriate column title to call into the SetCellA1() method. For example, if the column header of the second column is "CarValue," and in the currently iterated row the second cell contains the value 10,000, the workflow will set the value 10,000 into the named range CarValue.

The retry mechanism kicks in only inside the loop — if an error is encountered, the workflow goes to sleep for 20 seconds and sets the session to null (this will cause the session to be recreated at the top of the loop, starting from a fresh one).

The last important method in this class is the one responsible for saving the workbook. It is similar to the one that saves workbooks in the calculation workflow:

```
private void SaveWorkbok(string postfix, Session session)
{
    try
    {
        string workbook = Helper.GetPostfixedWorkbookName(postfix);
        workbook = Path.GetFileName(workbook);
        workbook = m_targetLibraryName + workbook;

        SPFile file = Helper.FindOrAddFile(workbook);
        Helper.WriteToLog("Getting workbook snapshot.");
        WorkbookData data = session.GetWorkbook(
            WorkbookType.PublishedItemsSnapshot);
        Helper.WriteToLog(
            "Saving binary to Sharepoint. Length = {0}",
            data.RawData.Length);
        file.SaveBinary(data.RawData);
    }
    catch (WebException webEx)
    {
        throw new RetryException(webEx);
    }
    catch (SoapException soapEx)
    {
        Helper.WriteToLog("Unable to get the workbook. Error was: {0}", soapEx);
        throw new RetryException(soapEx);
    }
}
```

The method uses the postfix passed into it (the postfix is determined by the leftmost column in the range used for generating the workbooks). It then uses the `Helper.FindOrAddFile()` method to get the `SPFile` of the generated report and saves the data retrieved from the workbook into it.

Deploying the Solution

This section explains the steps that are needed to successfully deploy the solution to the server.

There are three things that need to be done for the workflow to be used by SharePoint:

1. The assembly needs to be added to the GAC. For that, it needs to be strongly named using a key and dragged to the GAC on the SharePoint server machine.

It is also possible to use utilities such as the `GacUtil.exe` *provided with Visual Studio to do this or to add it to the setup process. The batch file that will be shown in this section will include an automatic way of GACing the assembly if* `GacUtil.exe` *is installed.*

2. SharePoint needs to be notified about the new feature being installed — this is done by creating a "feature" and making SharePoint aware of it by using the `stsadm.exe` utility. Features allow developers to package a fully functional definition of a feature and deploy it to SharePoint. The file will be named `Feature.xml`.

3. The `feature.xml` file contains a reference to a `workflow.xml` file, which contains the definition of the workflow. When the feature file is processed by the SharePoint administration utility, the workflow file will be picked up, processed, and installed on the system.

The names `feature.xml` *and* `workflow.xml` *are not set in stone. Their name can be anything as long as they are XML files following the correct schema.*

In this example, step one can either be done manually on the SharePoint server or automatically (if there's Visual Studio 2005 or .NET 2.0 SDK installed). Steps 2 and 3 will be done automatically by a batch file, which will be shown.

Feature.xml File

A feature file can contain multiple elements that need to be deployed to the server. In this case, it will contain a single element — the workflow.

```
<?xml version="1.0" encoding="utf-8"?>
<Feature  Id="{064585F8-3949-4d5f-91F8-AB66D3BE036A}"
        Title="Professional Excel Services Workflows"
        Description="Allows for various activities to take place when an Excel
2007 file is changed or added to a document library. Professional Excel Services
book."
        Version="12.0.0.0"
        Scope="Site"
        ReceiverAssembly="Microsoft.Office.Workflow.Feature, Version=12.0.0.0,
Culture=neutral, PublicKeyToken=71e9bce111e9429c"
        ReceiverClass="Microsoft.Office.Workflow.Feature.WorkflowFeatureReceiver"
        xmlns="http://schemas.microsoft.com/sharepoint/">
```

```
  <ElementManifests>
    <ElementManifest Location="workflow.xml" />
  </ElementManifests>
  <Properties>
    <Property Key="GloballyAvailable" Value="true" />
  </Properties>
</Feature>
```

The following tags and attributes are worth taking note of:

Tag/Attribute	Meaning
Feature tag/ Id attribute	A GUID that will uniquely identify the feature.
Title tag Description tag	Human-readable information about the feature.
ReceiverAssembly tag	The assembly that contains the class that knows how to handle the files defined in the ElementManifest tags.
ReceiverClass tag	The class that handles the files defined in the ElementManifest tags.
ElementManifests tag	A collection of elements that will be installed to the server.
ElementManifest tag	A file containing the definition of a single element inside a feature.

In this case, the Feature.xml file is only pointing to a single file containing workflow definitions — the file called Workflow.xml.

Workflow.xml File

When the Feature.xml file described in this chapter is processed by the SharePoint administration utility, it will find that it needs to process the Workflow.xml file. The contents of that file tell SharePoint exactly what workflows will be available:

```
<?xml version="1.0" encoding="utf-8" ?>
<Elements xmlns="http://schemas.microsoft.com/sharepoint/">
  <Workflow
      Name="Workbook Background Calculation"
      Description="Calculates workbooks that are saved to SharePoint and resaves
them calculated."
      Id="{C5507572-7459-4999-88D1-71F4DD39CB1C}"
      CodeBesideClass="Pes.ExcelWorkflows.CalculationWorkflow"
      CodeBesideAssembly="Pes.ExcelWorkflows, Version=1.0.0.0, Culture=neutral,
PublicKeyToken=70f77e400132c3ed">

    <Categories/>
  </Workflow>
</Elements>
```

The tags and attributes to consider in this XML are:

Tag/Attribute	Meaning
`Workflow tag`	Defines a single workflow process that will be deployed to the server.
`Workflow tag/` `Name attribute`	The name of the workflow — this is the string that appears in the list box when setting up workflows on a document library.
`Workflow tag/` `Description attribute`	The description of the workflow, as it appears near the list box, when the workflow is selected.
`Workflow tag/` `Id attribute`	Unique GUID identifying the workflow.
`Workflow tag/` `CodeBesideAssembly`	The assembly containing the code that implements the workflow.
`Workflow tag/` `CodeBesideClass`	The class inside the `CodeBesideAssembly` that implements the workflow.

Install.bat File

The `install.bat` file, when executed on the server, will run everything needed to install the workflow. This will probably not be an acceptable solution for deployment on production servers, but for development ones, it should be good enough.

The highlighted parts can be modified to make the batch file work with any feature.

```
echo Copying the feature...
Set FeatureName=PesExcelWorkflow
Set ServerUrl=http://oss
Set BinaryName=Pes.ExcelWorkflows

Set FeatureLocation=%CommonProgramFiles%\Microsoft Shared\web server
extensions\12\TEMPLATE\FEATURES\%FeatureName%
Set GacUtilExe=%programfiles%\Microsoft Visual Studio 8\SDK\v2.0\Bin\gacutil.exe

:: Step 1: Recreate the folder for the feature
rd /s /q "%FeatureLocation%"
mkdir "%FeatureLocation%"

:: Step 2: Copy the appropriate files to the feature directory.
copy /Y feature.xml  "%FeatureLocation%\"
copy /Y workflow.xml "%FeatureLocation%\"

:: Step 3: Try installing the assemblies to the GAC.
echo Adding assemblies to the GAC...

"%GacUtilExe%" -uf %BinaryName%
"%GacUtilExe%" -if bin\Debug\%BinaryName%.dll
```

```
:: Step 4: Deactivate and Reactivate the feature on SharePoint
echo Activating the feature...

pushd %CommonProgramFiles%\microsoft shared\web server extensions\12\bin

stsadm -o deactivatefeature -filename %FeatureName%\feature.xml -url %ServerUrl%
stsadm -o uninstallfeature -filename %FeatureName%\feature.xml

stsadm -o installfeature -filename %FeatureName%\feature.xml -force
stsadm -o activatefeature -filename %FeatureName%\feature.xml -url %ServerUrl%

echo Doing an iisreset...

popd
iisreset
pause
```

The first step makes sure the feature directory exist (the features must be located in the well known folder shown in the batch file). The second step copies the appropriate files into the feature directory. Next, the assembly is installed to the GAC (this will only work if the .NET 2.0 or Visual Sudio 2005 is installed). The fourth step uses the stsadm utility to install and activate the feature on the server. Finally, the batch file resets IIS so that the new features are accepted.

Summary

These two classes show how workflow can be used to take time consuming operations and move their execution to the server in a manner that is tightly coupled with the lifetime of the documents themselves.

These examples didn't even scratch the surface of the functionality of workflow — each of these workflows could have been componentized into separate activities, which could then be used in other workflows to create even more complex templates. On top of that, tools such as the SharePoint designer allow users who do not know how to code to generate their own workflow templates in a completely graphical manner. This chapter exists mainly to show developers how to start using a workflow in SharePoint and to show some of the really nice things that can be done with it.

21

EWA Projects

This chapter consists of multiple projects that can be done with EWA — some require coding; others do not.

Parameterized EWA Links

Chapter 17 showed you a technique that lets users apply parameters to a workbook directly, returning the modified workbook, which can then be opened in Excel (or downloaded for later consumption).

This project demonstrates a technique that allows for similar results but is based on a different use of the technology. The main differences between this project and that in Chapter 17 are:

❑   This solution requires no special deployment, nor does it require any coding. It is based solely on out-of-the-box SharePoint features.

❑   When used in conjunction with Excel Services, the solution in Chapter 17 can have a negative effect on caching and sharing in the system, making it perform less than nominally in some cases. This solution allows Excel Services to do as much sharing as is normally possible.

❑   This solution needs to be tailored to a specific workbook (or at least, to a specific set of exported parameters). Chapter 17's solution could be used on any workbook with any set of settable named ranges.

❑   Using the solution presented here, it is impossible to give somebody a simple link that will then be opened in Excel. The user will need to go through the EWA Open in Excel menu to do that.

How It Works

The idea behind this solution is to use Filter Web Parts in conjunction with EWA to change parameters that are exported in an Excel workbook. Expanding a bit on the Premium Quote example shown in Chapter 17, the authors now wish to use Excel Web Access to supply their clients with quotes instead of Excel client.

On top of that, the authors also want to show the client the difference between the state averages (for the client's age group) and the price they will end up paying. The workbook utilizes conditional formatting with icon sets to show the user whether the price being quoted with is well above the average (red dot), comparable to the average (yellow dot), or well below the average (green dot).

The following screen shot shows how the workbook looks when opened in the browser. In this case, the link to open the workbook is:

```
http://oss/Book/EwaApps/QuoteViewer.aspx?CarValue=20000&Age=80&Accidents=1&State=OR
```

Figure 21-1 shows the EWA in the browser with the information relevant to this quote.

These links can be sent to anybody with EWA access, showing them the data relevant to them.

How to Build

The first step (see Figure 21-2) involves creating a new Web Part page. In this case, choose the "Header, right column, body" template and the location is the EwaApps document library.

Once the page is created, modify the top caption to show some explanatory text by using the "Content Editor Web Part," and insert EWA into the body part (the left drop area) of the page. The EWA has been configured to show the appropriate PremiumModel workbook (by setting its Workbook URL property in the Web Part properties pane) and to not show the parameters pane (there's no need for it — the parameters will be set from the URL query string). This step should be similar to the page shown in Figure 21-3.

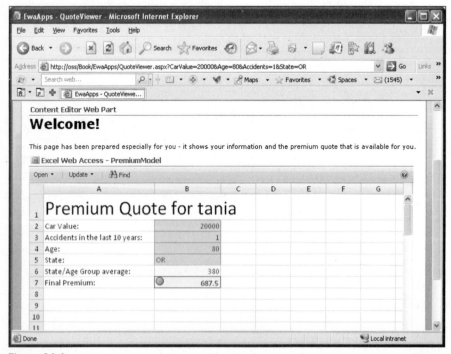

Figure 21-1

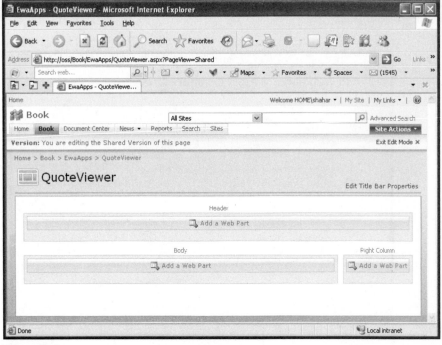

Figure 21-2

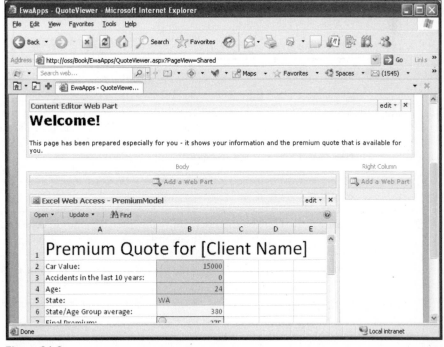

Figure 21-3

Figure 21-4 shows the next step. Adding a "Query String (URL) Filter" Web Part into the right-hand column in the Web Part page:

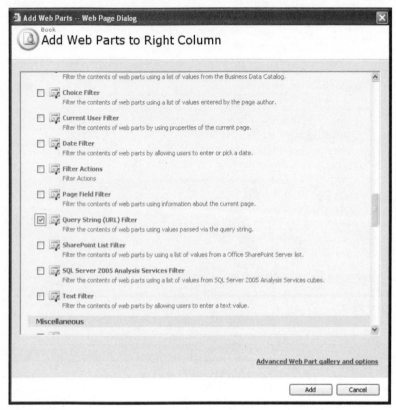

Figure 21-4

Once this is added, configure the filter to get its value from the appropriate query string parameter. The Filter Name property on the Modify Properties pane of the filter can be any arbitrary name that will help with remembering what the filter is all about (in this case, it will be called AgeFilter). The following table lists the properties that it is important to modify.

Property	Meaning
Filter Name	The name that will be used to identify the filter Web Part in code and when creating part-to-part (P2P) relationships.
Query String Parameter Name	The name of the parameter that the filter will use to get its value from.

Property	Meaning
Default Value	If the parameter is not located on the URL, this will be the value returned from the filter.
Title	This is optional (especially because these filter Web Parts are hidden when the page is viewed out of design mode), but it is useful to change this to some helpful string so that the page designer knows what each one holds.

Figure 21-5 shows a part of the web page that was configured according to the table above.

The filter Web Parts are added to the right column so that they are easier to manage. When the page is displayed out of design mode, these Web Parts will be hidden, and the right Web Part zone will be empty and thus hidden as well, allowing the EWA to take the whole width of the page.

Next, add three more Query String Filters for the car value, the number of accidents, and the state.

Once that is done, add a "Current User Filter" Web Part to the page, setting it up to show the first name of the user (see Figure 21-6). This will later be connected to the EWA in such a manner that it goes into the ClientName workbook parameter, which in turn will further customize the workbook to show the name of the client.

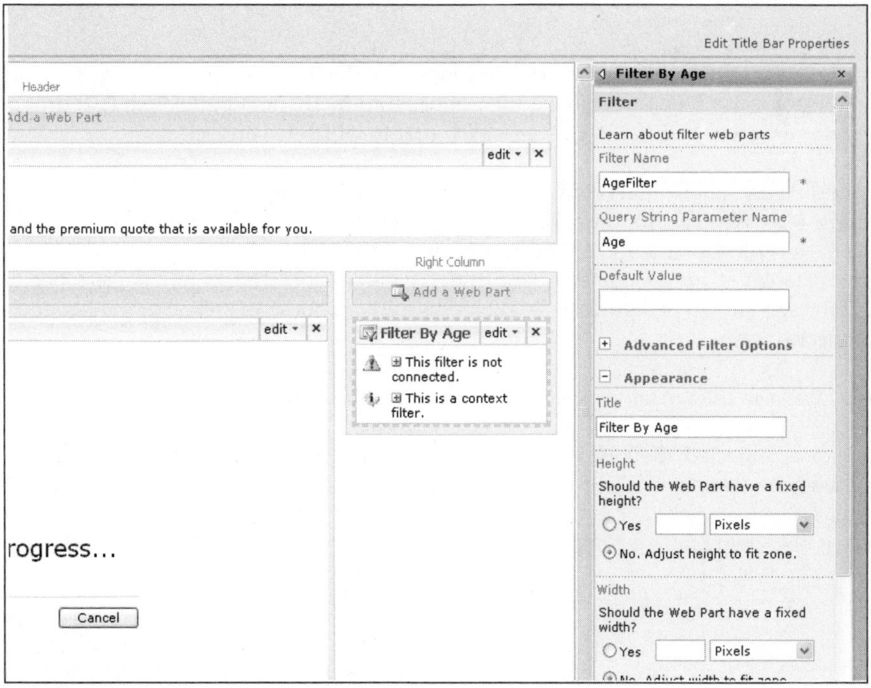

Figure 21-5

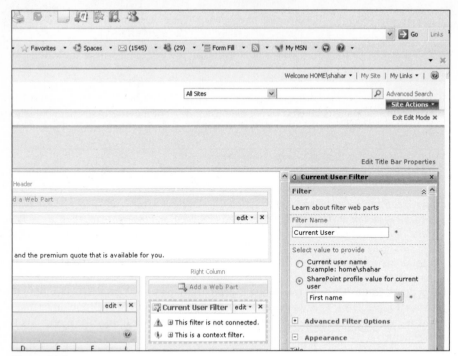

Figure 21-6

The last step in designing this Web Part is to connect all the Web Parts together via part-to-part communications. This can be done by choosing the Connections menu item in the Web Part dropdown and then selecting the appropriate Excel Web Access Web Part to which to connect.

The connection dialog box that comes up allows the user to choose how the connection is made. If going through the filter Web Part for the connection, the first page in the dialog that comes up will show the string Get Filter Values From, which is what's desired (the other options would allow the caller to set the workbook URL or the named object from the parameter). The second page (called "Configure Connection" and shown in Figure 21-7) will let the author choose the name of the parameter that needs to be connected:

> *Only workbooks that are saved inside SharePoint support using parameters in such a manner.*

Once they are connected, the Web Parts (both the filter and EWA) will show some text informing the user that they are connected. Figure 21-8 shows the page when all Web Parts are connected:

The page is now ready for consumption by users.

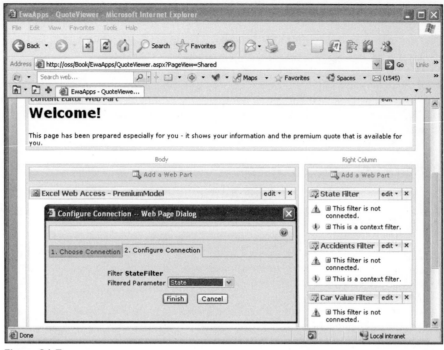

Figure 21-7

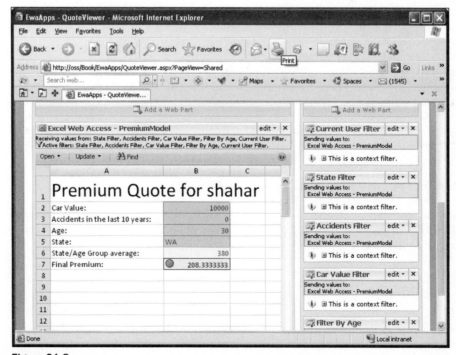

Figure 21-8

Custom XLViewer

The XLViewer page that ships with MOSS 2007 can be used to display a workbook and also allows the user who creates the link to choose which range/named object is viewed.

The rest of the parameters of the workbook are not accessible in the viewer page. They can be modified on a Web Part inside a Web Part page, but then they cannot be determined as URL parameters. This solution comes to solve this issue by creating a custom ASPX page that mimics the behavior of the XlViewer.

How It Works

In the following example, there's a workbook that contains stock information. The workbook also exposes a model and parameters; however, the author wants to send links to people so they can just see the data without being able to modify it.

> *It's important to understand that this is not a security precaution — it's simply a presentation mechanism. Any user who has the right to see the workbook and is technical enough to know what a URL is can modify it to remove these restrictions.*

Figure 21-9 shows the workbook when it's opened inside the regular XLViewer.aspx page when navigating to the following URL:

```
http://oss/Book/_layouts/xlviewer.aspx?id=http://oss/book/shared+documents/
StockAnalysis.xlsx&DefaultItemOpen=1
```

The various sheets are available for the users to view as are the parameters. Also, it is possible to sort the list and filter it. These may divert the attention from what the person who sent the link wants the users to see.

When using the custom Excel workbook viewer, however, the link can be formed in such a way so that the information that's not needed is not shown at all. The URL will be different, containing the options that need to be turned off:

```
http://oss/Book/_layouts/customxlviewer.aspx?id=http://oss/book/shared+
documents/StockAnalysis.xlsx&DefaultItemOpen=1&allowinteractivity=
0&allownav=0&showparameters=0&toolbar=3&rows=4&cols=4
```

The browser then presents the result shown in Figure 21-10.

Because navigation is disabled, the sheets are not available and the buttons that allow the user to scroll to different pages in the workbook do not exist. Interactivity being turned off means that it's impossible to sort or filter the list.

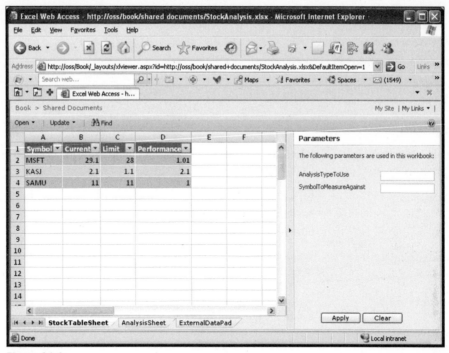

Figure 21-9

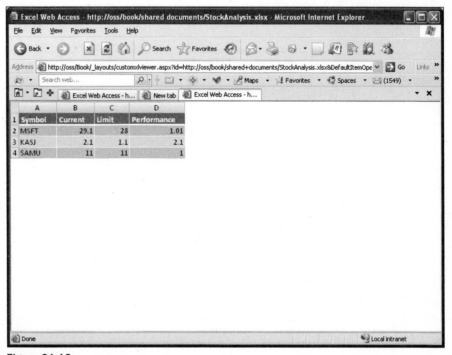

Figure 21-10

The following query string parameters are available on the URL (Those parameters that have "(preexisting)" near their names also work in the regular XLViewer page.)

Query String Parameter	Meaning
Rows	Limits the number of rows visible in the workbook. Defaults to 75.
Cols	Limits the number of columns visible in the workbook. Defaults to 25.
AllowFiltering	When set to 1, this allows filtering to occur inside lists and pivot tables. Defaults to 1.
AllowExcel	When set to 1, this allows users to open the workbook in Excel (if they have the authorization to do so) by clicking on the toolbar button. Defaults to 1.
AllowInteractivity	When set to 1, this allows users to interact with parts of the workbook. Defaults to 1.
AllowRefresh	When set to 1, this allows users to manually refresh data connections inside the workbook. Defaults to 1.
AllowNav	When set to 1, this allows users to navigate around the workbook. This includes using hyperlinks to hop around the workbook and navigating between sheets or inside sheets (page up and down, left and right). Defaults to 1.
AllowPivot	Specific for PivotTable navigation and interactivity. When set to 1, allows that functionality. Defaults to 1.
AllowRecalc	When set to 1, this allows users to manually recalculate the workbook from the toolbar.
AllowSorting	When set to 1, this allows users to change the sorting in the workbook. Defaults to 1.
ShowParameters	When set to 1, this will show the parameters pane, if there are any parameters in the workbook. Defaults to 1.
Toolbar	Can be set to an integer between 0 and 3 (inclusive):0: Full toolbar.1: Summary toolbar — only Open in Excel, Reload, and Refresh menu items.2: Navigation only — if the page is scrollable, the toolbar will show the arrows that allow to navigate page down and up, left and right.3: No toolbar at all.
Id (preexisting)	Sets the name of the workbook.

Query String Parameter	Meaning
Range (preexisting)	Sets the range to show. This can either be a named range or an Excel-style reference.
Refresh	Sets the interval (in seconds) where the workbook will refresh itself. Especially useful when a workbook contains automatically updating data (such as a periodic refresh data connection).
Reload	Sets the interval (in seconds) where the workbook will be reloaded. Useful for displaying workbooks that change often. Mutually exclusive with the Refresh query string parameter.
Title	This is optional (especially because these filter Web Parts are hidden when the page is viewed out of design mode), but it is useful to change this to some helpful string so that the page designer knows what each one holds.

Coding the Solution

The solution is based on the standard XLViewer.aspx page. To start, the file needs to be duplicated in the _layouts virtual directory and named CustomXLViewer.aspx. By default, the location of the file is:

```
C:\Program Files\Common Files\Microsoft Shared\Web server extensions\12\
TEMPLATE\LAYOUTS
```

> While this way of utilizing the Excel Viewer page (XLViewer.aspx) works, it's not fully supported by Excel Services. Because the page uses code-behind, which is part of Excel Services' binaries, the user has no real control over the code that happens to run. The next section shows another method of achieving similar results but without relying on the code-behind of XlViewer.aspx.

Once created, the file can be opened in any editor (Visual Studio 2005 provides some rudimentary Intelli-Sense capabilities). The first step is to change the AutoEventWireup attribute on the Page directive to be true:

```
<%@ Page language="C#" Codebehind="XlViewer.aspx.cs"
AutoEventWireup="false"
Inherits="Microsoft.Office.Excel.WebUI.XlViewer,Microsoft.Office.Excel.WebUI,Versio
n=12.0.0.0,Culture=neutral,PublicKeyToken=71e9bce111e9429c" %>
```

This will instruct ASP.NET to look inside the ASPX file and take what looks like events (which usually come in the form Object_Event with the appropriate signature) and wire them to the events on the system. In this case, the event that will be added is the Load event on the ASPX Page class. Since the code is embedded as part of the page (not code-behind), it lives inside a `<script>` tag with the `runat` attribute set to `"server"`:

```
<script runat="server">
    private int m_refreshInterval;
    private int m_reloadInterval;
    public void Page_Load(object sender, EventArgs e)
    {
        m_excelWebRenderer.RowsToDisplay =
            ParseInt(Request.QueryString["rows"], 75);
        m_excelWebRenderer.ColumnsToDisplay =
            ParseInt(Request.QueryString["cols"], 25);
        m_excelWebRenderer.AllowFiltering =
            ParseInt(Request.QueryString["allowfiltering"], 1) == 1;
        m_excelWebRenderer.AllowInExcelOperations =
            ParseInt(Request.QueryString["allowexcel"], 1) == 1;
        m_excelWebRenderer.AllowInteractivity =
            ParseInt(Request.QueryString["allowinteractivity"], 1) == 1;
        m_excelWebRenderer.AllowManualDataRefresh =
            ParseInt(Request.QueryString["allowrefresh"], 1) == 1;
        m_excelWebRenderer.AllowNavigation =
            ParseInt(Request.QueryString["allownav"], 1) == 1;
        m_excelWebRenderer.AllowPivotSpecificOperations =
            ParseInt(Request.QueryString["allowpivot"], 1) == 1;
        m_excelWebRenderer.AllowRecalculation =
            ParseInt(Request.QueryString["allowrecalc"], 1) == 1;
        m_excelWebRenderer.AllowSorting =
            ParseInt(Request.QueryString["allowsorting"], 1) == 1;
        m_excelWebRenderer.ShowWorkbookParameters =
            ParseInt(Request.QueryString["showparameters"], 1) == 1;
        m_excelWebRenderer.ToolbarStyle =
            (ToolbarVisibilityStyle)ParseInt(Request.QueryString["toolbar"], 0);
        m_refreshInterval =
                ParseInt(Request.QueryString["refresh"], 0);
        m_reloadInterval =
            ParseInt(Request.QueryString["reload"], 0);
    }

    private int ParseInt(string st, int def)
    {
        int result = def;
        if (st != null)
        {
            Int32.TryParse(st,
                System.Globalization.NumberStyles.Integer,
                System.Globalization.CultureInfo.InvariantCulture,
                out result);
        }
        return result;
    }
</script>
```

The `Page_Load()` method looks for the various query string parts, setting properties on the Excel Web Access control (called `m_excelWebRenderer`). The `ParseInt()` helper method returns either the value that was passed in or the default value if the query string does not contain the parameter. The reload and refresh interval are stored inside private members, which will be used later inside a client script block.

That's the only piece of server-side code that's needed. The next step is to get rid of the "breadcrumbs" section at the top of the page — see Figure 21-9. That section can be found in the ASPX page under the main table that's there for formatting reasons:

```
<table cellpadding="0" cellspacing="0" width="100%" height="100%" border="0">
    <tr>
        <td>
            <!— begin global breadcrumb —>
            <table
width="100%"
cellpadding="3"
cellspacing="0"
border="0"
class="ms-globalbreadcrumb">
<!— Removed for brevity —>
    </tr>
```

The highlighted line in the HTML represents the row that contains the "breadcrumbs" section in the page. It is impossible to completely remove this row because the page relies on it being there. Instead, it is possible to use HTML to make it invisible. Adding the display style to this element will make it invisible on the page:

```
<tr style="display:none">
```

For the reload and refresh optional parameters to work, the ASPX page needs to contain a client-side JavaScript block, which will take care of it:

```
<script type="text/javascript">
var reloadInterval = <% =m_reloadInterval %> * 1000;
if (reloadInterval != 0)
{
  window.setInterval("EwaReloadWorkbook('m_excelWebRenderer')", reloadInterval);
}

var refreshInterval = <% =m_refreshInterval %> * 1000;
if (refreshInterval != 0)
{
  window.setInterval("window.location.reload()", refreshInterval);
}

</script>
```

The script schedules functions to run at a given time. If the `m_reloadInterval` field is set to a value other than zero, the system will call the `EwaReloadWorkbook()` function after that interval has passed. This is one of the two client-side methdos exposed by the EWA to allow developers to interact with it (the second method will be discussed in the next section).

If the refresh interval is not set to zero, the script will make a call to `window.location.reload()`, which will cause the page to refresh, potentially showing new data.

Finding the Excel Web Access Control on the Page

The code written into the custom ASPX page uses a variable called `m_excelWebRenderer`. That variable is a field on the page class that runs in the code-behind of the ASPX. The control can be found in the page itself:

```
<WpNs0:ExcelWebRenderer id="m_excelWebRenderer" ...>
```

The `WpNs0` namespace is automatically generated by ASP.NET — looking at the top of the page, one can find that namespace declared using the `Register` ASP.NET directive:

```
<%@ Register Tagprefix="WpNs0" Namespace="Microsoft.Office.Excel.WebUI"
Assembly="Microsoft.Office.Excel.WebUI, Version=12.0.0.0, Culture=neutral,
PublicKeyToken=71e9bce111e9429c" %>
```

Manipulating the EWA Session

The previous section showed one of the two EWA client-side JavaScript APIs available for developers to call — the `EwaReloadWorkbook()` function.

This section will show how to use the second one, called `EwaGetSessionId()`, which, interestingly enough, returns a Session ID that is usable with Excel Web Services via SOAP. This section will show an example of how to combine EWA, AJAX-style calls to Excel Web Services and the `EwaGetSessionId()` method to build a solution that allows users to modify cells inside EWA. The solution is a mock stock analysis where the users select a stock they wish to analyze and the workbook displays relevant information. In this case, the workbook itself is just a mock-up of such an analysis — the important part is to see how all the parts work together.

The workbook shown here is the same one that was used in the previous section. This time, it has two parts that are of interest — a list of stocks that can be analyzed (shown in Figure 21-10) and a second sheet that will allow users to analyze the stocks.

How It Works

The web page that this solution presents contains two important parts. The top one is a combo box (SELECT element in HTML) that contains a list of all the stock symbols that are analyzable (which comes from the first sheet of the workbook). The second is the EWA, showing the page that analyzes the stock. While the EWA is loading, the combo box is disabled (as shown in Figure 21-11).

Once the workbook loads up (see Figure 21-12), the combo box is enabled and populated with the symbols from the first sheet.

Figure 21-13 shows what happens when the user selects a symbol from the list. The workbook is automatically updated and refreshed, showing the analysis.

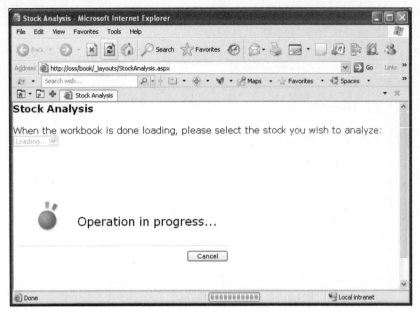

Figure 21-11

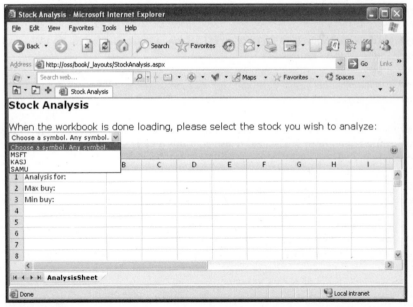

Figure 21-12

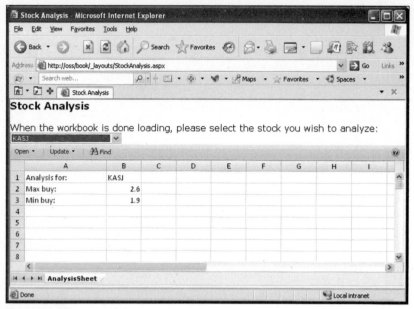

Figure 21-13

Coding the Solution

The first stage of this solution is to prepare an HTML page that will contain an EWA and will reside within the _layouts virtual directory.

In most installations, this means C:\Program Files\Common Files\Microsoft Shared\Web server extensions\12\TEMPLATE\LAYOUTS *on the server.*

The skeleton of the page will contain some prerequisites that are needed for an ASPX page with a Web Part to run inside SharePoint. The skeleton also contains a table with three rows. One for the title, one for the combo box, and one for EWA:

```
<%@ Register Tagprefix="WpNs0" Namespace="Microsoft.Office.Excel.WebUI"
Assembly="Microsoft.Office.Excel.WebUI, Version=12.0.0.0, Culture=neutral,
PublicKeyToken=71e9bce111e9429c" %>
<%@ Page language="C#" AutoEventWireup="true" %>
<html id="m_htmlTag" runat="server">
<head>
    <meta http-equiv="Content-Type" content="text/html; charset=utf-8" />
    <title>Stock Analysis</title>
</head>
<body style="overflow:auto;">
  <form runat="server">
    <table cellpadding="0" cellspacing="0" width="100%" height="100%" border="0">
      <tr>
        <td><h3>Stock Analysis</h3></td>
```

```
      </tr>
      <tr>
        <td valign="top">
          When the workbook is done loading,
          please select the stock you wish to analyze:
          <select id="stockToAnalyze" disabled="disabled"
            onchange="javascript:StockSelected()">
            <option>Loading...</option>
          </select>
        </td>
      </tr>
      <tr>
        <td id="webpartContainerCell" valign="top" >
          <WpNs0:ExcelWebRenderer id="m_excelWebRenderer"
            runat="server"
            WebPart="true"
            __WebPartId="{4F1D37E5-354C-4818-9A29-6B202A1FA56E}">
            <WebPart xmlns:xsi="http://www.w3.org/2001/XMLSchema-instance"
              xmlns:xsd="http://www.w3.org/2001/XMLSchema"
              xmlns="http://schemas.microsoft.com/WebPart/v2">
              <FrameType>None</FrameType>
              <Width>400px</Width>
              <Height>250px</Height>
            </WebPart>
          </WpNs0:ExcelWebRenderer>
        </td>
      </tr>
    </table>
  </form>
</body>
```

The Web Part section (the tag that's prefixed with WpNs0) is used to tell SharePoint to place the EWA on the page — when rendered on the server, that section will be replaced with the actual HTML that EWA produces.

The other tags that are inside the WpNs0:ExcelWebRenderer element act as property setters, determining some of the behavior of the Web Part. In this case, the parts that are interesting to us are the FrameType, Height, and Width properties. FrameType governs the HTML that surrounds the EWA. Setting it to none makes sure there's no unneeded HTML around it. Height and Width (which are only settable to pixels) govern the final size of the EWA.

There are two script blocks that are needed in this page. The first and simplest is server-side code that will make sure the workbook loads properly:

```
<script runat="server">
    public void Page_Load(object sender, EventArgs e)
    {
        m_excelWebRenderer.ShowWorkbookParameters = false;
        m_excelWebRenderer.WorkbookUri =
          "http://oss/book/Shared Documents/StockAnalysis.xlsx";
    }
</script>
```

This code runs in the server as the page gets rendered, making sure that the correct workbook is loaded and that there is no parameters pane showing.

Once the HTML lands in the browser, the usual "Progress window" shows waiting for the workbook to load.

The first step in the client-side script is to get the list of symbols that needs to be placed in the combo box. For that, the code needs to wait for the EWA to finish loading. This is done by polling the `EwaGetSessionId()` JavaScript function until it returns a non-null value:

```
<script type="text/javascript">

    function StartPolling()
    {
        window.setTimeout("Poll()", 100);
    }
    function Poll()
    {
        var id = EwaGetSessionId("m_excelWebRenderer");
        if (id != null)
        {
            FillFromSession(id);
        }
        else
        {
            StartPolling();
        }
    }

    StartPolling();
// …
</script>
```

The `StartPolling()` function is called in the script and it uses the `setTimeout()` JavaScript function to get the `Poll()` function to execute after 100 milliseconds.

When executed, the `Poll()` function tries to find the Session ID of the EWA. If it's successful (the return value is not null), it will call the `FillFromSession()` function. Otherwise, it will call the `StartPolling()` function, waiting for another 100 milliseconds to try again.

`FillFromSession()` uses AJAX to execute an Excel Web Services SOAP request for the values that are contained inside the column of symbols in the table shown in Figure 21-10. In this case, this is done by utilizing the `XMLHTTP` object to issue an asynchronous request to the server. The code ends up doing the same thing that the generated proxy classes in Visual Studio do — in this case, the process is more painful because all the details of the call need to be crafted by hand.

```
var request;
function FillFromSession(id)
{
    request = new ActiveXObject("Microsoft.XMLHTTP");
    request.onreadystatechange = FillFromSessionDone;
    var url;
```

```
    url = "/_vti_bin/ExcelService.asmx";

    var envelope = "<soap:Envelope" +
        " xmlns:soap=\"http://schemas.xmlsoap.org/soap/envelope/\"" +
        " xmlns:xsi=\"http://www.w3.org/2001/XMLSchema-instance\"" +
        " xmlns:xsd=\"http://www.w3.org/2001/XMLSchema\">" +
        "<soap:Body>" +
        "<GetRangeA1 " +
        "xmlns=\"http://schemas.microsoft.com/office/excel/server/webservices\">" +
        "<sessionId>" + id + "</sessionId>" +
        "<sheetName></sheetName>" +
        "<rangeName>StockTable[Symbol]</rangeName>" +
        "<formatted>true</formatted>" +
        "</GetRangeA1>" +
        "</soap:Body>" +
        "</soap:Envelope>";

    request.open("POST", url, true);
    request.setRequestHeader("Content-Type", "text/xml");
    request.send(envelope);
}
```

The first step creates a new XMLHTTP object so that it can create an asynchronous request. The second part places a callback in the onreadystatechange event, which is raised as the status of the request changes.

Next, the script builds up the request that will be sent. In this case, it is hand-crafting a SOAP request by generating the XML that will be sent to the server. The following table explains the meaning of each part of the XML.

Tag	Meaning
soap:Envelope	This is the top-level SOAP element, which acts as a container to the call. It's also used here to define the various potential namespaces that will be used.
soap:Body	Specifies the request body.
GetRangeA1	The name of the method being called. This could have been any of the methods defined in Excel Web Services. In this case, the code needs a range identified by a name. The namespace for this element is the one defined inside the xmlns attribute.
sessionId	Parameter of the web method call. The ID of the session that was harvested from the EWA.
sheetName	Parameter of the web method call. An empty element — the equivalent of passing an empty string in the sheet parameter to the GetRangeA1() web method.

Continued

Tag	Meaning
rangeName	Parameter of the web method call. The name of the range requested from Excel Services.
formatted	Parameter of the web method call. Indicates whether or not the result needs to be formatted to string.

The last three calls to the request object in this method cause the network request that will be received by Excel Web Services. The call to open() tells the request object that the HTTP action that is taken is POST (as opposed to GET), that the URL is "/_vti_bin/ExcelService.asmx" and that the call needs to be done asynchronously (that's third parameter).

The call to setRequestHeader() makes sure the HTML sent over will be recognized as something Excel Web Services can interpret. The last call to send() takes the XML that was created and sends it to the server.

As the state of the request changes, the XMLHTTP instance will keep calling the FillFromSessionDone() function (it was set as the callback at the beginning of the function). FillFromSessionDone() waits for the completion code (which happens to be 4) and then it will take the result, parse it using the XML DOM and place the parts that are important (the symbols) in the combo box.

The result coming back from the server is an XML that represents a SOAP response containing a jagged array:

```
<soap:Envelope
    xmlns:soap="http://schemas.xmlsoap.org/soap/envelope/"
    xmlns:xsi="http://www.w3.org/2001/XMLSchema-instance"
    xmlns:xsd="http://www.w3.org/2001/XMLSchema">
  <soap:Body>
    <GetRangeA1Response
        xmlns="http://schemas.microsoft.com/office/excel/server/webservices">
      <GetRangeA1Result>
        <anyType xsi:type="ArrayOfAnyType">
          <anyType xsi:type="xsd:string">
            MSFT
          </anyType>
        </anyType>
        <anyType xsi:type="ArrayOfAnyType">
          <anyType xsi:type="xsd:string">
            KASJ
          </anyType>
        </anyType>
        <anyType xsi:type="ArrayOfAnyType">
          <anyType xsi:type="xsd:string">
            SAMU
          </anyType>
        </anyType>
```

```
        </GetRangeA1Result>
      </GetRangeA1Response>
    </soap:Body>
  </soap:Envelope>
```

The highlighted part above represents the array. There are three arrays in it — each corresponding to a "row." Since each row has only one cell, there's only one anyType element.

```
function FillFromSessionDone()
{
    if (request.readyState == 4)
    {
        var dom = request.responseXML;
        dom.setProperty("SelectionNamespaces",
          "xmlns:soap='http://schemas.xmlsoap.org/soap/envelope/'" +
          " xmlns:xsi='http://www.w3.org/2001/XMLSchema-instance'" +
          " xmlns:xsd='http://www.w3.org/2001/XMLSchema' xmlns:es=" +
          "'http://schemas.microsoft.com/office/excel/server/webservices'");
        var list = dom.selectNodes("/soap:Envelope/soap:Body" +
            "/es:GetRangeA1Response/es:GetRangeA1Result" +
            "//es:anyType[@xsi:type='xsd:string']");
        var selectElement = document.getElementById("stockToAnalyze");
        while (selectElement.options.length > 0)
        {
            selectElement.options.remove(0);
        }

        var opt = document.createElement("OPTION");
        selectElement.options.add(opt);
        opt.innerText = "Choose a symbol. Any symbol.";

        for (var i = 0; i < list.length; i++)
        {
            var opt = document.createElement("OPTION");
            selectElement.options.add(opt);
            opt.value = list[i].text;
            opt.innerText = list[i].text;
        }
        selectElement.disabled = false;
    }
}
```

The first step is to call the SetProperty() method on the XML DOM so that, when using XPath to do selection, it will be using the appropriate namespaces. In this case, four namespaces are being added — one for Excel Services, one for SOAP, and two for XML schemas.

Next, the function builds an XPath query, which will return all the anyType elements that have string contents:

```
/soap:Envelope/soap:Body/es:GetRangeA1Response/es:GetRangeA1Result//es:anyType[@xsi
:type='xsd:string']
```

The call to selectNodes() returns the list of nodes that fulfill this XPath query. In the case shown above, this means that there will be three nodes that are returned.

For each such node, a new OPTION element is created and added to the combo box. The value and text are set to whatever the data that came from the range was.

At this stage, the page has the combo box enabled and is waiting for a user to select an item. Once selected, the StockSelected() method gets executed (it's on the onchange event on the SELECT element tag in the HTML).

```
function StockSelected()
{
    var selectElement = document.getElementById("stockToAnalyze");
    if (selectElement.value != "")
    {
        ChangeAnalysis(selectElement.value);
    }
}
function ChangeAnalysis(symbol)
{
    request = new ActiveXObject("Microsoft.XMLHTTP");
    request.onreadystatechange = ChangeAnalysisDone;
    var url;
    url = "/_vti_bin/ExcelService.asmx";

    var envelope = "<soap:Envelope" +
        " xmlns:soap=\"http://schemas.xmlsoap.org/soap/envelope/\"" +
        " xmlns:xsi=\"http://www.w3.org/2001/XMLSchema-instance\"" +
        " xmlns:xsd=\"http://www.w3.org/2001/XMLSchema\">" +
        "<soap:Body>" +
        "<SetCellA1 " +
        "xmlns=\"http://schemas.microsoft.com/office/excel/server/webservices\">" +
        "<sessionId>" + EwaGetSessionId("m_excelWebRenderer") + "</sessionId>" +
        "<sheetName></sheetName>" +
        "<rangeName>StockToAnalyze</rangeName>" +
        "<cellValue>" + symbol + "</cellValue>" +
        "</SetCellA1>" +
        "</soap:Body>" +
        "</soap:Envelope>";

    request.open("POST", url, true);
    request.setRequestHeader("Content-Type", "text/xml");
    request.send(envelope);
}
```

The StockSelected() function calls into the ChangeAnalysis() function, which issues a SOAP call, very similar to what FillFromSession() does. In this case though, the web method that gets invoked is the SetCellA1() method — it takes as a parameter the Session ID (which this time is retrieved directly using the EwaGetSessionId() JavaScript function). The selected symbol is passed as the value into the range in the workbook that represents the symbol that will be analyzed.

When the request is done, the ChangeAnalysisDone() function gets called.

EWA has no knowledge about the SOAP calls that are made to the server since these take place on a mechanism that is completely separate. Because of that, EWA has no way of knowing that the data in the workbook has changed and thus cannot refresh itself. That's why the solution needs to cause a refresh when the value gets set. The only supported way to cause an EWA refresh is to refresh the whole page. While that's the safest way to do this from a forward compatibility point of view, it is also not always desirable. As opposed to the previous example, in this one the EWA is part of a page rather than inhabiting it in its entirety. Instead, in here, only the EWA is refreshed, getting new values. It is important to understand that this behavior may break in a future release. Developers who are not willing to take this risk should refresh the whole page instead of just the EWA.

```
function ChangeAnalysisDone()
{
  if (request.readyState == 4)
  {
     RefreshEwa("m_excelWebRenderer");
  }
}
function RefreshEwa(id)
{
    var element = document.getElementById(id);
    FindIFrame(element).contentWindow.document.forms[0].submit();
}

function FindIFrame(element)
{
    for (var i = 0; i < element.childNodes.length; i++)
    {
        var child = element.childNodes[i];
        if (child.tagName == "IFRAME")
        {
            return child;
        }
        child = FindIFrame(child);
        if (child != null)
        {
            return child;
        }
    }
}
```

When `ChangeAnalysisDone()` is called, it checks to make sure the operation is done and then goes ahead and calls the `RefreshEwa()` function.

`RefreshEwa()` takes an ID of a Web Part (`m_excelWebRenderer` in this example) and calls the `FindIFrame()` function on it. This function will recursively search the elements under the Web Part element, finding the first `IFrame` there. This `IFrame` will just always happen to be the one that contains the contents of the EWA. Refreshing this `IFrame` wll cause the EWA to update itself. Once the EWA refreshes, it will show the most current information.

Reading in a book the phrase "always happen to be" is the first sign that an unsupported feature is being used. Changes to the product in future versions or even service packs may change this assumption, disabling this part of the solution.

Summary

While EWA does not supply a rich server-side or client-side object model, it is still possible to use it in a myrid of solutions.

Chapter 23 shows an even more elaborate solution that uses an Excel Web Services AJAX library to create a Mashup with Virtual Earth.

22

Excel Data Filter

Chapter 21 showed how to interact with the Excel Web Part to implement various solutions. Some of the solutions relied solely on the SharePoint Web Part page feature and showed how to create a rudimentary application using EWA and some filter Web Parts.

Other solutions showed how to interact with Excel Web Services from IE, using the same session EWA is using to both get information from a workbook (and place it in a combo box) and to set information back to the workbook and have EWA display it.

The project in this chapter shows how to create a filter Web Part that uses an Excel range in a workbook as the data from which users can choose. The filter can be integrated with an EWA placed on the page, or it can be used with any other Web Part that knows how to consume filters.

Overview

The filter can be set up so that it runs on the client (like in the "Manipulating the EWA session" section in Chapter 21) or on the server. It can be set up to work against a specific workbook or, if the filter is connected to an EWA, it can be set up to use the same workbook that the EWA is using (and the same session in some cases).

The filter has two modes in which it operates. The first is the "server-side" mode in which a new session is opened on the server and data is extracted, filling the combo box on the server. The second is the "client-side" mode in which the extracting of data and filling the combo box happens on the client (inside the browser).

The following section will show some ways of using the new Web Part that this solution creates.

Use

The first example shows how to use an Excel workbook containing a simple book list inside a Web Part page to create an application that allows the user to look at the covers of each book.

Creating and Setting Up the Page

Figure 22-1 shows an Excel workbook containing a table of books, where each row is holding the name of the book, the authors, and a link to the cover image.

Once the workbook is uploaded to a document library, the next step is to create a new Web Part page containing the Excel Data Filter Web Part (it will appear in the gallery when Add Web Part is clicked), a Picture Web Part and a Filter Actions Web Part. Figure 22-2 shows the page after the editing is done.

The next step is to edit the properties of the Excel Data Filter Web Part. After choosing the Modify Shared Web Part option in the dropdown menu of that Web Part, the pane shows all the properties of the filter. At the bottom there's a section called Filter Options. Figure 22-3 shows the contents of that section once it's opened up.

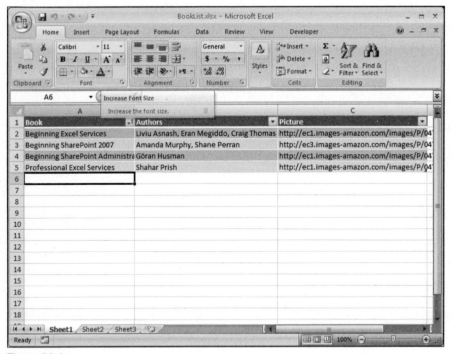

Figure 22-1

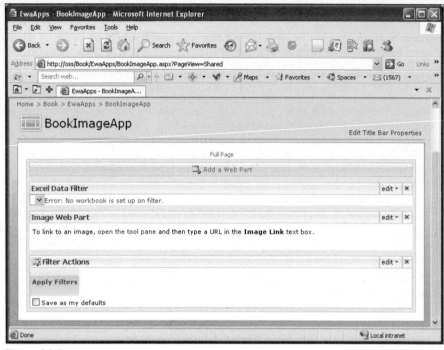

Figure 22-2

Figure 22-3

For the purpose of this example, the following properties are changed:

❑ **Filter Name.** Just as in Chapter 21, this name will identify the filter in the UI when it's being used to connect Web Parts. In this case, it will be modified to be BookImageUrl.

❑ **Workbook URL.** This is the name of the workbook that will be used for the data. In this case, it's the URL for the BookList.xlsx file that was saved to the document library.

❑ **Range.** The name of the range that will be extracted from the workbook. In this case, this is the named range of the table the workbook contains.

Using the name of the table as the range reduces the maintenance work that a workbook author has to do. If the table were to grow on the next save of the workbook, no other adjustments would be needed in the workbook.

❑ **Text column index.** The range that's returned from Excel is used to fill the combo box that is the filter. This property (and the next one) allows the author of the web page to determine which column will be used for the contents of the combo box. In this case, since the author of the page wants to see the name of the book, the first column is used (zero-based).

❑ **Value column index.** In this case, the value is the URL of the book picture, stored in the third column. The property thus is set to 2.

After the properties are modified in this manner, clicking OK on the Web Part properties pane should show the web page author the populated filter, as Figure 22-4 shows.

Figure 22-4

The last step is to connect the two Web Parts. Doing this is very similar to the way the EWA was connected to the various filters in the "Parameterized EWA Links" section of Chapter 21. Once connected, the page immediately refreshes to show the selected book (see Figure 22-5).

Selecting a different item in the combo box and clicking the Apply button will change the picture Web Part to show the relevant image.

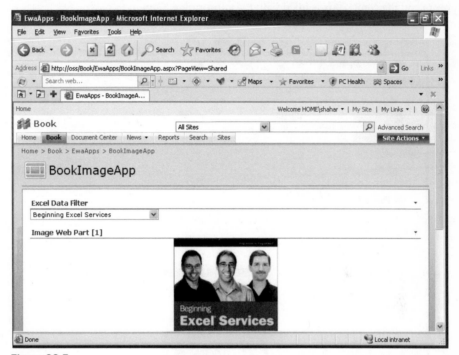

Figure 22-5

Client-side Connection

Depending on the size and complexity of a workbook and on the load on the server, it may sometimes take minutes for a workbook to load. The Excel Web Access Web Part is built in such a way that it does not slow the opening of the page down, even when the workbook takes a long time to open.

The Excel Data Filter Web Part can work in a mode where it also does not slow down the loading of a page — instead, it uses AJAX to call into Excel Services and get back the appropriate information, doing the rest of the work from IE.

Note: In some cases it may not be secure to do this. If it is important for the location of a workbook to be hidden from the viewers of a page, be aware that this approach will allow them to see the full workbook URL. On top of that, in some deployments, Excel Web Services may be disabled, making this method inapplicable.

To change the Web Part so that it issues the request from the client rather than from the server, the author of the page needs only to check the Connect to Excel Services from the client option on the property pane of the workbook. The Web Part will behave almost exactly the same — but instead of the values being immediately available on the page, it will issue the appropriate requests:

Figure 22-6 shows the filter with a status message reporting that the values are being fetched. Once the opening stage is done, the message changes to say that it's now querying the values. Finally, the message disappears and the combo box is filled with the appropriate range.

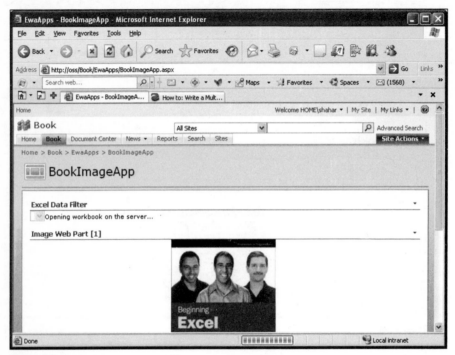

Figure 22-6

Using EWA with the Excel Data Filter

Chapter 21 showed how it is possible to bind parameters to filters to give a Web Part page a much more "application-like" feeling.

Much as the previous section did with the image Web Part, it is also possible to bind parameters in the EWA Web Part to an Excel data filter. However, when connected to an EWA Web Part, the filter gains some abilities it does not have when it's connected to other Web Parts.

In the case where the Excel data filter is connected to EWA, it is possible to tell it to use the same workbook that the EWA is using (and as will be seen later, the same session as well).

To see how this plays out, the following example uses the PremiumModel workbook to show how it is possible to navigate the various clients and see their insurance information on the page. In this case, the page contains three parts. The first part is the model that has been used throughout the book. The second is the user-facing sheet containing only the relevant information. That list is similar to the left part shown in Figure 22-6 (containing only the information about the clients such as their age and number of accidents).

Because the workbook contains both the list of clients and their information, the sheet that contains the model calculations will use it as the source of information inside the workbook. Figure 22-7 shows the workbook, where instead of expecting values to be inserted into the cells, the Excel VLookup formula is used to search for the relevant information.

The page needed for the next example will contain the EWA, the Excel Data Filter and the Filter Actions. The EWA will be configured to show the premium model (which is in Named Object mode so that it shows only the user-facing sheet containing the details of the premium). The parameters pane will be hidden. The filter will be configured with the following properties:

❑ **Use the connected workbook.** This should be checked — it will instruct the filter part to use the EWA to figure out the workbook name.

❑ **Range to use as filter information.** Set to "ClientTable" — that corresponds to the table representing the clients in the workbook.

❑ **Text column index/Value column index.** Both should be set to zero — the name that's needed visually and that is going to be set to the workbook are the same.

The last stage is to connect the EWA and the filter, as shown in Figure 22-8.

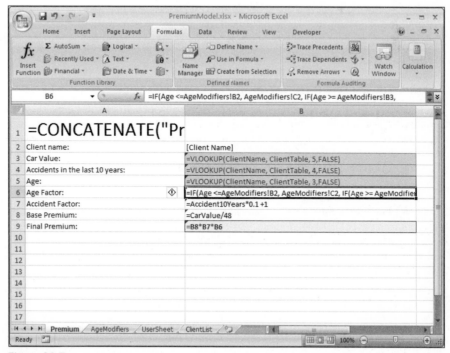

Figure 22-7

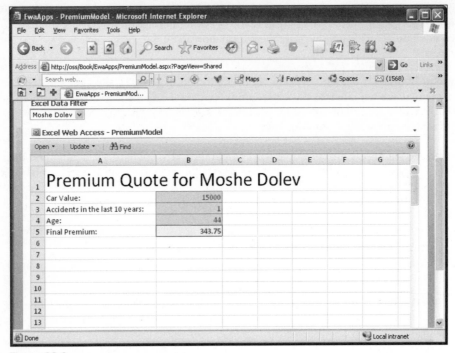

Figure 22-8

The filter is now tied to the EWA, using the same workbook as the EWA. If the page authors change the workbook that the EWA is using, the filter automatically starts using that instead (that may be a good thing or a bad thing, depending on the scenario).

Using the Same Session as EWA

Chapter 21 showed how the session EWA is using is accessible to script running inside the browser. It is possible to leverage that with the filter. Checking the Connect to Excel Services from the client check box will change the behavior of the filter to use the same functionality as Chapter 21 used to figure out the Session ID and then use it to issue the GetRange requests to the server. Once EWA is done loading the list box will be populated and shown to the user. Figure 22-9 shows the Excel Data Filter waiting for the EWA to finish loading.

There is an extra layer of behavior that exists in this mode, which is unique — because the filter shares the session with the EWA, it means that any changes made to the workbook inside the session may affect the values that the filter provides. Like before, how useful this is depends wholly on the scenario. In the case presented here, it does not really matter because the table will never be changed.

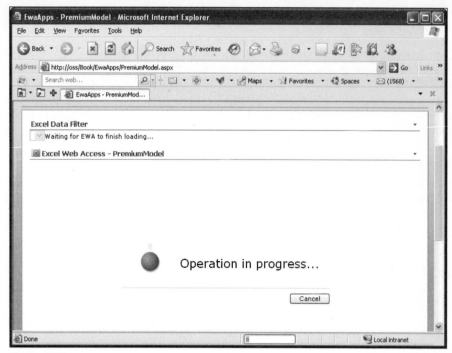

Figure 22-9

Coding the Solution

Due to the various modes this filter has, the code and structure of the solution are not trivial. On the server side, the code is in line with most of what this book has shown so far. On the client side, however, it is slightly more complex. This section will first discuss the Excel Services AJAX library, which is used to supply the client functionality, and then will show the whole implementation — server and client together.

The Excel Services AJAX library

Since the Excel Web Services are exposed as a SOAP over HTTP API, it is possible for browsers to call into Excel Web Services using AJAX.

AJAX stands for Asynchronous JavaScript And XML. It allows browsers that support script to issue HTTP requests to a web server and use the results to somehow manipulate the page they are in, giving a "rich application" feeling to the user. Some of the first implementations that were widely used are Outlook Web Access, Google Maps, and Virtual Earth.

Chapter 21 showed some of this in a very specific way — one of the examples in that chapter used AJAX to hand-craft and issue SOAP calls to Excel Services.

This section discusses the AJAX library, which is a single JavaScript file that can be used in any browser to give a page the ability to communicate with Excel Services.

The library follows the ideas behind the Excel Services library described in Chapter 7. On top of providing a simple mechanism for calling server methods such as `OpenWorkbook()` and `GetRangeA1()`, the library also allows the developer to create session objects that abstract the Session ID.

Including the Library

To use the library, you must first load it into the browser. To do this, make sure that the following tag exists in the header of the page. (There are other ways to do this. This seems to be the simplest and will be used later in the chapter):

```
<head>
<script src="/_layouts/ExcelServicesAjax.js" type="text/javascript"></script>
</head>
```

Using the ExcelServices Class

The `ExcelServices` class encapsulates all communication with the server, managing SOAP calls and maintaining a state for the user.

As an example, to open a workbook and display the Session ID that was returned, a developer may write the following code:

```
var es = new ExcelServices();
es.openWorkbook(
"http://oss/book/shared documents/blank.xlsx",
OpenWorkbookCallback);
function OpenWorkbookCallback(webMethod)
{
    alert(webMethod.result);
}
```

The first step is to create a new ExcelServices instance using the `new` operator. Then, the script calls into the `openWorkbook()` method, which takes two parameters — the name of the workbook and a callback that will be executed when the operation is done.

The pattern of passing a callback as the last argument to methods will repeat itself throughout this section. Because AJAX is asynchronous, it needs to notify the client when the operation is done — this is one way of achieving this.

When this occurs, the following sequence takes place:

1. The call to `openWorkbook()` causes a SOAP envelope to be created (much like the AJAX done in Chapter 21). That envelope is then sent to the server.

2. The server sends back a response, which the Excel Services AJAX library interprets and turns into a result that can be consumed by the developer.

3. The result is placed inside an instance of the `ExcelServicesWebMethodCall` class and passed in to the callback.

4. The callback, when executed, uses the `ExcelServicesWebMethodCall` instance to get to the result (which, in the case of an `OpenWorkbook()` call is the Session ID).

The code, however, is not perfect — it does not take into account any errors that may occur in the operation. To do that, the caller needs to probe first if the result is an error. Errors are represented by the `ExcelServicesError` class, which happens to have an `isError` property set to true. To check for an error and notify the user would change the code to look like this:

```
var es = new ExcelServices();
es.openWorkbook(
"http://oss/book/shared documents/blank.xlsx",
OpenWorkbookCallback);
function GetCellCallback(webMethod)
{
    if (webMethod.result.isError)
    {
        alert("An error has occurred:" + webMethod.result.reason);
    }
    else
    {
        alert(webMethod.result);
    }
}
```

The code now first makes sure that the result is not an error. If it is, it notifies the user about the error and gives the reason property (which contains the verbose error message).

Getting Data from Excel Services

To get a cell from Excel Services using the Excel Services AJAX library, the developer can use the `getCellA1()` method. The following example opens a session on the server and, once opened, uses the `getCellA1()` method to get a specific cell and alert the user about it:

```
function OpenWorkbookCallback(webMethod)
{
    es.getCellA1(webMethod.result, "Sheet1", "A1", true, GetCellCallback);
}
function GetCellCallback(webMethod)
{
    alert("Sheet1!A1 is " + webMethod.result);
}
var es = new ExcelServices();
es.openWorkbook(
    "http://oss/book/shared documents/blank.xlsx",
    OpenWorkbookCallback);
```

The code is similar to the one shown before, only this time, instead of showing the user the Session ID, the code tries to get a cell in the workbook. The call to `getCellA1()` is passed the Session ID (represented by the result passed into the `OpenWorkbookCallback()` callback method). It passes the requested range and the fact that the results need to be formatted (that's the fourth argument). The `GetCellCallback()` method is also passed in — it will be called when the operation of getting the value is done.

`GetCellCallback()`, when called, then uses the result in the `webMethod` parameter to access the contents of the returned cell.

Issuing Multiple Requests

Some requests can be executed together in the server. Because the various `GetRange`/`GetCell` calls are such requests, it is possible to call them concurrently from the client:

> *Due to the HTTP standards, most browsers and apps are configured to never issue more than two requests at the same time to a server. Once two requests are being processed on the server, clients will tend to queue up the rest, waiting for one of the running requests to return before continuing with the waiting ones. This limit is sometimes configurable.*

```
function OpenWorkbookCallback(webMethod)
{
     es.getCellA1(webMethod.result, "Sheet1", "A1", true, GetCellCallback);
     es.getCellA1(webMethod.result, "Sheet2", "A1", true, GetCellCallback);
     es.getCellA1(webMethod.result, "Sheet3", "A1", true, GetCellCallback);
     es.getCellA1(webMethod.result, "Sheet4", "A1", true, GetCellCallback);
     es.getCellA1(webMethod.result, "Sheet5", "A1", true, GetCellCallback);
}
function GetCellCallback(webMethod)
{
     alert("Result is " + webMethod.result);
}
var es = new ExcelServices();
es.openWorkbook(
     "http://oss/book/shared documents/blank.xlsx",
     OpenWorkbookCallback);
```

In this (somewhat nonsensical) example, the Web browser will issue five different requests to the server, with each request that comes back alerting the user as to the result.

User State in Requests

Consider the following code that sets a value in cell A1 and then reads the information from cell A2:

```
var sessionId;
function OpenWorkbookCallback(webMethod)
{
     sessionId = webMethod.result;
     es.setCellA1(webMethod.result, "Sheet1", "A1", 1, SetCellCallback);
}

function SetCellCallback(webMethod)
{
     es.getCellA1(sessionId, "Sheet1", "A2", true, GetCellCallback);
}
```

```
function GetCellCallback(webMethod)
{
    alert("Sheet1!A2 is " + webMethod.result);
}
var es = new ExcelServices();
var sessionId;
es.openWorkbook(
    "http://oss/book/shared documents/blank.xlsx",
    OpenWorkbookCallback);
```

This code is using a variable called sessionId, which was unneeded before. The reason for this is that without it, by the time the SetCellCallback() method is called, the script has already forgotten what the Session ID is. The sessionId variable solves this, but at a steep price. Consider what happens if there are two scripts calling into Excel Services in the same page. They both now have to define their own Session ID variables and need to make sure that these do not conflict. This can be compounded in scenarios where server controls are used and can emit code that might conflict with itself.

For this reason, the Excel Services AJAX library contains the notion of "user state," which can be attached to the ExcelServices instance. That state can be anything — from the Session ID to an object defined by the user.

The example, modified to take advantage of the user state will look like this:

```
function OpenWorkbookCallback(webMethod)
{
    var es = webMethod.excelServices;
    es.userState = webMethod.result;
    es.setCellA1(es.userState,
        "Sheet1", "A1", 1, SetCellCallback);
}

function SetCellCallback(webMethod)
{
    var es = webMethod.excelServices;
    es.getCellA1(es.userState,
        "Sheet1", "A2", true, GetCellCallback);
}

function GetCellCallback(webMethod)
{
    alert("Sheet1!A2 is " + webMethod.result);
}

new ExcelServices().openWorkbook(
    "http://oss/book/shared documents/blank.xlsx",
    OpenWorkbookCallback);
```

This code does not rely on any global variables — eveyrhing is encapsulated inside the ExcelServices instance, which itself is not held in any global variable.

The OpenWorkbookCallback() method takes the Session ID and places it inside the userState property of the ExcelServices instance. From that moment, that Session ID is accessible by any callback that will be executed because each executed web method will hold `excelServices` in its property, supplying access to it (and from it, to the Session ID stored inside the `userState` property).

Using the ExcelServicesSession Class

The session class encapsulates the Session ID, making it somewhat easier to call into Excel Services functionality. There are two ways to use it. The first is through the `openSession()` method on the `ExcelServices` class. The second is by instantiating it directly with a Session ID.

The following example shows how the same code shown before would look if it were written using sessions:

```
function OpenWorkbookCallback(webMethod)
{
     var session = webMethod.excelServices.userState;
     session.setCellA1("Sheet1", "A1", 1, SetCellCallback);
}

function SetCellCallback(webMethod)
{
     var session = webMethod.excelServices.userState;
     session.getCellA1("Sheet1", "A2", true, GetCellCallback);
}

function GetCellCallback(webMethod)
{
     alert("Sheet1!A2 is " + webMethod.result);
}

new ExcelServices().openSession(
     "http://oss/book/shared documents/blank.xlsx",
     OpenWorkbookCallback);
```

There are two major differences between the previous code snippet (that was not using sessions) and this one. First, in the session code, there is no need to pass the Session ID each time a call is made. Second, the `userState` property is preset to the session, making it slightly easier to use.

How Part to Part Works

Although it is out of scope of this book, the following is a simplified explanation of how part to part works in ASP.NET and SharePoint.

Part to part in general is a relatively simple mechanism that can be made very complex, depending on the amount of connections present.

1. When the page starts up, ASP.NET goes over all the connections it finds. For each connection, it checks which Web Part is the consumer and which one is the provider. From that information, it builds a dependency graph, which governs the order in which connections need to be resolved.

2. Using the tree, for each provider, ASP.NET calls the exposed method or interfaces to get the data the provider is pushing.

3. In each case, such data is then pushed to the consumer Web Part that's connected to the provider.

4. Once the tree is fully resolved (i.e., when all controls have been called with the appropriate data), the infrastructure continues to the render portion of the page.

Pes.Filter Project

The next step is to create the Web Part filter project that will provide the functionality shown at the beginning of the chapter.

The solution contains a single C# library project, which contains two classes. On top of that, the solution also comes with a JavaScript file that needs to be installed on the server. (ExcelServicesAjax also needs to be installed on the server.) Since the solution is a Web Part, it will need to be registered on the server so that it can be used (this will be shown at the end of the chapter).

ExcelDataFilter Class

In SharePoint, filters are simply Web Parts that support a specific interface. In this case, the ExcelData-Filter Web Part inherits both from the SharePoint WebPart class and from the ITransformableFilter-Value interface:

Because both ASP.NET and SharePoint each has their own WebPart class, the code distinguishes them by using two different aliases to their namespaces — AspWebParts and SPWebParts.

```
using System;
using System.Collections.Generic;
using System.Text;
using AspWebParts = System.Web.UI.WebControls.WebParts;
using System.Web.UI.WebControls;
using System.Web.UI;
using System.Xml.Serialization;
using System.ComponentModel;

using Microsoft.SharePoint.Utilities;
using Microsoft.SharePoint.WebPartPages;
using Microsoft.Office.Excel.WebUI;
using SPWebParts = Microsoft.SharePoint.WebPartPages;

using ExcelServicesLibrary;

namespace Pes.Filter
{
    [ToolboxData("<{0}:ExcelDataFilter runat=\"server\"></{0}:ExcelDataFilter>")]
    [XmlRoot(
        Namespace="http://prish.com/Pes/ExcelFilter/20061116",
        ElementName="ExcelDataFilter")]
    public class ExcelDataFilter :
        SPWebParts.WebPart,
        SPWebParts.ITransformableFilterValues
    {
        // ...
    }
}
```

On top of the inheritance, the Web Part also has two attributes — the `ToolboxData` attribute and the `XmlRoot` attribute. The first tells SharePoint (and Visual Studio) how the markup of the control looks when it's inserted into ASP.NET code. The "{0}" portion of the string will be replaced by whatever prefix is given to the namespace that the Web Part is using. The `XmlRoot` attribute declares both a namespace for the Web Part and an element name. These will be used in various places, such as when SharePoint serializes the control into the database and when ASP.NET renders the control.

The next part of the Web Part contains all the properties that are settable from the property pane in SharePoint. Each property thus exposed will have a set of attributes applied to it, telling SharePoint important information about it. The `FilterName` property, for example, looks like this:

```
[AspWebParts.WebBrowsable(true)]
[Category("Filter Properties")]
[DefaultValue(ExcelDataFilter.DefaultFilterName)]
[SPWebParts.WebPartStorage(SPWebParts.Storage.Shared)]
[XmlElement("FilterName")]
[FriendlyName("Filter Name")]
public string FilterName
{
        get { return m_filterName; }
        set { m_filterName = value; }
}
```

The following table explains the function of each attribute.

Attribute	Purpose
WebBrowsable	Tells SharePoint/ASP.NET that the property should be exposed to the user for modification in design mode.
Category	Specifies the category of the property. In SharePoint, each category will appear in the property pane with a little "+" sign near it, allowing users to browse the properties in a hierarchical manner.
DefaultValue	Used by the serialization mechanism to determine if the property needs to be written to the database or not. It is important that the value passed into the `Default` attribute is in line with the contents of the property when the class is first created.
WebPartStorage	Determines if the property can be personalized or not.
XmlElement	The name of the tag that will be used to serialize this property.
FriendlyName	The label that will appear in the design environment when the property is shown. SharePoint uses this, for example, when it shows the property pane.

Altogether, there are eight properties that control the behavior of the filter. The following table explains the function of each one:

Property	Purpose
FilterName	Will be used by SharePoint to identify the Web Part when showing the user the connection UI.
UseConnectedWorkbook	Instructs the filter to see if an EWA is connected to it, and if it is, to use the workbook or session that EWA is using as the source of data.
ClientSide	When set to `true`, tells the filter Web Part to emit script that will fill the combo box on the client. When `false`, does all the work on the server.
IgnoreFirstRow	When `true`, tells the filter to skip the first row of the returned table — useful for tables with headers.
	(In Excel, when a new table is defined, the named range that is automatically created and represents the table does not contain the header. This means this property is only useful for ranges that are not based on Excel tables.)
WorkbookUrl	The location of the workbook. Ignored if `UseConnectedWorkbook` is set to `true`.
Range	The name of the range to use.
TextIndex	The index (zero-based) of the column in the range that will be used as the textual representation of each filter value.
ValueIndex	The index (zero-based) of the column in the range that is used as the filter value.

The code will be shown in two phases. First, the pieces of code that are shared between server and client modes and the code specific for server mode (when ClientSide is false) will be shown.

ExcelDataFilter Class — Server and Shared Code

The overridden `CreateChildControls()` method is used as the launching pad for Web Part when in server mode. The method creates a new `ListBox` instance and sets it up to show the relevant information (the same `ListBox` is used in the case of client mode).

The created `ListBox` control (which translates to a `SELECT` element in HTML) is set to have single row (which means it will be a combo box instead of a list box). It's enabled if the control is in server-mode, and it is given an ID so that it can later be identified. It is then added to the child controls of the Web Part.

`AddExcelValuesToList()`, shown below, is called to make sure the list box contains the correct values. At the end, the method catches any errors and shows them to the user.

```
protected override void CreateChildControls()
{
    try
    {
        m_listBox = new ListBox();
        m_listBox.Rows = 1;
        m_listBox.Enabled = !ClientSide;
        m_listBox.ID = "FilterListBox";
        Controls.Add(m_listBox);
        if (ClientSide)
        {
            PrepareForClient();
        }
        else
        {
            AddExcelValuesToList();
        }

        base.CreateChildControls();
    }
    catch (Exception e)
    {
        Label label = new Label();
        label.Text = "Error: " + e.Message;
        label.ForeColor = System.Drawing.Color.Red;
#if DEBUG
        label.ToolTip = e.ToString();
#endif
        Controls.Add(label);
    }
}
```

(`PrepareForClient()` will be explained in the next section.)

The `AddExcelValuesToList()` method uses the Excel Library in `DirectLinking` mode to access the Excel Services API without going through the SOAP layer. The usage pattern is very similar to how the library has been used througout the book — a session is opened and then used to get the appropriate range. That range is then used to fill the list box with `ListItem` instances, which contain the text and values contained in the range.

```
private void AddExcelValuesToList()
{
    ExcelServices es =
        new ExcelServices(ExcelServicesType.DirectLinking);
    using (Session session =
        es.Open(GetInternalWorkbookUrl()))
    {
        RangeResult result = session.GetRangeA1(Range, true);
        if (result.ColumnCount < 2)
        {
            throw new FilterException(
```

```
                        "Range must contain two columns" +
                        " - first one for the caption and " +
                        "the second one for the data.");
            }

            foreach (Row row in result.RowCollection)
            {
                string text = (string)row[TextIndex] ?? "";
                string value = (string)row[ValueIndex] ?? "";
                m_listBox.Items.Add(new ListItem(text, value));
            }
        }
    }
```

`AddExcelValuesToList()` uses the workbook name returned by the `GetInternalWorkbookUrl()` method to figure out which workbook it needs to open. The method either returns the `WorkbookUrl` property or, if `UseConnectedWorkbook` is set to `true`, tries to find a connected EWA and use the workbook it's using by calling into the `WorkbookUri` property of the `ExcelWebRenderer` instance:

```
private string GetInternalWorkbookUrl()
{
    string result = null;
    if (UseConnectedWorkbook)
    {
        ExcelWebRenderer renderer = GetConnectedRenderer();
        if (renderer == null)
        {
            throw new FilterException("Filter is not connected to an EWA");
        }
        result = renderer.WorkbookUri;
    }
    else
    {
        result = WorkbookUrl;
    }
    if (String.IsNullOrEmpty(result))
    {
        throw new FilterException("No workbook is set up on filter.");
    }
    return result;
}
```

The method also takes the responsibility of throwing an exception if no valid workbook exists. While this helps simplify the code, it means that it should only be called when a workbook is really needed (and not, for example, to check if a workbook exists).

The call to `GetConnectedRenderer()` returns the connected EWA, if one exists. It uses the `WebPartManager` class to iterate over all the connections present on the page. When it detects one that has the filter on one side, it checks to see what's on the other side. If that's an EWA, it returns it:

```
private ExcelWebRenderer GetConnectedRenderer()
{
    foreach (WebPartConnection connection in
```

```
        WebPartManager.Connections)
    {
        if (connection.Consumer is ExcelWebRenderer &&
            connection.Provider == this)
        {
            return (ExcelWebRenderer)connection.Consumer;
        }
    }
    return null;
}
```

This concludes the pieces of code used to render the control when it's running in server mode. The next portion of the code is mostly shared and is responsible for the filter functionality, as required by SharePoint. The first part is the `GetConnectionInterface()` method, which is the entry point used by SharePoint to figure out what types of part-to-part communications the class supports. The method has the `Connection-Provider` attribute (which is how the entry point is found by ASP.NET and SharePoint) marking it as the providing end of a part-to-part connection. The method returns an `ITransformableFilterValues` reference to itself (since the whole functionality of the filter is implemented by the Web Part itself).

Web Parts that wish to provide multiple filter connection points can return references to inner objects, each representing a single connection.

```
[AspWebParts.ConnectionProvider(
    "Excel Data Filter",
    "ITransformableFilterValues",
    AllowsMultipleConnections=true)]
public SPWebParts.ITransformableFilterValues GetConnectionInterface()
{
    return this;
}
```

The first parameter to the `ConnectionProvider` attribute gives a name to the connection point. The second declares the connection interface supported by this connection point. The last named property in this case declares that the connection can be used by multiple consumers at the same time.

The `ITransformableFilterValues` interface provides five properties. The first four are relatively simple and define the behavior of the filter:

```
[WebPartStorage(Storage.None)]
public bool AllowAllValue
{
    get { return false; }
}
[WebPartStorage(Storage.None)]
public bool AllowEmptyValue
{
    get { return true; }
}
[WebPartStorage(Storage.None)]
public bool AllowMultipleValues
{
    get { return false; }
```

```
}
[WebPartStorage(Storage.None)]
public string ParameterName
{
    get { return FilterName; }
}
```

The `WebPartStorage` *attribute is applied to all the propeties, since they are public, but should not be serialized as part of the Web Part data.*

Property	Purpose
AllowAllValue	Some filters have a special value that stands for "All" the other values. Those filters return `true` from this property.
AllowEmptyValue	Some filters have the notion of an empty value, which means that nothing is selected. Because in some cases there may be no values in the range, this is supported by this filter.
AllowMultipleValues	There are filters and consumers that can handle multiple values. When that's the case, this property returns `true`.
ParameterName	Tells SharePoint what the name of the filter is. This is used to render more useful information to the user.

The final property is used by SharePoint to grab the actual contents of the filter. The property returns a read-only collection of strings. In the case of this filter, the code checks to see what the selected value in the list box is and returns that.

```
[WebPartStorage(Storage.None)]
public ReadOnlyCollection<string> ParameterValues
{
    get
    {
        if (m_listBox == null)
            return null;

        string selectedValue = null;
        if (ClientSide)
        {
            selectedValue = ClientSelectedValue;
        }
        else
        {
            selectedValue = m_listBox.SelectedValue;
        }

        if (String.IsNullOrEmpty(selectedValue))
            selectedValue = null;
        string[] selection = new string[] { selectedValue };
```

```
            ReadOnlyCollection<string> result =
                new ReadOnlyCollection<string>(selection);
            return result;
        }
    }
```

(The next section will explain what the `ClientSelectedValue` property returns.)

That's the final part of the shared and server-specific code. The next section goes into detail about the server code and client code that has to do with the client-side mode.

The client-side mode is driven by the server pushing the correct script to the browser.

ExcelDataFilter Class — Client Related Code

The first part of the client-mode code is the `PrepareForClient()` method shown in the previous section being called from the `CreateChildControls()` method. The main function of the method is to add the script call that will cause the web page to issue the Excel Web Services calls using the Excel Services AJAX library. On top of that, it determines if the script will connect to a running EWA or, alternatively, use a workbook URL. The generated script is placed inside a `Literal` control and added to the child control collection.

Literal controls simply output into the HTML whatever they contain. They are the easiest way of insert-ing arbitrary HTML in well-known locations.

The template for the script that is generated will be shown below the method:

```
internal const string ScriptForFillingList = "\r\n<script language=\"javascript\"
type=\"text/javascript\">FillComboBoxFromExcelServices(\"{0}\", \"{1}\", \"{2}\",
{3}, {4}, \"{5}\", {6}, {7}, \"{8}\");</script>";
private void PrepareForClient()
{
    m_span = new System.Web.UI.HtmlControls.HtmlGenericControl("span");
    m_span.ID = "messageSpan";
    Controls.Add(m_span);

    string workbookOrEwa = WorkbookUrl;
    if (UseConnectedWorkbook)
    {
        ExcelWebRenderer renderer = GetConnectedRenderer();
        if (renderer == null)
        {
            throw new FilterException("Filter is not connected to an EWA");
        }
        workbookOrEwa = renderer.ClientID;
    }

    string script = String.Format(
        ScriptForFillingList,
        SPHttpUtility.EcmaScriptStringLiteralEncode(m_listBox.ClientID),
        SPHttpUtility.EcmaScriptStringLiteralEncode(m_span.ClientID),
```

```
            SPHttpUtility.EcmaScriptStringLiteralEncode(workbookOrEwa),
            (UseConnectedWorkbook) ? "true" : "false",
            (IgnoreFirstRow) ? "true" : "false",
            SPHttpUtility.EcmaScriptStringLiteralEncode(Range),
            ValueIndex,
            TextIndex,
            SPHttpUtility.EcmaScriptStringLiteralEncode(ClientSelectedValue));


        LiteralControl control = new LiteralControl(script);
        Controls.Add(control);
    }
```

The script constant is:

```
internal const string ScriptForFillingList = "\r\n<script type=\"text/javascript\
">FillComboBoxFromExcelServices(\"{0}\", \"{1}\", \"{2}\", {3}, {4}, \"{5}\", {6},
{7}, \"{8}\");</script>";
```

The meaning of each parameter will be explained when the JavaScript method FillComboBoxFrom-ExcelServices() is shown.

The OnLoad() method is overriden to add two script libraries to the HTML. The first is the Excel Services AJAX library. The second is a small JavaScript library specific for this control (ExcelDataFilter.js). The reason for using the RegisterClientScriptInclude() method is so that if there are more than one instance of the Excel Data Filter on the page, the scripts will not be included twice:

```
protected override void OnLoad(EventArgs e)
{
    const string ExcelServicesAjax = "ExcelServicesAjax";
    const string ExcelDataFilter= "ExcelDataFilter";
    base.OnLoad(e);
    if (!Page.ClientScript.IsClientScriptIncludeRegistered(
        typeof(ExcelDataFilter),
        ExcelServicesAjax))
    {
        Page.ClientScript.RegisterClientScriptInclude(
            typeof(ExcelDataFilter),
            ExcelServicesAjax,
            "/_layouts/ExcelServicesAjax.js");
    }

    if (!Page.ClientScript.IsClientScriptIncludeRegistered(
        typeof(ExcelDataFilter),
        ExcelDataFilter))
    {
        Page.ClientScript.RegisterClientScriptInclude(
            typeof(ExcelDataFilter),
            ExcelDataFilter,
            "/_layouts/ExcelDataFilter.js");
    }
}
```

The last part of the server code is the property that returns the user selection in the client-side mode. The property access the `Form` property of the `HttpRequest` instance to get the actual result from the client (since the list box is not set up properly, it's impossible to use the automatic functionality of getting the posted-back value):

```
private string ClientSelectedValue
{
    get { return Page.Request.Form[m_listBox.UniqueID]; }
}
```

The next section goes through the contents of `ExcelDataFilter.js`, which is the JavaScript code that's executed inside the browser and uses the Excel Services AJAX library to achieve the client-side mode functionality.

The JavaScript function `FillComboBoxFromExcelServices()` is actually a JavaScript object. Because the operation of getting data from the server can potentially span multiple asynchronous calls, it is useful to have a state that remembers exactly what needs to be done. The object represented by the method will do that. The method has three stages. The first initializes the various members. The second declares some anonymous methods, which will be executed depending on the state of the object. Finally, the last section actually kicks off the asynchronous operation.

```
function FillComboBoxFromExcelServices(combo,
    messageElementId,
    workbookOrEwa,
    useEwa,
    ignoreFirstRow,
    range,
    valueIndex,
    textIndex,
    selectedValue)
{
    // Stage 1 -  Prototype
    this.combo = combo;
    this.messageElementId = messageElementId;
    this.workbookOrEwa = workbookOrEwa;
    this.useEwa = useEwa;
    this.range = range;
    this.valueIndex = valueIndex;
    this.textIndex = textIndex;
    this.ignoreFirstRow = ignoreFirstRow;
    this.selectedValue = selectedValue;
    this.session = null;
    this.ewaPollTimerId = null;
    this.setMessage = function(message)
    {
        var element = document.getElementById(this.messageElementId);
        element.innerText = message;
    };

    // Stage 2 - Anonymous methods prperations
    // ...
```

```
        // Stage 3 - Asyncronous operation kick off
        // ...
}
```

The method (which is the "constructor" to the object) first sets all the parameters it gets into member fields. It also stores some more members for easy retrieval such as the `this.session` member, which will hold an `ExcelServicesSession` instance and the `this.ewaPollTimerId` member (shown below).

The second stage creates a new `ExcelServices` instance and creates two anonymous functions. The first one that is referenced by the `callbackForWorkbook` local variable and is used as a callback in the case where the filter is set up to accept a workbook name as the data source. The second, referenced by `callbackForEwa`, is used as a callback if the filter is set up to integrate with EWA.

```
// Stage 2 - Anonymous methods prperations
var callbackForWorkbook = function(methodCall)
{
     objThis.session = methodCall.excelServices.userState;
     objThis.session.userState = objThis;
     objThis.session.getRangeA1(
         "",
         objThis.range,
         true,
         FillComboBoxGetRangeCallback);
     objThis.setMessage("Workbook opened successfuly." +
         " Getting range from server.");
};

var callbackForEwa = function()
{
     var sessionId = EwaGetSessionId(objThis.workbookOrEwa);
     if (sessionId != null)
     {
         var session = new ExcelServicesSession(sessionId);
         session.userState = objThis;
         objThis.setMessage("EWA found. Getting range from server...");
         session.getRangeA1(
             "",
             objThis.range,
             true,
             FillComboBoxGetRangeCallback);
         clearInterval(this.ewaPollTimerId);
     }
};
```

The main difference between the two functions is where their origin is. The `callbackForWorkbook` function is called as a result of a call to the `ExcelServices.openSession()` method. The `callbackForEwa`, on the other hand, is continually called until the EWA is done loading (`EwaGetSessionId()` returns a non-null value). Both callbacks call into the `ExcelServicesSession.getRangeA1()` method with the `FillComboBoxGetRangeCallback()` function as a callback parameter.

Depending on the whether or not the filter is connected to an EWA, the script does one of two things. It starts polling by calling the `window.setInterval()` method with the `callbackForEwa` anonymous

function shown above if the filter is connected to an EWA. Otherwise, it issues the `ExcelServices`
`.openSession()` asynchronous call to get back a valid session in the `callbackForWorkbook` anonymous function.

```
// Stage 3 - Asyncronous operation kick off
if (this.useEwa)
{
    this.ewaPollTimerId = window.setInterval(callbackForEwa, 100);
    objThis.setMessage("Waiting for EWA to finish loading...");

}
else
{
    es.openSession(this.workbookOrEwa, callbackForWorkbook);
    objThis.setMessage("Opening workbook on the server...");
}
```

The `FillComboBoxGetRangeCallback()` callback function is called when the `getRangeA1()` operation is completed. The code uses the result of the operation to to fill the combo box in the browser:

```
function FillComboBoxGetRangeCallback(methodCall)
{
    var objThis = methodCall.excelServices.userState.userState;
    var combo = document.getElementById(objThis.combo);
    var startIndex = 0;
    if (objThis.ignoreFirstRow)
    {
        startIndex = 1;
    }
    for (var i = startIndex; i < methodCall.result.length; i++)
    {
        var row = methodCall.result[i];
        var opt = document.createElement("OPTION");
        combo.options.add(opt);
        opt.innerText = row[objThis.textIndex];
        opt.value = row[objThis.valueIndex];
    }
    combo.disabled = false;
    combo.value = objThis.selectedValue;
    objThis.setMessage("");
}
```

Note: The code uses the `userState` *property on the* `ExcelServicesSession` *object to store the object represented by* `FillComboBoxFromExcelServices`.

Summary

The filter is a relativley comprehensive soltuion for both client-side and servert-side filtering of data on SharePoint Web Part pages. Because the data it uses comes from Excel workbooks, it's very easy to create data-driven or model-driven content for filtering other Web Parts.

23

Excel Services Mashup

A software book coming out in 2007 without at least a reference to mashups and Web 2.0 is like a software book coming out at the mid-nineties without a reference to "design patterns" or "object-oriented programming."

This chapter uses a lot of the skills shown in the previous chapters and shows how to put them to use to create an HTML/JavaScript application that brings together an Excel model encapsulated in a workbook, a UDF module, API calls, and EWA programming to give HR specialists the ability to easily find employees and partners home addresses on a Virtual Earth map by using their titles as a filter.

Overview

The solution is a single HTML file that contains three elements. The top element both allows users to select the job title of the people being sought and to change the current view to either an Excel workbook view or a Microsoft Virtual Earth view.

Use

Figure 23-1 shows the page as it looks when it is first navigated to.

The top-left part of the page has two buttons allowing users to navigate between map view (upper button) and EWA view (lower button). Once the EWA is done loading, the page fills a combo box with the various job titles available in the workbook (see Figure 23-2).

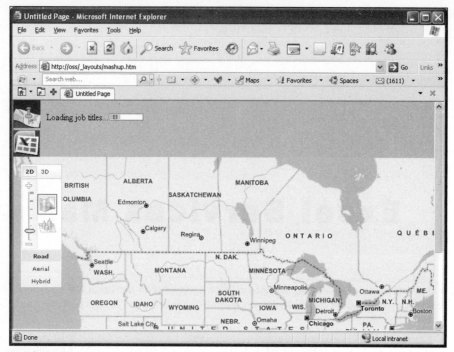

Figure 23-1

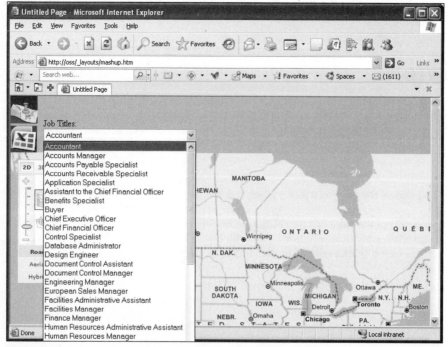

Figure 23-2

Once the page is loaded, the user can select a job title in the combo box — the page will update asynchronously (i.e., with no full-page refresh) to show the people and their addresses, as shown in Figure 23-3.

The information contained in the push pins that represent the various addresses is taken straight from Excel Services. It is then formatted from its tabular form to give the user of the mashup the ability to leverage the meaning behind the information. In this case, the application is linking the name of the person to their email (clicking on the name will bring up an email program). It also links the phone number to the telephone protocol so that if the machine displaying the web page has an integrated phone system, it can call the number with a click of a button.

It is important to note that the map is fully functional — all the features supplied by the component are available on the page. This includes panning, zooming, or viewing the map in other ways (as shown in Figure 23-4).

As shown in Figure 23-5, the last component in this infrastructure is the EWA, which contains the list of people in a spreadsheet.

The page does not have a whole lot of code. It uses industry-standard mechanisms for stringing together separate components, using the Web browser as the runtime environment and HTML/JavaScript as the development language/infrastructure.

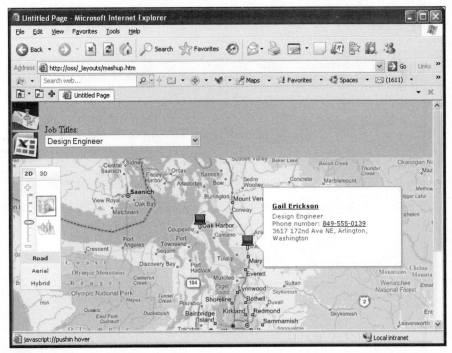

Figure 23-3

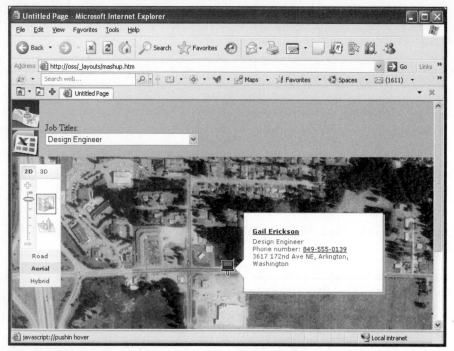

Figure 23-4

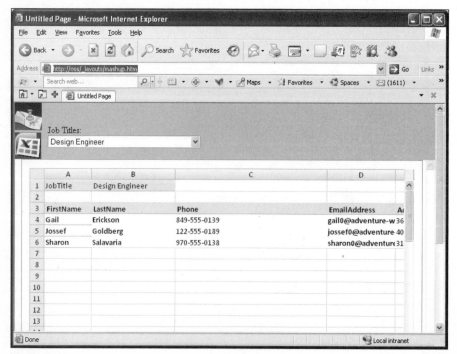

Figure 23-5

Coding the Solution

As explained at the beginning, the component is written in HTML and JavaScript. The model is written in Excel and is driven by EWA inside a Web Part page. The model is also using a UDF to calculate the longitude and latitude of the addresses.

Workbook Model

The model that's driving the solution is a workbook containing two PivotTables. The first PivotTable is set up to show the people in the company in a tabular fashion — it also includes a page-field filter that will allow the solution to filter the people by their job titles (see Figure 23-6).

The cells on the "I" column contain the concatenation of the fields in the PivotTable that represent the address of the person. The "H" column contains a call to the GetLongLatString() UDF (shown in the next section), which, when executed on the server, returns the coordinate of the address.

The ListOfTitles sheet contains another PivotTable, which contains the list of the unique job titles the table contains.

To finalize the model, the workbook contains three named ranges — one for the first 20 rows of the PivotTable (including the column containing the coordinates), one for the list of titles and one for the page field (named EmployeeTable, JobTitleTable, and JobTitleParameter, respectively). The page field is also defined as a parameter so that it will be modifiable in the EWA page.

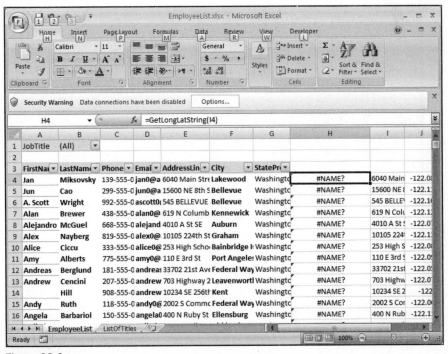

Figure 23-6

EWA Page

The EWA page is a regular Web Part page containing the EWA and a query string filter Web Part. The filter Web Part is connected to the JobTitleParameter named range in the workbook and uses the query string parameter JobTitle to get the value that needs to be set.

The ready web page is then edited in Microsoft Office SharePoint Designer to remove the standard SharePoint UI (all the menus, chrome, and so on). What remains, is a page containing only one visual component, which is the EWA. On top of that, the page is tweaked to have an appropriate size, and the ID of the EWA is changed so that it is discoverable when programming against the page (see Figure 23-7).

This page is hosted inside an IFRAME element in the HTML page that ties the solution together. This helps the system be more like AJAX, where the whole page rarely refreshes. When a new job title is selected, the IFRAME element will be modified to pass in a different parameter through the query string, bringing back the filtered list of employees.

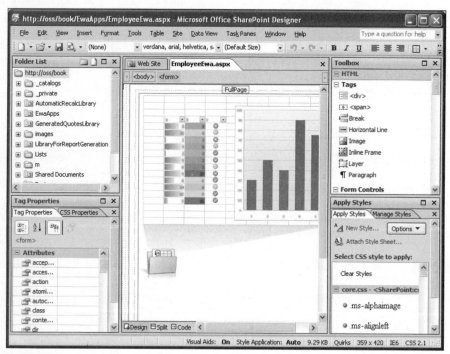

Figure 23-7

UDF Assembly

The UDF assembly contains a single method, which finds the coordinates of a member:

```
namespace Pes.GeoCodingUdfs
{
    [UdfClass]
    public class GeoCoding
    {
        [UdfMethod]
        public string GetLongLatString(string address)
        {
            MapPoint.FindServiceSoap findService =
                new MapPoint.FindServiceSoap();
            findService.PreAuthenticate = true;
            findService.Credentials =
                new NetworkCredential("[Name]", "[Password]");
            MapPoint.FindSpecification findSpec =
                new MapPoint.FindSpecification();
            findSpec.DataSourceName = "MapPoint.NA";
            findSpec.InputPlace = address;
            MapPoint.FindResults results = findService.Find(findSpec);
            MapPoint.LatLong location = results.Results[0].
                FoundLocation.LatLong;
            return String.Format(
                CultureInfo.InvariantCulture,
                "{0},{1}",
                location.Latitude,
                location.Longitude);
        }
    }
}
```

The method is using MapPoint services — it could just as easily use the Yahoo REST APIs for geocoding or any other such service. (It could also use a client-side mechanism for getting this information.)

HTML

The HTML in the solution contains two top-level DIV elements that correspond to the upper and lower part of the application. The top panel contains the buttons (images with onclick events attached to them), which switch between the two views. It also contains a label with a marquee-style progress bar, which is shown by default when the page is initially loaded, and a combo box (an HTML SELECT element), which will be filled with the job titles.

The bottom part contains the two components inside a DIV that is set up to hide any overflow that occurs. The DIV contains the two components, one after another — the Virtual Earth (VE) one on top and the EWA on the bottom. Because the VE component is sized to fit the DIV, it "pushes" the EWA page into overflowing, which in turn makes it hidden.

This little HTML dance is required because of the resizing code of IE6. In some cases, hidden components are not properly sized — in the case of the EWA, this can result in a real ugly and unusable Excel sheet. In the approach shown here, the component is visible from the point of view of IE but hidden (due to the overflow) from the point of view of the user.

```
<body onload="javascript:Initialize();">
    <!-- Top panel -->
    <div style="height:100px;overflow:hidden">
        <div
style="vertical-align:middle;height:100%;background-color:LightSkyBlue">
                <!-- Buttons -->
                <div style="position:absolute;top:0;left:0">
                    <div style="height:48px">
                        <img style="cursor:hand"
                            onclick="ChangeView('Map')"
                            src="PesMashup/map.png"/>
                    </div>
                    <div style="height:48px">
                        <img style="cursor:hand"
                        onclick="ChangeView('Excel')"
                        src="PesMashup/excel.png" />
                    </div>
                </div>
                <div style="position:absolute;top:20;left:60;width:300">
                    <!-- Loading Message -->
                    <span id="jobTitleMessage">
                        Loading job titles...
                        <img src="images/kpiprogressbar.gif" />
                    </span>
                    <!-- Combo-box -->
                    <span  style="display:none" id="jobTitleSpan">
                    Job Titles:
                    <select onchange="javascript:JobTitleChanged();"
                        id="jobTitleCombo">
                    </select>
                    <img id="changeJobTitleProgress"
                        src="images/kpiprogressbar.gif"
                        style="display:none""/>
                    </span>
                </div>
        </div>
    </div>
    <!-- Bottom Panel -->
    <div id="parentDiv" style="height:500px;width:100%;overflow:hidden">
        <!-- Virtual Earth placeholder -->
        <div id="clientMap"
            style="position:relative; width:100%;height:500px">
```

```
            </div>
            <!-- EWA page container -->
            <div id="excelView" style="display:block">
                <iframe id="ewaContainer"
                        src="/book/ewaapps/EmployeeEwa.aspx?"
                        style="width:100%;height:500px;"
                        frameborder="0"
                        scrolling="no">
                </iframe>
            </div>
        </div>
</body>
```

When the page finishes loading, the `Initialize()` JavaScript function is called. That function sets the page up and caches some global variables the solution will need later:

```
var map = null;
var ewaPollTimerId;
var originalIFrameSource;
var ewaPageIFrame;
var ewaSessionId;
var ewaSessionFoundCallback;

function Initialize()
{
    // Start checking for the session - this will load the list of job titles.
    StartPollForEwaLoadCompletion(EwaSessionFoundOnLoad);

    // Initialize Virtual Earth.
    map = new VEMap('clientMap');
    map.ShowDisambiguationDialog(false);
    map.LoadMap();

    // General caching
    ewaPageIFrame = document.getElementById("ewaContainer");
    originalIFrameSource = ewaPageIFrame.src;
}
```

The first part of the method polls for the EWA to finalize loading so that it can retrieve the list of job titles. The second part initializes the Virtual Earth map, using the Virtual Earth SDK.

When the EWA page is done loading and the workbook in the EWA is fully rendered, the `EwaSession-FoundOnLoad()` function will be called.

A new `ExcelServicesSession` object is created, using the session ID retrieved from EWA — that session is then used to get the named range `JobTitleTable`, which will return the full list of job titles. When that call is done, the `OnJobTitlesReceived()` function will be called.

```
function EwaSessionFoundOnLoad(result)
{
    if (result != null)
    {
```

```
            var session = new ExcelServicesSession(result);
            ewaSessionId = result;
            session.getRangeA1("", "JobTitleTable", true, OnJobTitlesReceived);
    }
}
```

`OnJobTitlesReceived()` takes the range that is returned from Excel Web Services and uses it to fill the combo box:

```
function OnJobTitlesReceived(methodCall)
{
    var jobTitles = document.getElementById("jobTitleCombo");
    var jobTitlesSpan = document.getElementById("jobTitleSpan");
    var jobTitlesMessage = document.getElementById("jobTitleMessage");

    jobTitlesSpan.style.display = "block";
    jobTitlesMessage.style.display = "none";
    for (var i = 0; i < methodCall.result.length; i++)
    {
        var value = methodCall.result[i][0];
        var option = document.createElement("OPTION");
        jobTitles.options.add(option);
        option.innerText = value;
        option.value = value;
    }
}
```

The next step is to see what happens when the user selects a job title in the combo box. In the HTML, the combo box has an event that is fired when the value of the combo box changes. The event is called `JobTitleChanged()`, and it changes the `src` attribute of the `IFRAME` element to include the query string parameter that will filter the list. It also starts polling for the EWA to complete loading again.

```
function JobTitleChanged()
{
    EnableJobTitleCombo(false);
    var value = event.srcElement.value;
    ewaPageIFrame.src = originalIFrameSource + "&JobTitle=" +
        encodeURIComponent(value);
    StartPollForEwaLoadCompletion(EwaSessionFoundOnTitleChange);
}
```

This time, when EWA is done loading, the `EwaSessionFoundOnTitleChange()` function will be called. It will make a request to Excel Web Services to get the first 20 rows or so of the PivotTable that's in the workbook, retrieving information about the people in the list:

```
function EwaSessionFoundOnTitleChange(result)
{
    ewaSession = result;
    var session = new ExcelServicesSession(ewaSessionId);
    session.getRangeA1("", "EmployeeTable", true, OnEmployeeTableReceived);
}
```

When the AJAX request for the `EmployeeTable` range is complete, it will call the `OnEmployeeTable-Received()` function, which will call into the Virtual Earth SDK and add push pins to the map. Each push pin will contain formatted information that comes directly from the received range:

```
function OnEmployeeTableReceived(methodCall)
{
    var result = methodCall.result;
    // Clear the push pins.
    map.DeleteAllPushpins();
    var lastRow = null;
    var locations = new Array();

    for (var index = 0; index < result.length; index++)
    {
        var row = result[index];
        if (!row[4] || row[4] == "")
        {
            break;
        }
        // If the first column (first name) does not contain a value
        // take that value from the previous row.
        if (row[0] == "" || !row[0] && lastRow)
        {
            row[0] = lastRow[0];
        }
        // Split the string containing the latitude and longtitude
        // and parse the two values out of it.
        var latLong = row[7].split(",");
        var lat = latLong[0];
        var lon = latLong[1];
        locations[index] = new VELatLong(lat, lon);

        // Create the push pin.
        var pin = new VEPushpin(
            index,
            locations[index],
            null,
            "<a href=\"mailto:" + escape(row[3]) +
                "\">" + escape(row[0]) + " " +
                escape(row[1]) + "</a>",
            GetRowDescription(row));
        map.AddPushpin(pin);
        lastRow = row;
    }
    // Make sure the map displays the best view for all the locations.
    map.SetMapView(locations);
    EnableJobTitleCombo(true);
}
```

Summary

This solution shows the strength of Excel Services from various angles at the same time. Here are the various areas where the unique value of Excel Services can be spotted:

❑ **The model is opaque.** There is nothing that the HTML writer needs to know about how the model is calculated other than the various interface points with it. The data comes from an unknown location (the list of employees may come from a database; it may be completely embedded in the workbook; it may refresh each time the workbook is opened; it may contain user-specific information — all that doesn't matter to the person writing the HTML code).

❑ **The function calls the model makes are opaque.** The logic in the UDF calls from the model are opaque as well — the name and password used by the service will never be visible to the end user because they don't need to be sent — all the logic for the completion of the model occurs on the server.

❑ **EWA can be used to gather information.** The session ID that is used to interact with the work-book is retreived from the running EWA. This allows the mashup developer to propagate any of the changes occuring there to the application. If there were another set of parameters that could be set by the user for example, using the EWA session would guarantee that the mashup used the most up-to-date data.

❑ **Excel Web Services.** The fact that Excel Services exposes a Web Services interface, allows devel-opers to call into it using AJAX patterns.

Index

Q

R

W